PROVINCIAL PATRIARCHS

Provincial Patriarchs

Land Tenure
and the Economics of Power
in Colonial Peru

Susan E. Ramírez

University of New Mexico Press, Albuquerque

333.3
R17 p

Library of Congress Cataloging in Publication Data
Ramírez, Susan E., 1946–
   Provincial patriarchs.

   Bibliography: p.
   Includes index.
   1. Landowners—Peru—History. 2. Haciendas—Peru—History. 3. Encomiendas (Latin America) 4.
Land tenure—Peru—History. I. Title.
HD554.R35   1985   333.3′0985   85-13934
ISBN 0-8263-0818-X

Library of Congress Catalog Card Number 85-13934.
International Standard Book Number 0-8263-0818-X.
First edition

Contents

Illustrations

Preface and Acknowledgments

In writing this book, I learned that research can be both rewarding and frustrating. It is satisfying to conceptualize and define a problem and to be able to find the data to flesh it out. It is gratifying to be able to write up one's findings and to bring the study toward a conclusion. But therein lies the problem. Research, in effect, can never be completed. There is always the possibility that sometime in the future another "lost" manuscript will be "found" that will refine one's previous research. I present this study while remaining very cognizant of that possibility. Nevertheless, a point is reached when reviewing old manuscripts brings diminishing returns. Although my research stopped at that point, I am confident that the story which follows accurately retells the history of the landowning elite in the Lambayeque region.

I wish to thank all the persons who made this study possible. John Leddy Phelan, Peter H. Smith, and Thomas E. Skidmore gave me the superb and rigorous training needed to carry out the project. The personnel in the archives of Peru, Colombia, Spain, Germany, England, and the United States deserve mention for their help in locating material. I thank the following persons for guidance and thoughtful suggestions about how to improve the original manuscript: my three advisors, Fred Bronner, Michael González, Michael Hamerly, Robert G. Keith, Meno Lovenstein, Murdo J. MacLeod, Keith Peterson, William Thiesenhusen, and Jorge Zevallos Quiñones. I, of course, take full responsibility for any faults and oversights. Keith Butt deserves a special word of thanks for the hours which he spent drafting and redrafting the map, genealogies, and graphs.

Finally, I would like to mention the foundations whose support turned the idea into reality: the Social Science Research Council, the Marie

Christine Kohler Foundation, the Sigma Xi Foundation, and the Fulbright-Hays faculty research grant program.

This book is dedicated to the memory of my grandparents, Edgar Freeman and Adelia H. McCartney, for their unfailing love and strength.

1   Introduction: Institutional History and Beyond

During the last thirty years, the work of a relatively small group of scholars has greatly increased our knowledge of the great estate or *hacienda* in Spanish America. As a result, it is now recognized as one of the most fundamental social and economic institutions in colonial America. Its formation speeded European settlement and the acculturation of the native population. Within a few decades of the conquest, the estate developed into the basic socioeconomic unit of production in an agrarian, preindustrial society. Under the aegis of owner and overseer, a subordinate labor force produced, first, livestock, wheat, and other foodstuffs to meet a local demand, and later, sugar, indigo, and similar products to supply a growing regional market and the Western world. Interpersonal relations within the confines of the rural domain reflected the hierarchical, multiracial society of the towns and cities. The estate served, in short, as a unit of social and economic organization, which linked countryside to city and various ethnic groups in colonial society.

The often detailed, monographic research of recent generations of scholars has allowed them to revise the early views of the institution advanced by the pioneers in the field.[1] The stereotype of the estate as a large, loosely administered and marginally profitable rural refuge for an urban-dwelling upper class, although not without a basis in fact, has been shown to be an oversimplification. "The" great estate did not exist. The term *hacienda* is a generic convention that, though useful at times, often masked the geographical diversity and obscured the dynamism of the institution. It is unsuited for discussing any single country, much less all of Latin America.[2]

In fact, the growing body of literature on the topic shows that the

1

colonial estate assumed many forms. Three main types predominated: the *estancia;* the *hacienda;* and the *trapiche,* or *ingenio.* Each type represents an agricultural enterprise which, by definition, was large in size and was characterized by a particular combination of land, labor, capital, technology, and social relations. The most clear-cut differences between the three types of estates lie in their principal economic activities and marketable products. *Estancias,* or ranches, are associated with livestock raising and the production of meat, tallow, hides, and wool. *Haciendas,* or mixed farms, combined the cultivation of cash crops with animal raising. The *trapiches,* or *ingenios,* were farm-mill complexes and prototypes of the present-day plantation. These units typically specialized in one agricultural commodity, produced in relatively large quantities for shipment to distant markets. These estates took their names from the particular type of processing facilities installed on the property. Ingenios, for example, were water-powered mills for crushing sugar cane; trapiches were animal-powered mills used for the same purpose.

This broad classification obscures somewhat the variation within categories. The diversity recognized by contemporaries is evidenced by now almost forgotten terminology. The *hato* in Cuba was the equivalent of an *asiento* in Chile and Peru; both became synonymous with and were eventually replaced by the word *estancia* in the seventeenth century. The *labor, huerta, chacra,* and *asiento de pan llevar* in Chile and Peru were variations of the *rancho* of Mexico. The term *hacienda* was used interchangeably with these expressions and rapidly displaced them.[3]

Each term connotes a variation on the myriad of details about the organization of production,[4] which persisted through time despite the spread of uniform terminology. Thus, haciendas, besides producing a wide variety of foodstuffs and several types of livestock, differed in degrees of self-sufficiency, specialization, profitability, and capitalization; in the source and nature of their labor force; and in their system of management and direction. In his now classic study, François Chevalier describes the hacienda (as opposed to the estancia) in northern Mexico as a large unit, producing grains, sheep, goats, and mules; self-sufficient in basic foodstuffs and building materials; and often managed by someone other than the owner. In contrast, William Taylor, in his important monograph on land tenure in the Valley of Oaxaca during the same period, found the haciendas to be modest in size and rarely economically self-sufficient or politically independent. The haciendas described by other prominent scholars fall within these two extremes.[5]

Similarly, the details of the organization of production of the third type, the commercialized farms, vary from one region to another. Thus, sugar estates on the eastern coast of South America depended almost exclusively on slaves for both skilled and unskilled labor and produced primarily for export. On the western coast and in Mexico, Indians provided sugar estates with temporary unskilled labor to supplement the work of slaves. Administrators hired skilled artisans, such as iron workers, masons, and tailors from nearby towns and cities. The Mexican ingenios, described by Ward Barrett, supplied an internal market. Those in Peru marketed some sugar within the viceroyalty, but also exported some to Tierra Firme, Upper Peru and Chile.[6]

Thus, far from leading to a consensus, these recent, in-depth characterizations of the estates located all over the Iberian colonial domain show variation on detail. These studies have provoked a lively debate, so ably synthesized by Magnus Mörner, on such specific points as financing, labor use, and forms of payment, and on the more fundamental issues of the relationship between the *encomienda*[7] and the hacienda and the seignorial or capitalistic nature of the hacienda itself.[8]

Attention to the origins and development of the estate helps to account for and explain the sometimes bewildering and growing assortment of findings and opinions on the institution. After the appearance of the first studies that explained the legal origins of the estate,[9] most writers explained the origins, evolution, and diversity of the estate on the basis of such factors as geography and climate; demographic trends; the existence of markets; the availability of land, labor, and capital; technological advances; and crown policy. In combination, these factors help explain why stock-raising estancias spread across northern Mexico, why indigo thrived in Central America, why wheat grew near the mines in Upper Peru, and why sugarcane predominated on the coast. These variables also help explain the continuum of development between the estancia, the hacienda, and the mill complex. In well-watered but isolated areas, without an abundant, cheap, and disciplined labor force, land was used for livestock raising. Sheep and goats fed on the natural scrub and grasses of the central Mexican plateau and coastal South America. Labor requirements for stock raising were minimal. Furthermore, animals walked to the slaughterhouse, or to the soap-making and tanning facilities. Wheat required fertile land, an abundant labor force, and a nearby market that would keep the cost of transportation by slow oxcart and mule train low. Sugarcane replaced grain when and where geographic and climatic factors permitted and market conditions merited the invest-ment of significant sums of capital in technology and skilled labor.[10]

Such factors also help to explain the lack of long-term development or prosperity and short-term adjustments in the operation of estates. The indigo-producing estates of Central America, for instance, re-mained relatively small, poor, and self-sufficient because the decline of the native Indian population created a severe labor shortage that, given the general economic conditions, was not readily remedied by importing blacks. Similarly, there is growing evidence suggesting that haciendas in northern Mexico and elsewhere lapsed into self-sufficiency whenever mining activities or market demand, in general, slowed.[11]

Many authors use these factors to account for the differences in interregional patterns of development. But the use of these factors leaves unanswered questions about the intraregional variation among estates, where general economic conditions, geography, and climate are more constant. It leaves unanswered, too, broader questions about the changing nature of the estates and their role in society. More and more scholars are realizing that no explanation of the origins and de-velopment of the estate and its associated diversity can be complete without considering the political dimension of the process of land trans-fer and use and the broader societal context in which it occurred. To understand why some estates changed their organization of production in response to successive governmental policies or fluctuating prices sooner than others; to understand how Indian communities lost land despite volumes of protective legislation and numerous royal officials supposedly charged with their well-being; in short, to understand more about variation and diversity in the colonial institution of the hacienda, one must identify the individuals and groups involved—that is, the landowners and the Indians—and examine their daily interaction. Only figuratively did the estates dominate the city and countryside. Within the confines imposed by the system, landowners responded to chang-ing conditions, made decisions, found means to expand their land-holdings where and when warranted, raised capital, organized labor, and experimented with new crops. Indians lost land. Their surplus production financed estate improvements. They furnished most of the agricultural labor in many areas.[12]

In an attempt to deepen our understanding of the agrarian situation in Spanish America, I will carry the analysis beyond conventional in-stitutional history and, as suggested by James Lockhart, present the history of the estate as a history of landowners. My views on the estate differ from the standard ones because I focus on the related themes of land tenure, power, and the powerful. On a local level, a knowledge of the relative wealth and power of certain individuals should broaden our understanding of the evolution of latifundia and the functioning of agrarian societies—both past and present.[13]

This approach represents the logical extension of the pathbreaking work of others who have called attention to the social history of the estate. Chevalier, Jean Borde and Mario Góngora, and David Brading, for example, recognize and discuss the importance of the landed elite in general terms. *Hacendados,* or owners of large estates, are identified as either New World counterparts of the European lord, who lived in a town or city, visited the estate periodically, and were uninterested in maximizing returns if it meant soiling their hands; or as entrepreneurs with wide-ranging commercial operations. Hacendados also functioned as *encomenderos,*[14] merchants, miners, government officials, and priests. Collectively, they constituted the privileged group in society.[15]

These authors agree that hacendados exercised considerable social, economic and political power over local affairs. For the hidalgo mentality of the colonists, landownership symbolized prestige; landowners embodied the social ideal; and, consequently, they enjoyed high social esteem and authority. The ownership of an estate in most areas implied at least a certain level of wealth as well as the potential ability to provide employment for professionals, artisans, and laborers. Land, according to Clarence Haring, Charles Harris, and Chevalier, provided the basis for the acquisition of local political power.[16]

The growing interest in landowners has led to research that attempts to detail or determine how hacendados used their power[17]—be it economic, political, or social—to protect and enhance their properties.[18] Many scholars equate the hacendados' power with their active participation in the *cabildo,* or town council. Research by Chevalier, Taylor, Lockhart, and Robert Keith shows that, first, encomenderos and, then, hacendados dominated the municipal councils in Mexico and Peru, respectively. These and other authors state that landowners used their positions on the council to protect their interests. "The hacendados," says André Gunder Frank, "were able to impose—through the cabildo . . . and the viceroy—the policies which suited them with regard to prices, indenture, vagrancy laws, etc." Chevalier states that hacendados used the cabildo to establish and confirm grazing rights, to grant themselves land, and to control the water supply.[19]

Others have focused on the basic question of whether real or fictive kinship ties were important factors used by the landed elite to extract favors. In the published literature, reference is made frequently to the influence wielded through allied family members and friends who held key bureaucratic, military, and ecclesiastical posts. P. J. Bakewell notes that to have certain high officials inclined to take one's own views could be most profitable. Harris reports that sympathetic hearing from royal officials in the north aided the Sánchez Navarros's empire building, although members of this family, intensely interested in politics, shunned open participation in political life. They preferred to work behind the scenes through relatives and an extensive network of correspondents, business agents, and informants. Taylor found that the friendship and advice of landowners in Oaxaca were frequently sought by political officials of lower social standing. This, he says, gave certain of them "subtle influence" in political matters beyond their tenure in office. Leslie Lewis's companion essay in the same volume shows that personal connections were important for economic advancement in Texcoco. Konrad's prize-winning study of the Mexican Jesuit estate of Santa Lucía shows that they, "like their secular hacendado counterparts, exploited their elite status and close ties with royal authorities to further [their] interests. . . ." They recognized the usefulness of maintaining close working relationships with the political and social elites to aid them in their ongoing battles with civil and indigenous authorities. "Controlling the local offices would 'eliminate' a thousand disputes with anticipation."[20]

Studies on Peru are less numerous than on Mexico, so many basic questions about the institution of the estate there remain to be studied. Few Peruvianists focus on the issue of landowners' power. It is not known to what extent or how long the estate owner participated in the local decision-making councils or whether he developed alternative means to control the local situation. Under what circumstances did hacendados use their wealth to influence decisions? To what extent did their near monopoly of natural resources affect the actions of others? Did the combination of wealth, political power, and social prestige place a relatively small number of men of Spanish descent above the law as compared to the Indian masses?[21]

Also unknown or largely neglected is the Indian side of the story. With few exceptions, historians dismiss this aspect of land tenure by reporting that the native population decreased rapidly and that those who survived were concentrated in new locations, away from what the crown considered the corrupting influence of peninsular society. Indians were assigned a passive role; and their response to continuing containment and incipient proletarianization, which paralleled in many areas the establishment and development of the estate, was lethargy, withdrawal, resignation, and fatalism.[22]

But the estate in most areas developed at the expense of the Indian community. The process involved the gradual replacement of the pre-conquest tradition of collective use and control of land with a system of private possession. As the estate took form, the natives lost land and their immediate postconquest function of supplying foodstuffs to the conquerors. Communities became important primarily as a local reserve of labor and a source of revenue for a few encomenderos or the royal treasury. Did the interaction between Indians and hacendados involve suffering, protest, and conflict? When did the Indians react to protect their interest? What were their alternatives?

These and other questions are examined in the process of tracing the economic and social history of the estate in one region on the northern coast of Peru during the colonial period. This region—extending on the south through the Pacasmayo Valley and bounded on the north by the Sechura desert and on the east by the Andes mountains—is an ideal laboratory in which to test hypotheses because of its long history as a major population and production center. Paul Kosok estimates that this area accounted for almost a third of the total cultivated area and population of the entire coast in ancient times. In the sixteenth century the area quickly became, and remains to the present day, one of Peru's major export-oriented agricultural enclaves.[23]

The legal and institutional histories of the estates in this region provide the framework within which to examine the human side of their evolution. I use the factors discussed above—(1) climate and natural resources; (2) labor: administrative, skilled or unskilled, slave or free; (3) capital: both physical and financial; (4) the level of technology or state of the arts: machinery, sources of energy, agricultural techniques or practices, new varieties of seed, and so forth; (5) market conditions, which, in turn, are affected by war, depression, and natural disasters; and (6) governmental policy on the continental, viceregal, and local levels—to determine how, in different combinations, they affected the changing physiognomy of the latifundia. By thus dissecting the process, I explore the conditions which gave rise to the different types of estates, and by extension, how this development affected the resource base of the Indian communities.[24]

Within this framework, I focus on the interaction of hacendados and Indian officials (as representatives of their communities) on questions related to the distribution and control of land, labor, and water. This study is designed to document, to the extent that surviving manuscript sources permit, the functional nexus between social and economic status and effective political power and influence. Biographical data on almost nine hundred landowners are used to examine the stereotypes of the hacendado to determine whether he was a New World counterpart of an Old World feudal lord, an entrepreneur, or some combination of the two. Information on career patterns and mode of land acquisition reveals at what point in life a person gained land and thus to what extent land served as an avenue of upward mobility. Analyzed collectively, the data have obvious implications on the composition, cohesion, and stability of the landed elite and on the process of capital accumulation and transfer over time. By determining whether the key to economic and political power was land or vice versa, and if and how estate owners used their position and power to manipulate the factors of production to protect their fortunes within one specific historical context, I extend the analysis beyond institutional history to suggest the underlying social relationships affecting the distribution of resources. This will lead, I hope, to a more complete appreciation of how land tenure affects the functioning of society, not only in colonial times but in many areas today.[25]

The organization of the text reflects this preoccupation with the social history of the estate. Each of the three following parts corresponds to a phase in the development of the estates: their origins (circa 1532–1594), their maturation and prosperity (1595–1719), and their decline (1720–1824). (See Appendix 4 on periodization.) The formation of a powerful landed elite parallels this development and is reflected in the chapter divisions. Part One is devoted to background material. It begins with a chapter on the establishment of the conquerors and their descendants as encomenderos with almost unrivaled authority over regional affairs, based on their control of native labor. The next chapter explains how conditions, largely outside of their control, undermined their authority. The last chapter of Part One deals with the appearance of a group of settlers whose economic base is land, not encomienda labor. They rapidly replace the encomenderos as the dominant force in the area. In the two chapters in Part Two, I recount how relatively small farms develop into large estates and how the power and position of the estate owners affected the process. Part Three focuses on the circumstances under which the established landowning elite is transformed by the incorporation of new members and the consequences of this transformation on the organization and functioning of the haciendas and on their relationship with the surrounding Indian communities.

PART ONE

Conquest Society and the Institutionalization of Spanish Domination to 1594

During the fifteenth and sixteenth centuries Spain was locked in a race with Portugal to discover and claim sovereignty over distant and supposedly rich lands outside the then-defined, civilized Western world. National pride and spices were not the only factors at stake. After the fall of Granada in 1492, Ferdinand and Isabella promoted further exploration, not only to seek a trade route to the spice-rich east and the profits such trade promised, but also because they realized that continued, extracontinental territorial expansion would provide a convenient escape valve to drain off the potentially dangerous, excess military energies left over from the reconquest of the peninsula. The occupation and settlement of Peru, and more specifically of the northern coast, must be placed within this larger framework.

In this first section, I examine the beginnings of conflict over the resources essential to agricultural production between the native inhabitants of the region and the conquering Spanish. To provide a backdrop against which to measure subsequent change, I provide one chapter on the arrival of the Spanish and the establishment of conquest society, based as it was on the control of native labor. The Spanish soldiers of fortune who were granted Indian communities in trust, the encomenderos, adroitly displaced the top Indian officials and used middle- and lower-ranking native bureaucrats to enforce their will. They created a bastardized Spanish culture by the selective importation of peninsular material goods and customs and superimposed their religion on that of the Indians.[1] In Chapters 3 and 4, I discuss the growing importance of land and the rise of agriculture as the basis of wealth, political position, and social status. By the 1560s and 1570s, changing circumstances led to a fall in the value of encomiendas and a parallel rise in the value of land; the successive transfer of land and rights to irrigation water from the Indian communities to the Spaniards; and the conscious efforts by the crown to establish a rival group of settlers which eventually came to dominate the area.

13

2   *The Encomenderos of Trujillo (to circa 1550)*

The history of Spanish land tenure in the Lambayeque region of Peru must be placed in the broader context of the conquest and settlement of America. This involves briefly shifting the focus of our attention away from Lambayeque to Trujillo. The latter became the heart of colonial life on the northern coast during the thirty years or so immediately following the conquest. During this brief period, encomenderos dominated society through their control of the economy, their monopoly of political office, and their position as the social ideal for the rest of the population. Indians, held in trust by encomenderos, produced foodstuffs and other household goods, which their masters used to maintain their families and sold to others. Indian production became the principal source of wealth and power in conquest society.

The young and ambitious men who risked life and limb to accompany Francisco Pizarro and, later, his partner Diego de Almagro in their exploration and conquest, came not to seek land but to search for gold and glory. Of lower nobility (*hidalgo*) or plebeian origin, these adventurers were responding to the military tradition and challenge established during the prolonged reconquest of the Iberian peninsula from the Moors. They were lured by promised opportunities to gain wealth and position in the service of the king. In Spain most would have faced a meager livelihood in an unglamorous occupation. The best educated among them were priests, clerks, accountants, and notaries. Some were merchants. Others were artisans, seamen, and farmers. Once in the service, all were mercenaries—true civilians at heart and men of the sword primarily for reasons of profit and upward social mobility.[1]

The plunder of the march and the treasures of Atahualpa's ransom made them fabulously wealthy by the standards of sixteenth-century

Iberian society. One afternoon at Cajamarca for the horseman Juan de Barbarán yielded 362 silver marks[2] and 8,980 gold pesos, or a total of nearly 15,000 pesos of eight reales. Melchior Verdugo's share included 136 silver marks and 3,330 gold pesos, or a total of almost 6,500 pesos, which was equal to less than half of Barbarán's reward, but still a princely sum for a common foot soldier. Like other mercenaries, they had dreamed of gold, and now they were richer than most could ever become in Spain, where an unskilled laborer earned about 1⅓ reales per day and a carpenter about twice that sum. Even the smallest share was enough, should its owner survive the dangers, to enable him to establish a family and live in respectable fashion back home. Given this booty, the sums needed to buy the basic necessities of life in Spain seemed small indeed. Olive oil (in 1532) cost six reales per *arroba*.[3] Wheat (in 1535) sold at exactly a peso per *fanega* and two pounds of bread cost less than one real. Wax candles cost slightly over 1 real per pound and 4.5 arrobas of wine could be purchased with a peso in 1532.[4]

The conquerors' rewards, then, were fortunes, especially in a land where the local *curacas,* Indian chieftains, provided food for free and Indians worked for nothing. The Spanish used their gold and silver primarily for trading amongst themselves—to purchase a good horse, armor, weapons, wine, or flour for bread. The Spanish who shared in this booty could easily afford imported foods, even at the high prices of the immediate postconquest years, when an arroba of white wine cost almost thirty-five pesos (in 1535) and a pound of wax for candles sold for over three pesos (in 1538). A good horse was the single most expensive item a self-designated conqueror could buy, costing an average of nine hundred pesos in 1535 and still nearly six hundred pesos two years later. These relatively high prices reflected the scarcity of these animals and the strong demand for them, given the Spanish belief that horses were essential for gentlemanly combat.[5]

But the booty of bullion proved insufficient to reward satisfactorily all the men who took part in the expeditions and campaigns during those first two or three years. So, Pizarro as governor and captain general of the kingdom began to grant his most deserving and loyal followers Indians in encomienda, the most valuable award that he could give them for their services. It immediately confirmed the recipient's important role in the settlement and pacification effort and conferred on him, in time, almost matchless prestige as a "conqueror." As the guardian or trustee of a specific Indian chief and his subjects, the grantee or encomendero became a glorified tax collector with unrivaled, though officially unsanctioned, authority to settle disputes. His word consequently gave him power over life and property. It gave him free rights or access to the personal services of the Indians. In fact, the major responsibility of the Indians became the support of the encomendero and his household. In exchange, the encomendero pledged to defend the Indians' material well-being and to send a priest to save their souls by teaching them the precepts of Catholicism. Inherent in the grant was the encomendero's promise to the crown to settle in the district and to keep a horse and weapons ready to defend the newly won kingdom.[6]

An encomienda was not a land grant. The geographical extent of a grant was not an immediate consideration. No one, not even Pizarro himself, had a clear idea at this time of the native concepts of tenancy or of the vastness of the area and how unwieldy it would be to administer and colonize effectively. The area was defined in terms of population, as separate groups of Indians. Furthermore, land was not a particularly scarce or valuable commodity before 1550. Encomenderos did not need agricultural land because the Indians produced most of what their new masters requested on land which they had formerly cultivated for themselves, for the Inca state, or for their religion. The only way an encomienda grant could be construed as a land grant— and then only in a restricted, unofficial jurisdictional sense—was that, in practice, the encomienda made an encomendero's word law in the area occupied by the Indians he held in trust. For the first ten to fifteen years following the conquest, then, the encomendero was known primarily as the master of people, not as an owner of land.[7]

Using the device of encomienda, Pizarro gave thirty-one men control over the coastal Indian communities between Santa on the south and Jayanca on the north and those in the highland provinces of Chachapoyas, Cajamarca, and Huamachuco. A third of these became masters of most of the Indians living in the Lambayeque area. On the northern fringe of the five-valley Lambayeque region, Pizarro awarded the community of Jayanca to Francisco de Lobo. He assigned Conoçique and his subjects in the Túcume area to Juan Roldán. Juan de Osorno received at about the same time the principales Ferriñafe, Chiclefe, and several others. In 1536, the Indians of Lambayeque were deposited in the keeping of Juan de Barbarán, Pizarro's loyal supporter and personal confidant. The Indians of Sinto, Collique (who were later resettled in Chiclayo), Chuspo-Callanca, and Reque were entrusted to Diego de Vega, Blas de Atienza, Francisco Luis de Alcántara, and Miguel de

Velasco, respectively. Pedro Gonzales received Jequetepeque. Captain Alonso Félix de Morales received title to the Indians of Saña, and Miguel Pérez de Villafranca Lezcano received Chérrepe on the northern fringes of the large Pacasmayo Valley.[8]

All but two of these men were among the original householders, or *vecinos*, of Trujillo, the Spanish town founded in late 1534 and named after Pizarro's birthplace. Trujillo became a symbol of European presence and permanence on the coast. The city served as a military outpost and center for the organization and direction of the region. Here, Pizarro awarded the vecinos choice house sites near the plaza, on the condition that they build a residence and live there at least four years, and small plots of land for gardens on the outskirts of town. Being granted Indians and named a householder of one of the first Spanish towns to be founded in Peru conveyed added status to these men of modest beginnings, turned soldiers, and provided them an excuse to settle down as respected citizens.[9]

The encomiendas became the economic base for these "conquerors" and their families, and for the increasing number of Spaniards who joined their households as personal retainers. Encomienda Indians left their communities to construct the encomendero's residence, served as domestics, and fenced and cultivated his garden plots around Trujillo. Those who remained in their communities worked on their traditional lands to produce food, cotton fiber, and the other products demanded by their master. These goods were later carried to Trujillo. The encomienda proved more than sufficient to supply labor for the needs of the encomendero and his household, and, had this been the Indians' only responsibility, the encomienda might never have evolved into the exploitative and oppressive institution it became.[10]

Alone, the encomienda made the encomenderos some of the richest men in Peru and certainly on the northern coast. Figure 2 lists the estimated monetary value of a dozen of the encomiendas in the region in 1548. These figures are extracted from an original document, signed in Cuzco by four vecinos of Trujillo on 16 April 1548 and prepared at the request of Licenciado Pedro de la Gasca, president of Peru, as a guide for the officials sent to compile the first itemized lists of tribute goods (*tasas*) for each Indian community in the kingdom. The four apparently used their own encomiendas as a gauge by which to estimate the value of the others and to rank them accordingly. The figures represent informed guesses of the value of the material goods delivered to the encomendero. Encomienda labor was unpaid; consequently, its

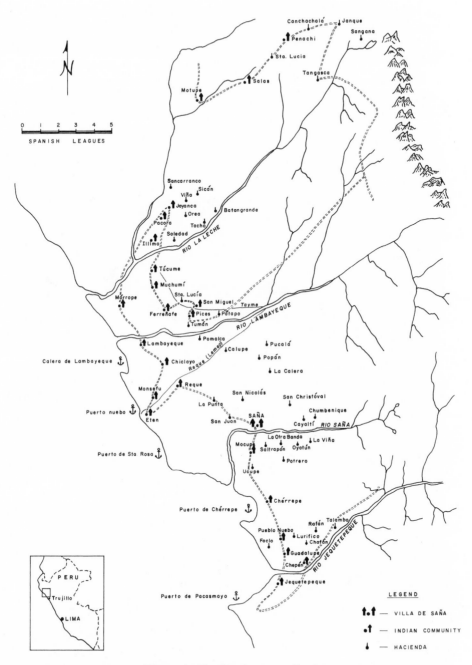

Figure 1. The Lambayeque Region

Figure 2. Value of Selected Encomiendas of Lambayeque in the Sixteenth Century

Encomienda	Year[1]	Value[2] in Pesos[3]
Collique	1548	2,702[4][5]
	1559–63	7,279[4][5]
	1568	4,963[4]
	1572	1,894
	1579–80	2,631[6]
	1589	1,444
	1591	1,814[7]
Chérrepe	1548	1,801[4][5]
	1556	4,592[6]
	1559–63	3,557[4][5]
	1566	1,760
	1569	1,324
	1591	465[7]
Chuspo-Callanca	1548	1,441[4][5]
	1559–63	4,053[4][5]
	1572	2,261
	1582	2,187
Ferreñafe	1548	2,162[4][5]
	1559–63	4,665[4][5]
	1572	1,831
	1591	1,278[7]
Illimo	1548	901[4][5]
	1559–63	1,357[4][5]
	1572	2,694
Jayanca	1548	7,206[4][5]
	ca. 1565–70	9,926[8]
	1572	3,985
	1589	2,750[9]
Jequetepeque	1548	1,801[4][5]
	1559–63	3,474[4][5]
	1572	3,047
	1575	3,320[10]

Encomienda	Year[1]	Value[2] in Pesos[3]
	1576	6,618[6]
	1589	2,593
	1591	2,057[7]
	1591	1,179[11]
	1595	299[11]
Lambayeque	1548	3,603[4][5]
	1559–63	5,542[4][5]
	1565	5,069[6][8]
	1566	1,318[6]
	1570	9,099[6][8]
	1572	9,265[6][8]
	1572	4,995
	1574	1,861[8]
	1574	11,374[6][8]
	ca. 1575	2,554[6][8]
	1591	5,091[7]
Pacasmayo	1548	1,801[4][5]
	1559–63	5,956[4][5]
Reque	1548	1,441[4][5]
	1559–63	3,640[4][5]
	ca. 1565	3,309[6][8]
	1572	456
	1591	1,729[7]
Saña	1548	2,702[4][5]
	1559–63	5,790[4][5]
	1563	2,647[6][8]
	1572	937
	1572	608[12]
Sinto	1559–63	3,805[4][5]
	ca. 1565	4,136[6][8]
	1572	2,180
	1578	602[11]
	1583	1,156
	1591	2,264[7]

Figure 2 (continued)

Encomienda	Year[1]	Value[2] in Pesos[3]
	1591	1,415[8]
	1595	409
Túcume	1548	2,162[4][5]
	1559–63	5,741[4][5]
	1566	9,529[6][8]
	1568	10,588[8][13]
	1568	4,235[7]
	1569	9,265[6][8]
	1569	3,706[7]
	1570	7,941[8][13]
	1570	3,176[7]
	1572	4,986
	1591	4,749[8]
	1591	2,696[7]

Notes:

[1]Unregulated prior to 1549. Note that when more than one estimate was found for any given year, all are shown.

[2]Net, unless otherwise specified.

[3]Rounded to nearest peso of 8 reales each. Conversion rates for various years are given in Appendix 1, under prices for pesos corrientes and ensayados. If the type of peso is not indicated, the conversion rate of 450 maravedis to 1 is assumed.

[4]Assumed: approximately a fraction of the true market value.

[5]The manuscript does not indicate the type of peso used. For conversion purposes, I assumed the pesos in 1548 equalled 490 maravedis each.

[6]Impossible to determine whether figures are gross or net.

[7]Net for the year equals the total tribute less the king's fifth and 40 percent for the costs of collection and contributions. For 1591, I assumed that costs remained at the same average level as those of 1572.

[8]Estimate.

[9]Low, because the official value of tribute cloth is assessed at only about half its true market value.

[10]Total tribute less the sum of officials' salaries, the church construction fund and the king's fifth.

[11]Fixed pension paid from the tribute to the encomendero.

Figure 2 (continued)

[12]Not including the *mitimaes* (Indian colonists, living apart from the main community) of Saña. One encomendero held Saña and the mitimaes of Saña
concurrently.
[13]Gross.

Reliability:
The 1548 figures must be considered a minimum and probably equal to only
a fraction of the encomienda's true value.

Sources:
BAH/ML: t. 82, 1548, 138–40; Muñoz, A–92, 1540, 66v–67; A–66, No. 211, 1591,
234–296v; ART/HO: 5–XI–1586; Mata: 26–VIII–1572; Vega: 3–X–1589; 1599 [1589];
CoO: 13–VII–1570, 112, 119v, and 301v; MT: 1573 [*sic* 1587]; 1574; BUSR/IV, No.
60, 323; ANP/R: 1. 2, c. 5, 1582, 129–35; 1. 7, c. 16, 1590, 1163–64; AGI/AL: 199,
n.d. [1563], 1v and 3; 203; 273, 168v; C: 1780b; E: 534A, 72 and 375; J: 418,
1573, 2v and 45; 420, 1574, II, 105v and 108v; 459, 2653 and 3030; P: 1. 97, r.
4, [1569], 10v, 16v–18 and 45v; 1. 108, r. 7, 1562, 51v–2; 1. 113, r. 8, 63; ASFL/
Reg. 9, No. 2, Ms. 21, n.d.; BNP/A157, 132, 135 and 138; A538, 1580; Rubén
Vargas Ugarte, "Fragmento de una historia de Trujillo," *Revista histórica*, VIII
(1925), 88–89; *Actas del Cabildo de Trujillo, 1566–71*, II (Lima, 1969), 102; Rolando
Escobedo Mansilla, *El tributo indígena en el Perú Siglos XVI y XVII* (Pamplona,
1979), especially 38–49; and Rafael Loredo, *Los repartos* (Lima, 1958), especially
250–58 and 265.

value was not included in the calculation. Because a market did not
exist for some of the goods produced as tribute, and the four encomenderos had no sure knowledge of the amounts requested by their
peers, the figures certainly reflect no more than a fraction of the true
value of an encomienda and can only be accepted with this in mind.
The figures are useful, however, to show that encomenderos, as a
group, were rich in comparison to other persons,[11] but within the group
their income varied considerably: from less than 1,000 to over 3,600
pesos per year, with the average at slightly over 2,000 pesos.[12]

Once the encomendero's personal needs for food, clothing, shelter,
and drink were met, he used the encomienda to launch complementary
economic and financial ventures. Francisco Luis de Alcántara and Pedro
Gonzales, not unlike their fellow encomenderos, quickly put their Indians to work in building houses and stores for lease on additional
land they received from the town council. The encomenderos' near

monopoly of native labor also made them the major labor brokers for the rest of society, regularly renting Indians to nonencomenderos for specific purposes. In addition, the encomendero required his Indians to plant cereals—especially wheat—to be sold in the developing urban market. By the end of the civil wars in the late 1540s, the Indians delivered enough goods to establish a significant regional trade between Trujillo and Lima and Tierra Firme.[13]

The encomenderos either reinvested the profits from these activities or lent them to other aspiring individuals. Among the most common uses for surplus capital was financing a voyage to Tierra Firme to buy wines, perfumed soaps, furniture, linens, velvets, and other imported luxury items. The encomendero rarely engaged in this long-distance trade directly, preferring instead to participate as a partner or outright sponsor of a trip. Such indirect participation in trade allowed the encomendero to avoid the disdain associated with merchants, while allowing him to share in the lucrative business. Juan de Barbarán's will, dated 1539, makes numerous references to this type of undercover participation in commercial life. It also leaves no doubt as to his role as early colonial financier. He died with more than three thousand pesos in outstanding debts, but more than thirty persons owed him about five times that much.[14]

The healthy profits from these ancillary activities added to the income derived indirectly from the unregulated encomienda allowed first-generation encomenderos to establish a free-spending tradition that would be the bane of many of their descendants. Some spent small fortunes to return to Spain themselves or to send someone in their stead to find family and friends. Others spent lavishly on conspicuous consumption, so determined were they to live in the imagined style of peninsular grandees or hidalgos—to be served by black slaves, to taste bread on silver plates, and to savor Castilian wine from golden mugs. Their involvement in suppressing Indian rebellions and their participation in the civil wars also required the resources to hire and provision men for months in the field. Encomenderos justified such expenses as necessary to live up to the unwritten pact made with the crown in return for their Indians and to establish themselves and their posterity with honor as the "first" families.[15]

Along with wealth and prominence, the encomenderos enjoyed an absolute monopoly of local political power. The status of Trujillo vecino carried with it the right and obligation to serve on the town council, or cabildo; and during the first two decades or so, council membership was limited to them alone. Pizarro named the original council of two magistrates (*alcaldes*), five aldermen (*regidores*), and a municipal treasurer and trustee (*mayordomo del cabildo y de consejo*), and continued to appoint them for a few years. Blas de Atienza and Diego de Vega sat as magistrate and treasurer, respectively, of the first council. Atienza served until 1536 at Pizarro's request. Three other encomenderos of Lambayeque, Roldán, Morales, and Alcántara joined the town council at that time as aldermen, bringing the representation of Lambayeque to almost half the membership of the council. This precedent became tradition during the 1540s, when the viceroy assumed the responsibility of selecting replacements from the nominations of outgoing members. As many as six encomenderos with Indians in Lambayeque served as magistrates and councilmen in the eight years between 1535 and 1550, for which information is available.[16]

Representation on the cabildo assured the encomenderos of a say on the issues brought before the only ruling body for the area, and they virtually regulated society as they saw fit. But contrary to generally accepted beliefs, participation during these first few years rarely directly affected the exercise of power over their distant encomienda holdings. The area within the jurisdiction of Trujillo was too large for the members of the council to govern effectively. Their preoccupation with the countryside diminished in direct proportion to distance from the city. Thus, frontier areas like Lambayeque were outside the purview of constant attention.[17]

The published minutes of the council meetings show that Atienza, Roldán, Morales, Lope de Ayala, and the other members rarely took any action beyond the immediate urban and suburban zone of the city, despite the fact that their jurisdiction included the Lambayeque area and a vast highland district. Urban planning and sanitation, all part of establishing and running the city, occupied the collective attention of the council during these early years. Encomenderos devoted entire meetings to discussing petitions from newcomers for vecino status and accepting qualified individuals;[18] granting house sites; establishing and maintaining a reliable, potable water system; founding and running the hospital; guaranteeing the food supply; and setting prices for these foodstuffs and the services of artisans and certain professionals. Encomenderos profited personally from participation by voting themselves additional house lots, garden plots, and allotments of irrigation water.[19]

Usually, they took action in the rural areas only to comply with a directive from Lima or another viceregal authority. Then, they chose a magistrate or another representative to go on an inspection tour (*visita*) to hear complaints, correct abuses, settle disputes, or report on the conditions of rest houses, roads, and bridges.[20]

This limited action was consistent with the interests of council members as individuals and encomenderos. The encomenderos assumed authority over the countryside largely by default: for years there were no other Spanish authorities in the area. The encomendero seemed omnipotent among the Indians. His word was law; he made the rules and settled disputes. The Indians rarely questioned his authority or appealed his actions or decisions to the occasional visiting Spanish dignitary. The encomenderos jealously guarded these prerogatives and did not welcome the idea of other encomenderos meddling in their spheres of influence.[21]

Council service also qualified them for other positions of power and responsibility in Trujillo. Magistrates, who were elected from among the other council members, served as judges of first instances. Moreover, in these early years before a royal bureaucracy had been established, councilmen doubled as royal treasurers and officials.[22]

These duties and the attending stature and preëminence of his person; a predilection for urban living and its comforts; pressing business concerns and personal affairs; and twenty-five leagues of rough terrain, whether traversed under the strong desert sun or under cover of night with its increased danger of attack, kept the encomendero's visits to his encomienda in Lambayeque brief and infrequent. The instruments of his power as far as the Indians were concerned were the Spaniards that the encomendero hired to live in Lambayeque in the communities under his control. The encomendero delegated his authority to a trusted servant or retainer (*criado* and majordomo), who worked closely with native officials to collect and transport tribute goods to Trujillo and otherwise carry out his orders. The priest, the encomendero's religious agent, said Masses and attempted to teach the sons of the native nobility Spanish and the rudiments of Christianity. Both the majordomo and the priest took advantage of any excuse for lengthy absences. Consequently, their supervising and acculturating activities were sporadic and largely ineffectual during these first few years.[23]

Other contact that Indians had with Spaniards was limited to vagabonds, travelers, itinerant merchants, and the occasional agents of the crown. Wanderers and travelers stopped at roadside inns which were permanently staffed and supplied by nearby communities. Merchants

visited the valleys, trading beads and other trinkets for grain and textiles. Official visits to the relatively isolated Lambayeque area at this
time were rare. Royal authorities passed through the region on their
way to Lima or arrived occasionally to conduct an inquiry. Such contact
apparently had little impact on the mass of Indians, for native officials
routinely dealt with arriving strangers and their visits were normally
brief.[24]

This interaction between Spaniards and Indians through the institution of the encomienda did not significantly affect the organization
of the Indian communities in Lambayeque. Agricultural practices remained basically unchanged. The Spanish rarely introduced European
technology; and the natives did not have the means to acquire it.
Encomenderos encouraged the cultivation of wheat, but otherwise the
Indians continued to grow cotton, corn, beans, and other traditional
foodstuffs.

The exceptions were the few Indians who learned to cultivate such
European crops as olives and grapes while working on the garden plots
(*huertas* and *chacras*) near Trujillo, under the direct supervision of the
encomendero and his retainers. Livestock raising was the major innovation in the communities. The Indians learned to raise pigs, goats,
sheep, horses, and mules, which they drove to Trujillo as needed.[25]

The Spanish presence did change Indian culture in certain respects.
Robed friars, for instance, declared the Christian god to be more powerful than the sun, the moon, and all the deities of the native pantheon
combined. Threats of divine punishment bolstered the position of the
conquerors. Catholic ritual gradually replaced what the conquerors
deemed "pagan" ceremonies.

These changes, however, were superficial. Most Indians lived as
before, under the direction of their officials. These chiefs continued to
distribute the land and organize and lead collective labor to produce
the surplus which provided the basis for the encomenderos' wealth,
political power, and status and sustained the growing Spanish community. They were the first to assume Christian names, to accept baptism, and to learn Spanish. They played key roles as cultural brokers
or middlemen between the Spanish and the mass of Indians, translating
and explaining.[26]

Their job grew more difficult over the years as the encomendero's
demands increased and it became more burdensome for the Indians
to fill their master's quotas. Indian officials had little choice but to serve
as the encomendero's willing accomplices. In exchange for cooperation,

the encomendero allowed Indian officials to retain some of their traditional privileges (such as exemption from tribute obligations), overlooking petty abuses and, later, outright corruption. Some Indian officials actually took advantage of the encomendero's leniency, their own power, and the lack of effective control to enhance their personal wealth and position. For example, Spanish ignorance of the extent of an official's preconquest authority allowed curacas to collect excess tribute, to increase the number of their personal servants, and to claim with impunity lands formerly planted in the name of the Inca state or religion.[27]

The tolerant attitude of the encomenderos toward the increasing abuses of cooperative native officials contrasts sharply with the attitude they assumed in regard to those officials unwilling or unable to satisfy their demands. An encomendero did not hesitate to replace an obstinate and uncooperative Indian official with another who would better serve his purposes. According to María Rostworowski de Diez Canseco's study of succession, encomenderos usually confirmed the choice of a curaca, chosen by the Indians according to their ancient custom. If a curaca proved recalcitrant, however, the encomendero did not hesitate to exercise his veto power and replace him. Fray Domingo de Santo Tomás reports that the Spanish "gave [the position of curaca] to whomever they thought would be a good administrator of the poor Indians in carrying out their will. . . ."[28]

One of the reasons why native officials often found themselves in a difficult position was the continued sharp decline in the numbers of their subjects. There are many reasons to believe that the native population of the region was already on the decline in 1532. On their way to Saña, Pizarro and his men passed abandoned buildings and fields. Oral tradition recorded by the early chronicler, Felipe Guamán Poma de Ayala, tells of strange diseases which destroyed families and entire lineages before the arrival of the first Europeans. Such diseases as smallpox and measles advanced faster than Spanish exploration and settlement, spreading from village to village through New Spain to Central and South America, perhaps carried by long-distance native traders. Huayna Capac, father of Atahualpa and Huascar, died of smallpox in Quito before Pizarro left on his first voyage of discovery to the Peruvian coast. In addition, the civil wars of succession between the two brothers undoubtedly took their toll. Henry F. Dobyns postulates that the population of the Inca empire may already have been reduced by more than half by the early 1530s. Nevertheless, the Indian population that greeted the Spanish conquerors was larger and denser than it would be again until at least the eighteenth century, as the population curves on Figure 3 show.

During the postconquest decades, the native population continued to drop sharply, faster on the coast than in the highlands. In a letter to His Majesty in July 1550, Santo Tomás estimated that in the last decade the indigenous population had fallen by one-third to one-half. The documented 85 percent decline in population of the community of Saña between 1532 and 1563 is probably typical of the region.[29]

Eyewitnesses attributed the continuing population decline to a combination of causes. A major Indian uprising on the coast in 1538 claimed many lives, and disease took its toll. Another frequently cited cause was the abuse of the natives by the Spanish and particularly by the encomenderos—their supposed protectors and champions. Until 1549 the encomendero was free to demand from his charges whatever goods and services he wanted and they could provide. Besides quantities of local products, some encomenderos demanded items exotic to the area. In such cases, curacas sent emissaries to other communities to exchange their products for the items the encomendero specified. Over the years, the growing domestic and export markets and the encomendero's desire to profit from this expansion motivated him to work his charges harder.[30]

The encomendero made demands regardless of the population loss suffered by the community. Ironically, his quotas increased at the same time that the Indians' ability to produce fell. As the native population declined, those who survived were forced to work harder to fill quotas. Indians who failed to meet the encomendero's demands were brutally punished. Many fled to isolated areas or to nearby cities or towns to escape the exigencies of the encomendero and his agents.[31] Thus, almost every year, the encomendero demanded more services than the previous year, yet each year fewer Indians remained to work. This became a perennial pattern for the years before 1550.[32]

Tribute remained completely unregulated, despite reports to the crown from humanitarian-minded priests and a few government bureaucrats of the encomenderos' harsh treatment and their unreasonable demands on the Indians. In the frontier atmosphere of the northern coast, there were hardly any individual or institutional checks on the encomendero's action. The few government bureaucrats in Peru lived in Lima, where they did not witness the heavy-handedness of the production and transportation of the tribute goods from the countryside. Furthermore, the position of these bureaucrats as urban consumers made

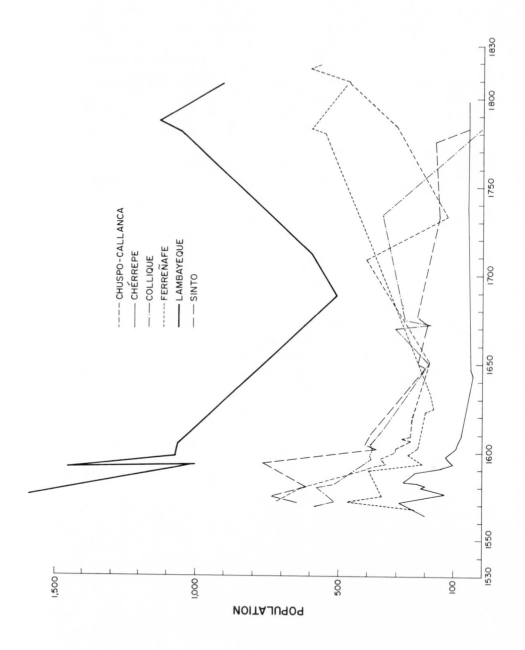

Figure 3. Tribute-paying Population of Selected Communities

Sources: Luis de Morales Figueroa, "Relación de los indios tributarios . . . del Pirú,", BAH/Muñoz: A-66, No. 211, 1591, 234–96v; 9-4664, 1549, 23v–24v; ART/ Mata: 1587; RH: 20-I-1788; IO: 8-VII-1793; 4-VI-1799; 18-X-1788, 14, 21 and 91; IC: 11-XII-1787; CoO: 13-VII-1570, 96–99v; CoAG: 29-XII-1622; and 24-I-1685; CoR: 30-VI-1576; CQ: 1698; 20-IV-1688; CoComp: 21-I-1721; Noble David Cook, "The Indian Population of Peru, 1570–1620," Ph.D. diss., University of Texas, Austin, 1973, 350; Domingo Angulo, "Diario de la segunda visita pastoral . . . ," Revista del Archivo Nacional del Perú, 1, no. 2 (mayo–agosto, 1920), 227–45; "Relación hecha por el Virrey Don Martín Enriquez dellos oficios q[ue] se proveen en la governación de los reinos y provincias del Perú," in Roberto Levillier, Gobernantes del Perú, Cartas y papeles (siglo XVI), 9 (Madrid, 1927), 206–10; ANP/R: 1. 2, c. 5, 1582, 131, 135, 138, 139v and 186v; 1. 22, c. 57, 1611, 706v–7v; DI: 1. 19, c. 483, 1793, 20 and 25; 1. 23, c. 675, 1809, 4; 1. 24, c. 684, 1606; 1. 39, c. 820, 1737, 14; RA: 1. 302, c. 2711, 1791, 53; Tributos: 1. 2, c. 25, 1734, 1v and 3; TC: 1. 5, c. 37, 1811–19, 3v and 19; Antonio Vázquez de Espinosa, Compendio y descripción de las Indias occidentales (Madrid, 1969), 458–59; ANCR/ 1787–88, 35v–41v, 104v and 114; 1808: 146v, 163 and 197; [1808]; Collús: [1807]; BP/343, 1789, 5; 2817, 1756, 4–7; Alejandro O. Araujo, "Reseña histórica de Saña," (Eten, noviembre 29, 1957), 30; Augusto D. León Barandiarán, Mitos, leyendas y tradiciones Lambayecanas (n.p. [Lima?], n.d. [1938?]), 142; BNP/C3028, 1787, 1v–2v; A310, 1572, 35v; C2195, 1756, 55, 60 and 70v; D6557, 1809, 3v; AGI/P: 1. 97, r. 4 [1596], 16v; J: 457, 851, 857v and 870; 464, 1583, 138; 420, 1574, II, 152v and 154v–55; and R: 1. 3, c. 7, 1582, 507; E: 517A, 1674–80, 8– 8v and 10v; 502A, [1607–11], 9; AL: 201, 1633; 320, n.d.; C: 1821, 1729–67; Rubén Vargas Ugarte, "Fragmento de una historia de Trujillo," Revista histórica 8, nos. 1–2 (1925), 88–89; Carlos Bachmann, Monografía de Lambayeque (Lima, 1921), 12; Luis Arroyo, Los Franciscanos y la fundación de Chiclayo (Lima, 1956), 32; Victor Arenas Pérez and Hector E. Carmona, eds., Anuario de Lambayeque (Chiclayo, 1947), 506 and 602; ASFL/Reg. 7, No. 2, Ms. 10, 1766; Reg. 9, No. 2, Ms. 26, 1647, 69; OCIL/Reque: 9, 22, and 63; "Títulos pertenecientes a las tierras y linderos de la comunidad del pueblo de Santa Lucía de Ferreñafe," Firruñap 3, no. 25 (1966), 25; Jacinto A. Liza Q., "La Ciudad de Ferreñafe," Firruñap 3, no. 25 (1966), 65; Centro de Estudios de Historia Eclesiástica del Perú, Monografía de la Diócesis de Trujillo 1 (Trujillo, 1930), 12; Ángel Mendez Rua, Boceto histórico de la iglesia de Lambayeque (Lambayeque, 1935), 41–45; ACMS/ 1654–1765, 13, 37v and 41; 1813, 6v and 93–94; Marco Aurelio Cabero, "El Capitán Juan Delgadillo, encomendero de Saña," Revista histórica 2, trim. 1 (1907), 94; and Justo Modesto Rubiños y Andrade, "Un manuscrito interesante: Sucesión cronológica . . . de los curas de Mórrope y Pacora en la Provincia de Lambayeque . . . (1782)," Revista histórica 10, no. 3 (1936), 306, 316 and 354; Manuel Burga, "San Jacinto de Ucupe: Una estancia colonial en el Valle de

Zaña," *Análisis* 2–3 (abril–diciembre, 1977), 193–95; Burga, *De la encomienda a la hacienda capitalista* (Lima, 1976), 63, 125, and 135; Günter Vollmer, Bevölkerungspolitik und Bevölkerungsstruktur im Vizenkönigreich Peru zu Ende der Konialzeit (1741–1821) (Zurich and Berlin, 1967), 252; Antonine Tibesar, *Franciscan Beginnings in Colonial Peru* (Washington, D.C., 1953), 63; AFA/Mocupe: c. 6, 9, 19 and 20; 1. 1, c. 10, 3–5; and 1. 2, c. 16, 3; *La Unión,* 14-V-1959, 1; Sebastián de la Gama, "Visita hecha en el Valle de Jayanca [Trujillo]," *Historia y cultura* 8 (Lima, 1974), 218 and 221; Fuentes, *Memorias de los virreyes,* Appendix VI, 6–7; AAT/Padrones: 1786; Javier Tord Nicolini, "El corregidor de indios del Perú: Comercio y tributos," *Historia y cultura* 8 (1974), 199; and Katherine Coleman, "Provincial Urban Problems: Trujillo, Peru, 1600–1784," in D. J. Robinson, *Social Fabric and Spatial Structure in Colonial Latin America* (Ann Arbor, 1979), 375.

---

them dependent on the encomenderos' supplies. The royal *audiencia* (the supreme executive, legislative, and judicial body seated in the capital) was established in the early 1540s, but this source of justice remained too distant and abstract to be effective.[33]

The few limitations on the exactions made by the encomendero were the tolerance of the Indians for work; the transportation, storage, and sale of produce; and his own conscience. The grant of the Indians of Túcume specifically stated that the encomendero's conscience should suffer all the burden and responsibility for mistreatment of the natives—not the soul or conscience of the king or of Pizarro. This provision probably did little to change the conduct and exactions of an encomendero while he was in his prime. As he grew old and began to fear death, however, guilt often surfaced. To alleviate this guilt and to make amends (*"por vía de restitución"*), an encomendero often made provision in his will for the welfare of his Indians. To ease the pangs Roldán felt for forcing his Indians to produce large quantities of alfalfa and chickens, he left them 1,575 pesos to be invested in real estate. The annual interest of almost 300 pesos on this principal was to be spent to celebrate church holidays and to purchase clothing and blankets for the poor. Likewise, Lope de Ayala, in one provision of his will dated 9 May 1551, mentions his agreement with other encomenderos of the Lambayeque area to found a monastery for Franciscan friars in Collique. He reiterates his desire to contribute to the funding and gives the authorities of Trujillo power to see that the monastery is constructed, equipped, and supplied as agreed. When Pedro Gonzales died in 1559, he left the Indians of Pacasmayo three houses and four stores, the annual rents of which were to be spent to supply the hospital of Jequetepeque that served the Indian communities to Pacasmayo, Lloco, and Puemape.[34]

By the end of the 1540s, this elite, created by the fiat of Francisco Pizarro, was firmly positioned at the pinnacle of conquest society. Despite the death of some of their numbers in Indian skirmishes, the civil wars, and other ennobling service to the crown, their survivors and the rest of the remaining twenty-odd first families looked forward confidently to petitioning the crown for coats of arms and further confirmation of their status. They were satisfied with the right which their control of the Indians in the hinterland gave them to participate in the town council and act as the judges, legislators, and executives of local colonial society. They benefited by setting prices for items they sold and by setting the rates for the services of artisans whom they employed. They controlled the unskilled urban labor supply, hired and dismissed administrators, and contracted for the services of priests. They, and especially the first generation, anxiously guarded their power—which gave them celebrity status in the eyes of their compatriots—and should it become necessary, they were determined to risk themselves and their fortunes to maintain their privileged position.[35]

But encomenderos remained relatively unconcerned with land: control of labor, not the soil, meant wealth. Along with a responsibility for the Indians' spiritual and material welfare, Pizarro gave the encomenderos power to order and direct the mode and level of production of the Indian communities; but the Spanish found little need to change the economic organization to meet their needs. The surviving hierarchy of Indian officials ably carried out their orders. Direct contact between the Spanish and Indians remained, therefore, limited. The major impact of the conquest on the communities was demographic, not organizational, but no less significant.

3   Landowning Encomenderos, 1550–1565

The phase of rarely countermanded encomendero power on the local level was short-lived. The efforts of the crown to check the hegemony of the encomenderos as a group, as well as a high native mortality rate, began to undermine seriously their position as early as the middle of the sixteenth century. These two factors and a third, the growth of markets, added land to labor as the basis of the economy. A separate group of landowners grew to the point where it eventually challenged the encomenderos' dominant social, political, and economic position. To the native inhabitants of Lambayeque, this meant the arrival and the permanent presence of additional Spaniards in the region and the establishment of units of agricultural production worked by paid laborers. These developments initiate a new phase of accommodation between the two cultures, marking the beginning of the end of conquest society and turning the focus of our attention back to Lambayeque.

Spanish interest in large grants of land on the coast and in encomenderos' economic troubles began with the depreciation of the encomienda. The crown had watched the uncontrolled growth of encomendero power, first in the Caribbean and then in New Spain and Peru. Disturbed by this development and the sometimes exaggerated reports of physical abuses, excessive tribute demands, and the continued suffering and high mortality rates of the native population, the crown began to enforce more vigorously its established policy designed to curb encomendero exploitation of the Indians, and, ultimately, to appropriate the tribute income for its own needs.

Initially, Carlos V mandated the eventual end of the encomienda. The New Laws he issued in 1542 contained the now-famous provision forbidding the giving of the institution in the future:

> We order and mandate that from this time forward
> no viceroy, governor, audiencia, discoverer or any
> other person grant Indians in trust by reason of any
> contract, cession, donation, sale, reward [*vocación*]
> or inheritance.

This provision was tantamount to the gradual confiscation of the economic foundation of the most powerful group in Spanish-American society at the time. It automatically abrogated the Law of Succession, which had given encomenderos jurisdiction over the Indians for two lifetimes. The existing encomiendas were to end with the death of the present encomenderos. Thereafter, the crown would assume the responsibilities for the well-being of the natives, and the Indians would produce tribute for the royal treasury.[1]

The emperor underestimated the reaction of the encomenderos. Ships originating in New Spain brought word of the New Laws before the first viceroy, Blasco Núñez Vela, arrived in Peru in 1544. His uncompromising determination to implement the imperial edict led to an encomendero revolt and his own death in the ensuing civil war. Licenciado Pedro de la Gasca, who replaced the viceroy, eventually defeated the rebels. He then proceeded to reassign and confirm the encomiendas, even to some rebels, in a calculated spirit of reconciliation designed to reestablish loyalty to the king.[2]

Realizing the impossibility of implementing the New Laws as written, La Gasca redefined the relationship between encomendero and community by specifying and limiting the Indians' obligations. This was consistent with the established policies of the crown. As early as 1536, Carlos V had instructed Pizarro to set limits on tribute exaction. Other humanitarians in Peru, such as Fray Domingo de Santo Tomás, had reminded the king that the tribute demands of the encomenderos were excessive and petitioned him repeatedly for regulation. Santo Tomás argued that "[the Indians] are not masters of their own wealth [haciendas], because they [the Spaniards] take it from them; nor of their own persons, because [the Spaniards] make them serve as if they were animals. . . ." Perhaps a little naively, he reasoned that if the Indians knew exactly what their obligations were, they would be less subject to extortion and exploitation.[3]

La Gasca defined the Indians' tribute obligations in terms of goods and personal services. Goods were restricted to items which the community itself produced or manufactured in abundance. The encomendero could no longer ask for exotic items. Lists (tasas) were compiled specifying the quantities of each good the encomendero could expect in a year. The items that the community of Saña had to produce for Rodrigo de Paz, their encomendero, in 1549 included cotton textiles, ranging from handkerchiefs and blankets to suits of clothes; foodstuffs; building materials; and furniture. Personal service was limited to planting and harvesting twenty-five fanegas of seed corn, ten of wheat and two of beans on community land. The curaca also had to provide sixty Indians to plant and harvest ten fanegas of corn and wheat on the encomendero's fields in the environs of Trujillo in each of the three annual growing seasons. Another fifteen Indians were to serve as domestics in the encomendero's house in Trujillo, and fourteen had to either cultivate his gardens or tend his livestock. In addition, the Indians had to transport most of the tribute goods to Trujillo.[4]

Indian claims that La Gasca's tribute lists were excessive were probably well founded, for the encomenderos of Lambayeque voiced no complaints about them. Their dissatisfaction stemmed, instead, from the fact that the mere existence of the tasas represented an infringement on their previously unrestricted rights to the labor of "their" Indians. They accepted the lists as a compromise solution rather than lose the encomiendas entirely, knowing full well that enforcement of the regulation would be uneven. Most Indians could not understand Spanish, let alone read it. Those few who could were pawns of the encomendero and could easily be influenced.

The 1549 regulation, however, was just the first of a series of tasas. Tribute, according to crown policy, was subject to periodic review and revision. Every few years the royal audiencia commissioned a local official or sent one of its members (an *oidor*) to count the native population and, on this basis, recompute the tribute to keep it proportional to the ability of the Indians to produce. Enumerators reduced the tribute obligations of the communities to reflect the prevalent demographic trends, although miscounting and other abuses were common. As a result, the income that the encomenderos derived directly from the encomienda decreased rapidly.[5]

Remarks by the encomenderos, and the available tribute figures, which are summarized in Figure 2 and selectively plotted on Figure 4 show the approximate magnitude of their losses. Despite the noted problems of the reliability and comparability of the numbers, the trend is clear. Income obtained directly from the encomiendas seems to have already peaked in the 1550s and early 1560s. The encomendero of Chérrepe first experienced the loss suffered later by all the others,

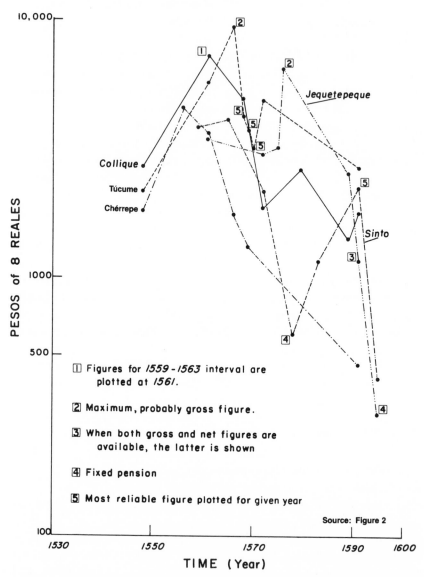

Figure 4. Value of Selected Encomiendas of Lambayeque, Sixteenth Century

probably due to the more rapid population decline of his Indians as a result of the direct and prolonged contact between them and the Spanish in the bustling port. The encomenderos of Íllimo, Jayanca, and Lambayeque were more fortunate in that the income produced by the Indians in those communities declined later and more slowly.

Already by the early 1560s, encomenderos complained that their incomes were low. As we shall see in Chapter 4, during the next ten years or so, viceregal officials took advantage of the reconfirmation process after the death of an encomendero to begin granting fixed pensions to the successors. Invariably, these pensions were significantly less than the total net income produced by a community and enjoyed by a grantee's predecessor. The heir of Sinto, for example, lost almost two-thirds of the net revenue from the Indians in this way, but retained the honor of being named the successor or *"encomendero propietario,"* a title still associated with high social status, prestige, and awe in 1570. This portended similar reductions to the encomendero of Jequetepeque in the 1590s and the rest of them in the seventeenth century.[6]

The encomendero's economic position was further weakened by the suppression of the unpaid personal services that the Indians provided him as part of the tribute and their replacement with paid labor organized along the lines of the old Inca institution of the *mita*. Shortly before his departure from Peru, La Gasca received a royal decree from Carlos V instructing him to abolish tribute labor completely. The difficulty of reforming and regulating the amount of tribute made La Gasca hesitate to add the loss of this valuable resource. The encomenderos considered the unrestricted use of their encomienda Indians as profitable as the sale of surplus tribute goods, and they were in no mood to have their privileged access to labor curtailed. La Gasca, therefore, prudently chose to disregard the royal will and allowed the tasas, which clearly limited the labor services of the natives, to stand.

Similarly, his successor, Viceroy Don Antonio de Mendoza, did little to implement the king's wishes, reasoning that the encomenderos were still too unsettled from the civil wars to accept such a radical change. After Mendoza's death, however, the audiencia tried to enforce the royal decree. Its implementation caused dissatisfaction and an immediate reaction. In what is a classic case of *"obedezco pero no cumplo,"*[7] the encomenderos of Trujillo, led by the magistrates Pedro Gonzales and Diego de Vega, dispatched a representative to Lima to protest the regulation of tribute labor before the audiencia in October 1553, reasoning that the decree was unrealistic under the present conditions and harmful to both Indian and Spanish republics. Elsewhere, encomendero discontent culminated in the revolts of Sebastían de Castilla and Francisco Hernández Girón. Although both uprisings were eventually quashed, with the help of some of the encomenderos of Lambayeque, they did succeed in delaying the implementation of the royal decree. Still, personal service was gradually phased out over the next few years.[8]

As an alternative to tribute labor, royal authorities revived and updated the mita to reflect changed conditions and needs. The mita was reintroduced as the Indians of a community were relieved of their labor obligations to the encomendero. Unlike the Inca mita, which was sporadically organized for extraordinary public works projects, the Spanish mita was systematic, constant, and coercive. Under the new regime, a certain percentage of the adult male population of a community worked for individual Spaniards or for the state. The specific percentage of a given community that served in the mita at one time and the lengths of service varied. In Trujillo, one-seventh of the adult males worked for a standard period of three months.[9] The curaca was responsible for sending the quota of *mitayos* for his community to Trujillo, where they were at the disposition of the town council for public works projects, such as maintaining the irrigation ditches that supplied the city with water. Others worked near the community on road repair or church construction. Another group worked locally for individual Spaniards. In theory, a magistrate, and later the corregidor,[10] distributed these mitayos among the Spanish—both encomenderos and non-encomenderos—who submitted petitions requesting labor, according to need. In practice, the individuals with the most power and influence (that is, the encomenderos) received a disproportionately large share.[11]

Mitayos, like the growing number of free laborers (*forasteros*), had to be paid. Before 1558 on the northern coast, ten Indians, when paid, worked for the standard wage of one peso ensayado (standardly defined as 450 maravedis or about 13 reales) per day. In that year Viceroy Marqués de Cañete sent the town council a modified wage scale for consideration and adoption. The members of the cabildo at that time, including the encomenderos of Saña, Íllimo, Collique and Túcume, agreed to adopt a wage scale, but not the one sent by the viceroy. They proposed, instead, to pay construction workers and farmhands half a *tomín* (28 maravedis or .8 of a real) and a ration of corn per day. Shepherds were to receive half a fanega of corn every twenty days and one change of clothes or 2 pesos corrientes (5.75 pesos of 8 reales each) every four months. This schedule of remuneration, which was some 25 percent less than that suggested in the viceroy's original proposal, was another compromise between royal authorities and local interests in this era of transition.[12]

The reestablishment of the mita signaled the end of the encomendero's labor monopoly. Henceforth, he was theoretically equal to any nonencomendero who requested mitayos. The continuing decline in the Indian population meant that the number of mitayos available to work fell annually. Mitayo labor became increasingly scarce and was generally insufficient to supply everyone who held a legitimate claim. Encomenderos fared better in the periodic distribution of mitayos than nonencomenderos, because either they or family and friends remained in control of the allotment. Despite this advantage, the supply of mita labor failed to meet all their needs.[13]

The overall regulation of the encomienda had profound and lasting effects on the economic position of the encomendero and the broader colonial economy. For the individual encomendero, the loss of tribute labor denied him an important resource he had previously employed in other business ventures. Instead of a source of income, Indian labor became a cost. Moreover, the encomendero received a smaller quantity of goods than he might have otherwise exacted had tribute remained unrestricted. Assuming a constant standard of living, this meant that his household consumed a greater proportion of these goods, leaving him with less of a surplus to sell in the growing local and export markets.

This gradual loss of a substantial amount of income came at a time when the few remaining survivors of the conquest and, now, the second generation were still engaged in lengthy and costly negotiations at court to gain titles, coats of arms, and other honors. They were also preoccupied with furnishing their rambling mansions in a style worthy of the peninsular royalty which had established itself around the viceroy and audiencia in Los Reyes. The encomenderos felt obliged to emulate the pomp and pretentions of the court to maintain their status, especially when their position was being seriously challenged locally by a growing number of prosperous merchants. Eventually, these expenditures forced the encomenderos to borrow from the merchants they considered their social inferiors, albeit in a manner so discreet as to keep the secret of financial troubles to themselves and the scribes of the notary's office.[14]

On the broader societal level, tribute regulation cut the supplies of marketable goods, precisely at a time of growing demand—both in Peru and in Tierra Firme. The population of Trujillo, Los Reyes, and other cities had increased rapidly. Thousands of Spaniards migrated to Peru before 1550, and more arrived each year. From an original eighty inhabitants (including the thirty-one vecino-encomenderos), the city had grown to approximately three hundred Spanish families and their Indian and black servants during the 1560s. The growing sector of merchants, bureaucrats, and artisans who lacked the time or interest in farming or in raising animals added to the pressure on supply. Tierra Firme, rapidly becoming one of the most important commercial centers in the Western Hemisphere, was an attractive and burgeoning market that drained supplies, especially of wheat, from the domestic market. Ships from many parts of the Spanish empire, the Iberian peninsula, and Africa periodically unloaded such luxury items as sugar, wine, soap, and slaves to exchange for flour and other products from the south. Encomenderos were among those who eagerly supplied this market to take advantage of the high prices and the coveted goods the profits could buy.[15]

The result of the restrictions imposed by the tasa, of the growing viceregal markets, and of the continued export of grain to Tierra Firme was that production proved insufficient to meet domestic demand. In contrast to the 1540s, when the food supply kept pace with demand because encomenderos forced the Indians to produce more of what was needed, the 1550s were years of recurring food shortages. The situation was aggravated by the fact that the Indians did not produce sufficient quantities of the items needed to satisfy the desires of the European population for wheat, meat, and wine. Furthermore, the tasas, to the extent that they were observed, did not allow encomenderos to substitute wheat for corn or other products, and Indians generally sowed only enough wheat to fulfill their tribute obligations.[16]

This unsatisfied demand was supplied by sea from Tierra Firme. Along with cargoes of slaves, silks, taffetas, and saffron came wine and olive oil at great cost. Red and white wine imported from Castilla, for instance, sold at just under 20 pesos the *botija* in 1549, down substantially from its high of some fourteen years earlier, but still a considerable sum. Such nonessentials as sugar cost over 120 pesos per *quintal* (retail) in 1537 and still close to half that much in the 1550s. Imported soap sold at 2½ reales per pound in 1550 in Los Reyes and cost even more in the provinces. From New Spain came hundreds of arrobas of tallow at 20½ pesos in 1554. Imported mules sold on the northern coast at over 550 pesos in the same year.[17]

The threat of abolishing the encomienda, and its subsequent regulation and declining yields, prompted the farsighted encomendero to respond to these price incentives. Because many had participated as silent partners in the burgeoning import and export trade, they knew of the profits to be made. Taking advantage of their knowledge of market conditions at home and abroad, they embarked on a strategy of import substitution that gradually interested them in organized, large-scale ranching and commercial agriculture. With this shift, control of land assumed new importance.

With no less than two-thirds of the encomenderos establishing estancias or corrals in Lambayeque before 1565, ranching proved to be among the most popular investments for the encomendero looking for new sources of income. Estancias were easy for encomenderos to establish, because ranching required little capital investment after the initial purchase of a herd, and because stock raising was not labor intensive. One shepherd, who could care for up to one thousand sheep at a time, earned less than the value of ten head per year. The encomendero's hired majordomo, who was already in charge of the seasonal collection of tribute, could oversee several herding operations at once. The additional cost of his salary, food allowance, and bonus—usually a percentage of the increase in the herds—was low in comparison to the value of the animals under his care. A final reason for the predilection toward ranching was that the encomendero could limit his involvement to a loose administrative overview and an appearance at the annual roundup and branding.[18]

Corrals or estancias became characteristic features of the Lambayeque countryside in the 1550s, although encomenderos of the region had begun raising stock in Saña informally as early as 1539. When the number of shepherds specified by La Gasca's tasa (for example, fourteen for Rodrigo de Paz) proved insufficient to handle their growing herds, they hired forasteros to supplement them. After the abolition of tribute labor, forasteros and mitayos guarded the herds. Decrees that limited the distance a mitayo could travel to work and that no longer required delivery of tribute goods to Trujillo were among the main reasons for the establishment of the estancias in Lambayeque, still about a four or five day ride from Trujillo. Such action guaranteed the encomenderos continued access to the relatively cheap mitayo labor and was also a way to utilize part of the tribute (that is, corn) without the expense of transporting it to urban areas.[19]

Although the cost of establishing one or more estancias fell well within the financial resources of most encomenderos in the 1550s, many who had multiple operations chose to set up some as partnerships for administrative expediency. Melchior de Osorno, the encomendero of Ferreñafe, and Francisco Pacho, a resident of Trujillo, organized a typical cooperative venture in 1561. They owned the 1,330 pigs, 206 sheep, 110 cows, and 375 goats jointly. Osorno contributed the corn grown by the Ferreñafanos as tribute for feed, and Pacho resided in the Túcume Valley to keep the accounts and to guarantee the good care of the animals. The partners decided to hire additional help, as needed, and divide the profits equally at the end of two years.[20]

The contract between Osorno and Pacho makes no mention of land. With the gradual suppression of tribute labor, the encomendero lost the use of community pastures. So when stock raising came under his direct supervision, he moved his animals onto the vast areas of open lands, which had been abandoned since the conquest, the so-called *tierras baldías*, or *vacas*. Most *estancieros*, or livestock raisers, did not have legal title to these lands; and stock raising did not imply exclusive rights to any, except *de facto* rights to those occupied by the corrals that were built to enclose the animals at night.

Few worried about the question of the ownership of land and pastures at this time. Indians seldom protested the establishment of estancias or livestock raising solely on the grounds that they occupied their traditional lands. Elsewhere, however, stock raising caused land disputes as early as 1541, when some persons occupied an area and tried to keep others from building corrals or grazing their animals nearby. Carlos V and his advisors became worried that if this practice spread all the good pastures would be partitioned within a few years and settlement of Peru retarded. Therefore, the king declared that, as was the custom in Spain, pastures were to be held in common.[21]

Common pastures were a great windfall to Spanish cattlemen, but the same was not true for the Indians. Very few had livestock. Any advantage to these few did not compensate for the damage done to the majority. Herds became a major source of conflict between the Indians and the Spanish when the latter allowed their animals to roam freely into the unfenced fields of Indians. Swine, in particular, were notorious for uprooting and destroying crops. Their depredations were

so well documented that Carlos V prohibited encomenderos from raising swine near Indian towns and fields in 1549, but Spaniards paid
little heed to decrees that were against their interests, where there was
little effective law enforcement by officials representing the king. In
fact, Spaniards sometimes purposely allowed their animals to graze in
Indian fields, defending this practice to the bewildered Indians by
citing the definition of "pasture": any vegetation except crops, including the stubble left after the harvest in Indian fields and the grass
growing between the rows.[22]

Livestock also damaged irrigation ditches. They stumbled and fell
when crossing, breaking down the walls and sending dirt and sand
into the bottom. To prevent damage to the city water supply, the town
council ruled that no one could corral animals near irrigation canals
above the city; but, in more remote areas like Lambayeque, the damage
to the irrigation infrastructure continued. Indians brought the problem
before Dr. Gregorio Gonzales de Cuença, a judge of the audiencia,
when he arrived in the area on an inspection tour in 1566. They petitioned him to put a stop to such practices. In response, Cuenca ordered several estancias moved, noting that because of the vast areas
of vacant land with abundant pastures this should cause no major
hardships.[23]

Similarly, the encomenderos reacted to the local grain shortages and
the growing markets in Tierra Firme by planting wheat on some of
their chacras near Trujillo. Continued expansion near the city proved
impossible when the decrees that limited the distance which mita labor
could travel to work began to be implemented. This regulation prompted
them to start planting near the communities in the Lambayeque region
as early as 1551–52.

Pedro de Olmos de Ayala, Luis Atienza, Francisco Luis de Alcántara,
and no fewer than thirteen other encomenderos established *labores de
pan sembrar* (or *de pan llevar*) in the Lambayeque area before the middle
of the 1560s. Mixed farms included land planted in grain and land left
as natural pasture for grazing animals. To create a labor required a
much greater capital outlay to purchase handtools, plows, oxen, and
carts than to establish an estancia. Wage costs were also greater, because as a labor-intensive activity farming required constant and specific administration to synchronize and coordinate plowing, planting,
weeding, and irrigating various fields at once by large numbers of
workers. As the labor shortage became more acute, those who could
began to spend large sums to purchase slaves to maintain and expand

production. Supervisors also directed the storage of produce until ready for the slow trip via oxcart to the port or for the trip overland to Trujillo. Improperly stored grain was quickly damaged or ruined by mildew.[24]

The mita system and the establishment of estancias and labores brought a clear change in the organization and relations of production on the northern coast. Indian labor no longer worked under the direction of the curaca or other native officials; workers now took orders from a Spanish administrator or slave steward. Planting was no longer celebrated with the rituals and ceremonies of communal efforts, and ceased to be a major social occasion. Mitayos from one community worked with mitayos from another. Work lost its sense of personal obligation to the encomendero and became a matter of selling one's toil for a ration of corn and a wage.

To secure these investments in labores, the encomenderos began seeking ways to establish their rights to the lands they occupied. At first, encomenderos planted on recently abandoned land that was easy to clear and required relatively little work to restore the irrigation network. Because vacant land was abundant and easy to obtain, there was no need for encomenderos to encroach on land still being used by the Indians. They also took advantage of the creation of the Spanish mita system to acquire land. They simply remained in possession of community land that tribute labor had previously farmed, once the mita system was established. Because mitayos were replaced by others every few months, the land became identified with the encomendero who occupied it continuously and quietly assumed its control and disposition. This resulted in a *de facto* transmittal of property rights over the years.[25]

Like their counterparts in Mexico, the encomenderos of Lambayeque used an ostensible rental arrangement as another ploy to acquire land. Spaniards leased Indian lands and later asserted that the rental was a sale, claiming that possession throughout the intervening years constituted proof of ownership.[26]

Gradually, however, the legal uncertainties associated with these strategems and a prohibition against encomenderos owning lands near their encomiendas led the encomenderos to prefer formal sales. Juan Roldán Dávila, the younger, like several other encomenderos, purchased land from Indian chieftains for token payments, despite royal disapproval and at least one decree prohibiting such transactions. In 1566, Dr. Cuenca specifically prohibited the sale of land by curacas and other Indians, unless absolutely necessary.

> Item, because the curacas, without having power to
> do so, sell on their own authority the lands of their
> communities as their own, thus causing their
> subjects great harm . . . and because, if the Indian
> population ever increases in numbers there will be
> a scarcity of land, it is ordered and mandated that
> no curaca or Indian official can sell community
> lands to Spaniards or any other individual, unless
> the sale is of urgent necessity or of evident utility
> to the community. . . .

Cuenca realized that if such sales were not banned the Indian population would lack sufficient land to provide for its own needs if the population ever increased to previous levels. But, in later years, Spaniards took advantage of the provision's loophole to continue these purchasing practices.[27]

Encomenderos were not alone in wanting land. A significant number of adventurers who arrived after the initial phase of the conquest fought in the civil wars and joined expeditions to discover new territory. After active combat ended, these men congregated in Los Reyes, Trujillo, and other major cities to petition authorities for encomiendas, pensions, or other rewards for their services. Some moved into the homes of friends or relatives to await the outcome of their petitions. Others joined the households of encomenderos as quasi-permanent guests and became retainers. Too many others, local authorities complained, remained idle or underemployed.[28]

These late arrivals found it impossible successfully to petition the crown or viceroy for stipends or other rewards even with a distinguished service record. There were far more individuals who wanted encomiendas than there were encomiendas available as rewards. Military service was no longer sufficient to merit such an award. To be a successful petitioner, an outstanding military record had to be combined with seniority in the conquest, social background in Spain, and good connections with governors and royal authorities. Other traditional rewards were also in short supply. The spoils of armed conquest belonged to previous decades; encomenderos monopolized local positions of power; and the royal treasury could not provide every aspirant with a pension from its limited resources. One encomendero of Lambayeque, disappointed at the pension assigned him after the death of his predecessor, complained bitterly that the promise of another pension was valueless given the number of others awaiting the same.

The dimensions of the problem were clear to the Marqués de Cañete: the population of Peru included over eight thousand adult Spanish males in 1555 by his own estimate, fewer than one thousand of whom could be satisfied with an encomienda (the approximate number of encomiendas was 480 at this time), appointment to government office, or a pension. Because of the superabundance of aspirants and their reluctance to work as artisans or laborers, unemployment, vagrancy, and vagabondage began to trouble the authorities.[29]

One way the crown devised to defuse this disturbing situation and compensate the ex-soldiers was by making land grants, or *mercedes*. From the individual Spaniard's point of view, land grants were acceptable rewards. With the possibilities for plunder and treasure already gone, agriculture offered a practicable alternative for earning a living, especially considering the healthy demand for foodstuffs and the now available supply of mita labor. This was an advantageous solution for the authorities as well, because mercedes implied relatively small outlays by the treasury to cover administrative costs and served the purposes of alleviating social unrest, settling the land, and increasing the food supply. Perhaps more important, the authorities viewed mercedes as a means of creating an independent group of nonencomendero farmers, or *labradores*. The formation of such a group became part of the crown's strategy to check the power of the encomenderos. The crown reasoned that a new and enlarged group of farmers whose wealth was based on land rather than the direct control of Indians would eventually serve as a societal counterweight to the encomenderos.[30]

The Spanish monarch's authority to make mercedes emanated from the discovery and conquest and his succession to the titles and rights of the Incas. In theory, the Spanish king's claim to eminent domain[31] was based on Pope Alexander VI's bull *Inter Caetera Divinae Magestatis*, issued 4 May 1493. It granted the Catholic monarchs Ferdinand and Isabella and their heirs and successors the lands, cities, forts, places, rights, and jurisdictions to all the islands and continents discovered up to 100 leagues west of the Cape Verde Islands. The bull's only restriction was the prohibition against the usurpation of lands belonging to a Christian prince. The Treaty of Tordesillas (4 June 1494) subsequently moved Spanish jurisdiction 270 leagues further to the west.[32]

Using this authority, the Spanish monarchs confirmed the Indians' communal use and possession of land (dominio útil), thus legitimizing their previous tenuous tenure, based as it was solely on occupation. According to the climate of opinion, the Indians were minors and dependents to be provided for and protected. Therefore, the monarchs never gave them absolute, fee-simple property rights to the land.

Land grants to Spaniards, in contrast, implied both dominion and usufruct rights, provided certain provisions were met. Land grants became valid titles, for example, only after the grantee had cultivated the land for a specified number of years. The grantee was also enjoined from selling the land to another individual for a definite period and prohibited indefinitely from selling or donating the land to the church. Moreover, land grants were subject to royal confirmation, although few grantees bothered to seek confirmation at this time. Finally, mercedes were issued with the condition that they cause no harm to third parties (for example, the Indians); authorities were repeatedly cautioned not to disturb the possession of lands of the Indian communities.[33]

The Spanish monarchs delegated their authority to make land grants to governors, viceroys, and certain town councils. Pizarro distributed both urban and suburban real estate around Trujillo. The town council of Trujillo later assumed this power, making liberal grants of house sites to encomenderos and nonencomenderos alike. The council rarely denied its members or other encomenderos land on which to grow grain or other products. Viceroy Don Antonio de Mendoza made the first known grant of about fifty fanegas de sembradura[34] to a nonencomendero of Trujillo for agricultural purposes in 1550, while he traveled overland to Lima to assume office. In the following years, the cabildo, too, partitioned abandoned tracts of land among recent arrivals. These settlers, referred to as "poor farmers" ("*labradores pobres*") by the council four years later, used the land to grow wheat and other foodstuffs.[35]

The municipal council had been making grants since the departure of Pizarro without the official sanction of the king or any other authority. In 1558 the Viceroy Marqués de Cañete, in an effort to formulate the first coherent land distribution policy, questioned the legality of the council's actions and apparently moved to annul the grants. Pedro Gonzales, with power of attorney from the council, hastily departed for Lima to persuade the viceroy to confirm its previous actions. Under pressure, the Marqués allowed these unauthorized grants to stand in a royal decree issued in Lima on 21 February 1558. The minutes show that the council continued to make grants near the city until at least the end of the 1560s.[36]

Nevertheless, the records of the council meetings reveal that it rarely granted land outside the immediate vicinity of the city. Only one encomendero received a merced in the Lambayeque area from the council. Lambayeque was considered a distant frontier district, only vaguely known to anyone except the encomenderos with holdings in the region and persons who actually lived there. Grants in Lambayeque to anyone but those with the access to the capital necessary to start production would have been of little but subsistence value. Except for this one, none of the titles of landholdings in the Lambayeque region date from this time, and there is no extant evidence that any new settlers established estates there before the 1560s.[37]

The ability to exploit the land profitably varied according to the capital resources available for investment. Labradores without the resources to buy slaves, hire large numbers of day laborers, or invest in capital equipment worked the land personally with little or no help. In theory, they qualified for mita labor; in practice, they rarely received their rightful allotment. The labor shortage thus restricted their farming to a few hectares at a time. Chacras gave these early labradores an independent economic base and a means of subsistence, but few became wealthy. Those few who did make enough money to become active participants in city life (the *vecino-ciudadanos*)[38] did not become rich from their landholdings alone; they invariably had other sources of income (for example, commerce), an education, or special skills.[39]

While Carlos V and his advisors were gradually regaining control of the encomiendas, they were also taking action to reestablish their political control over the viceroyalty. In Trujillo, one of the manifestations of this was the appointment during the 1540s of a salaried official, the corregidor, to serve as the crown's direct representative in the provinces. His duties and responsibilities were vast and multifarious. As chief justice, he superseded all judicial officers, including the magistrates of the town council. As the top executive, he had power to enforce royal decrees and punish infractions of the law. To maintain public order and decency, he could ban gambling and forbid entertainment at night or immoral plays.[40]

The corregidor was an established feature of the administrative hierarchy of Trujillo by 1549, with at least theoretical jurisdiction over all the territory within the district of the city. Given the enormous size of this area, his control over the countryside was tenuous at best during those early years. He made no pretense of being able to administer it effectively from Trujillo. The multiplicity of his duties forced him to routinely delegate authority to lieutenants, who assumed his place in Trujillo when he visited the countryside to implement royal decrees or check up on subordinates. The corregidor's presence ended the period when encomenderos exercised almost unrivaled political and judicial authority on the northern coast.

Unfortunately, the minutes of the town council sessions that might reveal the initial reaction of the encomenderos to the appearance of the corregidor have not survived. In later years, however, the council did not hesitate to appeal to the central authorities whenever the corregidor threatened its traditional prerogatives as an institution.[41]

Toward the mid-1550s, however, a feeling of common interests between corregidor and encomenderos replaced the initial resistance and distrust. Encomenderos began to serve as the corregidor's guarantors; that is, an encomendero guaranteed that the corregidor would appear at his *residencia*, a judicial review at the end of his term of office at which he had to answer any charges of incompetence or misuse of power. Such arrangements compromised the impartiality of the corregidor and generally made him a less zealous representative and advocate of the crown's interests. As a result, it became common practice for a corregidor to appoint a guarantor his lieutenant. In May of 1559, for example, Francisco de Samudio, encomendero of Túcume, guaranteed Pedro Pacheco as corregidor and chief justice of the city. In August, when Pacheco left on an official visit to a northern district, Samudio assumed his duties, including presiding over meetings of the municipal council and sentencing court cases. These are the first instances of a developing strategy on the part of the encomendero elite to co-opt royal bureaucrats and gain their cooperation.[42]

Another manifestation of declining encomendero power was the opening of the town council membership to others. Before 1557 council members had been encomenderos. The first time a nonencomendero sat on the council occurred that year, when the cabildo members themselves elected Bachiller Pedro Ortiz an alderman. Ortiz was a well-educated and respected member of the community. He and his brother had received one of the first land grants in 1550 from Viceroy Don Antonio de Mendoza near Trujillo. During his year in office, Ortiz served as interim magistrate and lieutenant of the corregidor, while the men normally holding these positions were absent. The following year, Ortiz's brother, Alonso, was elected alderman, and in 1559, Captain Baltazar Rodríguez served in the same post.[43]

This participation in the town council by nonencomenderos anticipated an official decree of 1560 which ordered the cabildo to elect at least one nonencomendero member each year. The decree was accepted with only one dissenting vote. In 1567 another royal decree was brought to the attention of the cabildo on the day of elections. It had been found buried and apparently purposely forgotten in the city archive. This decree ordered that half of the council members be "vecinos-ciuda-danos," that is, nonencomenderos. The response of those present clearly indicated that the decree had been neglected on purpose: the protest against such a provision was strong and unanimous. The meeting ended with the election of new members, none of whom was a vecino-ciudadano.[44]

On the whole, the vecinos-ciudadanos remained a numerically small and weak group in society vis à vis the encomenderos. Members of the council had to be men of independent means, because neither magistrates nor aldermen received any regular remuneration. This fact, and legislation prohibiting all councilmen from engaging in trade without royal permission, effectively limited membership. Moreover, vecinos who sought council positions identified with the encomenderos and copied their style of life to the extent their resources permitted. This, added to the fact that vecino-ciudadanos served on the cabildo at the pleasure of the encomendero members, assured the encomenderos that the former would not threaten their political position.[45]

The reason that the encomenderos doggedly resisted encroachments on their political power and the exercise of their traditional autonomy is not difficult to understand. For almost three decades, the encomenderos had regarded the council as an exclusive club. They used the cabildo to grant themselves land near Trujillo and sites within the city for houses, gardens, and mills; and to set prices for goods and services which they produced and consumed. Of late, they had used the authority and prestige of the cabildo to defend their position before royal authorities in the capital. In 1552 the cabildo sent a representative to Lima at the city's expense to plead for the perpetuity of the encomienda, which was clearly of concern only to the privileged few. The encomenderos took similar action in the following year in regard to the establishment and regulation of mita labor. The encomenderos understood that the regulation of the encomienda and the challenge to their political power affected their position as the elite of society.[46]

A united front facilitated their defense. By the middle of the 1560s, the encomendero families formed a group with a common economic base, shared interests, and years of participation on the cabildo, all of which—when reinforced by kinship ties—helped overcome a few interclan rivalries and strengthened intergroup coherence and cooperation. Figure 5 shows that Juan Roldán, for example, founded a family which, in time, included holders of seven encomiendas in the Lambaye-que area and at least three others with encomiendas outside Lamba-yeque, but within Trujillo's jurisdiction—in total, about one-third of all the encomenderos in the region.[47]

Blood relatives served as executors of each other's wills and gave each other power of attorney to represent them in court, to collect debts, and to buy slaves. An unspoken code virtually assured that a request between relatives for financial assistance, intercession with a friendly authority, or other favor would not be denied, if it seemed helpful to the family as a whole.[48]

This tradition held with equal strength for affinal relatives. Marriage, besides allying families within the elite, became a mechanism for se-lectively admitting deserving outsiders into the privileged circle. Mar-riage was not as much a matter of romantic love between two individuals as an association of families, wealth, and position. Parents arranged marriages of their children after a careful examination of the potential partner's family background and social position, assets, income, and political connections. Once married, the relatives of one spouse became the relatives of the other. Privileges and favors followed.

The match between Francisco Pérez de Lezcano and Doña Luisa de Mendoza, shown in Figure 5, illustrates this concept of marriage. Lez-cano was born in Spain, the legitimate son of Captain Miguel Pérez de Lezcano and Catalina Pérez. He settled in Trujillo in 1551, after a distinguished military career. The cabildo elected him attorney general for the city in 1552 and granted him land on which to build a house and construct a flour mill. By 1555 he was a major exporter of flour and sweetened biscuit. In that year he presented a decree from King Carlos V and was accepted into the town council as an alderman. When he married Doña Luisa, sometime within the next four years, his estate was worth over 33,000 pesos and included several houses and mills, fields near Trujillo, black slaves, gold and silver jewelry, and household furnishings. Doña Luisa's parents, Francisco de Samudio and Leonor de Requera, gave her a dowry of about 16,550 pesos—including a house on the plaza, over twenty-five slaves, a garden and a mill in Trujillo, and two more flour mills and herds of cows and droves of swine in Chérrepe.

Both parties gained from the marriage. Doña Luisa married a pen-insular Spaniard from a noble family with good political connections who could administer her property. He gained social acceptance by

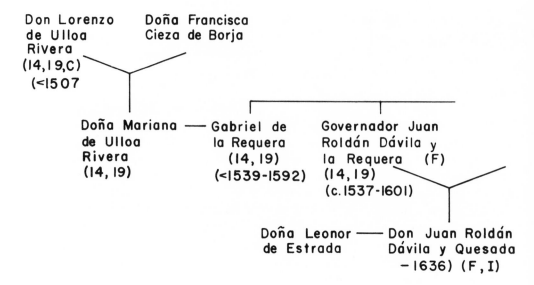

Don Lorenzo   Doña Francisca
de Ulloa   Cieza de Borja
Rivera
(14,19,C)
(<1507

Doña Mariana —— Gabriel de   Governador Juan
de Ulloa   la Requera   Roldán Dávila y
Rivera   (14,19)   la Requera   (F)
(14,19)   (<1539-1592)   (14,19)
                                 (c.1537-1601)

Doña Leonor —— Don Juan Roldán
de Estrada   Dávila y Quesada
                -1636) (F,I)

ESTATES		ENCOMIENDAS	
I.	San Lorenzo el Real	A.	Casma la Alta
2.	La Candelaria	B.	Casma la Baja
3.	Aberru	C.	Catacaos and Guambos
4.	Collasos	D.	Cherrepe
5.	Pátapo	E.	Chuspo - Callanca
6.	Luya	F.	Íllimo
7.	Mamape	G.	Jayanca
8.	El Molino	H.	Lambayeque
9.	Santiago de Miraflores	I.	Requay
10.	San Cristóbal	J.	Saña
11.	Leviche	K.	Túcume
12.	Oyotún	L.	Moro
13.	Chumbenique		
14.	Íllimo		
15.	Charcape		
16.	Geigipe		
17.	Tulipe		
18.	Pomalca		
19.	Sasape		

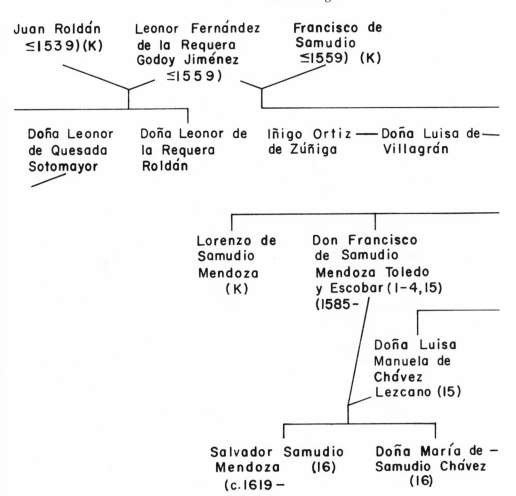

Figure 5.

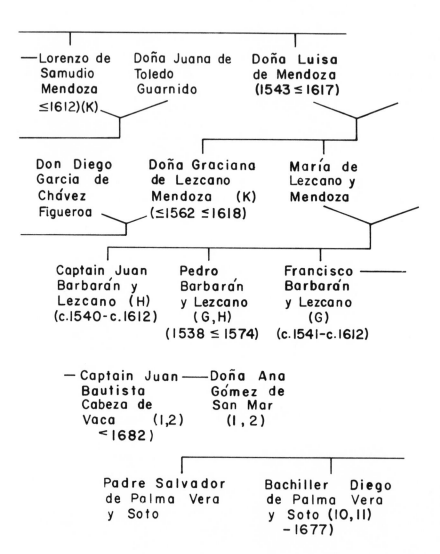

Figure 5, continued.

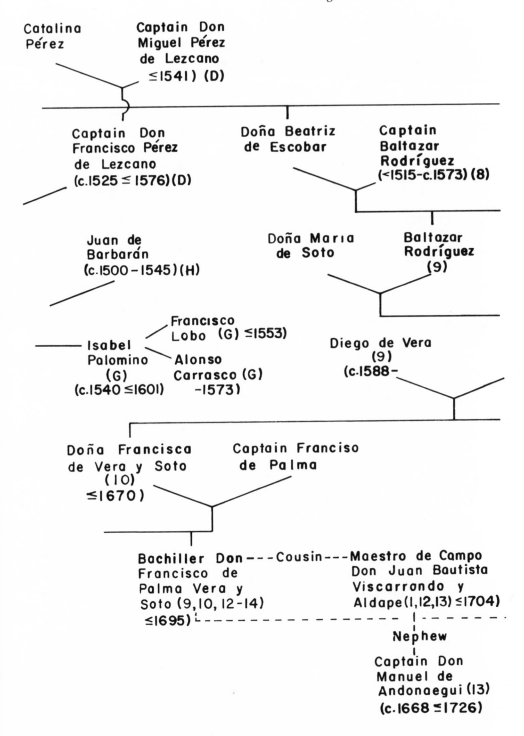

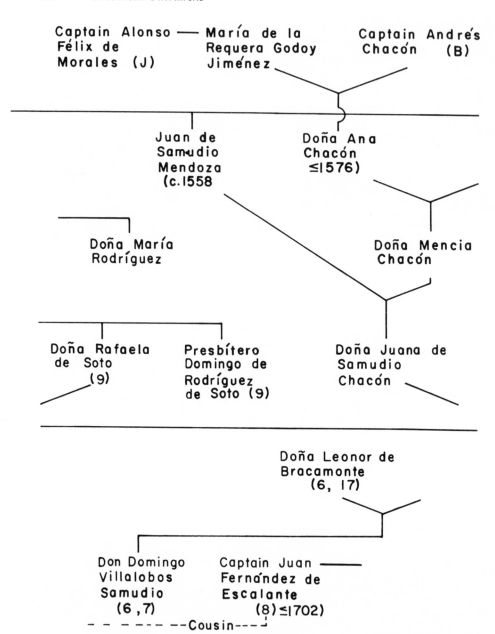

Figure 5, continued.

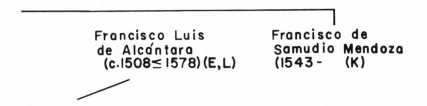

Francisco Luis
de Alcántara
(c.1508≤1578)(E,L)

Francisco de
Samudio Mendoza
(1543- (K)

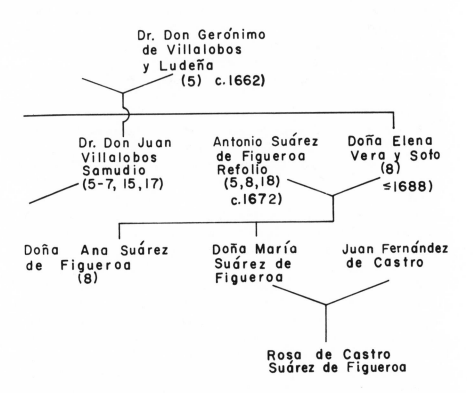

Dr. Don Gerónimo
de Villalobos
y Ludeña
(5) c.1662)

Dr. Don Juan
Villalobos
Samudio
(5-7, 15,17)

Antonio Suárez
de Figueroa
Refolio
(5,8,18)
c.1672)

Doña Elena
Vera y Soto
(8)
≤1688)

Doña Ana Suárez
de Figueroa
(8)

Doña María
Suárez de
Figueroa

Juan Fernández
de Castro

Rosa de Castro
Suárez de Figueroa

marrying into one of the founding families of Trujillo. This confirmed his place in the elite and opened the way to future positions of honor and responsibility on the cabildo. In 1559, he served as interim magistrate and was chosen probate judge (*tenedor de bienes de difuntos*). He later served as a lay official of the Inquisition, sheriff, and lieutenant of the corregidor. In these capacities he undoubtedly served his greater family well.[49]

Elite families were also linked through friendship and business dealings. It was quite common, for example, for one unrelated encomendero to give his power of attorney to or post bond for another. Captain Melchior Osorno put up the bond so that Pedro Gonzales de Ayala could serve as lieutenant of the corregidor in 1558. Salvador Vásquez guaranteed Luis Roldán as the tithe collector of Túcume, Íllimo, and Ferreñafe in 1563. Encomenderos also patronized the flour mills of friends.[50]

The encomenderos used this informal network of family and friends, their wealth, and their control of the town council to meet the political challenge and maintain their position vis à vis the rest of society. They acted as individuals and as a group to win the allegiance of the corregidor and to uphold their traditional prerogatives against the threatening innovations he sponsored. When an encomendero acted as the corregidor's lieutenant, he took the opportunity to resolve court cases in favor of friends and relatives. Well-considered marriages integrated energetic outsiders into the family network. By this means and their control over the membership of the cabildo, the encomenderos guaranteed that, instead of challenging their hegemony, vecinos-ciudadanos would cooperate to maintain their privileged position. Thus, the elite of encomenderos and their families, although no longer as powerful as during the first heady years after the conquest, remained the dominant social, political, and economic force in society despite the regulation and falling yields of the encomienda, the presence of the corregidor, and the participation of "vecinos-ciudadanos" on the council.[51]

The major change in the economy of coastal society between 1550 and 1565 was that control of land became as vital as control over labor. Shrewd encomenderos of Lambayeque responded to the regulation of the encomienda and falling incomes by establishing labores and estancias near the communities. Their financial resources, administrative ability, and knowledge of markets permitted them to overcome the limitations of the labor shortage to begin production to take advantage of market opportunities. Farming and livestock raising generated rev-

enue that compensated, in part, for the income lost from the encomienda and allowed the encomenderos to maintain their position as
the major purveyors of foodstuffs for urban society and to continue
exporting to import the luxury items necessary to support their way
of life. Nonencomenderos benefited from the crown's land-giveaway
policy, but they lacked the resources and know-how to profit fully from
the favorable economic conditions. Land gave them an independent
economic base, but few made fortunes strictly from agriculture before
1565.

Growing Spanish interest in land had two major harmful effects on
the Indians. First, livestock raising meant depradations of their fields.
Second, large-scale agricultural production and the mita brought a
change in the conditions of their labor. Labor lost the aura of being an
almost sacred duty to a master and became an almost undisguised
economic exchange. But the loss of land did not yet concern the Indians.
For the moment, they continued to have more than enough to meet
their needs.

4 Saña and the Origins of a Local Landholding Elite, 1566–1594

During the next thirty years, significant developments affected the land tenure patterns and the expansion of agriculture in Lambayeque. The founding of a new Spanish town, the *villa* of Santiago de Miraflores in the Valley of Saña, opened the area to systematic settlement beginning in 1563. The Spanish presence and the opportunities to profit from expanded agricultural production created a favorable environment for the prompt execution of Viceroy Francisco de Toledo's plan to relocate the native population. The resulting concentration of the scattered Indians into a few communities freed large tracts of land for planting and livestock raising. The citizens of Saña invested their modest savings in chacras and herds. Encomenderos, with more private resources and access to credit, enlarged their estancias and built processing facilities to make soap and tan hides. They also constructed *molinos* near the wheat fields to mill flour, and they planted cane and erected trapiches and ingenios to produce sugar. Settlers and encomenderos shared control of the area into the 1570s. Gradually during the next decade, the balance of power in Lambayeque shifted from the old encomendero elite to the settlers, and land assumed added importance.

The Founding of Saña

The establishment of Saña was another dimension of the crown's design to speed the settlement of Peru and reduce the power of the encomenderos. As noted above, in older cities, such as Trujillo, these objectives meant that settlers received grants of land and access to the labor needed to work it. To fortify the economic position of Trujillo's settlers, the crown opened the membership of the town council to allow them to participate in local decision making.

In frontier zones, such as Lambayeque, Carlos V's policies involved founding new towns. Following instructions from Spain, the Viceroy Conde de Nieva ordered the establishment of several new settlements as regional nuclei for agricultural and commercial activities. One of these was to be christened Santiago de Miraflores in 1563. The corregidor of Trujillo, Licenciado Don Diego de Pineda Bascuñán, commissioned Captain Baltazar Rodríguez, a wealthy vecino-ciudadano of Trujillo who had married into the Roldán clan, to found Miraflores in the Saña Valley. (See Fig. 5.) Rodríguez chose the rest house on the old Inca highway, near the customary ford of the river, as the site for the town square, and he took possession of the entire valley in the name of the king. The valley was a logical choice since within its area were algarrobo forests for firewood and wooden beams, fertile and well-watered land, natural grasslands for grazing, lime deposits for building and construction, and the other natural resources necessary for settlement. A second attraction of the site was its low population density. Less than 15 percent of the estimated preconquest inhabitants remained. A new settlement, according to the official reasoning, might be less disruptive in this valley than one established in an area where larger numbers of natives survived. Finally, the valley was central to the northern region, a factor that would soon establish Miraflores as a major regional capital rivaling Trujillo in importance.[1]

The Conde de Nieva's instructions clearly specified that the town was to be established without harming the Indians. Undoubtedly, Rodríguez's claim to the entire valley evoked strong protests, which eventually reached the viceroy's successor, Licenciado Lope García de Castro. For this and other reasons, he abruptly cancelled Rodríguez's commission, in December 1564, and named an alderman of Trujillo, Miguel Rodríguez de Villafuerte, to complete the work. Rodríguez de Villafuerte assumed control of the land north of the Saña River and relegated the Indians to the southern bank. Next, he extended the territorial jurisdiction of Saña leagues up the coast to the community of Jayanca and from two to three leagues south to Pacasmayo. Chérrepe became the official port.[2]

The provisions for founding Saña, as the new town came to be called, resembled those which had governed the establishment of Trujillo. The layout and system of governance were almost identical. Saña, like Trujillo, was surveyed and planned following the grid pattern. Each citizen received a house site of 140 by 210 feet, an area four times as large for a garden, and approximately 40 *fanegadas*[3] of farmland. Settlers who had served the crown and who had not been previously granted an encomienda, pension, or other reward were preferred in the distribution. The conditions for residency included moving to the town within four months and having sufficient financial resources to begin working the land. The provisions prohibited the sale of this property to subsequent arrivals for four years and to each other for ten.

The provisions ensured the town considerable autonomy and minimal control from Trujillo. The town council—made up of two magistrates, two aldermen, and one chief constable—voted for twice as many candidates as there were vacancies on the cabildo. The corregidor of Trujillo chose the officials for the coming year from these nominations. Here the corregidor's power over Saña ended. There was to be no corregidor or lieutenant appointed from Trujillo. Instead, magistrates held the supreme positions, with almost absolute power over urban affairs and considerable jurisdiction over rural ones. They acted as judges in the first instance of both criminal and civil cases. Equally important, they controlled the local supply of wage laborers. The viceroy instructed the curacas of eleven communities north of the valley to send mitayos to Saña instead of to Trujillo. Anyone desiring access to this pool of more than three hundred laborers petitioned one of the magistrates.[4]

The establishment of Saña offered its citizens the opportunity for upward social and economic mobility which had been denied them in Trujillo, where the encomenderos and their families practically monopolized status and position. Hence, more than forty applicants presented themselves to Rodríguez for consideration. Those who could not appear personally rushed to the notary's office to give their power of attorney to others to represent them. Rodríguez accepted a good mix of individuals, including professionals, artisans, merchants, one woman, and at least one farmer. The majority of the thirty-nine chosen to be householders had been living in Trujillo. Some had arrived recently; others were longtime residents, who had applied for vecino-ciudadano status in the early 1550s. Almost one-half had firsthand knowledge of the Saña region, because they had been or were then employed by a local encomendero and had spent varying amounts of time there. Some probably had served—or believed they had served—the crown in some significant capacity, since service was a criterion for citizenship according to the instructions of both the Conde de Nieva and García de Castro. They had undoubtedly been disappointed when they failed to win what they considered to be an adequate situation or stipend. In Trujillo, such men earned their living as confectioners, upholsterers and carpenters, small shopkeepers, or clerks. Frustration over their fortune was probably compounded by the slim prospects for future advancement in Trujillo. Saña promised them an opportunity to start anew, gain the prestige of being among the town's founders, and acquire formal political power through participation on the cabildo.[5]

The biography of Simón Beltrán conveys the feeling of frustration over the lack of opportunities in Trujillo. He had been a vecino-ciudadano for five years when, backed by a guarantee of over 3,700 pesos from the physician of the city, he assumed the responsibility for establishing the municipal granary for the town council. After two years, Beltrán's initiative had not paid off. So, he petitioned the cabildo for a six-year extension, saying that he had bought the right to establish the granary, had done all the work, but had not profited. The cabildo acquiesced, but his earnings remained low. In 1564, at the end of six years, Beltrán decided to move north to begin anew in Saña.[6]

Men who were in better social and economic positions than Beltrán moved to Saña with the same expectations. Captain Baltazar Rodríguez, who as royal treasurer and merchant with agents as far afield as Tierra Firme had used his considerable wealth and influence to win the hand of a daughter of one of the first families of the city, welcomed the opportunity to lead the royal enterprise to found Saña and thus establish a respected position in his own right. The Ortiz brothers, among the first persons without encomiendas to receive grants of land and sit on the cabildo of Trujillo, decided to leave the city and their considerable holdings (several lots, a flour mill, and at least one chacra) when they determined that future upward mobility would be difficult. The deciding factor in their case was the Conde de Nieva's reassignment of part of their landholdings to another settler.[7]

Encomenderos were not among the original vecinos of Saña. Viceroy García de Castro ordered

> that no person that holds Indians in trust in the
> [old jurisdiction of the] said city of Trujillo or in any
> other location can have a house or citizenship in
> the said town or go to live in it.

This order prevented the confirmation as a citizen of Alonso Gutiérrez, the encomendero of Casma la Alta, who had joined the first group of settlers. But it did not discourage others from moving their families north. Despite the prohibition, their illegal status, and vociferous protests from those encomenderos who remained behind, Captain Juan Delgadillo, Salvador Vásquez, Alonso Pizarro de la Rua, and Luis de Atienza, among others, moved to Saña with the intention of staying. The encomenderos already had economic interests in the area; and, because of its proximity, Saña promised to be a much more convenient center of administration and residence than Trujillo. Their action effectively split the regional social establishment in two.[8]

During the next decade Saña became the center of a growing agricultural zone. Settlers established modest chacras to provide for their own subsistence and take advantage of the market conditions which had encouraged the encomenderos to establish labores in the area ten or more years before. Fields were carved out of land grants and sowed with wheat, beans, rye, and chickpeas. Vineyards, olive groves, and orchards were planted.[9]

But development proved uneven. Like their counterparts in Trujillo, settlers in Saña at first lacked the financial resources and labor to develop an entire merced. Tools, plows, oxen, and carts required for farming their holdings were beyond the financial reach of many. At least initially, a scarcity of capital also prevented them from directly benefiting from the higher prices in Trujillo, Los Reyes, and Tierra Firme. Those with surplus crops lacked the cash or credit necessary to pay for its carriage to these central markets. Most sold surpluses to merchant-middlemen who made shipping and commercialization of the region's agricultural products a business.[10]

Labor was the second factor restricting the expansion of farming among the settlers. Most had not come to follow oxen across a field, and the supply of mitayos was inadequate to meet the labor needs of both town and countryside. This shortage encouraged settlers to hire forasteros and to keep them on their land. These helped, but remained a numerically insignificant source of labor for at least a decade. Nor was slave labor a possible alternative for the settlers. At more than seven hundred pesos for a prime-aged male, blacks generally remained too expensive for them to acquire.[11]

Thus, the experience of the settlers of Saña paralleled that of the early settlers in Trujillo. Mercedes were underutilized; farming was confined to a few intensively worked fields. Livestock grazed on the remainder. Settlers produced enough to supply their own needs and a modest surplus in good years, but not enough to make farming

comfortably profitable. Many supplemented their income by continuing to work for the encomenderos or as independent artisans. Juan
Calderón Lascano, Diego de Segovia, and Pedro Tinoco set up shops;
and many others continued to engage in petty trade among the Indians.
One citizen ran the inn. Life in Saña was a struggle during its first
decade; for the twenty-odd settlers who persisted through those first
ten years, however, the hardship was well worth the effort for the
eventual power, wealth, and prestige it would bring some of them and
their descendants.[12]

A few gave up their citizenship within two years. Antonio Andeyro
and Alonso Gallegos apparently had been caught up with the excite-
ment of Saña's founding, and on a speculative impulse they petitioned
Rodríguez along with the others so as not to miss out on an opportunity.
Neither showed any intention of moving. Shortly after confirmation,
they transferred their rights and property to others: one, for fifty fanegas of flour; the other, in payment of debts. Simón Beltrán recon-
sidered his decision and decided to remain in Trujillo. Others were
either dissatisfied with their lot in Saña or forced to leave by other
considerations. Diego de Olivares, for example, remained in Saña less
than a year. He returned to Trujillo where he still owned four city lots,
became active in the town council, and served as alderman in 1565 and
magistrate in 1566. Juan del Castillo took advantage of his appointment
as a policeman by Corregidor Íñigo Ortiz de Zúñiga to return to Trujillo
in 1566. Alonso Ortiz deserted Saña when the cabildo of Trujillo elected
him alderman. He subsequently purchased the position and served
until his death (circa 1601). Finally, Diego de la Serpa returned to the
city when the council offered him a license as one of its five tavern
keepers. All shared a better than average socioeconomic position, and
each of the last four returned to assume a position of authority on the
town council or to take advantage of a business possibility. The cabildo
of Trujillo openly used the tactic of granting absent encomenderos
special economic concessions or electing them to positions on the council to entice or force them to return. This may have been the strategy
of the council members in regard to nonencomenderos as well.[13]

In contrast to the modest investments of the settlers, the encomenderos, yet to feel the full impact of declining tribute revenues, invested
heavily in their labores and estancias. In the mid-1560s most encomenderos had accumulated capital from their encomiendas and related
business ventures; officeholding; mills and rental properties in Trujillo;
and the estancias and labores in Lambayeque, which had been func-

tioning, in some cases, for over a decade. Although exact annual income figures for encomenderos are not available, the sums that Pedro Gonzales de Ayala, the younger, received from various sources typify the intake of some of the richest and most active. Figure 2 shows that tribute, although already declining, still averaged nearly 3,000 pesos per year between 1572 and 1589. Although they probably overstated a little, his mother and four other knowledgeable persons estimated his income from his export-import business, rental properties, and office-holding at between 9,000 and 10,000 additional pesos per year. The sale of the office of inspector of weights and measures alone brought him nearly 3,400 pesos in 1564.[14]

He also received income from the *diezmo,* or tithe. Every year or two, ecclesiastical authorities auctioned the right to collect the tithe in an area to the highest bidder. Tithe collection was a speculative investment. The amount offered reflected the anticipated value of the products that the *diezmero* expected to collect, less a comfortable profit margin. Theoretically, the tithe equalled 10 percent of the gross yield from farming and livestock raising. In practice, tithe collectors bargained with producers for as much as they could get—often less than a tenth. Even so, tithe collecting was generally profitable in the sixteenth century. The tithe collector either paid the church in advance or more commonly presented a guarantor to stand surety for the whole amount. The diezmo for Trujillo was leased to one individual, who, because of Trujillo's vast area, often subleased the right to collect in particular valleys. Encomenderos frequently bought the right to the tithes in the area of their encomienda and used their agents to collect the agricultural products from both Spaniards and Indians. The goods were later sold to recoup the original investment and, the encomenderos hoped, at a profit.[15]

Yet, as large as Gonzales's income seemed, it did not always cover the cost of maintaining his established business enterprises, extended household, and intended investments. Out of his annual income in the 1570s, Gonzales paid almost 750 pesos to his mother for her support and more than 2,050 pesos to his estranged wife for alimony and child support. These extraordinary expenses aggravated occasional cash flow problems. As early as 1562, when petitioning for the confirmation of his encomienda, he was already complaining, rather arrogantly, of not having enough income to live on. Indeed, one source puts his accumulated debt at over 13,000 pesos, although no one seriously questioned his credit worthiness until a decade later.[16]

If overextension was not yet a problem for most encomenderos, Gonzales and many of his cohorts had to resort to borrowing to make the large financial commitments needed to expand production in Lambayeque. This they easily accomplished. Due to their position and considerable property holdings, encomenderos had access to mortgage funds normally unavailable to settlers. One such source was the cash accumulated in the *cajas de comunidades* (general treasuries of the Indian communities). The cajas contained money from the sale of surplus tribute and the rental of community lands. Officials spent part of the income to pay the tribute of deceased or absent members; to support the hospital; to pay for the repair of irrigation canals, roads, and bridges; and to aid the widowed, maimed, sick, and poor. In addition, hundreds of pesos were periodically lent to individuals for private purposes at the prevailing annual interest rate of 7.14 percent. Francisco de Samudio and Salvador Vásquez took advantage of such funds, mortgaging their estates to secure the loans.[17]

Capital was also available from funds left to establish *obras pías* (acts of charity and good works). Wealthy persons left thousands of pesos to be invested in real estate, considered one of the safest forms of long-term investment. The annual interest was used to finance religious celebrations, to establish dowries, to supply wax and incense for the altar of a favorite saint, or to do other pious works. In 1588 Juan Roldán Dávila, the younger, borrowed 4,950 pesos from a fund that his parents had established in their wills to benefit the Indians of Túcume. He guaranteed the funds by mortgaging his real estate holdings, which included houses, stores, chacras, and two sugar mills, and assumed the payment of the yearly interest.[18]

The encomenderos borrowed these funds to invest in their labores and to increase the size of their herds. Judging from inventories of estancias and labores, it appears that the encomenderos employed most of the funds to increase wheat production. On their labores, they built molinos, or flour mills, locating them near major irrigation ditches, to take advantage of waterpower to turn the grinding stones, and as near the geographical center of the fields as possible to minimize the distance that the grain had to be transported. Melchior de Osorno, the encomendero of Ferreñafe, and at least eight others established molinos in the early 1560s. Apparently it was easier and more economical to grind the wheat into flour in Lambayeque, near the fields, than to transport the wheat to Trujillo for milling, sale, and export.[19]

The local price of flour, shown in Figure 6, though subject to fluctuation, remained profitably high. Prices in the capital and in Panama were even better. Encomenderos planted wheat in acreage formerly sown in beans, rye, and chickpeas—thereby turning labores or mixed farms into specialized estates dedicated almost exclusively to one crop.

Within a decade or so, these molinos, as both the mills and surrounding wheatlands were called, developed into elaborate estates. Pedro Gonzales de Ayala's mill, established before 1566, is typical of the others. At the center, or asiento, of the estate were located his residence, the mill, and holding corrals for his carrying stock and draft animals. Equipment included two carts, three yokes, handtools, and ten plows. The size and importance of this molino and others in the area is suggested by their annual output. Gonzales's molino, for example, produced one thousand fanegas of flour per year in the early 1570s, worth about two thousand pesos at the mill and about twice that much in Tierra Firme.[20]

Investment capital also gave the encomenderos some advantage over the settlers in coping with the labor shortage. In addition to mitayos, encomenderos hired community Indians, recruited by the curaca, to work on a temporary basis and forasteros to work for one- and two-year periods for an average of about fifteen pesos and from eleven to twelve fanegas of corn per annum. Incentives which encomenderos offered forasteros to stay on as permanent agricultural laborers included the right to plant a garden and graze a few head of livestock. Under the direction of Spanish, mestizo, and black overseers, Indians guarded livestock, built corrales, slaughtered animals, planted fields, cleaned irrigation ditches, transported supplies, and picked sticks and stones from wheat before milling. Encomenderos also had the resources to purchase the equipment and draft animals needed to maximize the available labor. By increasing the productivity of each worker, they could bring additional land under cultivation.[21]

Thus the establishment of Saña provided the impetus to develop land in the surrounding Lambayeque region, an area that had previously been only a marginal area within Trujillo's domain. Settlers developed chacras to the extent their resources permitted. Encomenderos, with financial resources of their own and access to credit, invested on a much grander scale, upgrading labores to molinos and expanding their herds.

Toledo's Reducción (*Reduction*) Policy
After the establishment of Saña, the arrival of Viceroy Francisco de

Toldeo in 1569 brought the second most significant change to the valleys of Lambayeque in this period. Toledo disembarked in the port of Paita in September 1569 and traveled overland to Los Reyes. In the two to three weeks it took him to reach Trujillo, he collected information about the places and people along his route. In Trujillo, he inquired about the population density, the conduct of authorities in their relations with the Indians, the collection and amount of Indian tribute, and the condition of the royal treasury. His observations along the road convinced him of the need for a total reorganization and systematization of the kingdom. Accordingly, he sponsored a visita to gather more information on Indian history and customs, to count the native population, to review the Indians' tribute obligations, and to relocate the Indians in more accessible places.

Toledo's visita had two major effects on the inhabitants of Lambayeque. Toledo redefined the term *tributario* (tribute payer) as an able-bodied male between eighteen and fifty years old. Previously the criteria had varied in different areas of the empire; and in Lambayeque the cutoff ages had been set at seventeen and forty-seven. He and his representatives also updated the tasas, taking into account the Indians' declining ability to produce. These adjustments had the cumulative effect of lightening the Indians' obligations and further reducing the encomenderos' incomes.[22]

Second, Toledo sent Spanish officials to resettle the natives in a few conveniently located villages. Dr. Cuenca had begun to implement this policy on the coast in 1566, but not on the scale envisioned by Toledo. Old World diseases, overwork, and flight had continued to decimate the population, until remnants of Indian families were left scattered over what was once uniformly and densely settled land. Uprooting and reconcentrating the Indians in a few larger settlements, the viceroy reasoned, would facilitate religious indoctrination and acculturation,

---

Sources: ANP/RA: 1. 10, c. 35, 18; 1. 173, 1668, 923; LC: 1. 140, 1808, 4v; 1. 141, 1809, 13v, 14v, 17v, 22, 23v, and 44v; 1811, 50v and 52; 1. 143, 1816, 3-3v and 5v; and 1. 138, 1794, 10v and 24v; ART/CoO: 26–IV–1646; and 24–I–1596, 75; CaO: 29–III–1588; Palacios: 14–II–1611; E: 3–X–1814; and Mata: 1596; ANCR/ Dapelo: 1800; AAL/AT: 15b–IX, 1678, 1; BNP/B357, 1668, 264–64v and 266v; A538, 1580, 229; and B137, 1601; *ACT,* I, 42; II, 36 and 89; III, 196; Guillermo Lohmann Villena, "Apuntaciones sobre el curso de los precios de los artículos de primera necesidad en Lima durante el siglo XVI," *Revista histórica* 29 (1966), 86–88; and *Libros de Cabildo de Lima* 3, 85; and X, 6 and 358.

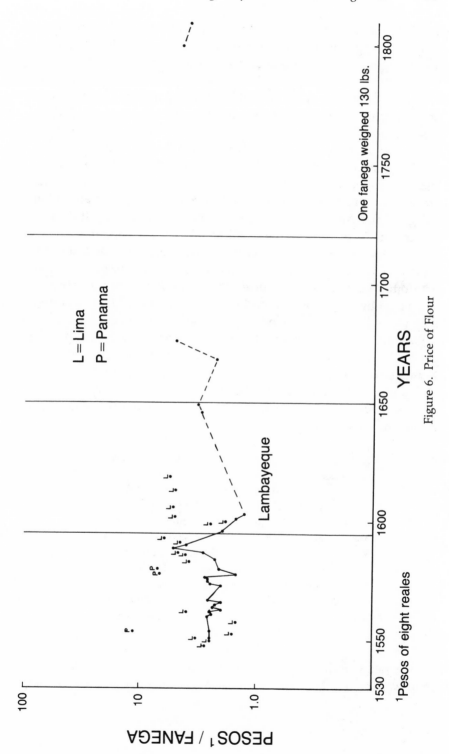

Figure 6. Price of Flour

and help maintain the segregation of Indians from the mistreatment and corrupting influences of the Spaniards. A less publicized but nonetheless significant reason was administrative expediency—facilitating tax collection and control.[23]

Official statements regarding the reducción program, as the relocation plan and the settlements themselves were called, stressed its positive features—saving the infidels and protecting them from direct Spanish exploitation through segregation. Laws governing the program promised added safeguards. Indians were not to lose their lands; and an *ejido*, or reserve, with a diameter of one league for communal grazing and future urban expansion, was to be designated around all villages. Land was to be set aside for communal cultivation. If the new settlements were far from their traditional fields, making daily access difficult, Indians were to receive new ones near the reducción. The Indians on whose land the new town was built were to be recompensed with other land. Toledo instructed the visitors to respect the private lands held by Indian officials and to allow them to sell the property if they wished. Abandoned land was to be held in common.[24]

Juan de Hoses, Toledo's visitor in the Lambayeque area, explained and rationalized his decision to resettle the residents of the village of Ñoquique (one of the three settlements of Chérrepe)[25] in these terms. He stated that Ñoquique was unhealthy and so isolated that the priest rarely visited, a condition which allowed Indians to practice their pagan rights unmolested.

> It [Ñoquique] is next to some swamps that cause
> sickness and high infant mortality and it is
> surrounded by hill-shaped shrines [*huacas*] which
> are damaging to the religious beliefs of the Indians,
> [because] many Indians—[both] commoners and
> nobles [*parques y principales*] go to said settlement of
> Ñoqui[que] to celebrate and dance according to
> their ancient rites . . . and there is no one to
> disturb them. . . . Also, because of its small
> population a priest does not ordinarily reside there
> nor visit often, and the Indians do not hear mass as
> regularly as is convenient. . . .

He stressed that the move was for the Indians' own physical and spiritual welfare. He ordered the farmers of Ñoquique to rebuild their dwellings around the monastery of Nuestra Señora de Guadalupe and the fishermen to reestablish themselves in Chérrepe.[26]

The Indians protested the reducciones. The inhabitants of Chérrepe, for example, petitioned the viceroy and royal audiencia almost ten months before the actual order for them to move was given. They sent representatives to Lima

> to ask for favorable decrees and justice for the well-
> being and conservation of the Indians and town of
> Chérrepe and especially [to ask] . . . that the town
> in . . . the port of Chérrepe not be moved or
> removed from where it is located because of the
> benefits the location . . . gives to said Indians for
> the commerce [*contrato*] of the sea. They know from
> experience that the Indians benefit daily from
> working in the sea and those who venture inland
> for one work [or another] daily come to less and
> this is what is asked.

Their request was partially accepted. When it came time to move, Hoses spared Chérrepe, but the residents of Ñoquique were given twelve days in which to rebuild in a new location. If they obeyed promptly, the *visitador* (inspector) promised to excuse them from one-third of the yearly tribute. If they did not comply with his order, Hoses threatened to collect the full amount and burn their old homes.[27]

Like Ñoquique, Callanca was completely dismantled and abandoned, with its population resettled downstream in the hamlet of Monsefú. The communities of Sinto and Collique moved from their locations in the upper Lambayeque Valley to the site of the Franciscan monastery in the lower valley (where the town of Chiclayo grew).[28]

Although theoretically sound, reducciones had a negative effect on the Indians in practice. Without a known exception, the Indians moved to the lower parts of the valleys, precisely the areas with the most unhealthy climate and poorest agricultural potential. On the low-lying lands near the ocean a heavy mist, or *garúa*, the closest approximation to precipitation in a desert environment where rain falls on the average of once every twenty-five to forty years, accompanies the formation of fog banks during the six-month winter season, from approximately April to September. The fog and heavy mists promote the growth of harmful fungi and insects and encourage the spread of disease.[29]

The Indian chronicler Poma de Ayala's condemnation of Toledo for the reducción policy seems written with Lambayeque in mind.

> Viceroy Don Francisco de Toledo ordered the
> abandonment and resettlement of the towns of this
> kingdom that had been built on sites selected by
> the most important native wisemen, doctors and
> philosophers and approved by the first Incas for
> their climate, lands and water to [best ensure the]
> growth of the population. Since then, the Indians
> in their new towns have died and are disappearing.
> Where there were ten thousand persons—soldiers
> of war, without [counting] the women, old men
> and children—now there are not ten tribute-paying
> Indians. . . . In [some] parts, the high mortality
> rate of the Indian population is caused by [their
> resettlement on] humid land, subject to disease-
> carrying, stinking winds that come from the
> sea, . . . In other parts, it is caused by the sun or
> the moon or the planets. . . .[30]

As a result of these moves, Indians also began to suffer from a lack of water for irrigation. Because of the absence of rainfall, the inhabitants of the area relied almost exclusively on rivers, originating in the mountains, to provide the water necessary to sustain their lives and to irrigate the soil for farming. Water became a problem during the dry season in the mountains, when water flow to the coast decreased to a trickle, sufficient at times to irrigate only the lands in the upper parts of the valleys. Problems during this period, however, stemmed from the distribution system, not from an absolute shortage, and were more occasional than continuous. But some groups of Indians found themselves at the mercy of the Spanish farmers living along the irrigation canals above them, who because of their position had access to water first. If the Spaniards took more than their allotment, the Indians further downstream obtained proportionately less. The situation became especially acute during periodic droughts.[31]

Worse yet, the Indians lost their best lands. In contrast to the middle and upper reaches of the valleys, where the semitropical climate and year-round sun make it possible to harvest two and even three crops per year on irrigated land, the fog and mists nearer the ocean cut the sun off from the earth, retarding plant growth. Furthermore, strong sea breezes cause erosion. Heavy grit and sand are dropped after short distances, whereas fine particles of soil are carried far inland. Poor drainage and salinity, caused by the high water table, are also problems of land near the beach.[32]

Indirect evidence makes it clear that the reducciones in Lambayeque were carefully planned, based on a thorough knowledge of the geography of the area. Although no written evidence of collusion between the visitor and the Spanish in the area has been found, reconstruction of the circumstances of the reducciones and the pattern of subsequent Spanish settlement supports the conclusion that Hoses consulted with the settlers and encomenderos and kept their needs and desires in mind. Thus, if not an explicitly stated motivation, the transfer of land from Indians to Spaniards was not an unforeseen consequence. In effect, the reducciones were frequently little more than a pretext to move Indians to clear and consolidate large tracts of the best land for the expansion of Spanish agriculture and livestock raising.[33]

This underlying consideration is proven by the transcripts of the reducciones. A copy of the visita of Chérrepe places the town of Ñoquique right next to the encomendero's molino. Once the Indians left Ñoquique, the encomendero expanded his fields onto their land. The next encomendero of Chérrepe, Diego García de Chavez, still had a molino at the site twenty years later. In the seventeenth century, the molino became the hacienda and estancia of Ñocotín.[34]

Many of the properties which later became the largest estates in the valleys took form after the reducción. Pátapo and Mamape were established on lands of Sinto. The molino of Collús was erected on the traditional lands of Chuspo-Callanca. Luya was an estancia established on lands of the ancient Indian community of Farcap. Pampa Grande and La Punta were carved out of the lands of Collique. Lands called Namor served as an open range on which to pasture livestock until the late seventeenth century, when they were cleared to become the hacienda of Ñanpol.[35]

Freeing large tracts of fertile land in the 1570s proved a real boon to agriculture. Induced by the rising or almost steady prices of livestock, as plotted in Figure 7, the inhabitants of Saña eagerly invested to expand their herds. They moved into the areas vacated by the Indians and set up estancias to accommodate their multiplying stock.

The additional opportunities drew new settlers to the area, some of whom became prosperous ranchers by the end of the 1570s. At least eight got their start as paid administrators on the estancias of others.

Administrators may have had an advantage over other settlers in establishing estancias because they had experience and usually received as part of their salary a fraction of the annual increase in the herds. Enterprising and ambitious individuals could, in a few plague-free years, accumulate several hundred head with which to go into business on their own.[36]

The life history of Alonso de Mingolla illustrates the success of one settler in establishing himself in the valleys. A peninsular Spaniard by birth, Mingolla was not among the founding citizens of Saña, although he was in the area at the time, probably already in the employ of the encomendero Pedro de Barbarán. Mingolla's hard work as Barbarán's resident agent, and his loyalty in helping his master evade an embargo of his tribute and property a year later, were rewarded. Before the end of the 1570s he owned his own animals.[37]

During the next five years, he established several estancias and did so well that he left Barbarán's service and moved his residence from the Indian town of Lambayeque, where he had been living as the encomendero's agent and the overseer of his pork ranch, to the town of Saña to become a full-fledged citizen and magistrate. In the following two decades he served several more times on the municipal council, for example, as magistrate in 1595, and as lieutenant of the corregidor and chief justice of the province in 1586 and 1592. He began lending money to such persons as his former employer's wife, and in 1598 he posted bond for the corregidor, Sancho de Marañón.

By the 1590s he had five or six estancias, including Supián, Penso,

Sources: AGI/AL: 100, [1646]; J: 458, 1851v and 2327; 459, 2443v and 2445v; and 462, 1738 and 1740; AFA/1. 1, c. 8; c. 19, 174, 176 and 179; and c. 20; 1. 2, c. 1; ART/Mata: 9–III–1562; 20–VII–1562; 2–IX–1562; [VIII–1563], 387; 23–XII–1563; 7–VII–1565; 1593; 1596; [1598]; CoO: 30–I–1564; 5–I–1566; 6–XII–1560; 4–IV–1573; 18–I–1574; 11–VIII–1582; 15–I–1583; 9–X–1591; 18–XI–1596; 4–XII–1596; 31–I–1598; and 2–V–1598; CaO: 24–I–1587; CoAG: 27–XI–1586; LC: 21–IV–1559; 1561; 22–X–1561; 26–VI–1564; Escobar: 1609; AAT/T: 1717; 1738, 32; 1742; 1746; 1775; 1776; and 1784; Causas: 1633, 11v; BP/2817, 1756, 7; ANCR/Collús: 1643, 131v and 137v; Álvarez: 23–V–1663; and Rivera: IX–1707; ACMS/n.d.; 1723; and 1736; Guillermo Lohmann Villena, "Apuntaciones sobre el curso de los precios de los artículos de primera necesidad en Lima durante el siglo XVI," *Revista histórica* 29 (1966), 86–88; and José Ignacio de Lecuanda, "Descripción geográfica de Lambayeque," Manuel A. Fuentes, ed., *Biblioteca Peruana de historia, ciencias y literatura* 2 (Lima, 1861), 265.

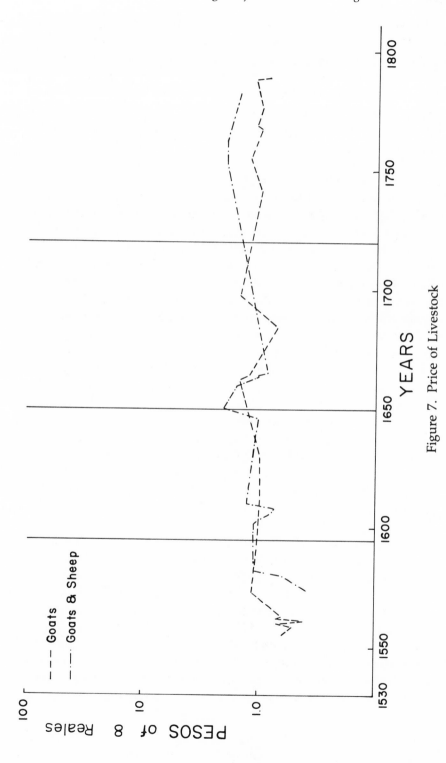

Figure 7. Price of Livestock

and Picsi, on lands once held by the communities of Lambayeque, Sinto, and Collique. Friends estimated the size of his herds in 1584 at fifteen to sixteen thousand head. On Picsi alone he regularly held five thousand head of sheep, goats, and pigs. He no longer supervised the day-to-day operations of his estancias; a salaried administrator, Diego de Soria, took over those activities.[38]

Mingolla's position as a respected member of society—a breeder of goats and sheep, and owner and "lord" of Picsi—was the result of hard work, luck, and the personal ties he had cultivated over the years. His former residence in the community of Lambayeque and his dealings with the curaca gave him an advantage in recruiting laborers. As lieutenant of the corregidor, he granted Indians special dispensation from paying tribute when they were sick, and he issued licenses for travel. As magistrate and judge, he settled minor disputes and took inventories of the estates of the dead. He also maintained contact with the Indians through business dealings. For instance, he purchased corn from the curaca of Collique to feed his pigs. His financial ties to the corregidor obliged that official to give him preferential treatment in the distribution of mitayos and to help him in securing other favors. In the 1590s Mingolla, according to one statement, had more resident peons and mitayos working for him than did any other settler in the valleys, allowing him to expand his operations during the next decade into the contiguous northern district of Piura.[39]

Mingolla was not uncommonly successful. Juan Domínguez Corso was another of Barbarán's employees who rose from the rather obscure background of a majordomo to become a "rancher" (*ganadero*). He even surpassed Mingolla in accumulating property. By the end of the century, he owned no fewer than eleven estancias, a vineyard, wheatfields, a soap factory, and a lime furnace. Many of the other settlers had similar, if less spectacular, success.[40]

Again, a limiting factor to the expansion of ranching by the settlers was the scarcity of labor. Desperate settlers went to extremes to secure the labor they needed. Court cases of the period recount the ways in which settlers threatened and pressured Indian officials to get mitayos. When such tactics were unsuccessful, overextended ranchers had to break the rate of expansion and even cut the size of their herds. Andrés Martín Pizarro, a settler with herds as large as Mingolla's, allowed his goats and sheep to dwindle between 1584 and 1588 because two-thirds of the kids born each year died from exposure and improper care due to the scarcity of shepherds. He describes a gruesome picture of buzzards killing the defenseless young, despite the efforts of shepherds to protect the animals. Attacks by wild dogs and a species of wildcat (*"leones"*) also increased his losses as the herds became too large to be guarded successfully.[41]

But again here, as with the establishment of Saña some ten years before, the encomenderos benefited much more than the settlers from the immediate opportunities that arose as a result of Toledo's reducción policy. Their financial resources allowed them to take advantage of the newly opened land to expand their herds to the point where it was economically feasible to build their own on-site soap-making facilities (*tinas*) and tanneries (*tenerías*). They thus profited from both the ranching and the processing aspects of the livestock business.

These facilities were built right on or close to the existing corrals. Because of royal legislation making it unlawful for estancias to be built near cultivated fields or Indian communities, and the heavy concentration of chacras, labores, and molinos near Saña, most of the corrals were located in the valleys north of the town. Local processing facilities ended the need for the long cattle drives to Trujillo, where soap-making and tanning operations had functioned since the early 1550s. The savings in wages and herd mortality more than compensated for the additional cost of transporting the tallow, hides, and soap between Lambayeque and Los Reyes.[42]

The estancias, tina, and tenería operated by the encomendero Juan Roldán Dávila, the younger, and later sold to his nonencomendero, younger brother Gabriel de la Requera (see Fig. 5), are typical of large-scale operations in the 1580s and 1590s. Roldán operated six estancias with approximately fourteen to sixteen thousand head of sheep and goats in the Túcume Valley. His tina-tenería had the capacity to process between two and three thousand head each year. On average, he employed sixty-five Indians at a time to guard and brand the stock, to drive them to the slaughter, to build corrals, and to transport firewood. Indians slaughtered, stripped the fat from the skins, and cooked it with ash to produce a paste, which when treated repeatedly with salt formed a hard soap. The hides were soaked in limewater solution to remove the wool, treated with tannin, and dried. Two black slaves—a master soap maker and a master tanner—supervised the activities. Equipment was simple—several large copper kettles, clay jars for storing fat, scissors, axes, knives, and a large scale. As shown in the accounts presented by the administrator, this animal-based, agro-industrial complex yielded over 20 percent per annum on a gross of about 12,300 pesos.[43]

Tinas y tenerías became the centers of a bustling regional economy. They provided direct employment on a short-term, seasonal basis for Indians from the surrounding communities. Indirectly, they provided work for Indians who produced and transported salt, ash, and tannin; for Indian weavers who provided cloth for sacks and reed baskets for packing the soap and tallow; and for Indian potters who fashioned and fired clay jars. At the tina-tenerías, Indians sold wheat, corn, beans, and fish to feed the laborers and cotton garments to clothe the slaves. Indians transported to Túcume the lime that was produced in Saña. Skilled metal workers came from Saña to cast the boiling kettles needed for soap production, and itinerant merchants arrived to sell scissors, knives, and axes.[44]

While stock raising and its derivative industries developed for the most part north of the Lambayeque River, the encomenderos were busy planting sugarcane and building trapiches and ingenios on the fertile soil closer to Saña. Two encomenderos, Salvador Vásquez and Luis de Atienza, started planting sugarcane near their molinos in the Saña valley in the 1570s. In the following years, although the molinos continued to function, wheat and flour production increasingly took a subordinate place to the manufacture of sugar, syrup, and fruit preserves.[45]

Sugar mills were larger and more complicated than any enterprise that had existed in the area previously. Their establishment involved more sophisticated technology and sizable expenditures for capital equipment and slave labor. Technology and know-how were not problems. The first ingenio on the northern coast was established by Diego de Mora and his wife, Ana de Pizarro, in the Chicama Valley before 1558. The encomenderos probably commissioned the same carpenter shop to build their first wooden trapiches, while purchasing other equipment from the same suppliers.[46]

Labor was another story. The encomenderos could not employ Indians (had there been a surplus) after Bartolomé de las Casas and other humanitarian-minded priests barraged the king and the Council of the Indies with propagandistic writings describing the exploitation of the Indians by the Spanish. Hacienda records include accounts of Indians losing fingers, hands, and even arms while feeding cane into the trapiche; of Indians being splattered and burned by the hot, bubbling cane juice as it boiled in its copper cauldrons; and of Indians worked to exhaustion cutting sugarcane from dawn to dusk. The government reacted with an edict that declared sugar-making too dangerous for natives and prohibited their employment near trapiches. This prohibition, although honored in the breach initially, eventually forced encomenderos to import entire crews of black slaves.[47]

Sugar works proved beyond the private financial resources of most individual encomenderos. Given the declining yields of encomiendas and the continuing expense of maintaining their standard of living, capital accumulated from their other business ventures proved insufficient to meet initial expenditures. So they began to tap alternative financial reserves. Vásquez, for example, borrowed over three thousand pesos from the community treasuries of Licapa (Pacasmayo) and Chicama and from a private investor to purchase black slaves trained in the sugar-making process, all the while claiming to need twice as much capital as was available.[48]

Investors and trustees in charge of monitoring funds felt safe in loaning Vásquez and the others the money because domestically produced sugar was rapidly replacing the more expensive imported product during the 1570s and 1580s. Prices, though dropping, were relatively high and markets in Los Reyes and Trujillo were growing. Some far-sighted individuals already looked forward to the day when sugar would overtake flour and textiles as the major export to Tierra Firme and the south.[49]

Furthermore, the molinos and sugar mills themselves served as collateral. In 1582 Vásquez's estate near Saña consisted of an ingenio, six fields of sugarcane, his original flour mill, fifty fanegas de sembradura of wheat, and his residence. Huts of Indian laborers and slaves, several crude storehouses, and sheds surrounded the mill. The entire estate, according to several estimates, was worth about 15,000 pesos. Moreover, maintaining the production of wheat and flour at close to previous levels guaranteed the encomenderos income, while they invested in sugar. With profits on each fanega of flour exported to Guayaquil at about 5 pesos, the Vásquez estate yielded over 9,925 pesos annually, even in the first years of sugar production. Its value, boasted a seemingly confident Vásquez, increased daily. Vásquez's eloquent verbal blustering did not fool everyone. A few realized that although his estate was a sound investment Vásquez had seriously overextended himself and was on the brink of grave personal financial disaster, which would soon force him to sell the property.[50]

Ten years later, the new owner, a merchant originally from Trujillo, had increased the cane fields to nine—enough to keep three wooden trapiches busy at once. The flour mill was still functioning, but its capacity was unchanged. Capital equipment included three kettles of various sizes; two copper cauldrons for boiling cane juice into syrup; two sieves; seventeen large clay jars for molasses; five hundred clay forms for the crystallizing syrup; and miscellaneous pieces of furniture and handtools. A separate *casa de purgar* (purification house) had been built to store the raw sugar during the crystallization and whitening process. The owner kept four teams of oxen and several horses and mules. The labor force numbered sixteen male and three female slaves, an unknown number of resident Indians, and a fluctuating number of temporary employees.[51]

Thus, by the mid-1590s, the Lambayeque zone was a prosperous agricultural area. At least forty chacras and labores, ten molinos, and two or three ingenios operated in Saña and the adjacent Jequetepeque and Lambayeque Valleys. Over fifty named estancias, several with their own processing facilities, dotted the open ranges, especially toward the north. This pattern represented an efficient use of the natural resources of the zone. Intensive agriculture had expanded to the limits imposed by the availability of labor and technology. Goats and a few sheep grazed on the grasslands, and pigs fattened in the algarrobo forests. Bacon, lard, hides, tallow, soap, sugar, molasses, and even

---

Sources: ASFL/Reg. 7, No. 2, Ms. 12; *ACT,* I, 285, 308 and 315; ART/O: 1592; Álvarez: 27–VI–1684; Rios: 1579; CoJV: 6–XI–1612; CoAG: 3–XI–1615; and 8–II–1616; Mata: Registro, 1594; 19–VI–1602; 1588, 311v; VII–1595, 302v; and 26–X–1595; MT: 1578; and CoO: 22–I–1598; ACMS/1642; 1666; 1766; and 1811; AGI/AL: 1417, 1765–66; ANCR/1680; and 1668; Rivera: 23–VIII–1686; 15–VII–1694; 10–VIII–1694; 1–X–1694; 23–XI–1694; 12–I–1700; 13–III–1704; 1–VI–1704; 20–XII–1704; and 3–II–1705; ANP/RA: 1. 24, c. 225, 1819, 8 and 42; 1. 33, 1594; and 1. 194, 1676, 78; Gremial, 1743–50; Temporalidades: Capellanías, 1. 132, 1770–76, 100; 1. 106, 1767; AAL/AT: 1. 18–IV, 1682; and 1. 23-X, 1706; AAT/C: 1796, 2v; T: 1697; 1704; 1742; 1744, 60 and 131; 1746; 1776; and 1779, 23–24 and 179; Causas: 1756; 1736; n.d.; Capillas: 1830; Guillermo Lohmann Villena, "Apuntaciones sobre el curso de los precios de los artículos de primera necesidad en Lima durante el siglo XVI," *Revista histórica* 29 (1966), 99; José Ignacio de Lecuanda, "Descripción geográfica de Lambayeque," Manuel A. Fuentes, ed., *Biblioteca Peruana de historia, ciencias y literatura* 2 (Lima, 1861); Miguel Feyjoo de Sousa, *Relación descriptiva de la ciudad y provincia de Trujillo del Perú* (Madrid, 1763) 79; José Matos Mar, "Las haciendas del Valle de Chancay," Henry Favre, *et al., La hacienda en el Perú* (Lima, 1967), 328; and Woodrow W. Borah, *Early Colonial Trade and Navigation between Mexico and Peru* (Berkeley, 1954), 48 and 85.

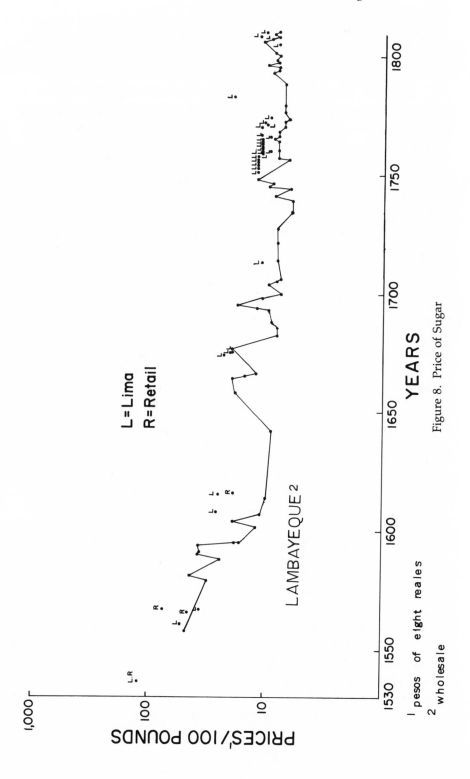

Figure 8. Price of Sugar

fruit preserves had been added to the traditional exports of flour, beans, and cotton textiles.[52]

The Changing Balance of Power

The settlement and development of the region by settlers and enco-menderos met, however, with hostility and stubborn resistance on two fronts. The abrupt arrival of the Spaniards and the expansion that followed meant conflict with the Indians beyond the weak, formal protests mentioned above. Landownership itself was still rarely an issue. Indians complained about continuing problems with harsh treatment, overwork, and occasional water shortages, but the damages caused by livestock were, by far, their most serious grievance. Apparently, Dr. Cuenca's 1566 orders to move estancias away from Indian fields were either not enforced or distance proved a poor deterrent.[53]

Mounting intercultural friction between the Spanish and the Indians and the fact that there were few disinterested authorities in the provinces to whom the Indians could appeal to for help were two of the reasons why Governor García de Castro appointed a *corregidor de indios* to govern the district in 1566. Whereas a *corregidor municipal* exercised jurisdiction over the Spanish and mixed population of the Spanish cities and towns, the corregidor de indios supervised the Indians and dealt with the problems of intercultural contact at a salary equal to less than half that of the corregidor municipal of Trujillo.[54]

As a cultural broker and ombudsman in the district, the corregidor de indios had an ambiguous role. Theoretically, the welfare of the Indians was his primary responsibility. He was to be an impartial authority to whom they could appeal for justice. His duties included enforcing labor laws which prohibited Indians from working as porters or mill hands, making sure mitayos were promptly paid, and monitoring the encomenderos' collection of tribute. The encomenderos' interference with this last duty prompted the governor to give the corregidor the additional task, in 1568, of collecting the tribute directly from the curacas. This eliminated the need for the encomenderos and their agents to maintain a residence in the area and eventually ended the encomendero's personal contact with his Indians.[55]

The corregidor de indios did not solve the Indians' problems with the Spaniards. One of his duties, for example, was to distribute mitayos—previously a task assigned to one of the magistrates. He forced the curacas to fill community quotas and punished those who failed, because the Spanish blamed him if the mitayos did not show up for work. In another case, spokesmen for the communities of Chérrepe and Pacasmayo appealed to local authorities for payment of damages to their corn and cotton fields and irrigation network caused by the livestock of Pedro de Morales and Gaspar de Coria. Cabildo officials had ignored them. When they approached the corregidor, Don Diego de Valverde, he stalled. To make matters worse, at the insistence of Morales, Valverde ordered the Indians whipped and shaved. To the Indians, cutting of the hair was second only in severity of punishment to exile. Then, to reassert his authority, Valverde sent them to work as mitayos for Morales. In another instance, the refusal of Captain Francisco de Coronado to recount the Indians of Íllimo and Túcume, to bring their tribute into line with the diminishing population, cost them three to four thousand pesos in unjustified tribute payments.[56]

In each of these cases the attitude of both officials and corregidor is explained by conflict of interest. Magistrates were farmers and livestock raisers, whose own animals damaged the Indians' fields and irrigation networks just as the animals of other settlers did. The corregidor's inaction can be explained by his clear identification with local interests. The corregidor, theoretically an outside, impartial representative of the crown and protector of the Indians, was by the 1570s and 1580s participating in the agricultural bonanza. Santo Toribio de Mogrovejo, the archbishop of Lima, wrote to King Philip II from the Lambayeque valleys in February of 1590 to report that corregidores commonly forced Indians to plant fields for them and grind wheat into flour. Moreover, the corregidores used the Indians to generate revenue to supplement their salaries. They regularly asked Indian weavers to fabricate cotton garments for them, which they later sold. Furthermore, the communities constituted a captive market for horses, mules, wine, and other goods which the corregidor could force the Indians to buy, sometimes at exorbitant prices.[57]

Personal ties to influential people in the area also affected the corregidor's impartiality. The encomenderos and leading citizens of Saña posted bond so that the corregidor could assume office. The encomendero of Saña, Captain Juan Delgadillo, sponsored the corregidor de indios, Pedro de Murguía, in 1568. Pedro de Olmos de Ayala, encomendero of Chuspo-Callanca and later of Jequetepeque, sponsored Don Alonso Osorio de Figueroa in 1580. Such sponsorships were tantamount to buying influence. Invariably, the corregidor exercised jurisdiction over the area where his sponsor held his Indians or property. Financial obligations made it difficult for a corregidor to take action against a bondsman.[58]

In addition to personal influence, being the sponsor of a corregidor sometimes gave the encomendero and settler the opportunity to resolve conflicts directly. Copying the practice in Trujillo, the corregidor often named his guarantor as a lieutenant, thus giving him official jurisdiction over his own interests. Over the years, this pattern became so common that being the guarantor of a corregidor became equivalent to purchasing the position.[59]

Bribes and threats also influenced the action of the corregidores. Francisco Luis de Alcántara, one of the encomenderos of Pacasmayo, paid the corregidor over eighty pesos to cooperate in a dispute over an irrigation canal. Eighty pesos was no small sum to a corregidor earning a base salary of fifteen hundred pesos per year. Later, Alcántara reminded him to "watch what you do" and vaguely threatened bodily harm if he should take the wrong action. It is not surprising, then, that the Indians rarely got results when they appealed to the corregidor or local officials for help.[60]

The Indians, however, were not always unsuccessful in getting redress for their grievances. Before the local elite was firmly established, corregidores acted more independently. One prosecuted the encomendero of Chuspo-Callanca in 1570 for the back wages of the Indians who worked on his farm, perhaps in anticipation of the pending arrival in the district of Toledo's visitador. Corregidores also punished curacas who cheated the Indians by charging more than the specified amount of tribute or who were uncommonly cruel. These corregidores, in short, took action in favor of the Indians when enforcement of the law would not unduly upset the Spanish or when the abuse was overt and serious enough to draw the attention of higher authorities.[61]

Visiting officials and authorities of Lima were much more sympathetic to Indians' complaints than were local authorities or corregidores who became beholden to local interests. Toledo's visitor in the Lambayeque area fined several encomenderos substantial amounts for maltreating Indians. Melchior de Osorno, Lorenzo de Samudio, Pedro de Lezcano, Captain Juan Delgadillo, Pedro de Olmos de Ayala, and several others each paid fines ranging from 150 to more than 3,000 pesos to the royal treasury. Such fines are extraordinarily high, given the income of the encomiendas at the time. Dr. Cuenca, as noted above, heard the complaints of Indians against the Spaniards and ordered remedial action. Unfortunately for the Indians, local officials were often unreliable and reluctant executors of orders. Manuscripts tell of more than one instance in which well-intentioned decrees from Los Reyes were conveniently ignored.[62]

The distance from the viceregal capital and the infrequency of visits by outside authorities allowed corregidores and local officials to act, in most cases, in their own interest. In a sense, the corregidor, those he appointed as his lieutenants and agents, his guarantors, and the wrongdoers were all involved in a cover-up. The records of the extant judicial reviews show that they became increasingly prescribed, ritualized farces in Lambayeque in the late sixteenth and seventeenth centuries. They exposed little because neither officials nor witnesses benefited from exposure. Spaniards and curacas testified on the corregidor's behalf, answering questions briefly and summarily regarding his fairness while in office. The judge of the residencia was uninterested in finding malfeasance because he was usually the incoming corregidor: he knew he would undergo the same examination when his term expired. A sympathetic judge usually declared the corregidor and officials innocent of all but the most blatant abuses of power. In the few cases where injustices were substantiated, the corregidor could appeal to Los Reyes and, eventually, Spain. This procedure took years and often ended in acquittal or, at worst, a fine.[63]

Other reasons why the Indians' protests were not more vocal and were generally ineffectual are many and varied. The fact that the top Indian officials were so closely identified with the encomenderos and later with the corregidor left the mass of Indians without effective leaders possessing the knowledge and experience to function in the Spanish system. Few other Indians understood the Spanish institutions and mentality. Moreover, the public crier announced in Spanish an impending visit by a judge or authority from the capital, and few Indians, other than the curacas, were bilingual.[64]

Although the crown's policies generally failed to improve the lot of the Indian communities, its settlement program did have its desired effect in regard to the balance of power among whites in the area. Paralleling the agricultural development was the assumption of power by the settlers. As discussed above, the encomenderos, traditionally the dominant group in the area, established labores and estancias years before the Conde de Nieva's order to found the town of Saña. The viceroy anticipated a situation in which they would move into the area and assume control by backing the formation of a group of citizens theoretically independent of the encomenderos' control. In keeping with this, he denied the latter the right to change citizenship and barred them from living in Saña and participating on the town council. Only settlers sat on the cabildo in Saña. There is no evidence that the encomenderos participated formally.

During the first ten to fifteen years that they lived in the area, however, the citizens of Saña were not impervious to encomendero influence. The wealth, position, and reputation of the encomenderos enabled them to influence aldermen and magistrates indirectly, especially during the first years of the council's existence. The citizens' modest economic base and inexperience made them weak and hesitant at first. They looked to the encomenderos for guidance and asked them for advice. The settlers respected the encomenderos as members of Trujillo's wealthiest, oldest, and most socially prominent families, as "conquerors" deserving enough of the king's esteem to merit the services of Indians. Encomenderos were recognized as "honored and eminent men." Pedro Gonzales de Ayala, for example, had the reputation among his own friends and relatives of being a "powerful and very favored person in the said city of Trujillo who ordinarily served as either magistrate or lieutenant of the corregidor. . . ." His power and connections made others consider him above the law. The citizens of Saña probably regarded him as even more formidable than did his peers.[65]

The encomendero, while barred from participation in the cabildo, maintained a strong position in Lambayeque, at least until the middle of the 1570s, by serving as the corregidor's lieutenant. Encomenderos also rented housing to settlers and lent them money or guaranteed loans. The encomenderos later used such arrangements to exert pressure on local politics. Juan Delgadillo, the third encomendero of Saña, allegedly bribed the magistrate Alonso de Paz and used his friendship with an alderman named Gaspar Fragoso to influence their votes to elect his handpicked slate of candidates to the cabildo.[66]

The exposure of this incident was due in part to growing pressure from a second front, which eventually rendered the encomenderos' influence on local politics ephemeral and forced them to reestablish their residence in Trujillo. The massive departure from Trujillo of the encomenderos with Indians in Lambayeque turned those who remained into a vocal group of detractors. Led by Rodrigo Venegas and, from behind the scenes, by Diego de Mora, they used the town council of Trujillo as a focus of resistance to the establishment of Saña. As early as 1566, they protested before Dr. Cuenca that Saña would generate little revenue for the crown and would retard Trujillo's development by dividing its jurisdiction. The cabildo asked not that Saña be abandoned, only that its status be reduced to that of a town subject to the city. Despite their efforts, the cabildo became desperate as more and more encomenderos of Lambayeque left the city to take up permanent residence in the town. They complained to the viceroy that the best educated, most conscientious, and highest quality citizens, from the oldest and best families, had moved to Saña and refused to return. The cabildo feared the abandonment of the city, probably a gross exaggeration but indicative of the concern felt by those who remained.

Several tactics were used to induce the absent encomenderos to return to Trujillo. In response to their petition and the crown's overall policy objectives, the viceroy issued a decree in January 1567 establishing heavy fines of more than two thousand pesos for those persons who were elected to the Trujillo council but did not accept the position. A year later, the continued absence of the encomenderos of Lambayeque prompted the cabildo to ask the viceroy to enforce royal decrees that threatened the encomenderos with the loss of their encomiendas if they did not return to the city.[67]

The cabildo's efforts had their desired effect. Outgoing council members elected absent encomenderos to office and forced them back. Salvador Vásquez and his family, for example, had been living since 1558, first sporadically and then permanently, in Saña near his encomienda of Reque. He was elected alderman of Trujillo twice (in 1558 and 1559) while out of the city and unable (and unwilling) to take the position. After the imposition of the fines, Vásquez's son and heir could not afford to disregard the mandate, given his growing financial problems. Another encomendero returned in 1568 for the same reasons to take charge of the city's finances and in 1569 to assume the position of alderman.[68]

Other changes contributed to the erosion of the encomendero's position in the valleys. The gradual enforcement of a Toledan decree that prohibited encomenderos from having lands and mills close to their encomiendas, and financial problems similar to those that faced Vásquez, forced Gonzales de Ayala to sell his molino to Antonio Durán, a citizen of Saña, to raise funds needed to pay off thousands to his creditors. Other encomenderos died, and their heirs—often schooled in Trujillo and accustomed to the prestige associated with their line—refused to return to what they considered a frontier outpost without culture or social life. They sold their property in Saña to prosperous settlers. One encomendero who was not encumbered with debt simply left his son in charge of his Lambayeque concerns when he moved back to Trujillo.[69]

As the actions of Vásquez and Gonzales de Ayala illustrate, during the last quarter century the settlers strengthened their position vis à vis the encomenderos to the point where they were in a position to purchase the encomenderos' properties and no longer needed the encomenderos' counsel. There was no one formula for success. Original vecinos who were artisans, shopkeepers, and clerks in Trujillo began their careers and fortunes with the land grant and whatever capital and skills they had brought with them. Some of these made money in merchandising. Martín de Arana and Juan Calderón Lescano earned good incomes as town scribes. Of the settlers who arrived after 1564, one made enough as a tithe collector in 1579 to purchase land and by 1583 owned a molino. The most typical career pattern for settlers in Saña was **(a)** employment, usually in the service of another; **(b)** establishment of an estate; **(c)** entrance into merchandising; and **(d)** service on the cabildo. By the mid-1590s, landholding settlers as a group had developed their chacras to the size and importance of the labores established by the encomenderos before the founding of Saña and had established themselves as some of the largest ranchers in the region. They controlled the town council and assumed many of the other functions previously performed by the encomenderos, such as guaranteeing the corregidor and serving as his lieutenant, and contracting for the tithes, with all the responsibility and influence these activities implied.[70]

As powerful as the encomenderos were in Trujillo, the northern coast, and Peru, in general, they were no match for the power of the crown. The influence of the encomenderos in Lambayeque gradually diminished as a result of the implementation of policy decisions on the peninsula, peer pressure to force them back to Trujillo, their subsequent absence from Lambayeque, and mounting economic difficulties. The return of the encomenderos to Trujillo marked the end of the era dominated by conquest society—the heyday of the encomenderos, their relatives, and employees, when labor was wealth and landownership was relatively unimportant. After the establishment of Saña, encomenderos and landholders shared control over the area for ten to fifteen years. The encomenderos based their influence primarily on wealth; the settlers' position initially rested primarily on the control of the cabildo. The continuing favorable market conditions encouraged encomenderos to invest in wheat and sugar production, establishing the first molinos and ingenios in the district. Early settlers lacked the financial resources and personal connections needed to secure large loans or an adequate supply of labor, so their chacras and animal-raising ventures were modest in comparison. But by the mid-1570s, settlers had begun to turn their modest holdings into sometimes lucrative agricultural enterprises. Their start in fortifying their position through interpersonal relations and in building their fortunes enabled them to form a new elite which paled in comparison to the status, wealth, and political clout of the elite of Trujillo. Nevertheless, local landholders by the mid-1590s clearly had become the new controlling force in the area.

PART TWO

Landed Society and the Development of the Great Estates, 1595–1719

The benign neglect of viceregal authorities, coupled with the growth of markets and good prices for local products, favored the expansion of the agricultural economy and the establishment of estate owners as the most influential residents of Lambayeque between 1595 and 1719. In contrast to its efforts during the second half of the sixteenth century to break the power of the encomendero elite by fostering the growth of a rival group of landowners and by sending royal officials into the provinces to directly implement its directives, the crown rarely intervened in local affairs during this period. Once the king and peninsular policymakers felt successful in eliminating threats to royal imperative, they turned their attention to more pressing matters elsewhere. The most noteworthy occasions of direct royal intervention in the provincial administration of Lambayeque during the next century and a quarter were the *visitas de la tierra* by viceregal officials sent to the provinces to review and legalize land titles. These visitas were not designed to check on the conditions or the efficiency of local administration, to alter the local balance of power, or to report on the situation of the Indian population as much as to simply generate additional revenues for the king. The viceregal bureaucrats' nearsightedness, self-interest, and disregard for the conduct of local affairs allowed the hacendados and provincial administrators to work out a mutually beneficial governing arrangement which guaranteed peaceful coexistence, cooperation, and collaboration.

Meanwhile, sure markets and the alleviation of the labor shortage by the normalization of the slave trade permitted the steady growth of the estates. Unusually high sugar prices at midcentury signaled the start of a sugar boom, characterized by the spread of cane cultivation, latifundia, and slavery, as well as heralding the beginning of an era when landowners played central and active roles in local affairs. Hacendados upgraded their standard of living in an obvious attempt to emulate the encomendero ideal and to capture the imagination and respect of the other sectors of society. They purchased public office and assumed commanding positions in the local militia. They consolidated their formal positions of leadership and power by establishing close personal ties with other professionals and government bureaucrats. With the latter's help, landowners extended their influence and control, sometimes by quasi-legal means, over the additional natural resources and labor necessary to expand their estates.

The Indians, in fact, abandoned by their designated protectors and unwilling or unable to appeal to higher courts successfully, retreated.

Consequently, Spaniards and Indians came to live as two separate and unequal groups, with cross-cultural interaction limited to the provisioning of the estates by the Indians with basic foodstuffs, supplies, and labor.

5 Formation of the Latifundia and the Local Landed Elite, 1595–1649

The year 1595 is a convenient breaking point in the continuing economic and social history of the Lambayeque region. In the economic sector, it signaled the beginning of a period of growth and technological improvements on the estates, facilitated by the regularization of trade, the review and legalization of precarious possession, and easier credit. The estates assumed the form they would retain with slight variations through the wars of Independence; and the use of the term *hacienda*, denoting a large estate or latifundio, became current. Socially, the period continued to be one of transition, marked by the end of encomendero dominance and an initial instability of land tenure. Improved conditions about 1630 established the surviving landowners as a local landowning elite. By the end of this period, the size and productivity of the agricultural units turned labradores into hacendados and estancieros. Owners acquired the trappings of wealth and prestige and established the personal connections that distinguished them as social and economic leaders. For the Indians, in contrast, 1595 began a period in which able-bodied laborers were increasingly forced to do double duty on the estates, working as both mitayos and hired help. As the Spanish landowners gained power, Indians lost control over traditional community lands, and irrigation water assumed new importance as an issue of contention.

By the last decade of the sixteenth century, the labradores and estancieros of the Lambayeque region had become unfinished versions of gentleman farmers, enjoying a comfortable if not extravagant life in the houses once owned by the encomenderos of the region. Black slaves, visible symbols of the labradores' economic well-being, replaced Indians as domestic servants in their households. Landowners continued to serve on the municipal council and assumed commanding though essentially ceremonial roles in the local militia. For these reasons and others, the ranchers and farmers who doubled as the leaders of the Spanish community enjoyed growing prestige and status. Yet these same men, who dressed uncomfortably in imported linens, woolens, and velvets to attend the ever more infrequent cabildo meetings or to accompany their wives and families to Mass or other religious festivities, also spent much of their time and energies on their estates, directly involved in the business of raising livestock and growing wheat and sugarcane. Indeed, they seemed to prefer the dust of the rural setting to the relatively sophisticated and overly polite manners of urban life. Their commitment to the development of the agricultural potential of the region was serious and all-encompassing because their livelihood and that of their families depended on it. The vecinos who strolled around the plaza of Saña in 1595 remembered or had heard about those few who had fulfilled the dream of accumulating the fortunes necessary for the move to Los Reyes. But reminders of hardship and failure surrounded them, as they realized how few of the representatives of the original settlers were still among them after thirty years.[1]

From Labores to Haciendas, Trapiches, and Estancias

During the next fifty years or so, these landowners of 1595 and those who gradually replaced them faced trying conditions. First among these were the increasingly unpredictable markets for the products of the region in Chile and Tierra Firme and, to a lesser extent, in Lima and the highlands. It was true that markets were growing. Continuing Spanish immigration and the natural population increase kept demand expanding throughout this period. The viceregal capital alone had grown from a few hundred inhabitants in the middle of the sixteenth century to over 23,000 by 1614. Moreover, Philip III's desire to eliminate American competition for the products of the peninsula and other Spanish possessions sold in the New World prompted him to order the demolition of sugar mills within six leagues of Lima. This change in crown policy and Viceroy Esquilache's (1615–21) subsequent prohibition on the importation of sugar mills and related equipment created, in essence, an additional market for the sugar output of the area.[2]

But, with the above-mentioned exception, competition in other areas also grew. The inflated prices of many of the products that had been imported from Spain and from older parts of its American empire in the immediate postconquest decades and their associated bonanza profits plunged, as domestic production grew and displaced the higher priced imports. Imbalances between supply and demand, especially frequent until the sporadically arriving imports tapered off, caused local prices to fluctuate tremendously over the years. Most affected was the price of imported sugar, an obvious luxury, which fell dramatically and almost continually until domestic production satisfied demand and prices stabilized. Competition, with highland wheat in the local market and Caracas production in distant Tierra Firme, also caused the collapse of the once-important local flour industry. Flour prices proved far more volatile than those of sugar. Unlike the latter, however, flour prices fell to the point where wheat no longer was an important cash crop in the area. Gradually, farmers replaced wheat with cane. Ironically, the reduced supply helped local flour prices to recover somewhat by 1650; whereas the expansion depressed sugar prices further, until heightened demand overtook supply and initiated a boom at midcentury.[3]

In contrast to sugar and flour prices, those of livestock and their by-products remained relatively stable. Goats on the hoof sold at prices which averaged about one peso per head, depending on the quality, age, and mix of animals and whether or not corrals and the right to mitayos were included in the sale. The price of supple, tanned leather (for which Lambayeque became famous) remained steady for years, before falling after 1615 by almost one-quarter as herds multiplied and cheaper Chilean imports flooded the markets. Local hog prices initially increased by one-third as soap makers bid up the price of tallow. Eventually, hog raisers, who had been in the business since the 1540s, were forced out by steadily lower prices for soap (see Fig. 9), by relatively high labor costs, and by the combined pressure from agriculturalists and other ranchers, who were incensed at the damage caused by swine to fields and natural grasslands.[4]

Thus, although prices in the uncertain years of the sixteenth and early seventeenth centuries fluctuated greatly, depending on such factors as the arrival of ships from Tierra Firme and Mexico, they were undoubtedly falling. But this trend is deceptive in that the lower prices did not have the disastrous effects on the economy of the region that might have been anticipated. Production was redirected. Cane cultivation spread to former wheatlands. Goats replaced pigs in the algarrobo forests and on the range. And the drop in sugar prices for domestic producers was actually less than the plot of Figure 8 indicates, because the high prices of the 1590s represent the average for the expensive imported and cheaper domestic product. Furthermore, the fall was cushioned by increasing sales of such sugar by-products as syrup and preserves. Compensating for the drop, too, were the prices of such inputs as copper, which fell even more rapidly from a high of 10 reales per pound in 1596 as deposits on the southern coast came into production. Oxen, so necessary for milling and transporting products to port, also declined in price from 22.5 pesos in 1568 to 5 pesos by midcentury.[5]

Like the fall of sugar prices, the decline in prices for most of the other products of the region reflected the fall of the prices for imports as domestic production increased. At least until the first decade of the seventeenth century, imported soap sold for as much as twice the price of domestic soap, giving local production a lucrative comparative advantage. Leather continued to be imported long after importation of animals on the hoof ceased in the 1570s. The decline in its price in the second decade of the seventeenth century coincided with a change in the laws which, some believe, gave Chilean products greater access to the Peruvian markets. In general, then, domestic production reached a level in this period sufficient to meet local and viceregal demand with a surplus for export to such areas as Tierra Firme. So ended almost a century during which local production had developed under the protective umbrella of high import prices.[6]

The commentaries and actions of the landowners indicate that the

---

Sources: ANP/LC: 1. 139, 1795, 10v; and 1801, 14–15; 1. 140, 1808, 5v, 13 and 20; 1811, 20v; 1. 141, 1809, 4v, 14, 17v; and 1811, 9–9v, 20v, 23v, 31, 41, 48, 49v; and 1. 142, 1812, 2v; 1. 341, No. 1220; and No. 1105, 14, 19, 28, 42v, 67 and 77v; RA: 1. 14, c. 71, 1575, 223v; 1. 22, c. 74, 1608, 1, 26, 54 and 57; 1. 24, c. 82, 1609, 1, 13v, 28v–30v, 132v; 1. 33, 1594; 1. 173, 1668, 923; T: 1. 232, 49v and 73v; BNP/B357, 1668; B1562; B4045; D10709; ANCR/GG: 23-VI–1804; Rivera: 2–VIII–1698; Lino: 30–IV–1722; Polo: 10–I–1748; VM: 24–VII–1775; and Collús: 1643; ART/Palacios: 12–IX–1610; 16–X–1610; 19–X–1610; 29–X–1610; 30–X–1610; 4–XI–1610; and 24–II–1611; and CoO: 24–I–1596, 71; AGI/J: 461, 1207, 1213v and 1221v; BCH/[1788]; AAT/T: 1746; 1775, 121–25; 1776; 1779, 141–45; 1784; 1794–95; and Guillermo Lohmann Villena, "Apuntaciones sobre el curso de los precios de los artículos de primera necesidad en Lima durante el siglo XVI," *Revista histórica* 29 (1966), 98; José Ignacio de Lecuanda, "Descripción geográfica de Lambayeque," Manuel A. Fuentes, ed., *Biblioteca Peruana de historia, ciencias y literatura*, II (Lima, 1861), 265; *Libros de Cabildo de Lima* 3, 600; 10, 149 and 195; and 14, 891–92.

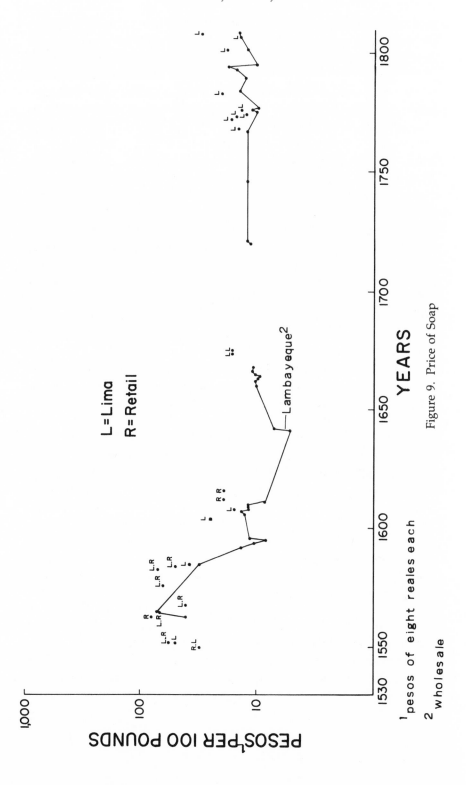

Figure 9. Price of Soap

PESOS[1] PER 100 POUNDS

YEARS

L = Lima
R = Retail

Lambayeque[2]

[1] pesos of eight reales each

[2] wholesale

profits of producing livestock, leather, soap, and sugar stabilized by the mid-1630s and remained acceptable even after the end of the import-substitution process, largely because local exports continued to command profitable prices in distant markets such as Tierra Firme, while prices of imported inputs were falling as fast or faster. Profit per unit of production, however, was probably down from the highs recorded in the sixteenth century.[7]

Fortunately, a general review and legalization of landholdings occurred at the start of the period which, despite initial misgivings and apprehension, encouraged labradores to invest to develop the agricultural potential of their holdings and maintain earnings. The excessive cost of Spain's continental warfare with England, France, and Holland; the destruction in 1588 of the great Armada; the resulting depletion of the royal treasury; and the reports of widespread illegal possession of crown lands in America prompted King Philip II to order a thorough review of land titles, a visita de la tierra, in 1589. The first of two visitas in the Lambayeque area during this period was the single most important event separating the pattern and conditions of land tenure of the conquest period from the second phase of landowner domination and control.[8]

The imperial decrees and the accompanying instructions for the visitas were designed to generate income for the king's treasury and bring order to the land tenure system. Philip II gave the viceroy, in consultation with the audiencia, the responsibility for appointing visitors to tour the kingdom to conduct the review.[9] The law required all persons, except Indians, to exhibit to the visitor for confirmation the titles to the land they occupied. If the titles proved defective[10] or illegal,[11] or if a landholder had no titles, the law provided that proprietary rights to the land in question either revert to the crown or be legalized (or *compuestos*, literally "repaired") by a payment of a "just" and "moderate" sum to the royal treasury. Thus, labradores had to pay if the visitor found more land than that in the original merced. Persons without titles had to pay a fee to legalize possession to all the lands they occupied.

The instructions further stipulated that vacant land—including land which had been assigned to the Indian communities at the time of the reducciones of Toledo that was now in excess of that actually needed and used—belonged to the crown, that is, was baldía and *realenga*. To raise additional funds, Philip II empowered and encouraged the visitor to sell as much of the vacant land as possible, taking care only to reserve the necessary area for the future urban expansion of Spanish towns and cities and for the agricultural needs of the Indian communities. The only condition for purchase was that buyers have the means and intent to cultivate it. The law clearly outlined the procedure for such sales. Prospective buyers submitted bids to the visitor for possession of the vacant land of their choosing. After verifying that the land was indeed abandoned, the visitor notified the owners of adjacent property to discover any objections to the sale. The town crier then announced the sale publicly on thirty separate occasions. On the day of the last such advertisement, a candle was lighted and additional bids were accepted as long as it burned. The highest bidder got the land. As we shall see, this elaborate procedure was not always followed in practice.[12]

News of these decrees and the impending visita unnerved landholders. Many realized that according to the law, the only sufficient titles to land were the *títulos originarios*, or titles for concessions, which emanated directly from the king or some person or institution with his explicit authority; for example, the governor, a viceroy, and certain town councils. Landlords with grants from the town council worried that their titles might be considered illegal, because the grants had been made without official sanction. Spaniards whose only titles were bills of sale or donations from the Indians realized that these titles could be declared defective. Spanish law regarded the Indians as minors. The king had never granted them dominion or absolute ownership of the land; Indians had purely usufructuary rights. Curacas had been allowed to sell private property, but this practice had been prohibited after the widespread sale of community lands in the sixteenth century. Consequently, only bills of sale or donations, dated after Dr. Cuenca's visita to the area in the 1560s and accompanied by the sworn statements of the corregidor and various informants that the lands were not needed by the Indians, would not be challenged as illegal. Finally, ranchers worried about their status and continued access to pastures and forests, because by royal decree grazing lands were communal and open to all. Many stockmen had no titles whatsoever, and hence only squatters' rights to the land on which they had built stock pens and huts.[13]

The settlers' fears were intensified by the circulation of exaggerated, near hysterical rumors that the visita was a scheme to return all the land to the Indians and that the land of many Spaniards would be confiscated; in fact, however, the king was willing to sell off large areas of the royal domain to raise funds. Viceroy Cañete's reaction to the order for the visita reflects the landholders' anxieties. He wrote Philip II a strongly worded letter, dated 27 May 1592, outlining the possible disruptive effects of his decrees and suggesting their slow and cautious implementation.

> the landowners include the richest and earliest discoverers and conquerors of the Kingdom, their children and descendants, and other persons to whom they have sold property. All these persons have plowed, cultivated, planted and improved the lands with buildings . . . at first everyone received land without contradiction; the viceroys and governors encouraged and aided those who dedicated themselves to exploiting and planting them. . . . Now nothing could cause more scandal and uneasiness in all the Kingdom among the most prestigious, valuable and able citizens than to try to take the land away from them when it represents all the wealth. Seizure of the encomiendas touches two-hundred persons who know that they hold the Indians for only one or two lives. They will not feel the deprivation as much as they would if you took away all the lands that they enjoy and hold as a secure and permanent possession.

The only lands that should be affected, he argued, were those no longer needed and used by Indian communities.[14]

The landholders' anxiety was unfounded: none of the predicted dire consequences of the visita came to pass. The visitor, Don Rodrigo de Ampuero, while outwardly maintaining a solemn and disinterested air, probably exaggerated the consequences of not regularizing land titles to encourage anxious landholders to come forward and thus accomplish his true and overriding purpose of raising as much money as possible for the royal treasury. Ampuero confirmed as legitimate and sufficient titles the original grants made at the time Saña was founded and their subsequent sale and donations. For a fee, Ampuero issued titles to excess lands and corrected and legalized defective titles. A modest sum also made landholders without titles legal landowners. A few Spaniards took advantage of the opportunity to purchase vacant land at auction. Juan Fragoso, for example, paid 45 pesos for three fanegadas of lands and the legalization of the bill of sale for nine others he had previously purchased from the curaca of Chuspo-Callanca.[15]

Judging from the extant records of the visita, livestock raisers were the group of Spaniards most affected. Ampuero issued clear title to estancias and corrals throughout the region for sums ranging from 42 to 190 pesos per fanegada. These titles gave the ranchers ownership of enough land for their center of operations and stock pens, but they did not give the owners exclusive rights to pastures and woodlands. Titles contained the clause that pastures and forests were to be held in common. The titles of the estancia of Picsi, for instance, included land for an administrative center and sites for corrals one-and-one-half to two leagues away. The need to move animals periodically to fresh pastures made corrals at these sites necessary to minimize the distance the herds had to travel each evening for protection. Subsequent legislation prohibited the establishment of the center of a new sheep and goat ranch within one league or that of a new swine ranch half that distance from an existing center of operations. Because of the recognized distinction between pastures (plants and fodder) and the lands (soil) on which the grasses grew, this regulation did not affect the tenure of the farmers with fields between corrals. Grazing stock did not differentiate between stubble and crops, resulting in continuing disputes on this account. Eventually laws were issued specifying that no new estancias could be established within a league of cultivated land and that fields be fenced.[16]

The records show that for the Spanish the visita merely legalized a *de facto* situation and did not change the pattern of landholding significantly. It made landowners of landholders. For the Indians, the visita meant yet another lesson in the idea of private property and a loss of unused land. The visitor, following his instructions, left the Indian communities with enough lands for their current needs, but without sufficient reserves for future population growth. All excess land was publicly declared the domain of the king.[17]

The visita, by providing the landowners with security in tenure, encouraged them to invest. The extant records show that the landowners' equity and the prospects for future growth made them eligible for mortgage funds and willing to borrow from many of the same sources that had previously supported the encomenderos' agricultural expansion. Readily available mortgage funds, then, must be counted as another stimulant of the growth and development of the estates at this time.

Landowners borrowed from funds left by individuals for charitable works (obras pías) and chantries (*capellanías*) and from funds accumulated by such ecclesiastical institutions as religious brotherhoods (*cofradías*), monasteries, and convents. The establishment of a chantry was very similar to that of an obra pía or other religious trust, in that the founder left a certain amount of money to be invested in real estate. In a society and economy based on agriculture, the money was often lent to estate owners. The annual interest paid a priest, usually one of the founder's relatives, to say Masses for someone's soul and to make certain that other conditions of the perpetual trust were met. The founder named as trustee either himself or another relative or friend. The church invariably became the trustee and ultimate beneficiary when those designated in the founding document died or were incapable of performing the obligations. This form of trust was very popular because it provided the founder with spiritual life insurance (to borrow the phrase of the late John Leddy Phelan) and the means of providing a guaranteed annual income for at least one relative. When, as very often happened, landowners established a trust, the principal of which was imposed on his own property, no money actually changed hands. The founder merely assumed the obligation of paying the annual interest on the principal. When a landowner set up a chantry, the principal of which was invested in an estate other than his own or when a non-landowner founded one, the principal was treated as any other investment capital and delivered to the estate owner in return for a promise to pay the premium. These sources provided the landowners with sums ranging from a few hundred to several thousand pesos, usually at a rate of 5 percent annually.[18]

Besides administering endowments earmarked for charitable works and chantries, the church offered large loans from funds acquired through pious donations and bequests, rental income from rural and urban property holdings, fees for religious services, and the weekly contributions of the faithful—making it the single most important lending institution in colonial society. But, unlike the funds from obras pías and capellanías, which had no set repayment date as long as the interest was paid, church loans usually had to be amortized in a specific number of years.

Another factor conducive to the development of agriculture in the region was the availability of an alternative source of labor. The labor shortage had become so acute at the end of the sixteenth century that the problem required the attention of officials at the highest levels of administration both in Peru and the metropolis. The existing system of mita labor proved unsatisfactory to king, landowners, and Indians alike. The crown disliked the system ostensibly because of its harmful effects on the Indians. Landowners complained more forthrightly that it did not provide them with a reliable supply of workers. The Indians resented the system because it forced them to work far from their homes for relatively low wages.[19] They had to be pressured to conform. In 1601 Philip III actually decreed an end to the mita, hoping that it could be replaced with voluntary wage labor. The Indians, however, were reluctant to hire themselves out, despite the fact that changes in the encomienda system during the last twenty years favored the alternative. Beginning in the late sixteenth century, Indians were given a choice of meeting their tribute quotas in specie rather than in kind. In some cases in the seventeenth century, cash equivalencies for goods were written directly into the tribute lists. In Lambayeque, tribute was assessed at the official rate of 5.5 to 6 pesos[20] per tributary in 1614–15, part of which Indians paid in cash and part of which they delivered in goods. For the corregidor, cash payment facilitated collection and eliminated the need to assemble large quantities of commodities for which he had to find buyers. For the Indians, cash payments meant a need for money and, hence, a need to work for the Spanish. Yet, despite the curaca's efforts to encourage temporary work on the estates, voluntary wage labor fell far short of providing enough Indian workers to maintain production levels. Philip III reestablished the mita in 1609, and thereafter, able-bodied males served both as mitayos and seasonal wage laborers. However, even this double duty was not enough to supply the growing demand for labor.[21]

Viceregal officials experimented with alternative solutions to the labor problem. As early as the 1570s, Viceroy Francisco de Toledo tried to force mulattoes, mestizos, and other mixed bloods to work, without notable results. He instituted the collection of tribute from forasteros, albeit at a lower rate than for community Indians with land, to force them into the money economy. Although this did increase the number of Indians willing to work on the estates, the measure proved insufficient to solve the labor shortage. In the seventeenth century, the crown asked the mixed bloods to pay tribute, hoping that this measure would increase the supply of the employable, but this too met with stubborn resistance and proved inadequate.[22]

Landowners, also, tried new schemes to attract Indian labor, especially after 1603 when Viceroy Luis de Velasco excused Indians from the mountain provinces of Cajamarca and Guambos from serving the mita of Saña because of their susceptibility to lowland diseases. One way that landowners devised was to send agents to recruit in communities by advancing Indians cash and supplies, in a system known today as the *enganche*, from the Spanish verb *enganchar*, meaning "to hook." Such efforts helped, but labor remained a problem.[23]

The continuing shortage of voluntary wage labor forced the crown, albeit reluctantly, to expedite the wholesale importation of blacks as the only practicable alternative. Black slaves had been imported in the sixteenth century, but never on a grand scale. During the seventeenth century, the supply of slaves reaching Peru became nearly sufficient in volume to meet the needs of the kingdom. Frederick Bowser, in his exhaustive study of the black in colonial Peru, reports that ships stopped at Saña and other ports on their voyages south from Tierra Firme to Lima, selling slaves along the way. The supply reaching Lima increased to the point where the capital market was glutted and prices were depressed in a few selected years. But the same was not true in provincial Lambayeque, where prices remained relatively high, reflecting the strong demand for agricultural labor in the area. Prices ranged from 470 to almost 700 pesos and averaged more than 550 pesos between 1597 and 1648. Occasionally landowners willingly paid 1,000 pesos or more for a skilled soap maker, confectioner, or seasoned agricultural worker. The easing of the labor shortage due to the increased availability of black laborers at affordable prices freed agriculture from a very serious constraint and is one of the major reasons for the expansion of the agricultural sector and, in particular, the spread of sugarcane cultivation.[24]

Together, these factors—price stabilization, tenure regularization, and mortgage and labor availability—fostered three changes in the agricultural panorama of the region. First, production on most estates was capital intensified. Landowners equated savings and profits with an increasing output. Accordingly, many enlarged the processing facilities of their estates. The capacity of several estancias, for example, increased about threefold by the middle of the seventeenth century. Because estancia owners found the rate of natural increase of their animals too slow to satisfy their actual and projected needs, they began sending agents to the province of Piura, immediately to the north, to buy herds of goats for fattening and processing in Lambayeque. Similarly, trapiche and ingenio owners intensified production by increasing the capacity and elaborateness of their sugar works. Owners increased the number of mills and substituted metal mills for the less durable and inefficient wooden ones. They kept carpenters and metal workers from Saña busy fabricating other needed equipment. This expansion in production capacity presupposed an increase in the area planted in cane and a corresponding increase in the size of the labor force. Landowners spent thousands of pesos to acquire slaves to man the processing facilities and help the Indian laborers plant, irrigate, weed, and harvest. The growth in the labor force is summarized in Appendix 3.[25]

Some estates experienced both a quantitative and qualitative change. In such instances changes in primary function meant major transformations. Between 1595 and 1649 estancias became haciendas when the owners, secure in the possession of the land in and around their corrals and able to secure the requisite labor, began to clear and cultivate fields. The visita of the estancia of Picsi in the 1590s makes no mention of cultivated land. An inventory of the hacienda of Picsi in 1642 mentions fields as well as the corrals and buildings at the original asiento. With the construction of a molino, haciendas became known variously as "haciendas y molinos" or simply as "molinos." Some estancias evolved into haciendas and then became specialized farms, all within this period. Other estancias assumed the title of "tinas y tenerías" with the construction of tanning and soap-making plants.[26]

Lending records for the period show a clear correlation between these transformations and the dates on which landowners mortgaged their property. Assuming all the mortgage funds were spent to renovate the estate, the reconditioning and transformation of Mingolla's old haunt, the estancia of Picsi, into a hacienda cost more than 3,000 pesos of borrowed funds. The owner of the hacienda of Cojal assumed a debt of 600 pesos at the time he established his molino. By the time the estate was producing sugar, the debt had risen to nearly 8,700 pesos and continued to rise to over 10,000 pesos in the 1650s. Owners of the ingenios and trapiches that had been established before 1595 also increased their indebtedness to expand their productive base. Thus, the debt recognized by the owner of sugar-producing San Lorenzo rose from about 3,000 pesos in the 1580s to over 11,000 pesos in 1643.[27]

Because the value of a property generally increased at a faster pace than the encumbrances, the total indebtedness never represented more than a relatively small proportion of its worth. Cayaltí's debt in 1622 equalled only 5.5 percent of its sale price. Popán's debt almost tripled between 1617 and 1627 as its owners intensified and expanded production, but still equalled only about one-fifth of its worth. Only Pomalca and Ucupe registered debt as high as one-half their value.[28]

Growing out of the intensification of production and the transformation of some estates was a third dimension of agricultural development: the need to acquire more land or pastures and the subsequent annexation of one estate to another. Given the fixed carrying capacity of land, an increase in herds eventually required additional pastures. Ranchers, therefore, acquired adjacent estancias, which gave them ready-made corrals at varying distances from one central asiento and, in effect, expanded their sphere of operation and the natural resources at their command. Likewise, the shift from cultivating wheat and other grains to sugarcane required a large investment to acquire a highly skilled slave crew. To keep the work force busy, the owner increased the number of fields to provide enough cane for year-round production. This, in turn, implied a need for larger reserves of irrigated land for rotation purposes. This territorial expansion also served to limit competition, if the land had been owned by another Spaniard, and would, in the long run, in more cases than not, increase the supply of labor if the land had been used by the Indians.

Thus, when the owner of the estancia of Calupe acquired the estancia of Fellupe, circa 1616, he integrated the corrals, stock, and shepherds of both into one larger estancia. The asiento of Calupe became the center for the entire operation, and the enterprise assumed that name. Thereafter, the name Fellupe occasionally appeared in the bills of sale as a toponym, but as a reference to a separate agricultural unit it was rapidly forgotten. The asiento of Collús became the center of a huge complex which eventually included the molino of Callancas; fifteen fanegadas of land called Chichip (Geigipe); the estancia of Añáñala, incorporated in the 1630s; fifty fanegadas of land called Coscupián, acquired in 1647; and at least seventeen other corrals.[29]

The typical pattern of consolidation brought two or more units under one management for the more efficient production of sugar, grains, or livestock. The lands of Aberru, for instance, were annexed to the trapiche of La Candelaria as early as 1618. By 1643 the owner of La Candelaria, Fernando de Obregón, had acquired the neighboring trapiche of San Lorenzo el Real, one of the first sugar mills established in the valleys. He installed the equipment from San Lorenzo at La Candelaria's center and thus consolidated the two operations into one. The ownership of several formerly separate estates by one person, however, did not always imply such a unification. When Juan Vásquez de Saavedra coordinated the administration of a sugar mill and two neighboring farms planted in tobacco and rice, each retained its separate identity, work force, capital equipment, and majordomos.[30]

The evolution of the estates in Lambayeque is presented schematically in Figure 10. It shows the formation and development of the three basic types of estates. In the sixteenth century, agricultural enterprises took the form of corrals, asientos and sitios—all basically livestock ranches; huertas, chacras, labores, fincas, and ranchos—all synonyms for small mixed farms; and molinos, ingenios, and trapiches—farms specializing in either grains or sugarcane. At the end of the sixteenth century, ranch owners built processing facilities near their corrals and the estancia became a reality. Simultaneously, mixed farms became known as haciendas as they grew in size and complexity. Some estates whose owners rationalized production were transformed into specialized farms producing wheat, sugar, or wine. The individual histories of the estates of the valleys show typical progressions from estancia to hacienda, and from hacienda to molino or trapiche; from estancia to hacienda to molino to trapiche, or any of several other variations. Most of the transformations took place between 1595 and 1649.

Figure 10. Evolution of the Estate in Lambayeque, Colonial Period

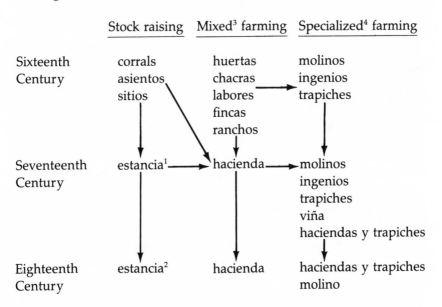

[1]Tinas y tenerías established on the estate
[2]Tinas y tenerías established near towns
[3]Estates producing both cash crops and livestock
[4]Estates producing one cash crop and no livestock

The three estate histories that follow illustrate the possible variations in the process of development, which culminated in the formation of the great estates, or latifundios, and the disappearance of the chacras and labores. At the beginning of the period, Calupe was one of several estancias dotting the countryside on the south side of the Lambayeque River, about four leagues inland from the Indian settlement at Chiclayo. Its corrals held some five thousand head of sheep and goats valued at more than 6,700 pesos. About 1616 Calupe increased in area to almost four times its original size by absorbing the estancia of Fellupe with legal title to one hundred fanegadas of lands. When part of these lands were cultivated, Calupe became a mixed farm, or hacienda. By the time of the second visita de la tierra in the early 1640s, Calupe encompassed 433 fanegadas of land, of which only about one-third were irrigated and suitable for planting. Cane had been planted and a trapiche was functioning at the site of the original asiento. Calupe had evolved into a trapiche.[31]

Not every estate, of course, became a trapiche. Picsi exemplifies an estancia which first increased in size and capacity and then changed in function to become a hacienda. Under Alonso de Mingolla, the estancia of Picsi initially consisted of an asiento and three outlying stock pens with a resident population of one Spaniard, six peons, eight mitayos, and twenty other "persons." Five years later, in 1595, Picsi included six corrals, located up to two leagues from the center. During the next twenty-five years, the estancias of Chumán, Sontocap and Tumán were added; and although the primary activity of the estate remained raising goats for soap and leather, the owner put some of his laborers to work planting part of the soil. Picsi became a hacienda with legal titles to 130 fanegadas of land, unofficial jurisdiction over many times that amount of pasturage and woodland, and a total population approaching one hundred. The number of livestock varied tremendously from year to year, but usually numbered in the tens of thousands. In the 1640s the huts of Indians, animal pens, warehouses, slaughterhouse, garden, orchard, and alfalfa fields, surrounding the owner's residential complex and its adjoining chapel, were testimony to continued expansion and intensification of production. Various estimates placed the population at between one and two hundred persons.[32]

The history of the third estate, Cojal, shows the effect of annexation. Similar to Calupe in that it had been an estancia in 1590 with a work force of only two mitayos, Cojal over the next thirty-five or forty years became a hacienda, then a molino, and finally a trapiche. In 1642 it displayed a complexity unsuspected from its title of "trapiche" alone. The owner had purchased two nearby farms and continued the production of wheat and other grains after the introduction of cane and the installation of the sugar mill. The inventory of the estate in 1642 mentions the owner's large house as the center of the enterprise; a nearby church, completely equipped with altar, images of saints, and paintings; a separate house for the majordomo; a group of huts around a small courtyard, which accommodated almost seventy slaves; a warehouse; and a sugar purification and storage center. Capital equipment included four metal trapiches; five carts; two large scales with bronze weights; miscellaneous carpentry, smithy, and hand tools; and over sixty draft animals. The assessors considered the flour mill and its equipment an integral part of Cojal, but listed separately its contents, related equipment, animals, and slaves. The inventory included the lands, rights to irrigation water, pastures, and almost 750 goats and sheep. The tobacco and rice fields, twenty slaves, draft animals, and other equipment at the place called Chumbenique were also inventoried separately, although they were still considered part of the larger whole.[33]

The similarities in the pattern of growth and elaboration, however, were not reflected at first in the terms used to designate the new units. The magnitude of the changes in their organization of production, the diversity of their functions, and the differences in timing and pace of development resulted in the use of a confusing array of descriptive terms to identify estates, such as "estancia y labor," "estancia y molino," "estancia y hacienda," "estancia e ingenio," "estancia y trapiche," "hacienda y molino," and "hacienda y trapiche." The terms "estancia y labor" and "estancia y hacienda" referred to mixed farms or estates on which part of the land was cultivated and part was grazed. The other terms referred to estates characterized by a combination of stock raising, cultivation, and processing.

By midcentury, the terminological potpourri had been simplified and reduced to three or four basic terms: *estancia, hacienda, trapiche,* or *ingenio.* In general, "estancia" referred to a livestock ranch, with or without tanning and soap-making facilities and with the understanding that the pastures were common (at least in theory). "Ingenio" and "trapiche" designated an estate with at least one cane mill, and whose principal products were sugar and its derivatives, regardless of whether or not any of its area was used for other purposes. "Hacienda" referred to a mixed farm on which part of the land was cultivated and part was used for animal raising, and whose main product was not sugar. The term "hacienda" was applied to these estates whether or not they included any former estancias or had a flour mill on the premises. Another purpose of Figure 10 is to show the progressive simplification in terminology, which is specific and unambiguous by the eighteenth century with regard to the type of estate to which it refers.

Also by midcentury, consolidation and transformation had drastically changed the landscape of the region. As shown in Figure 11 less than half the units that existed at the time of the Ampuero visita survived intact. Although the size of the herds had not diminished, ranching was increasingly combined with cultivation. Molinos and *viñas* (vineyards) as separate specialized units of production tended to disappear, given the prevailing economic conditions. The latter could not compete with the growing vineyards of Pisco to the south. The number of sugar producing estates doubled, although the figures mask the trends. During the first half of the period, the number of trapiches and ingenios actually dropped as estates were merged. The number grew thereafter, due to a rise in sugar prices at midcentury, which underwrote the costs of transforming viñas and haciendas into sugar-producing units.[34]

The size and function of the haciendas and trapiches of midcentury distinguished them from the chacras and labores of the previous pe-

Figure 11. Evolution of the Estates, 1595–1649

Type of Estate	Before Consolidation/ Transformation		After Consolidation/ Transformation	
	No.	%	No.	%
Estancias	65	78.3	10	28.6
Haciendas	3	3.6	12	34.3
Trapiches	6	7.2	12	34.3
Molinos	5	6.0	1	2.9
Viñas	4	4.8	0	0
Total	83	99.9	35	100.1
Unknown	5		6	

Source: Appendix 3.

riod. The estancia now averaged about fifty fanegadas in size, the haciendas twice that much, and the ingenios and trapiches a third more. Their actual sphere of influence, however, could be much greater. Thus, although the owner of Calupe had legal title to 433 fanegadas in 1643, he boasted that his estate included "[an area] more than three and a half leagues [long] and one league wide, encompassing more than 2,000 fanegadas of land." If the averages seem small in comparison to the size of estates of later years, contemporaries considered them impressive when compared to the two fanegada holding of Indians and the size of the original mercedes.[35]

Furthermore, the number of resident laborers and their families made some of these estates population centers, approaching the size of some of the Indian communities in the district. Whereas labradores generally worked the land themselves with the help of a few hired Indians and slaves, haciendas and sugar mills employed an average of 27 slaves, in addition to mitayos and resident peons. Cojal, an exception, had a slave population of 68 and a resident Indian population of 17 in 1642. Counting the labor force of the adjacent tobacco fields owned by the same man, the slave population totaled 88.[36] As mentioned above, the population of the hacienda Picsi numbered more than 100 throughout the period. In 1619 the 100 residents included at least 40 Indian laborers and their families. In the 1640s, 20 permanent Indian laborers and their families, a manager and his family, and 29 mitayos from the communities of Lambayeque and Collique resided on the estate. The priest and lieutenant corregidor reported a population of 260, but evidence from other sources suggests this figure may be too high.[37]

A final distinguishing factor between a chacra and a large estate was its function. Previously labradores produced foodstuffs for the local market. Account books and administrative records show that now the Indian communities increasingly assumed that task. Haciendas and trapiches specialized in supplying Tierra Firme and Lima with grains, sugar, and molasses. Estancieros continued to sell their meat locally or to ships which anchored in Chérrepe, but exported most of their tallow, hides, and soap to these same distant markets.[38]

Without a more complete set of account books for the period, the level of productivity and profitability of the estates is impossible to calculate precisely. Especially in the first thirty years or so of the period, the instability of tenure and the disappearance of a large number of separate properties indicate that many proved not to be viable. But in the second quarter of the seventeenth century the situation steadied.

The continued expansion and growth of the surviving estates; the increase in mortgages—which indicates that the larger and more efficient estates were financially sound and probably current on their interest payments; and the rarity of instances of foreclosure and bankruptcy indicate the generally improving health of the economy. Saña came to epitomize the thriving countryside. By the middle of the seventeenth century, the city boasted six monasteries and convents, a well-appointed church, and a large town hall and jail. Two-story town houses of the landowners lined the central plaza.[39]

Another indication of the incipient prosperity of the growing economy was the eagerness of the tax farmers, some of whom were landowners themselves, to bid on the right to collect the tithes in Saña and Chiclayo, especially as the production of sugar accelerated after 1620. Bidding for the right to collect the sugar and syrup of the estates was keenest around Saña. Investors considered Chiclayo prime territory for collections, too, as the sugar industry began to spill over into the adjacent valley from Saña. The two curves, plotted in Figure 12, closely parallel each other. But Chiclayo was definitely second choice to Saña, because included in the district were Indian communities. The value of the foodstuffs they sold in the local market was far below the commercial value of latifundio production.

The sugar-based prosperity of some was not shared by all. Bids for

Sources: For Chiclayo—ART/Mata: 3–XI–1584; HAG: 6–VI–1641, 13v–14; ID: 17–IV–1811, II–1, 58v; AGI/AL: 1417; ANCR/VM: 1780; Collús: 1643, 147v; Álvarez: 11–VIII–1663, 69; Lino: 4–X–1718; 3–VIII–1722; 6–V–1730; and 6–IX–1730; AAT/Diezmos: 1626; 1629; 1637; 1638; 1643, 3v; 1650; 1653–54; 1657–58; 1697; 1705–07; 1709; 1718; 1757; and 1795; AAL/AT: 1673. For Saña—ART/Mata: 2–X–1563; Vega: 1599; O: 11–VI–1617, 230v; 1619; HAG: 30–XII–1636; 6–VI–1641, 13v–14; Escobar: 5–VII–1617; CoD: 8–III–1770; and 4–II–1784; ID:19–IV–1801; 28–V–1802; 2–III–1804; 21–II–1806; and 22–II–1808; IC: 17–XI–1800; AGI/AI: 1417; ANCR/Mendoza: 1–IX–1637; AAT/1627; 1629; 1641; 1650; 1653–54; 1697; 1699–1702; 1706; 1708; 1720; and 1724; AAL/AT: 1. 18–IV, 1682; 1. 23–X, 1706. For Illimo—ANCR/Rentero: 1–V–1654; Álvarez: 27–II–1663; Lino: 19–VI–1730; 26–IX–1718; 3–VIII–1722; 28–VII–1730; AGI/AL: 1417; and ART/HAG: 6–VI–1641, 13v. For Lambayeque—AAT/D: 1697; 1703; 1705; 1626; 1706; 1707–08; 1757; and 1795; ART/IC: 23–VIII–1816; LC: 1560; CoD: 21–I–1780; ID: 28–III–1800; 22–II–1808; 21–II–1810; 7–III–1812; 12–III–1814; 2–IV–1816; 17–XII–1817; and 21–X–1819; HAG: 30–XII–1636, 11v; and 6–VI–1641; BNP/PB 562459, 1793, 27v; ANCR/Lino: n.d. [1718]; 19–VIII–1730; and AGI/AL: 1417.

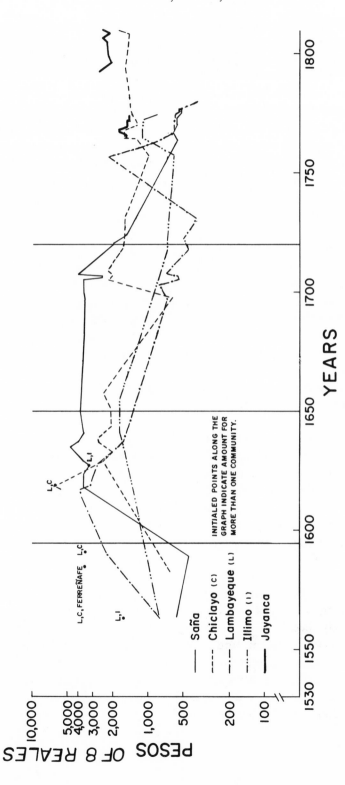

Figure 12. Bids for the Right to Collect Tithes

Lambayeque peaked about 1617, reflecting the end of an early heyday for ranching. Once the easiest way to build a modest stake into a solid social and economic position, the competition for capital and resources pushed the estancias off the best land and into the drier marginal areas. The once profitable hog industry died rapidly as a result of the price trends, the diminishing supply of Indian corn needed for feed, and the bitter conflict (noted above) over pastures with sheep and goat raisers. The steady demand for the more adaptable goats and their by-products meant that the value of the tithes in the district of Íllimo—with its concentration of haciendas, estancias, tinas, and tenerías—remained remarkably stable.

The Formation of a Landed Elite

As the labores and chacras were combined to form haciendas, trapiches, and ingenios; and as a number of separate corrals merged under one administration to form giant estancias, the labradores of the mid-1590s became hacendados and, collectively, a local landed elite. Gone were all but a few descendants of the once haughty encomenderos, victims of limiting regulations and the decline of the native population. In their stead were the descendants and successors of the original settlers, who had become rude gentleman farmers and moved into the dominant position by default by the end of the sixteenth century.[40]

Uncertain economic conditions took their toll. The key to survival was efficiency and access to investment funds. Success and wealth awaited the confident who invested profits (in the years there were any) and other income and borrowed money to increase the productive capacities of their land and, they hoped, generate a return. They used this income, in turn, to finance another round of investment and profit. Each investment in the estates represented an investment in their personal fortune, and, by extension, generated business and income for other groups in society.[41]

Although competition forced them to invest or risk survival, they did not live poorly. Some of their funds were spent to import luxury items which had once been the hallmark of their encomendero predecessors. The accounts of a commercial partnership formed between Andrés Gutiérrez of Saña and Francisco Migueles of Lima in the 1590s record the nonessential consumer goods that Migueles regularly shipped to his partner for sale: stocks of saffron, silk, satin, china, hats, sword belts, wine, paintings, and linens. The manner in which the landowners and their families dressed, the jewels they wore, the houses in which they lived, and the number of their domestic servants distinguished this group from the subsistence and small-scale farmers or labradores, the middling sector of artisans and shopkeepers, and the Indians. Over the years the gap between the wealth of the landowners and of these various groups increased visibly.[42]

Some landowners, of course, were richer than others. The poorest among the elite of local society left relatively modest fortunes at their death. Alonso Fernández Mellado's family, for instance, inherited the house, a slave, a few horses, an estancia at Leviche with a few flocks of goats and sheep, and the service of three mitayos from Túcume. Such individuals dowered their daughters moderately. Miguel Sánchez Sid, the owner of an estate near Saña, could afford to provide less than three thousand pesos in several hundred head of livestock, two pieces of land, a few draft animals, and furniture and clothing when his daughter married in 1599.[43]

One of the richest landowners was Juan Vásquez de Saavedra, a Spaniard by birth who died in 1642 at early middle age, leaving very extensive holdings. At the time of his marriage in Lima to Doña Ana María Gutiérrez de Espinosa, a native of Saña and daughter of the owner of Calupe (see Fig. 13), he was already wealthy, with a personal fortune of approximately seventy thousand pesos accumulated in trade. Doña Ana brought with her a dowry amounting to thirty thousand pesos, which was increased to forty thousand pesos by a generous wedding gift from the groom. At the time of his death, Vásquez owned the trapiche of San Ildefonso de Cojal with its annexed flour mill, a rice mill and farms, and a total of 105 slaves. His holdings stretched inland into the mountains of Cajamarca, where he owned the estancia of Udima. Besides his rural landholdings, he owned warehouses in the port of Chérrepe, half-interest in two ships, and one-quarter interest in a third—all three complete with their respective slave crews. Pending were sales and shipment of two thousand loaves of sugar, nearly five hundred cases of soap, one thousand fanegas of flour, thirteen thousand bundles of tobacco, and bales of woolen goods and cotton thread. When in Saña he lived in a large house with a private chapel, furnished in palatine fashion with upholstered sofas, ivory inlaid and lacquered chests, tapestries, and paintings. His staff of twenty-one domestic slaves served him from gold-plated silver tableware. Despite the semitropical heat, he dressed in imported silks and linens. Vásquez de Saavedra was more typical of the landowners who saw the end of the period, Fernández Mellado more representative of those who started the era.[44]

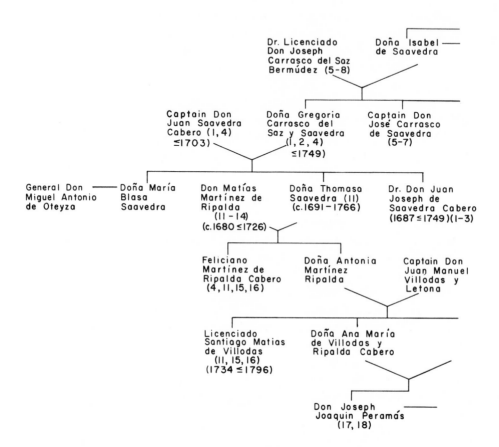

Figure 13.

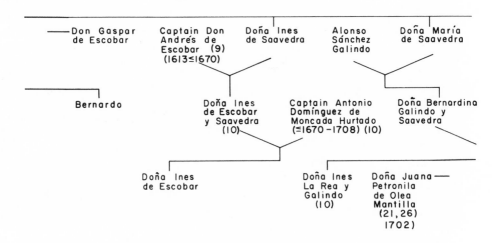

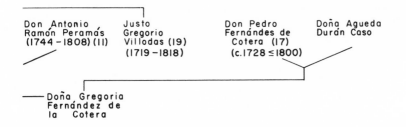

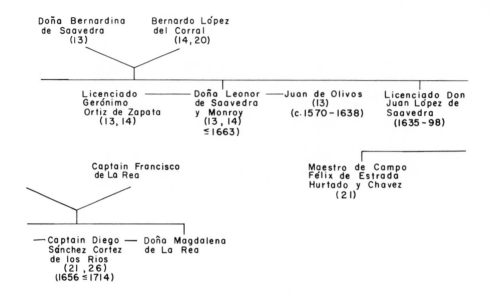

Figure 13, continued.

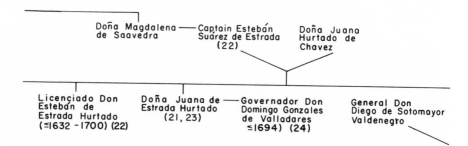

ESTATES

1. Sancarranco	25. Rafán
2. La Viña	26. Corbacho
3. Cadape	27. Coxal
4. Sialupe	28. San Nicolás
5. Collús	29. San Cristóbal
6. Añáñala	30. Chumbenique
7. Pomalca	31. Callanca
8. Samán	32. Ucupe
9. Calupe	33. Solcupe
10. Sárrapo	34. Collique
11. La Punta	35. Herrepon
12. Selenique	36. Misque
13. Íllimo	37. Mamape
14. Sasape	38. Popán
15. Pampa Grande	39. San Lorenzo
16. Saltur	40. Luya
17. Cayaltí	41. Sololipe
18. Calach	42. Lulincapuc
19. Santa Lucía	43. Sangana
20. Sodo	44. Tangasca
21. San Juan	45. Muchumí
22. Unidentified	46. Miraflores
23. Palomino	47. Sipán
24. Ramalpón	

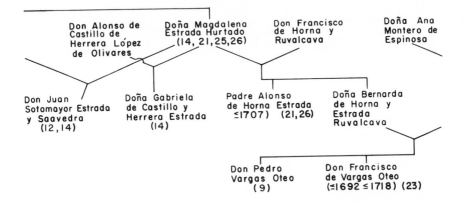

Figure 13, continued.

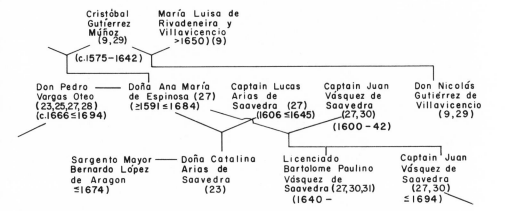

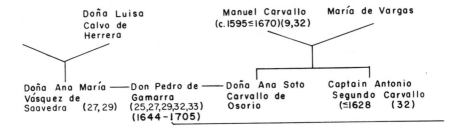

Figure 13, continued.

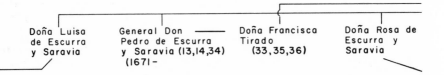

Doña Luisa
de Escurra
y Saravia

General Don ———
Pedro de Escurra
y Saravia (13,14,34)
(1671 –

Doña Francisca
Tirado
(33,35,36)

Doña Rosa de
Escurra y
Saravia

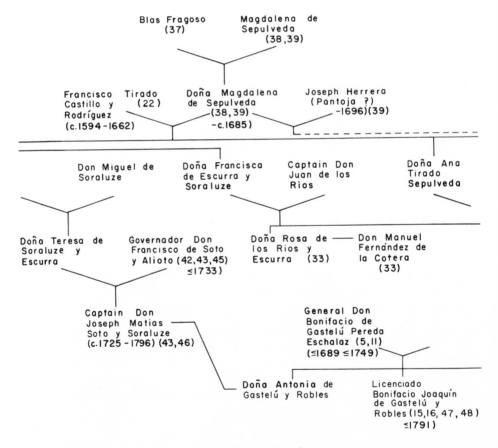

Figure 13, continued.

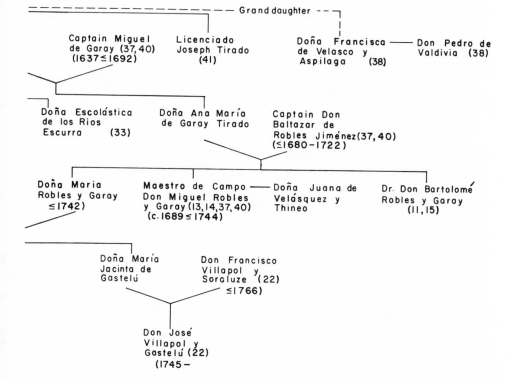

Like Vásquez de Saavedra, many of his cohorts had multiple economic roles. Being a "farmer" or "rancher" in the context of the seventeenth century implied more than a strict interpretation of the terms would suggest. The organization of production on the estates automatically made owners manufacturers of sugar, preserves, soap, and fine leather. Many often marketed their own products, contracting with ship captains to transport goods to Tierra Firme or hiring muleteers to take the produce to Trujillo and Lima. Some also personally arranged to import the raw materials, slaves, and luxury items they wanted.

Aside from these activities naturally associated with running the estates, more than one-third of the male landowners, Vásquez de Saavedra included, had other occupations. Figure 14 shows that one-fifth were merchants, with stores or import-export businesses. Twelve priests, one-half the ecclesiastics in the whole region and nearly 20 pecent of the landowners, owned estates. Significant numbers were self-employed as notaries. Others had worked for the crown as high-level bureaucrats or worked for others as majordomos.[45]

These economic roles made landowners the central and dominant force in society. As animal raisers and farmers, they were the largest employers of temporary unskilled labor in the region. They hired and fired majordomos, who ran the estates from day to day. These managers carried out the owner's instructions, assigned work to the mitayos and peons, and traveled north to Piura to buy stock, but had little decision-making power of their own. Most owners personally supervised estate operations at this time, because they distrusted majordomos, who "routinely altered the accounts in their own favor. . ." if not closely watched. An owner who was uninterested in or incapable of managing an estate personally, like most widows, for example, either hired an administrator—an employee of higher rank than a majordomo, who was given much more autonomy and responsibility in the direction of the estate—or rented out the property. Neither alternative proved satisfactory and, consequently, both were avoided, except under unusual circumstances.[46]

Activities as merchants, government officials, notaries, clerics, lawyers, miners of lime and saltpeter, and town barber enhanced the landowners' pivotal social position by bringing them into daily contact with members of other groups and providing them with important additional sources of cash receipts.

Their economic position also allowed them to continue participating on the cabildo. Although the landowners gave up the monopoly they

Figure 14. Known Occupations[1] of Landowners, 1595–1649

	No.	Percent	Other Occupations
Priests	12	17.9	financier
Merchants	14	20.9	notary, private accountant, bureaucrat; lawyer–priest; bureaucrat, shipowner
Miners	3	4.5	
Financiers	7	10.4	majordomo; bureaucrat, shipowner; diezmero
Lawyers	3	4.5	bureaucrat
Bureaucrats: major—	6	9.0	
minor—	2	3.0	
Notaries	9	13.4	merchant
Majordomos	7	10.4	
Other	4	6.0	
Total	67	100.0	

[1]By major occupation, as determined by self-declaration, reputation, or schooling.

Source: Biographical Index: Landowners [BIL].

had once enjoyed over the town council, they remained its most vocal and united group. More than one-half of the known council members were landowners, and they held more and higher positions than non-landowners. The fact that offices were sold meant that membership was restricted to the well-to-do, but almost any male with money, time, and proper connections could sit on the council if he chose. The fact that landowners did not completely monopolize the council indicates two changes in local political realities from the sixteenth century. Land-owners' interest in formal participation waned because the town council no longer significantly affected their economic base. During the period, its members lost the right to make land grants, lost control over the irrigation infrastructure, and no longer distributed agricultural mitayos. Price-fixing only tangentially affected the estates, given the importance of distant markets. The council regulated the price of food-stuffs and other basic consumer products, such as candles, but no regulated product represented a significant proportion of estate output. Fixing the wages and salaries for labor was one issue still of concern to landowning members, and sitting on the council ensured them a voice in such decisions. Any income from the positions was probably regarded as a fringe benefit of decreasing importance and not as a motivating factor for participation. In an increasingly status-conscious society, landowners served for the prestige value of the seats. Also, formal involvement was not absolutely necessary for political hegem-ony. If a hacendado did not sit on the cabildo himself he invariably had a relative or friend who did and was willing to present his views.[47]

In addition, landowners assumed the commanding positions in the local militia, despite the fact that officers often bought a commission and paid their men. Landowners eagerly joined the militia when it was organized in the seventeenth century, because military rank had been an important index of elite membership since the days of the first conquerors. One seventeenth-century source reports a force in Lam-bayeque numbering more than four hundred, 10 percent of whom were officers. Twenty-five percent of the eligible landowners were commis-sioned officers, two-thirds with the rank of captain or above. More than defense, the militia provided the landowners with the opportunity to don uniforms and parade at the head of columns of men on ceremonial occasions, to the delight and awe of the spectators.[48]

The image of the landowner was further enhanced by his convictions and support of the church. The voluntary position of *síndico*, a lay representative and trustee, for example, was typically filled by a landowner. Landowners vied for the prestigious position of *familiar* (lay representative) of the Inquisition. Several widowers joined the church, taking their growing sons to reside with them in the monasteries. Landowners became notorious for their bequests, the size of which was an index of their wealth and status. In the long run, however, religion robbed the elite of progeny and often meant the disappearance of a line. So ended one branch of the dignified Samudio family that went back to the legendary days of Pizarro and Atahualpa.[49] (See Fig. 5.)

But the landowning group was not yet an established class, as had been the hereditary encomendero group which preceded it. The local elite of Lambayeque was still in the process of formation. Throughout the period this cumulative process of investment and the modest stake needed to enter agro-business, especially at the start of the century, kept the landowning group relatively open to monied and well-born newcomers, like Vásquez de Saavedra and scores of others. Figure 15 shows that fewer than one-third of the recorded land transactions represented the transfer of wealth within the existing landowning elite, or "old" wealth;[50] sales between relatives or between members of other landed families and inheritance accounted for four-fifths of these. The remainder, more than two-thirds, represented opportunities when an outsider acquired an estate. This second group, labeled "new" in Figure

Figure 15. Mode of Estate Acquisition by Elite Status, 1595–1649

Mode	Old		New		Total	
	No.	Percent	No.	Percent	No.	Percent
Composición/ Denuncia	5	11	17	16	22	15
Donation	1	2	2	2	3	2
Dowry	1	2	13	13	14	9
Inheritance	19	41	5	5	24	16
Sale	20	43	64	62	84	56
Other	0	0	3	3	3	2
Total	46 (31%)	99	104 (69%)	101	150	100
Unknown					103	

Source: Appendix 3.

15 and outnumbering the descendants of the original settlers and their successors, entered the ranks of the landed by acquiring property directly from the crown or, more commonly, by purchase from an unrelated person. These newcomers were the nouveau riche, who benefited indirectly from the agricultural development. They accumulated enough wealth through commercial or professional pursuits to join the propertied class.

Most of the newcomers began their careers as merchants, royal bureaucrats, or professionals who arrived to live and work in Saña from other places. When the number of individuals who engaged in casual trade is added to the number of outright shopkeepers and merchants, the percentage of landowners with some commercial income rises to 40 percent ($n = 26$). Other members of the "new" elite were treasury officials and corregidores named to meet the needs of the growing central administration. The crown filled bureaucratic vacancies with persons preferably recruited from outside the area in which they were to serve, intending in this way to minimize fraud and collusion and to ensure a measure of honesty in local administration. Corregidores, with few exceptions, had always been strangers to Lambayeque, but even their lieutenants were outsiders now. Instead of appointing deputies from among their local guarantors, as was once the custom, corregidores arrived to take office with an entourage of friends and relatives who they named as their lieutenants, tribute collectors, and assistants. Legislation specifically prevented the corregidores from appointing local inhabitants to these posts, although locals were occasionally deputized in emergencies. Also prominent among the socially mobile were majordomos, notaries, and priests. Educated elsewhere, notaries bought licenses to practice in the locality. Priests were assigned benefices there.

But these positions did not guarantee entrance into the elite. A relatively small proportion of the professionals and bureaucrats acquired land and stayed. Two provincial treasurers and one corregidor joined the landowning class. Approximately one of seven of the corregidor's assistants did so. A notary had a slightly poorer chance.[51]

In general, the socially mobile were more active in the public[52] affairs of the province than those who already had land in the family. Before acquiring land, the nouveau riche typically held several different positions in the bureaucratic hierarchy, in the militia, or on the town council. Diego de Mestanza, for example, served for years as public advocate and lieutenant corregidor, and participated actively in the militia, before acquiring an ingenio in 1632. These activities undoubtedly aided the group in their ascent and suggests that land was the visible manifestation of a successful career.[53]

In comparison to "new wealth," "old wealth" was not yet very old. As a result of the upward social mobility and the rapid turnover of estate ownership, very few elite families could trace their landowning status back to even the original settlers, let alone the encomenderos of the region. One of the few who could was Dr. Don Gerónimo Villalobos Samudio, the owner of Pátapo in the 1640s. Figure 5 shows that among his illustrious forefathers was the encomendero of Chuspo-Callanca, Francisco Luis de Alcántara, who had served in Honduras and Nicaragua before continuing on to Peru, where he helped put down Indian rebellions and fought bravely with Blasco Núñez Vela and President La Gasca. Francisco de Samudio, one of the founders of his line and encomendero of Túcume, pacified the provinces of Chachapoyas, Guaylas, and Conchucos; joined Licenciado Vaca de Castro against Diego de Almagro; and then participated with La Gasca on the royalist side. Lorenzo de Samudio Mendoza, his son, left his son, Don Francisco de Samudio Mendoza Toledo y Escobar, in charge of his properties in Lambayeque, which included the ingenio of San Lorenzo, el Real, when he moved back to Trujillo. With shrewd foresight, Lorenzo purchased the post of chief constable for Don Francisco, and at Lorenzo's death, Don Francisco inherited the ingenio. Don Francisco was thus guaranteed a distinguished place in the local landed elite of Lambayeque. Don Francisco and Don Gerónimo's uncle, Captain Baltazar Rodríguez, the elder, established a molino soon after founding Saña. His son and namesake expanded and transformed the molino into the ingenio or trapiche of Santiago de Miraflores. Other members of Don Gerónimo's immediate family figured prominently in the best circles of Trujillo, and he himself, following family tradition, had studied in Los Reyes before returning to Lambayeque to oversee his estate and serve as a lawyer and judge.[54]

But Don Gerónimo was the exception. Only one or two descendants of the once dominant encomenderos still lived in the district by the 1630s. Most other individuals and their families remained in the elite for only one or two generations. Reasons for the disappearance of once prominent persons from the ranks of the propertied varied. Some landowners, such as Roque de Saldaña, married, but left no heirs. The sons of other landowners joined mendicant religious orders and renounced all claim to worldly goods. Out-migration accounted for the disappearance of other, once eminent local names. Sons of several landowners, like Don Gerónimo, became lawyers, but unlike him, they chose to remain in Lima to establish practices. Daughters married men from other places and moved away. A few landowners, like Pedro de Flores, the elder, left the area when they had made their fortunes. For many others, such as Juan Martínez Palomino, the reason was purely economic. They lacked capital and eventually sold out.[55]

Indicative of the advent of the age of the hacendado and the demise of the landed gentry is the manner in which some landowners expanded their operations. In the early seventeenth century, when mortgage money was first becoming readily available to nonencomenderos and mortgage rates were still 7 percent or higher, landowners entered into partnerships with family or friends as the easiest way to finance the transformation and consolidation of their estates. La Candelaria from 1609 to 1618, Popán in 1617, Luya in 1619, Cayaltí and Miraflores in 1624, and Calupe and Collús in 1628 were run as partnerships. They were generally short-term arrangements and began to disappear in the 1630s when individuals could afford to become sole owners of the estates. This, of course, implied that one-half of the owners rose in status at the expense of their partners. Over the years, movement into the elite was less frequent than movement downward and outward, especially as the process of expansion and consolidation quickened.[56]

Despite the lack of family pedigrees and the fluidity of group membership, identification as a landowner—whether a member of the town council, a provincial bureaucrat, professional or militia officer, or not—made such persons prominent and respected individuals in the locality. Contemporaries referred to Juan Rodríguez de Fuentes, Juan Rodríguez Vejete (his cousin), Captain Juan de Olivos, Amaro Gonzales, Pedro de Oquendo, Pedro Márquez de Vargas, and others as "lord[s] of estancias and breeder[s] of cattle." In 1629, Captain Juan Fernández Dávila was identified as a "gentleman" ["*caballero*"]. Blas Gonzales and Manuel Carvallo called themselves "owners and lords of . . . estancias." During this period, landholders assumed the title of "hacendado," a description which immediately distinguished them from the landless bureaucrats and professionals of Saña with whom they had daily contact. The awe such personages evoked in the ranks of the masses is evident from one remark made by an Indian in 1648, who described Juan de Arriola as a "powerful manipulator in this province and in the City of the Kings [Lima]."[57]

"Powerful manipulator" proved a fitting description for many landowners, who, like Arriola, maintained personal contacts that permeated the district and reached as far as the royal audiencias of Los Reyes and Panama. Like the great clans founded by the encomenderos, the extended family was becoming a major source of power and influence by the middle of the seventeenth century. Trusting relatives lent each other capital and pooled resources and talents in business ventures. Cabildo positions passed from father to son or from uncle to nephew. Not solely out of humanitarian consideration did hacendados help landless but aspiring brothers, cousins, and nephews to acquire positions in the bureaucracy, on the cabildo, and in the church: such help extended their own radius of informal power. Establishing a capellanía to support a son or nephew while a seminary student paid rich dividends later as much for advance information on available mortgage funds as for a channel of communication with the hapless Indians of the parishes. Having a cousin who was the lieutenant corregidor, sheriff, or rural constable guaranteed prompt execution of directives or quick apprehension of runaway slaves.[58]

Because family members often proved an important reserve of influence and resources, and because affinal kinship ties were typically as strong and binding as consanguineal ones, landowners carefully planned marriages as strategic moves which would enlarge their range of contacts. In addition to joining two individuals, marriage made all the relatives of one spouse relatives of the other. Marriages between landowning families were frequent. Juan Rodríguez Vejete, the owner of the estancias of Pomalca and Calupe, for example, married his daughter to Fernando de Obregón, the owner of the trapiche of Nuestra Señora de la Candelaria. Juan Martínez Palomino, the owner of a vineyard in Sárrapo, arranged for his daughter Clara to marry Roque de Saldaña, the owner of an adjoining horse ranch.[59]

Marriage was also a means of making purposeful alliances with the top bureaucrats and the rich merchants of the region. Among these merchants and bureaucrats peninsula-born newcomers were prime candidates for the hand of a landowner's daughter. Francisco Tirado was incorporated into the Fragoso clan of Jayanca and Motupe by marrying Doña Beatriz de Sepúlveda. (See Fig. 13.) Cristóbal Gutiérrez Muñoz, himself a Spaniard, celebrated his daughter's marriage to a rich merchant from his homeland with a festive wedding and a rich dowry. Diego de Vera, a treasurer of the Real Hacienda, married the daughter of his partner and eventually acquired sole ownership of the trapiche of Santiago de Miraflores.[60]

The most visible ties between landowners, after kinship, were eco-

nomic, commercial, and legal. Landowners lent one another money
and served as each other's debt collectors, factors, and bondsmen. They
supplied each other with goods and facilities. Partnerships in estates
and other large undertakings were common. Vásquez de Saavedra, for
example, in an effort to integrate his estates vertically with his overseas
commercial ventures, purchased one ship with Captain Juan de Medina, the owner of Ucupe, and another with friend and confident Lucas
Arias de Saavedra, who after Vásquez's death married his widow and
thus acquired control of his former partner's vast holdings and wealth.
Landowners guaranteed each other for public office, and given their
similar wealth and experience, were logical choices as executors and
trustees. Gerónimo Días Navarrete, for example, settled the estate of
Diego Rodríguez de Vargas; and Manuel Carvallo became the guardian
of Juan Vásquez de Saavedra, the younger, until he reached the age
of majority and assumed the direct administration of his considerable
inheritance. *Compadrazgo* often reinforced these ties with inviolable
obligations of family.[61]

In the 1630s and 1640s, these multiple ties distinguished the landowners in the eyes of the general population as a small and seemingly
cohesive group and implied some collaboration for the promotion of
mutual interests if not total friendship among the largest families. Although occasionally split over grazing rights, the distribution of irrigation water, or the purchase of a choice position or key appointment,
the hacendados overcame resentments to forge a defense against threats
to their common well-being. Landed representatives on the town council, for instance, appointed and financed two agents in Lima to ask for
the renewal of their traditional right to elect a water commissioner in
1638, when the viceroy tried to assert control over this position. The
best example of this type of cooperation to advocate an issue of primary
concern to all was the meeting in which twenty landowners empowered Captain Juan de Medina to represent their views regarding a
change in the laws regulating the mita before the royal officials in
Lima.[62]

As the instances of marriage between old and new wealth prove,
the landowners were willing to share power. Indeed, it was a necessity,
given their numbers and crown policy. Not all the successful merchants
and top bureaucrats, whether or not they had held land before the
marriage, could marry a landowner's daughter, but the fact that these
occasions arose fostered hope for similar success in others. Unsuccessful pretenders were kept satisfied in a generally expanding econ-

omy where newcomers and even the downwardly mobile second and third sons of the landed found positions as priests, minor bureaucrats, administrators of an estate, or, at worst, clerks in a store with a stipend sufficient for a respectable living.[63]

To maintain an amalgamation of interests and to guarantee that land-less persons remained willing allies, the landowners sought opportunities to befriend unrelated persons who held positions of authority in the area. In this respect, the contradictions in the governing system worked to their advantage. Although landowners were prohibited from serving with the corregidor, the practice of landholders guaranteeing him and other royal officials continued. Furthermore, because salaries of crown officials from the corregidor downward were generally too low to give them the means to live in a style commensurate with their aspirations, and because payment of their salaries was sometimes years in arrears, many royal officials—particularly those without opportunities to collect incidental fees with which to defray daily expenses and those at lower levels of the bureaucratic hierarchy—became dependent on the landowners for loans, credit, and subsidies. Landowners often extended credit to officials when their salaries were delayed. To the official, this represented a special personal favor, but to the landowner it constituted a small courtesy, which implied relatively little risk or cost. Favors and help that bureaucrats accepted from the landowners undermined their impartiality.[64]

Landowners also bonded professionals, such as the surgeon-druggist and notary, guaranteed nonlandowners as guardians, and named them as the executors of their estates. Such relations tied the professionals in Saña to the lords of the land.[65]

The number and identity of the business associates of Juan Vásquez de Saavedra, the older, illustrate the range of one landowner's potential influence. Vásquez de Saavedra, himself a regidor, was the son-in-law of another, and had accounts with two others and with the chief judge of the district. Several militiamen owed him money or had been his partners in business deals. He was a friend of the royal accountant and allowed the notary to board in his house in return for keeping his books. He imported wine as a special favor to the corregidor, who sold it at high markups to the Indians.[66]

Landowners' ties to the Indians, however, usually took other forms. Juan Martínez de la Serda and his wife, like many other elite couples, patronizingly became compadres to Indian children, thus establishing mutual obligations between themselves and their parents. Juan Romero de Arnedo, the younger, bought cattle from Don Diego Saavache, an Indian official of Lambayeque in 1619, as Mingolla had done in the past. Growing specialization of the estates also meant an expanding local market for Indian-grown produce, the distribution of which afforded more frequent and personal contact between the two major ethnic groups in the area.[67]

The range of the landowners' contacts extended beyond the geographic limits of Lambayeque and as far away as Lima and Quito. Licenciado Joseph de Carrasco de Saz, the son of a judge on the audiencia of Panama, had a brother-in-law who was the dean of the cathedral in Trujillo. Juan de Olivos was the nephew of a lawyer of the audiencia in Lima. Dr. Don Gerónimo de Villalobos, as mentioned above, actually served as a lawyer before the audiencia prior to returning to Lambayeque and an estate at Pátapo. Vásquez de Saavedra was godfather to the children of several of his factors in Lima and Callao and was also a cousin to a judge of the audiencia in Lima. Ties to the elite of Quito were established when Licenciado Don Gerónimo Ortiz de Zapata, a member of the Council of the Indies and a judge on the audiencia of Quito, married into an important landowning family.[68]

The Exercise of Power

This range of personal contacts, built around their dominant economic position, enabled the landowners to secure additional natural resources and labor. Not all the estates developed at the same rate and to the same extent; theoretically, however, economic conditions, security of tenure, availability of mortgage funds, and labor supply affected the entire Lambayeque area and did not discriminate among the estates. The differences in development on the local level between one estate and another were due, in part, to the capability of the owners themselves in maneuvering within the region to acquire the resources they needed for development.

Access to labor, for example, depended on good relations with the corregidor (or, in his stead, the lieutenant) and connections in Lima. Labor at the beginning of the period was still in short supply. Mitayos, the preferred type of labor because they worked for less than hired labor and did not require a capital investment as did a slave, never satisfied the demand; and the landowners were still in the process of purchasing a full complement of blacks. Except for the few years when the mita was abolished, the corregidor apportioned mitayos to local petitioners after a brief inquiry to find out if they were actually needed and with the condition that each such grant be confirmed by the vice-roy. The number of mitayos had been pegged at one-sixth the tributary population of the coast, which meant that the number was falling. If a landowner with a grant of mitayo labor died, his allotment fell vacant and could be requested by another. The corregidor granted the mitayos temporarily, until the landowners received confirmation from Lima. The information forwarded by the corregidor influenced the viceroy's decision on confirmation; hence, the need for good relations between the corregidor and the landowners, and hence, the willingness of the landowners to serve as his sponsor, despite the fact that they no longer served as his lieutenants.[69]

The corregidor used the distribution of mitayos to buy the land-owner's silence about his own transgressions against the Indians. Because the position of corregidor could cost as much as ten thousand pesos and the annual salary was usually too low to recoup the initial investment, pay expenses, and still yield a profit, the corregidor sought additional income. As his predecessors had done, the corregidor raised money by forcing Indians to buy goods, such as wine and mules, at above the fair market price and by commissioning them to work for him in a form reminiscent of the putting-out system of cottage industry in Europe. Corregidores, such as Don Bernardino Perales and Don Francisco Gonzales de Mendoza, established the only legal taverns in Lambayeque, Chiclayo, and Guadalupe, in which they sold wine, purchased for two or three pesos per unit, at from twelve to fourteen pesos. They provided Indians with raw cotton and paid them a piece rate to spin thread and weave cloth, which the corregidores then sold at a sizable markup. The corregidor, in short, neither gave the Indians what they paid for nor paid them adequately for their work; in this way, he recouped and profited from his initial investment. Viceroy Don Luis de Velasco prohibited the corregidor from selling merchandise to Indians, but the corregidor rarely observed the proscriptions. These abuses and the continuing practice of using Indians to plant made him vulnerable to local pressures. The hacendados apparently remained silent as long as the corregidor kept them satisfied. In at least one instance, the corregidor willingly asserted his authority to force Indian officials to provide the Spaniards with more mitayos than the law required.[70]

The Indians were helpless. Personal friends of corregidores were immune from their complaints and civil suits. Corregidores, like the encomenderos who they replaced, used their authority to remove re-

calcitrant and uncooperative Indian leaders. The power of the corregidor to excuse an Indian from paying his tribute by certifying that he
was too sick or disabled to work gave him yet another mechanism of
control. The corregidor threatened, bribed, jailed, and even physically
abused them to insure their silence. When they did testify before outside authorities, interpreters did not translate faithfully.[71]

On the rare occasions when Indians' complaints against landowners
got past local authorities, connections at court often prevented remedial action. The accusations of the curaca of Lambayeque against
Captain Juan Vásquez de Saavedra for abusing mitayos came to naught
because Vásquez's cousin, Don Fernando de Saavedra, a judge on the
bench of the Supreme Court and expert in criminal law, blocked the
investigation.[72]

The landowners' position and personal contacts were also helpful in
securing additional irrigation water. The supply of irrigation water had
until this time been a relatively minor problem. Occasional disputes
had arisen over water pollution and damage to the canal infrastructure,
but few resulted from an absolute scarcity of the precious liquid. In
the early seventeenth century, the first symptoms of chronic short
supply appeared. The problem was not one of drought in the mountains or absolute shortage, but rather one of accessibility. There was
enough water in the rivers to irrigate all the land then under cultivation
and additional land, but the existing irrigation ditches were incapable
of handling an increased volume. Consequently, much water remained
in the rivers and was lost to the sea.[73]

Water would not have been a problem if landowners had been able
to build additional irrigation ditches. Opening an irrigation ditch was
far more complicated than simply digging a channel off the main canal
that ran past a field. Theoretically, all the water in the existing system
was allocated to certain parcels of land. An increase in the supply of
irrigation water, therefore, required a new canal, which, considering
the gradual incline of the land, required that it branch off the river
kilometers above the land it was to irrigate eventually. The labor requirements and other costs put the construction of a major new canal
beyond the means of most single individuals.[74]

Because of this water "shortage" and the difficulty of increasing the
water supply, the inhabitants of the region had to adjust production.
Spaniards redistributed their water allotment to enlarge the area of
land they could plant. Sugar mill owners redesigned their water-powered mills so that they could be driven by oxen or mules. Ingenios

became trapiches and, in so doing, freed water to irrigate additional fields. Landowners also rented community land, not for cultivation but for access to the water assigned to it; then they diverted the water from the rental plots to their own land. The Indians of Collique became wary of such rentals because renters "make themselves lord[s] of the water."[75]

When even these measures proved insufficient, landowners simply began taking more than their share of water. Early in the period hacendados countered Indian protests against this usurpation by threatening to disembowel anyone who disturbed the water flow. Such threats of violence became rarer over the years as hacendados established their power and adopted more subtle means to accomplish the same ends. The hacendados, through the cabildo, elected the water commissioner until 1638, and even afterward they contributed to his salary. Understandably, he hesitated to take action against those whom he knew were cheating, despite the fact that this usurpation caused the Indians farther downstream to suffer. The Indians of Collique and Sinto complained that the usurpation of water upstream forced them to lose several crops and eventually to abandon some land.[76]

Usurpation of water became a problem for the community of Ferreñafe, one of the last to receive water from the Tayme canal. In 1648 the community sued the owner of Tulipe, Tomás Gonzales de la Torre, because he opened an irrigation ditch off the canal to irrigate a portion of his newly acquired lands, without obtaining proper permission from the authorities. The Indians of Sinto and Collique also objected, saying that the irrigation ditch Gonzales de la Torre opened

> is harmful and damaging to us, because it is near
> the beginnings of the Taimi [canal]; [therefore] the
> said Tomás Gonzales de la Torre will receive a lot of
> the water, while we will not receive enough to
> plant our fields because we are below him.

In self-defense, Gonzales de la Torre claimed that the water he brought to his land represented no more than what the Indians usually wasted. He declared that if the Indians really needed the water they should clean the Tayme, to remove the debris and silt to facilitate the flow, and repair the canal in two places where water was lost through seepage. In the course of the testimony, other instances in which Spanish landowners had taken water from the Indians in the recent past came to light. Apparently, the Indians' defense was ignored. The judge, Captain Don Diego de Novoa Feijoo, and his assistant, the ex-lieutenant corregidor and onetime rancher, Captain Luis de la Barrera Aguilar, ruled that the water in the Tayme canal was of sufficient quantity to allow Gonzales de la Torre to continue irrigating.[77]

Indicative of the shady dealing involved was the fact that no notary was present. The proceedings were recorded by a witness. They were probably too irregular for a notary to risk his reputation and office by signing his name to the records. A person who was not a notary could claim ignorance of the law and, if the case were appealed, he had little or nothing to lose by serving as interim scribe. This example should not give the impression that notaries were above questionable trans-actions or showed magnanimity toward the Indians. Sources reveal that notaries hid legal papers from the Indians to help creole friends and even changed the wording of manuscripts to the advantage of others. Poma de Ayala describes the typical notary, as follows:

> The notary enters and leaves from the towns and
> homes of the Indians like a stalking cat; very tame
> little kitty. The owner is unaware of what this cat
> takes from him quietly, very quietly. He takes all
> the Indians' wealth, all that he can. The notary is
> always writing without cause and he says [pay me]
> silver, all [in] reales and he twists the documents
> and His Majesty's orders. . . .[78]

The landowners' power, position, and advantage over the Indians is perhaps most evident in the records concerning land; and, once again, the landowners' formal positions of power on the town council or in the militia were of less importance to their successful acquisition than key personal contacts. The territorial growth of the estates referred to above was not as simple as an outright purchase of land would imply. Unlike private sales of property between Spaniards, sales of privately held Indian lands were allowed only with the approval of the Indian commissioner in Lima and of the local corregidor and protector. The sale of communal lands, once considered indivisible and inalien-able, was also permitted, subject to approval from Lima, to public and prior announcement for thirty days, and to auction if they were worth more than thirty pesos. If the lands were worth less, the corregidor alone had the authority to allow the sale. The law then placed the corregidor and protector in pivotal positions as far as the sale of Indian lands to Spanish hacendados was concerned. The records of sales— between Diego de Soria and the curaca of Lambayeque in about 1600; and between Juan Romero, Jr., and Don Francisco Llontop, the curaca of Chuspo-Callanca, and Don Diego Saavache, an Indian official of Lambayeque, in the late 1590s and 1615, respectively—indicate that the two officials were usually cooperative.[79]

The corregidor was also the person most able to help the landowners acquire land from the crown. The standard legal procedure to acquire property between visitas was for persons to apply to Lima for a title to vacant land. To do this according to law, the corregidor had to see the land, estimate its worth, and hold public hearings to discover if such a grant would be prejudicial to third parties. The corregidors of Saña did not always bother to ascertain whether or not the land was part of a community's domain and often vastly underestimated its value. Two years before the visita of 1642–43, one corregidor sold land for less than 3.5 pesos per fanegada, compared to the 10 pesos and more charged by the visitor. The corregidor reported his actions to the capital, but the viceregal officials in charge of issuing titles did not know the exact whereabouts of the lands in question in relation to the Indian communities or the real price or value of the land. They had no basis on which to challenge his word or actions. The collusion of landowners and officials, therefore, reduced the size of the community holdings and cost the royal treasury substantial sums of money.[80]

The landowners' growing wealth and position and their ties to the corregidor again proved beneficial during the second visita de la tierra in 1642–43. The second visita, like the first, was ordered as a means of raising revenues for the king during the term of the Viceroy Conde de Chinchón (1629–39). In the royal decree dated 27 May 1631, Philip IV ordered that the possession of untitled lands be legalized and new titles granted. The king, in short, was sanctioning the *de facto* but technically illegal possession of lands in the hands of the Spaniards. Vacant land, theoretically part of the royal domain, was to be sold to the highest bidder. Persons with legitimate titles were not to be disturbed. The king cautioned the visitors to leave the Indians enough land and irrigation water to support themselves. Philip IV declared that Indians should be preferred to private individuals in the proceedings, if they offered as much as a Spaniard. Another decree even allowed the Indians under certain circumstances to have the land for less than the amount a Spaniard bid. Indians were also exempted from presenting written titles, since the king had considered verbal testimony to the effect that the Indians had possessed the land since before the conquest as sufficient proof of ownership.[81]

The viceroy appointed a judge of the royal audiencia, Don Pedro de Meneses, who was a close friend and ally, to tour Lambayeque and the surrounding districts of Cajamarca, Conchucos, and Guaylas. Meneses arrived in the Lambayeque district in 1642 to begin reviewing the titles and selling land. The complete records of the visita and the transcript of Meneses's residencia have not been located, unfortunately; but enough information is available to allow reconstruction of the sequence of events and to show that Meneses's actions fell within the letter of the law, if not its spirit, and that he tolerated many irregularities which worked in favor of the Spaniards and to the detriment of the Indians.[82]

Interpreting His Majesty's decrees very strictly, Meneses accommodated the surviving Indian population on land in and around their communities. He allotted them enough land for subsistence and declared the vacated land the property of the state, when, in fact, the king had expected the Indians to be left with extra arable lands and sufficient water to irrigate them.[83]

He gave the landowners, in contrast, ample opportunities to legalize their titles, pay for excesses, and purchase vacant lands. The process of legalizing the excess lands of the estates, one of the objectives of the visita, is a case in point. The expansion of the estates in area has already been mentioned and is apparent from the figures in Appendix 3. Meneses found large discrepancies between the actual sizes of the estates and the sizes they were supposed to be according to their titles. These differences were explained in two ways: Indians and their partisans claimed that the Spanish usurped vacant land adjoining their estates; the estate owners and officials claimed that the discrepancies were due to inaccurate surveys. Meneses himself dismissed the differences, saying that measurements of the same piece of land were imprecise,

> and as if the [surveyor's] profession consisted of
> infallible principles, when it is known from
> experience that in the same site different surveyors
> find different areas: one finds four fanegadas of
> land, another six and another nine, as is seen in
> court cases. . . .

He argued that surveyors had to find excesses so they could collect their salaries. He claimed that if there was a survey every year

> the commissioned [surveyors] would find excess
> lands where none exist with which to justify their
> salaries even if it meant falsifications, offenses and
> abuses, and they would use illicit means with the
> pretext and guise of utility to the Royal Treasury so
> that they could keep their jobs.

He added that lands covered with brush and forests could not be measured accurately with a cord, thus adding to the possibility of error.[84]

Both explanations have some basis in fact. The owner of the estate of Calupe, for example, had legal claim to only 30 fanegadas at the time that his land titles were confirmed in Lima in 1599. One hundred fanegadas were added to Calupe with the addition of the estancia of Fellupe in the early seventeenth century. Yet in 1643, the estate measured 433 fanegadas. Some of this land was undoubtedly acquired through the unchallenged possession and use of adjacent Indian lands. Some was due to the confusion over the term *fanegada* and its past areal definition. Some of the excess, but certainly not all, can also probably be attributed to poor measurement, since 300 fanegadas were "covered with brush" as a result of damage and loss of an irrigation canal years before, and therefore, undoubtedly difficult to survey.[85]

It appears certain, however, that significant discrepancies were due to illegal possession rather than to errors in measurement and that the landowners had expanded their properties considerably in the previous half-century or so through usurpation at the expense of the Indians. Collús grew from 9 fanegadas to over 50 by 1647. Saltur measured 100 fanegadas in 1597 and 133 in 1640. Usurpation was relatively easy since the population of the Indian communities had continued to decline and more and more of the land formerly cultivated by them had been abandoned. The visitor obligingly declared the excess lands vacant (if they had belonged to the Indians) and sold them to their possessors for a fee.[86]

Not all such transactions were uncontested. The transcript of the sale of Tulipe contains evidence of the quasi-legal and illegal practices tolerated and perpetuated by Meneses to declare vacant the land of the community of Sinto and offer it for sale to the highest bidder. When the Indians found out about the sale they objected, basing their claim on willful wrongdoing. They stated that the only witness to the sale was the surveyor, that the surveyor did not measure the property until the day after Meneses arranged the sale, and that the survey had been done on paper and not on the site.[87]

Emotions ran high, but by reading between the lines it becomes clear that both sides exaggerated their defense. Indians stressed that they were left with "no" land when, in fact, they had enough to sustain themselves. Meneses did not deny the accusations. He even admitted accepting oral declarations in violation of the law and his instructions, but he justified the procedure as a cost- and time-saving measure. To dissemble his actions, he continually stressed his unfailing loyalty and service to the crown. He reported charging up to twenty-seven pesos per fanegada to issue clear title to lands, whereas the titles themselves show at least two instances when owners paid only ten pesos and only a single person who paid over twenty-seven.[88]

Another example of the injustices perpetrated during the visita is the case of Picsi. Meneses reviewed a Spaniard's petition for these lands, despite the Indians' opposition then and as late as 1649. Apparently their early complaints were ignored, because the petition was granted with the condition that pastures, forests, and waters be common. Viceregal officials in Lima eventually issued a *pro forma* order restoring the Indians' rights to the lands, but the order, which temporarily mollified their protests, was never enforced.[89]

Other titles of dubious validity were reviewed and legalized by Meneses. One series of manuscripts dating from 1622 documents the gradual alienation of Indian lands. The parish priest of Reque, Padre Francisco Gómez de Montalvo, became the trustee of lands disputed by two of his Indian parishioners, Don Lucas Ispilli and Juan Anaya for as long as the case remained unsettled.[90] In the interim, Gómez de Montalvo paid 8 pesos per year, four to each Indian, as *rent* for the use of the land. The rent served as testimony to the fact that he was not the owner, with the right to use the land only temporarily. A few months later (13 April 1622) he *sold* his rights for 320 pesos to Doña María de Cervantes, the titular encomendera of Reque, with the written stipulation that she continue to pay each Indian 4 pesos per year. The bill of sale was written in the same technical and legal jargon as any other, with no clear indication that she was purchasing the usufruct rights, except for the fact that she continued to pay the yearly rent. Doña María *resold* the property to Padre Gómez de Montalvo's successor, Don Pedro de Prado y Escobar, on 2 June 1623 with a *mortgage* payment of 8 pesos per year written into the contract. The receipts for these payments show that the Spanish buyer of the property paid the yearly rent until shortly after one of the Indians died. Rental payments stopped between 1626 and 1632. Apparently, after both of the original Indians died, their heirs did not collect the annual fee. The original conditions of the transfer and the fact that only usufructuary rights were in question were forgotten and the Spanish owners assumed complete control of the property and had the titles confirmed by the visitor.[91]

The dispute over the lands called Pololo also reveals some of the irregularities of the visita. Pololo was part of the lands the Indians of Collique were assigned after the reducción of Viceroy Toledo in the 1570s. Meneses declared them vacant and the property of the king and sold them at auction to Diego Sánchez del Barco without notifying the Indians of his action. The location and timing of the public announcements required by law and the auction did not give anyone in Collique time to object. All the proceedings took place in the town of Lambayeque, not Chiclayo, where the Indians of Collique lived. Only ten announcements were made, rather than the customary thirty, and all ten were given in the space of two days rather than one per day as was usual. Moreover, the announcements were made in Spanish, which only a few Indians could understand. The auction took place after the tenth announcement on the second day, and the buyer was the only person who bid on the land. The Indians learned of the auction later in the day and objected the same evening, even though their protector, the official charged with safeguarding their welfare, was conveniently absent, and despite the fact that the law prohibited them from initiating legal action without his presence and supervision. The Indians were probably emboldened to take action, where they normally would not have, by the hope that the visitor would be more responsive to their complaints than local officials.

No action appears to have been taken on the complaints, under a viceroy who by his own admission thought the Indians had more lands than they needed, until news of the fraud and abuses of the visita reached Spain and caused a scandal. Then, four years later, the audiencia sent a specially commissioned judge to collect testimony on Meneses's activities. During the investigation, both sides presented witnesses. Sánchez del Barco testified that the Indians were interested in Pololo only after he had constructed an irrigation channel, planted alfalfa and olive trees, and constructed a mill. The Indians quickly countered by reminding the judge that they had protested, in writing, on the day of the sale. One of Sánchez del Barco's witnesses claimed the community had over three thousand fanegadas of excess lands and did not need Pololo. The Indians supported their contention that they were using the lands in question by presenting court cases and wills dating back to the 1590s and as recent as 1643. The case was finally brought before the Tribunal de Tierras, a special court which had been established in Lima to settle claims over lands that had resulted from the visita in Lambayeque and other areas. Pressures from the Council of the Indies to settle the case and Meneses's clear disregard for the law made the officials eventually order the corregidor of Lambayeque to declare the sale null and restore the lands to the community.[92]

Allegations by the Indians of Collique that the visita was fraudulent and harmful to them were not the only complaints to reach Spain. Other communities with the help or perhaps at the urging of Captain Juan Medina, a landowner himself who had a grudge against Meneses and other high officials at the Lima court, brought suit against the visitor for selling their lands—or what they considered their lands—which had been left fallow for several years. Charges and counter-charges filled reams of paper with allegations, legal arguments, and rhetoric. The allegations against Meneses included: (1) auctioning land at unjustifiably low prices, and specifically, selling one piece of land worth 1,000 pesos for 500 and another valued at over 10,000 pesos for 2,000 "because it was for [his] confidant"; (2) making Indians pay higher prices for land than the Spaniards; (3) preferring friends of friends in the sale of lands; (4) making 15,000 pesos himself by selling products he probably brought with him from Lima; (5) accepting "fees" for special consideration; and (6) assigning Indians the poorest lands and declaring their good lands vacant and subject to sale. The Indians of Chiclayo claimed that they lost lands closest to their homes in exchange for "uninhabitable" ones, which required more work and sweat than those which had been sold.[93]

In his defense, Meneses claimed that he left the Indians plenty of fertile land and irrigation water. He gave each head of household 2 fanegadas of land and more to the Indian officials "according to their rank." After giving land in the best places to Lambayeque and the other surrounding communities, he admitted that he had declared 8,360 fanegadas vacant, as the king's decrees had instructed. He sold 303 fanegadas of these to various persons, including 80 to Manuel del Arze.

He gave the excess land to the Indians in usufruct until such time that buyers could be found. Meneses claimed he did not sell a single fanegada of "Indian land" and finished his statement with a certification from the Tribunal de Cuentas to the effect that his visita had yielded the royal treasury over 265,852 pesos.[94]

Despite the fact that Meneses was found officially innocent of wrongfully selling Indian lands in 1649, the investigation dragged on into the 1650s, when another judge, Padre Maestro Fray Francisco de Huerta, was sent to investigate Meneses's actions and to rectify some of his wrongdoings. Huerta found that many of the allegations were true, and his follow-up investigation revealed other irregularities. Huerta learned that Meneses had intentionally and systematically underestimated the area of various pieces of property, making the excesses smaller than those which actually existed. Meneses's actions can be readily explained as a compromise between the crown's interests and those of the landowners. The landowner paid a fee to legalize the declared excess, which in reality represented only part of the surplus that existed. To give them less land, Meneses undercounted the Indians. Related to this, boundaries of lands sold to Spaniards were sometimes left deliberately vague in the new titles so that future discrepancies could be blamed on the incompetence of the surveyor. Both the visitor's reputation and the landowner's possession were thus safeguarded.[95]

Huerta also found that at least one citizen of Lambayeque had been bribed, threatened into silence, and then told what to say to the judge of one of the previous investigations of Meneses's actions. Captain Alonso Larias refused to testify for fear of gaining an unnamed but allegedly powerful enemy. Another Indian official was paid to testify about the corregidor's handling of the transactions between the visitor and the landowners. Another Indian declared:

> I am certain that no Indian or witness dares or will
> dare to testify in this case, because of the fear, force
> and threats of said corregidor and the lieutenant
> Don Josep de Sahebedra and Antonio Núñez who
> is the corregidor's compadre [godparent to the
> corregidor's child] and Juan de Guevara his
> executive assistant [*su acedor y negociador de sus
> cosas*] and Don Andrés de Acauache [the curaca]
> who, in particular, all the Indians fear because he is
> to them as cruel as they [the corregidor and his

assistants] and it will be necessary to order them to
leave [the area] so that an investigation of the truth
will be possible. . . .

Huerta uncovered evidence that the judge of the real audiencia and
confidant of Viceroy Macera, Don Fernando de Saavedra, had foiled
attempts of the Indians to get a hearing because he used his position
to gain access to the records of the visita and the follow-up investigations and then filed them away in his private archive. Saavedra's
actions are explained by the facts that the corregidor had married his
daughter and that he himself was directly related to propertied interests
in the area, as mentioned above. These findings underscore once again
the importance of the informal power structure. Despite the laws,
personal connections facilitated the landowner's legal acquisition of
Indian lands.[96]

The cumulative effect of these sales and of the visita in general was
to place a premium on the cleared, irrigated, and fertile land available
to the communities and cause a growing amount of conflict among the
Indians themselves. When ordinary Indians found out that Collique
no longer had communal lands, they confronted their officials. The
desperation some Indians felt is revealed by the records of fights and
even murders over land possession. Less violent but nonetheless serious were disputes between Indian communities and outsiders (forasteros). An Indian raised in Lambayeque, but whose parents had come
from Collique, went to court against the community to keep the lands
he was planting. In another case, the corregidor was asked to decide
whether María Gil could claim the rightful use of lands she possessed
in Ferreñafe as the daughter of an Indian official.[97]

Land scarcity, as in the case of water scarcity, was not absolute: it
was more accurately a deficiency of arable land. The scarcity of good
land varied from community to community. Collique and Sinto had
no reserve lands, while Reque had an excess which it rented to its
landless neighbors. The effects of this short supply and of the mita,
which removed community Indians from their homes for months at a
time, were the breakdown in the traditional communal pattern of tenure to the point that Indians sold land among themselves and one
community sold or rented land to another. Such practices undermined
the authority and legitimacy of the traditional Indian leaders.[98]

Thus, an understanding of the deteriorating quality of community
life and the economic and social development of the Spanish creole

sector depends on the identification of the landowners and an appreciation of their economic and political positions and personal connections. The rhythm and timing of the transformations and growth of estates were not only a function of the quality of the land and the availability of irrigation water; the availability of labor, technology, and capital; government policy; and prices and markets; but also of the power of the landowners themselves. In the final analysis, those responsible for acquiring land, irrigation water, and sufficient labor to make an estate a profitable asset at the right time were the landowners, who directed the estates and decided when to invest, what to plant, what to purchase, where and when to sell, how to spend the income, and how to allocate their fund of social capital.

Differences in the position and economic standing of individuals explain the differential growth of the separate estates: why one estate (given comparable resources) remained an estancia while another was transformed into a mill, and why one developed faster or at the expense of another. It was no coincidence that labradores of modest means disappeared from the landowning group in the course of the period. The hacendados who established themselves as such and survived to the middle of the seventeenth century engaged in other activities and, therefore, had additional sources of income. Merchants had capital, a network of agents, and other contacts that proved beneficial in marketing the products of the estates and in acquiring the material they needed. Secular priests received stipends from the royal treasury, fees for performing the sacraments, income from chantries, and other religious trusts and contributions.[99] Almost all the individuals whose families endured and became prominent in the second half of the seventeenth century had other professions, and most participated in the town council. Extra income and the status and honor associated with public life gave one individual the advantage over another in securing loans and in acquiring additional labor. Wealth, land, political power, and prestige were almost inseparable: one tended to reinforce the other.

Over the years economic circumstances and the bureaucratic system itself favored the wealthiest and best-connected individuals. The procedure for acquiring mitayos and confirmation in Lima of the grants made by the corregidor required considerable expenditures, which could only be borne by those producers whose connections facilitated the paperwork. If it is true that mitayos were granted according to need, small producers would not have been eligible for as many mitayos in the first place, so the expenses incurred in procuring confirmation would have been proportionately higher. This was undoubtedly a factor that tended to force some farmers out of production.[100]

The same holds true for the legalization and confirmation of land titles. The visitor was more likely to settle for fewer pesos per fanegada when dealing with a large tract than when dealing with a small one. The wealthiest individuals were also more likely to have the knowledge of procedure and ties in Lima necessary to facilitate such proceedings.

In conclusion, unstable market conditions set the tone for an era of intense competition over natural resources in the first half of the seventeenth century. Price trends and relatively high labor costs forced most wheat and hog producers out of business. Another influence in the latter case was hostile reaction to the damage done to the range and farmlands by droves of pigs. The security of tenure gained in the first visita, the availability of mortgage funds, and a steady supply of black slaves, which eased the labor shortage for some, provided the conditions in which the intensification of production on some estates and the transformation and consolidation of others could take place. Cane cultivation and sugar production spread, although agriculture remained diversified, with no one type of estate or product predominating.

Not all the landowners survived these conditions. Especially at the beginning of the period, the economic situation of many landholders was precarious. A small margin coupled with pressure to maintain their standard of living, intensify production, and transform their estates forced many to enter into partnerships or to borrow. Without large capital reserves, landowners were subject to the vagaries of the market. Many could not withstand sudden price fluctuations or other prolonged crises. Beginning in the 1630s, some individual landowners were in a strong enough position economically and socially to make partnerships for investment purposes unnecessary. Those unwilling or unable to adapt passed into undocumented existence as their property was absorbed into other estates.

The labradores who endured to become hacendados were, as a rule, more active in public life and, therefore, better connected and better able to mobilize the resources needed to build up and keep their estates. Accumulating wealth and authority provided them with the direct power and indirect influence to affect crucial decisions and to modify the implementation of crown policy on the local level in their favor. After the landowners' economic position, interpersonal relationships and the possibilities for exerting informal pressure they implied proved more important than their formal positions as magistrates, aldermen, field marshals, and generals in the acquisition and control of the natural resources and labor without which the productive development of the estates could not have proceeded. Agricultural development continued to marginalize and subjugate the Indians because it implied a redistribution of resources in which they lost.

6 The Sugar Boom and the Entrenchment of the Landowning Elite, 1650–1719

High prices for sugar and preserves and, to a lesser extent, livestock and their by-products initiated a seventy-year era of unprecedented prosperity in the Lambayeque region, beginning at about midcentury and lasting until 1719. What amounted to boom conditions early in the period encouraged estate owners to continue intensifying production and expanding their estates. Owners spent earnings and borrowed money to purchase capital equipment and slaves and to hire unskilled Indian labor and master artisans. In so doing, they spread the beneficial effects of the sugar boom to other levels and groups in society. The prosperity of the era gave landowners the means to establish their families to the point where certain patronyms became synonymous with wealth, land, prestige, and formal political power. In comparison to the first half of the seventeenth century, the landed elite became wealthier, more homogeneous, and more stable; there was a sharp rise in the acreage and wealth which stayed in a family from one generation to the next. The landed elite, however, was not completely closed. A few new members joined its ranks from the group of government bureaucrats, priests, and businessmen with whom the landowners had close, constant social and economic contact. In fact, hacendados were as dependent as ever on their informal personal ties to assure themselves of a steady supply of labor and to further their efforts to acquire irrigation water, lands, and pastures. The possibility of upward social mobility, however small, along with the aura of owning land, fostered the identification of persons from the landless sectors of society with the landed and increased their willingness to cooperate. As in the past, laws, rules, and regulations were interpreted and used to benefit the Spanish landowners at the expense of the Indian communities.

159

The Sugar Boom

The landowners' investments in the estates during the first half of the seventeenth century paid off handsomely in the second as already favorable conditions improved. Strong demand for the products of the region and the availability of the factors of production provided them with the circumstances necessary to quicken the pace of agricultural development. Landowners' eagerness to invest, especially before 1680, made this an era of hurried, almost frenzied activity. The most dramatic increase occurred in the price of sugar (shown in Fig. 8), which rose spectacularly during the first decade of this period and hit levels unmatched since the sixteenth century. As noted previously, an initial price surge and profits stimulated and facilitated the rapid conversion of some of the grain-producing haciendas in the Saña Valley into sugar mills during the 1640s. The high sugar prices of the 1650s marked the start of a sugar boom that hastened the spread of cane cultivation into the adjacent valleys as other hacendados followed the lead of their neighbors. Prices for sugar peaked twice more before rising output brought prices down by the end of the period.[1]

The market for the products of the pastoral industry remained favorable. The available data show soap selling at more than ten pesos per hundredweight in the 1650s and 1660s and the price of leather remaining about steady at the same level as in the previous period. Like sugar, however, prices after 1700 were lower than at midcentury, bringing down average prices for the industry as a whole by almost 10 percent from the previous period.[2]

But even at the lower prices at the end of the period, the estates remained viable because the average cost of inputs was declining steadily at an even more rapid pace. The outlay for raw materials—the second most important input after labor—plummeted. The price of lime, necessary for both the tanning and sugar-making processes, declined 46 percent from the prices of the previous period. Copper, the metal used to fabricate the huge cauldrons in which the cane juice was boiled down into syrup and a metal combined with others to make trapiches and handtools, fell almost three times as much from a high of 125 pesos per hundredweight to an average of less than 25. The cost of purchasing draft animals was down by an average of 17 percent from the previous period. Although the "hard" economic data are too fragmentary for a complete and sophisticated economic analysis, they and other indirect evidence support the conclusion that the savings in the procurement of raw materials helped maintain earnings in both the sugar and the stock industries until about the turn of the century.[3]

Bolstering earnings, too, was the solution of the heretofore perennial labor shortage. Governmental deregulation of the slave trade increased the supply of blacks arriving in Saña and brought the price of an unskilled, prime-aged male down to about five hundred pesos. These imports proved inadequate to service the area, given the rapid expansion of the relatively labor-intensive sugar industry at midcentury; hence, landowners instructed their factors in Lima to buy slaves, or they financed trips to Tierra Firme to purchase them in lots of up to fifty-eight at a time. As a result, the number of slaves on Calupe doubled, while the slave population of Cayaltí almost tripled. Nevertheless, landowners in Lambayeque complained that they could not secure as many slaves as they needed.[4]

Because slave labor alone was never sufficient to work the estates, landowners and their agents recruited large numbers of Indians and racially mixed workers under different conditions and in different capacities to supplement the work of the blacks. Population counts for the second half of the seventeenth century are rare, but the available figures and other indirect evidence indicate a distinct reversal of the previous downward demographic trend among the natives. Figure 3 shows that between the middle of the seventeenth century and its end the population of some communities reached a nadir and began a slow recovery. The size of the mestizo and mulatto population had been rising slowly but steadily since the sixteenth century. This natural increase considerably eased the tight labor market by creating a growing pool of local workers which the hacendados tapped as needed.

Community Indians continued to work as mitayos and free wage labor. Landowners preferred the former for agricultural work and herding, despite their small numbers and the difficulties of obtaining them, because they remained one of the cheapest sources of labor available. Mitayos worked for one real and a ration of corn per day until 1656, when their cash wages were officially doubled. Even at two reales per day, mitayos were as cheap or cheaper than other wage laborers, who earned from two to six reales.[5]

The use of mitayo labor, however, decreased during the last years of the century. Because the number of mitayos was pegged at one-sixth of the tributary population, the number available for service remained small and far below potential demand. The maximum number assigned to a single estate for which we have records, was thirty-seven on Sasape in the 1660s; few other estates employed even half as many.

Furthermore, a corregidor's grant of mitayo labor required licensing and confirmation in Lima, a lengthy and expensive bureaucratic procedure worthwhile only for significant numbers of mitayos and best afforded by the strongest producers. Moreover, the use of mitayos was restricted. Legislation long on the books prohibited their assignment to the boiling house, the milling area, or other dangerous locations on sugar-producing estates. Officials in Lima probably made it more difficult for sugar producers to get grants because they knew that the regulations were systematically violated; for example, mitayos granted for herding were used for field labor and those granted for planting were sometimes used in or near the mill. The threat of detection decreased the popularity of this source of labor. Indicative of this fact is that when the mitayo system was abolished in Lambayeque circa 1720, there is no evidence that the landowners mounted a protest.[6]

Indian communities also supplied the estates with workers hired on a temporary basis. Legislative changes during the first half of the seventeenth century required Indians to pay their entire tribute assessment in cash. This worked in favor of estate owners because it forced community Indians to participate in the local money economy to a greater extent than ever before. Curacas and other Indian officials served as labor recruiters, sending gangs of day laborers to estates to plant, weed, cut cane, and build corrals to earn cash. Landowners sometimes hired individual Indians to plow or perform other specialized tasks. Indians were preferred for such tasks because they provided the draft animals for plowing. Should a majordomo assign a slave to do the same job, custom required the estate to provide the beast.[7]

Landowners also tapped the group of forasteros, mestizos, and mulattoes who resided in the towns and cities to round out their work force. Their need for cash to pay tribute made more of them willing to accept employment on the estates. Landowners enticed free laborers into service with yearly pay of 40, 45, or 50 pesos and promises of clothing, housing, provision ground, medicine, and food rations. Others were settled on plots of marginal land, especially near the outer limits of the estates, in return for a specified number of days of work per month or part of their crops.[8]

Another inducement to join the hacienda work force was credit. Landowners instructed their managers to advance the laborers goods and cash. Workers often consumed more than they could repay and in so doing became almost permanently indebted to the estate and its owner. A list of the amounts owed by eleven Indian peons on one estate shows that debts ranged from 30 to 100 pesos each; the combined total equalled 679 pesos or an average of about 62 pesos. In addition, ten owed the owner one year's tribute (9 to 13 pesos per year depending on whether or not the Indian had rights to community lands);[9] the eleventh owed him for six months. Even at the highest known salary of 50 pesos per year, such debt represented an obligation difficult indeed to repay.[10]

These imported and local laborers enabled the owners to react to the market incentive to expand production and were diverse enough to allow them to rationalize and maximize their use. Black slaves, who probably represented one of the most expensive forms of labor in both initial capital outlay and year-round maintenance cost, were purchased and trained primarily for specialized tasks in the manufacture of sugar and soap. Master confectioners and soap makers were well worth several hundred pesos more than an unskilled slave and were given monetary rewards and special privileges to assure careful work. Successfully turning boiling cane juice into sugar, for instance, depended on a critical decision about when the syrup had reached the point of crystallization. Other blacks fed the cane into the mill, stirred the boiling syrup, skimmed the froth and impurities off the top, emptied the boiling liquid into smaller pots for cooling, and filled and stored clay molds for the process of purging molasses from the forming sugar crystals. Landowners preferred Indians for the heavy fieldwork of plowing, harrowing, planting, and cutting cane in order to spare the blacks. Indians did not represent a significant capital outlay that would be lost if the worker became ill or died. The replacement of Indians with new recruits, while not always easy, cost landowners far less than a serviceable slave. Landowners hired workers as needed and employed them only long enough to complete the task. Skilled craftsmen—founders, masons, carpenters, and blacksmiths—were usually contracted in Saña to reside on the estate and work on specific projects, such as making copper cauldrons and building or repairing carts. Only the largest estates, such as Calupe, had slave artisans whose full-time job was to serve as carpenters or ceramicists.[11]

On the estancias, too, the division of labor followed racial lines. Gangs of slaves were in charge of making soap and tanning hides; mitayos and hired laborers worked as unskilled or semiskilled labor, performing such tasks as guarding stock or cutting bamboo for corral building. They also slaughtered the animals, dried and sold the meat, and depilated the hides.[12]

Easy credit was another factor underpinning the expansion so evident in the two or three decades right after midcentury. The prosperity which began before 1650 had a multiplier effect which brought extra income to shopkeepers, churchmen, and other local residents. Following the example of the landowners, these persons earmarked funds to found chantries and religious trusts to ensure their spiritual salvation. These foundations and other church funds helped finance, in turn, the continued expansion of the estates. It is also during this period that we see individuals investing surplus capital directly in the estates to generate long-term income. Lent to the estate owners, some of this money paid for acquisitions of equipment, improvements in the infrastructure, and labor. Figure 16 shows the degree to which the various estates assumed mortgages as a percentage of their sale price or value. All but one of the estates for which we have data show a marked increase in debt burden over the first half of the century. Pomalca, the exception, reduced its debt by almost half. Collectively, they increased their average debt dramatically, to almost four and one-half times the previous levels (from 9.5 to 40.2 percent, respectively), as Figure 17 more easily shows. Oyotún's debt climbed rapidly as the owners spent some of the available funds to transform the estate into a sugar producer. The amounts of these encumbrances indicate, first, that owners were willing to borrow heavily to expand production, confident of being able to repay the 5 percent interest and the principal; and, second, that others shared their optimism.[13]

Conditions, then, allowed landowners to orient the development of the hacienda system toward sugar production. The disparity between the profits from sugar and those from livestock raising was apparently significant, and this difference was reflected in the uneven investment in the two industries. Although the returns of the pastoral industry favored the continued expansion of the herds and the concomitant increase in the capacity of tinas y tenerías, the surge to invest in soap and leather manufacturing was not as great as the surge to invest in sugar production. Estancias expanded their operations, with several adding processing facilities, but most of the large operators tended to put their energies and resources into sugar and relegated stock raising to a secondary position. Eventually, sugar production grew until it overshadowed, at least to the outside world, all the other productive activities in the area.

Most of the changes on the individual estates reflect this emphasis on sugar production. Windfall sugar profits of the 1650s induced some landowners to intensify production and initiated another round of converting haciendas and estancias to trapiches. The history of Cayaltí epitomizes the intensification of production and renovation taking place on sugar mills which had been established before 1650. A major estate in 1622, Cayaltí consisted of cane fields, a garden, and an alfalfa field surrounding the owner's house; a purifying house; a boiling house; and several sheds. Twenty slaves ran the two wooden trapiches and five hundred head of livestock grazed on the land not then under cultivation. By 1657, the number of slaves and equipment had been increased. By 1705, a slave crew of fifty-four produced one-third to one-half more cane. Three bronze mills had replaced the two wooden ones. The number of carts, handtools, buildings, and draft animals had also risen proportionately. Growth continued as thirteen new cane fields were added to the forty-four then in existence during the next twelve years.[14]

The effect of the boom on estates like Cayaltí, Popán, and Sárrapo, which were already producing sugar at the time of the boom, was not as dramatic as its effect on others. As land once reserved for grains and livestock was planted in cane, haciendas and estancias were transformed into "haciendas y trapiches." The owners of Calupe and Oyotún were among the first to react to the economic incentives of the 1640s. On Calupe, this transformation entailed replanting tobacco fields in cane and purchasing mills and other equipment; and in building a boiling house, a purifying house, and warehouses. Soon after the owner Manuel Carvallo decided to switch to a new cash crop, he and his successors increased the number of slaves steadily from thirteen in the 1650s to forty-six and fifty in the 1690s and over double that number before the end of the period. They were needed to keep all three mills running year-round. By 1701 Calupe had supplanted Cayaltí as the epitome of efficiency, partially due to a greater number of healthy new cane fields and partially because of the energetic direction of its owner. Oyotún developed similarly, but later and on a smaller scale.[15]

The conversion of the estancia of Pomalca was far more complicated, due to a water shortage that prevented cropping. In 1650 Pomalca was used as intensively as its natural resources would permit and economic conditions merited. Twenty years later, the owner of Pomalca, Captain Martín Núñez de Arze, a man who had already made a considerable fortune from sugar production on Cayaltí, decided to invest to expand his sugar operations in the adjacent Lambayeque Valley. Knowing that before he could plant cane on Pomalca he had to remedy its water

Figure 16. Debt Burden as a Percentage of an Estate's Value

Estates	Before 1594	1595–99	1600–1609	1610–19	1620–29	1630–39	1640–49	1650–59	1660–69	1670–79	1680–89
Calupe		0		0	0	0	0				
Callanca										16.7	
Cayaltí					5.5						
Cojal											
Collús						0	0		32.5		
San Christóbal										23.1	
Chongoyape											
Chumbenique											
Isco	0	0	22.2								
San Juan	21.2										
San Lorenzo						12.8					
Luya				0	0						
Molino				0	0	0		29.3			37.5
Otra Banda										38.3	
Oyotún			0	0			13.8		14.3	33.3	
Pampa Grande							47.4				
Pomalca					36.0						
Popán				13.3							59.2
Pucalá											
La Punta											29.2
Saltur											
Sangana											
Santequepe				29.2		5.7					
Sárrapo			11.1								
Sialupe											
Sicán											
Sipán										42.9	
Tumán											
Ucupe				0		12.8	55.9				
Average*	10.6	0	11.1	6.1	10.4	5.2	19.5	29.3	23.4	30.9	42.0

*Averages are of known mortgages only. Estates with no mortgages are excluded. Had the latter been included, averages would have been lower.

Estates	1690–99	1700–1709	1710–19	1720–29	1730–39	1740–49	1750–59	1760–69	1770–79	1780–89	1790–99	1800–1809
Calupe	26.5	36.4	71.7	115.0	37.5	71.2				20.8		
Callanca							100+			8.3		
Cayaltí		77.2	93.1	40.0	57.5							
Cojal									43.3			
Collús	35.4	57.0		30.4	65.5			80.0				
San Cristóbal	24.4						44.4	38.6				
Chongoyape	27.1											
Chumbenique												
Isco												
San Juan												
San Lorenzo	33.3	61.4	35.0	100.0		55.1	100.0					
Luya		21.1			29.2		79.2	17.6				
Molino		55.8					90.9	91.8	100.0			
Otra Banda												
Oyotún	44.4					100.0				62.5		
Pampa Grande									81.3			
Pomalca	24.5	22.2				62.5	83.3			59.1		
Popán					57.5							
Pucalá					60.0		0					
La Punta				33.3				33.3	100.0	72.4		
Saltur					15.4	31.2		81.3		94.4		
Sangana							60.3					
Santequepe												
Sárrapo	47.6			89.7								
Sialupe												66.7
Sicán							81.5	114.5	98.3	62.3		
Sipán	40.0							4.5				
Tumán		55.6							79.1	79.4		
Ucupe											110.4	
Average*	33.7	48.3	66.6	68.1	46.1	64.0	71.1	57.7	83.7	57.4	110.4	66.7

Source: Appendix 3.

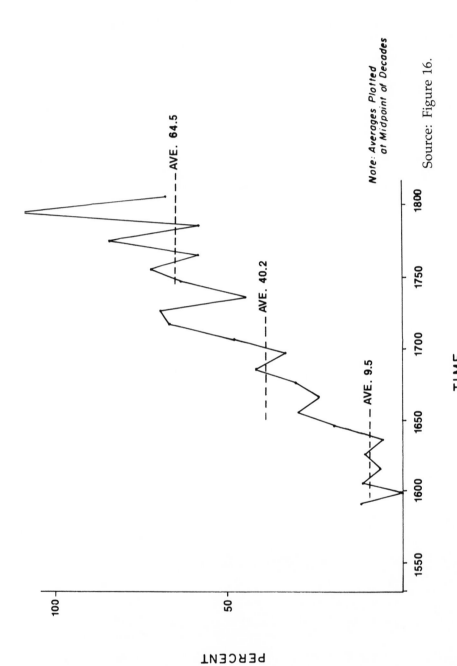

Figure 17. Debt Burden as a Percentage of an Estate's Value

problem, Núñez de Arze decided to acquire irrigated land and divert the water to Pomalca, an expensive prospect, but one apparently well worth the price to this sagacious businessman. Núñez de Arze had been leasing 150 fanegadas of pasturelands near Pomalca, called Nampón, Focodam, and Lonope, from the Indian community of Callanca-Monsefú. These grazing lands had been cultivated before a flood during the 1620s had destroyed the irrigation system. Since the damage had not been repaired, the lands had lain fallow and been allowed to revert to natural grasses and scrub forest. The lands, however, had not lost their customary right to a share of water. Between 1667 and 1672 Núñez de Arze successfully petitioned Viceroy Fernández de Castro Andrade for a license to reopen the irrigation canal to water the lands, while negotiating with the Indians for their sale. The Indians, with the approval of the corregidor and protector, finally agreed to sell the usufruct rights to the lands through a legal arrangement known as a *censo enfiteútico,* an agreement by which the owner transferred the usufruct to another in return for a yearly rent. Such sales were usually for one or more lives or, as in this case, in perpetuity. If the rent were not paid, the usufruct reverted to the original owner or his successor in the *dominio directo.* The agreement between Núñez de Arze and Callanca-Monsefú stipulated that the former would acquire the usufruct for a yearly rent of 5 percent on a principal of 750 pesos, or 37.5 pesos per year. The viceroy approved the sale in 1676, with the condition that the principal be increased to 1,000 pesos and the yearly rent to 50. After obtaining this approval, Núñez de Arze spent over 10,000 pesos in wages and materials to open the water channel before he actually planted cane or installed a single mill. Production of sugar on Pomalca began in the early 1680s and continues today.[16]

The conversion of Pomalca also exemplifies the tendency of the sugar estates to grow in size. Landowners annexed one property to another to limit competition, to force Indians into the labor market, and to acquire water and land resources. The latter became important to some because cane quickly sapped the soil of vital nutrients and left it exhausted after a few years of continuous cultivation. A system of rotation and an adequate reserve of arable land became imperative. Before the end of the period, additional lands, often in the form of an established estancia or hacienda, had been added to each sugar estate.[17]

To the 90 fanegadas of Luya and Tulipe, for instance, Captain Miguel de Robles Garay, the owner, added Supián with 60 fanegadas and Pátapo with 10. The size of Pomalca increased from 50 fanegadas to over 200 with the annexation of the estancias of Samán and Filtum and the saltpeter works called Santa Rosa, not counting the 150 fanegadas leased from Callanca-Monsefú. Captain Francisco de Seña Chirinos added another 122 fanegadas with the purchase of Arcarleche from the Jesuits in 1717. The results of these and other acquisitions are summarized in Figure 18.[18] Note that these figures are the official measurements of the estates and that most were actually much larger. Before the visita de la tierra of 1711–12 (discussed in detail below), the estancias that were added to the estates gave the owners legal title to but a fraction of the area which they had come to represent. In addition to the land on which buildings and corrals were located, titles to an estancia gave the owner *de facto* control over the pastures and, to a certain extent, the lands between his center of operations and the corrals he had scattered over the countryside, which were often located more than one league away. For example, although the owner of Calupe officially owned 433 fanegadas, one contemporary pointed out that he controlled over four square leagues of pasturelands.[19] The size of the estates listed in Figure 18 for the years prior to the visita, therefore, must be considered a minimum, because all the sugar mills consisted of a mill with cultivatable lands at the core and one or more annexed estancias. The sharp increase in size of Luya and Collús after the visita reflects the opportunity offered by the visitor, Don Antonio Sarmiento de Sotomayor, to acquire titles and the legal ownership of the pastures, as distinct from the lands on which they grew.[20]

Figure 18. Size of the Estates, 1650–1719

Estate	Year	Size[1]
Calupe	1704	433
Cayaltí	1705[2]	130
	1717	155
Collús	1706	190
	1712	843.5[3]
Luya	1692	90
	1713	150
	1715	683[3]

Estate	Year	Size[1]
Molino	1655	15
	1688	20
Oyotún	1658	375[2]
Pátapo	1692	10
Pomalca	(1649)[5]	5
	1712[2]	203
	1713	213
	1717	335
La Punta	1711[2]	133
		433[6]
Saltur	(1650)	133
	ca. 1711	300
Samán	1650	10
Santequepe	1651	231
Sárrapo	1655	360
Sialupe	1714	115
Sipán	1714[2]	100
Tumán	1680[2]	453[4]
Ucupe	1711	3

Average size[5]: Estancias: before visita   119
                                after visita   763
                Haciendas y trapiches   331

Notes: [1] In fanegadas, maximum extent reached before 1719.
     [2] Haciendas y trapiches.
     [3] Includes area with pasturage rights only.
     [4] Without Chongoyape.
     [5] Numbers in parentheses are added for perspective.
     [6] With Saltur.

Source: Appendix 3.

Owners planted cane on land previously used to grow grain and foodstuffs, or they diverted the water from the newly acquired land to fields closer to the mill. This centralization of production was a rational measure designed to minimize the distance heavy cane had to be moved by slow oxcart over bumpy, rutted trails; but it also meant that the surrounding land, deprived of its water, was allowed to revert to natural grasses and scrub forest.

The realities of an agrarian economy based increasingly on the cultivation of cane gave the sugar producers a use for the surrounding land and provided them with the motive for continued land concentration after the initial acquisitions. Sugar prices that had been steadily rising for almost a quarter of a century jolted the landowners with disbelief when they plummeted in the late 1670s. Fortunately for them, the drop proved ephemeral. Prices began to recover almost immediately, but took over a decade to regain previous heights. But the initial drop awakened the owners—many of whom were relatively new to the sugar business—to the fact that the higher profits associated with the production of a luxury good also brought much higher risk than with other products. The instability of the sugar market encouraged producers to use their pasturelands for grazing. Although stock raising remained secondary, it proved a superb complement to sugar production because the greater price stability of animal products acted as a hedge against the sometimes violent fluctuations of sugar prices. Furthermore, the acquisition of an estancia with its corrals, animals, and shepherds meant that the owners did not have to invest much additional capital to commence operation. Herds were processed, if necessary, in independent tinas y tenerías that were beginning to appear near Indian towns like Chiclayo and Lambayeque. If sugar producers could not be bothered with raising livestock themselves, they rented their pastures to others.

With the wedding of sugar production to stock raising, the sugar estates became "haciendas y trapiches," producing from three to five thousand arrobas of sugar and processing from several hundred to several thousand head of sheep and goats per year. At the four to five thousand arroba per year level, producers could count on net earnings on the sales of sugar and syrup alone of two thousand pesos or better. This figure can be multiplied several times for estates like San Cristóbal and Calupe that produced fourteen thousand arrobas per year. With this development, the estates had evolved into a mature form whose dimensions and organization of production remained almost unchanged into the nineteenth century. The phrase "hacienda y trapiche" accurately reflects the fact that none of the estates produced sugar exclusively. Undeniably, their primary cash crop was sugar, but sheep and goats grazed on the pasturelands and most had orchards to provide fruit with which to make preserves and alfalfa fields for the draft animals. This hybrid form reflected not a displacement of one activity by another, but rather a pragmatic reorganization toward the more efficient utilization of local natural resources and toward the economic security of the owners.[21]

Estancias had felt the effect of the trend toward concentration and development, too, as Figures 18 and 19 show. By the eighteenth century, the estancias of the region had become part of six huge ranching enterprises, some with a few fields planted in alfalfa or provision crops, usually for internal consumption. Estancias with herds in the fifteen to twenty thousand range usually slaughtered three thousand or more goats per year. Sales of the meat, hides, and soap yielded from 6 percent (considered poor) to 13 percent (considered average) profit in the 1660s, depending on the richness of the pastures and disease. Indeed, because stock raising was dependent on weather, losses could be staggering during periods of drought. The number of "haciendas" shown in Figure 19 overrepresents the importance of farming: most of the estates were predominantly livestock ventures with a small portion of their land in

Figure 19. Number and Types of Estates, 1650–1719

Types[1] [2]	No.	Percent
Estancias	6	19
Haciendas	12	38
Haciendas y Trapiches	14	44
Total	32	101

Notes: [1]By the latest available information. I only count estates that existed as separate units after 1700.
   [2]For contrast, see Figure 11 for numbers for the previous period.

Source: Appendix 3.

foodstuffs, tobacco, and cotton. The balance between farming and stock raising depended on the quality of the land, the availability of irrigation water, and the size and composition of the labor force.[22]

Commercial wheat production and molinos, with one known exception, disappeared from the Lambayeque region before the beginning of the eighteenth century. The one estate that continued to grow wheat as its primary cash crop was a small one, appropriately called "El Molino," which produced for the local market. After competition and low prices, contemporaries believed that the earthquake of 1687 was primarily to blame for the disappearance of wheat production. Antonio Ulloa, Jorge Juan y Santacilia, and Oscar Febres Villarroel report that the quake left the land on the coast unsuitable for wheat. Speaking of the lands near Lima, Ulloa states:

> Before the earthquake in 1687, when this city
> suffered in so deplorable a manner, the harvests of
> wheat and barley were sufficient to supply the
> wants of the country without any importation,
> especially of wheat, but by this convulsion of
> nature, the soil was so vitiated, that the wheat
> rotted soon after it was sown, occasioned, probably,
> by the vast clouds of sulphureous particles then
> exhaled, and the prodigious quantities of nitrous
> effluvia diffused through it. This obliged the owners
> of the lands to apply them to other uses, and
> accordingly many of them were turned into
> meadows of clover, plantations of sugar canes, and
> other vegetables, which they found not subject to
> the same misfortune.

Although much the same language described the northern coast, growing evidence suggests that, rather than the quake itself, wheat smut actually destroyed the crops.[23]

But this one example of an industry in decline must not detract from the fact that for the owners, as well as for others associated with the export economy, the more efficient estates made money. Contemporaries remarked that the 1650s and 1660s were decades of windfall profits, which, though they later declined, remained healthy nonetheless. The frequency of founding and the amounts of the chantries and other trusts (reflected indirectly in Fig. 16) also indicate regionwide prosperity. The growth in size and importance of Saña and its fame as a rich city attracted the attention of the English pirate Edward David, who landed with his men in the port of Chérrepe on 4 March 1686 and spent six days sacking it and transporting its treasures to his waiting ships. A final indicator of prosperity is found in the amounts paid for the right to collect the tithes in Saña, where most of the sugar estates were located. They remained high and stable until after 1700. The short-lived upward trend evidenced for Chiclayo corresponds precisely to the spread of cane cultivation into that valley in the 1650s.[24]

Landed Society

Behind these developments were the landowners. As entrepreneurs, they were dedicated, despite other activities, to the continued expansion of agribusiness in the region. For many (especially before about 1680), their first and most important preoccupation was administering their property, and this interest contributed to the prosperity and profitability of agriculture on which their position was based. Typically, hacendados ran the estates themselves from Saña, through their majordomos. Contemporaries recognized the personal attention of the owner to the management of the estates as very beneficial. Among the reasons for the reputation of Cojal as one of the finest estates in the Saña Valley were the personal supervision and dedication of two of its owners, Captain Juan Vásquez de Saavedra (the younger) and Don Pedro de Vargas Oteo. Over the years, however, the employment of one or more professional majordomos to run the estates increased as technology became more complex and the scale of operations grew to the point where the owner had to delegate the decision-making power for daily operations. Rentals of entire estates, as in the previous period, were neither frequent nor lasting, although many owners leased pasture to the growing number of independent cattle raisers without grazing rights.[25]

Landowners were rewarded for their concern. As never before, they became conspicuous in the local setting as the richest individuals in the region. Their estates alone represented thousands of pesos of capital. The average value or selling price had increased almost threefold in the last fifty years or so to about 30,000 pesos. The owners of several estates were worth much more. Núñez de Arze's estates, for example, represented a fortune of over 158,000 pesos. The value of Don Francisco de Palma y Vera's landholdings totaled well over 175,000 pesos.[26]

Besides the estates and their appurtenances, landowners owned townhouses, comfortably furnished with tapestries, paintings, and cushioned divans. Palma y Vera, for example, lived between the convent of La Merced and the central plaza in a mansion filled with rugs, upholstered furniture, and gold-framed mirrors. He took pride in his silver service, complete with candelabras; his personal chapel, containing a valuable collection of oil paintings and statues; and his library. He dressed in the finest fabrics, imported from England, Naples, and France. Despite owning estancias and tinas that produced thousands of pounds of soap per year, he preferred to wash with imported soap and dry his hands on English towels. To travel, he either mounted a mule, fitted with silver-adorned saddle and stirrups, or rode in a carriage with scarlet curtains.[27]

Such landowners were rich enough to fulfill their dreams. They sent their sons away to seminary and university, often with stipends equal to or higher than the annual incomes of many local bureaucrats. In contrast to the situation fifty years before, when a few landowners could not sign their name, the number of individuals with a complete seminary education numbered about a dozen (7.6 percent), and only one person held a doctorate; now almost all the landowners were functionally literate[28] and one-quarter had advanced degrees. At least twenty-two (17 percent) had finished seminary, and most of these had combined theology with training in law. Seven (6 percent) more had graduated and practiced law. Two (2 percent) held doctorates. Since no school existed in Saña at the time, an education implied years of residence in Trujillo or Lima, which gave them the added distinction of being the most widely traveled. For the daughters of the family, landowners arranged marriages to other persons of rank, like the sons of the judges of the royal audiencia or even to the judges themselves. Rich dowries of more than sixteen thousand pesos, which included everything needed to set up a household and enough jewels and clothing to last a lifetime, also assured beneficial matches.[29]

They could also afford to found more chantries in honor of their own souls and those of relatives and friends. Landowners were prodigious in this respect, especially toward the end of the seventeenth century, founding capellanías in the name of their parents and grandparents and others long since dead. The annual income guaranteed a son the funds for higher education or a daughter the dowry needed to gain entrance into the prestigious convent of Santa Clara in Trujillo or its counterpart in Lima. In establishing these on their own estates, though, no funds changed hands, and no improvements were made. They represented impositions, uneconomic mortgages, which in later times would add to an oppressive burden of debt payments. But few thought of that possibility for the moment.[30]

The gulf between the standard of living and personal wealth of these landowners and the professionals, minor bureaucrats, and the Indian masses was enormous. No water commissioner or Indian commissioner with an annual salary of two hundred pesos could live like Palma y Vera. Majordomos, who besides their annual salary of two to three hundred pesos received food, housing, and the use of pastures and a plot of irrigated land, could not afford to educate a son in Lima. A salary of more than two hundred pesos paid to the curaca of Lambayeque made him a rich and respected individual among his Indians; and, in the smaller communities, such as Jayanca, Pacora, and Mórrope, salaries only one-half that size gave officials similar status. Such salaries could not compare, however, with incomes in the Spanish creole sector.[31]

This wealth and education enabled the "hacendados," as they liked to be called, to establish themselves as a hereditary elite within which was concentrated the power and prestige of the area. Nearly every aspect of local politics and the economy was influenced by a landowner either in his role as an agribusinessman; priest or opinion maker for society; lawyer or judge who interpreted decrees and rulings from Spain and Lima; or bureaucrat, from corregidor on down, who selectively enforced the decisions on these directives. Over 40 percent of the males (up significantly from the previous period) had other occupations (see Fig. 20). In comparison with the first half of the seventeenth century when it was not uncommon for merchants and notaries to double as landowners, they now tended to be in the liberal professions. The number of churchmen and lawyers, both prestigious and lucrative professions, had doubled. This trend reveals the lessening, though continuing, social prejudice against merchants and commerce prevailing since the conquest.[32] Economic prosperity gave members of the landed elite more choice. They could acquire an education and become professionals, eliminating the need to engage openly and directly in trade. Merchants' sons did not take over the family business. Instead, fathers encouraged them to become lawyers or priests. That the number of lawyers is so low probably reflects the fact that many who studied law in Lima remained there to practice and that those who returned were also priests.

Hacendados dominated the provincial bureaucracy—either directly,

Figure 20. Known Occupations of Landowners, 1650–1719

Occupation	No.	Percent	Other
Priests	22	42	diezmero; financier, administrator; 17 lawyers
Merchants	4	8	financier; bureaucrat, financier; administrator, ship captain
Financiers	4	8	
Lawyers	7	13	
Bureaucrats: Major—	6	12	bureaucrat; bureaucrat; minor bureaucrat, innkeeper; financier; bureaucrat; bureaucrat, notary; minor bureaucrat
Minor—	4	8	
Notaries	3	6	diezmero
Miners	1	2	
Other	1	2	
Total	52	101	

Source: BIL.

by holding the highest and most important positions; or indirectly, through informal ties with these administrators. Indeed, the size and elaboration of the estates also limited the entrance of bureaucrats into the landed elite to the highest ranking and best paid. Landowners served as treasurers and accountants in the local treasury office, and corregidores and judges. These positions conferred on the holder wide and extraordinary powers and the social standing inherent in an appointment or confirmation signed by some of the highest civil and religious authorities in the realm.

Over the years, too, the cabildo became as exclusive as a private club. Membership passed from father to son, to son-in-law, or, occasionally, to nephew or cousin. A few families dominated. No longer was it possible for almost any wealthy individual, whether or not he owned land, to participate. Now landed interests clearly predominated both in the numbers of individuals who served and the numbers of different positions held. The chances that a magistrate was a landowner were better than eight to one. For other positions, the chances were better than two to one. Nonlandowners' potential interest in the cabildo was high. Many would have liked a seat, not for the power to affect urban organization because few substantive issues remained to be decided during this period, but for the prestige and the limited duties associated with the post. Meetings were irregular and as infrequent as twice per year. But the sale of public office now effectively excluded all but a handful of individuals and families, as office, like land, passed down through the generations of a family, excluding not only nonlandowners but 75 percent of the landed class as well.[33]

Closed out of public office, many landowners turned to the militia as a means of enhancing their image and fulfilling an ingrained sense of "service to the king." The militia apparently had more room, so landowners eagerly joined. Almost seven out of ten landowners eligible for such service held some position of command. They dominated by outnumbering the nonlanded in equivalent positions from Sergeant Major upward by as many as eight to one. The right to appear in a position of authority was no longer the major incentive for joining. Militiamen now had the right to trial by their peers (*fuero*), which usually meant more lenient treatment than in the civil courts. Another important consideration was the right to use military rank as a title. Prefixing a name with a military title of sufficient rank greatly enhanced a person's prestige in the eyes of the local inhabitants. Those unable to assume the title of a post on the town council (for example, alderman) used their military title to add respectability to their name and generally preceded the use of the title *don*, the Spanish term for "gentleman." In some cases, a father identified himself as general or captain and his son assumed the title of don.[34]

A single landowner was often active in several spheres of local life at once. As the "owner" of Chérrepe, Juan Bautista Cabeza de Vaca, for example, began his career as the caretaker and administrator (*alcaide*)

of the warehouses in that port before 1658. Within five years, he purchased the estate called San Lorenzo el Real and thereafter married
into the old and prestigious Samudio Mendoza family, served as permanent alderman and inspector of weights and measures on the town
council (1668), and was commissioned as a captain in the local militia.
Between 1668 and his death in 1682, he filled the posts of chief constable
(1675) and public defender (1680) of Saña and acquired the estate of
La Candelaria and the lands called Collazos.[35]

A second individual, Don Juan Bonifacio de Seña, was a peninsular
Spaniard from Burgos who arrived in Motupe before 1661. Soon, he
and another relative owned extensive estates in Piura. His first involvement in Lambayeque appears to have been his marriage to a local
woman. He then served in the militia as a captain (1670), as a governor
of arms (1694), and as a general and field marshal (1697). He was
appointed military reviewer in 1681, served as lieutenant governor of
the province in 1684 and again in 1694, and as corregidor in 1696 and
1697. At the end of his term as corregidor, he purchased the estates of
Pomalca and Samán and the saltpeter works known as Santa Rosa de
Acarleche.[36]

Not all of the estate owners were as active or in a position to exert
pressure in so many aspects of local life as Cabeza de Vaca or Seña.
Priests by virtue of their vows could not sit on the municipal council
or join the militia. Women were barred from participation in public
life. Yet, priests and women were the exceptions rather than the rule.
Over three-quarters of all the male landowners had professional training, engaged in nonagricultural business activities, sat on the municipal
council, commanded the militia, or accepted positions in the bureaucracy at one time or another.[37]

Increased concentration of wealth, formal power, and prestige in the
hands of a few was not the only way in which the character of the elite
had changed from the previous period. The sugar boom and the consolidation of property meant the increased exclusivity of the landowning class and fewer opportunities for upward social mobility for the
landless. Figure 21 shows that 91 (69 percent) of the property transfers
between 1650 and 1719 were between landed family members (indicating old wealth), while only 40 (31 percent) were between established
landowners and new, first-time owners—a ratio of better than two to
one. The significance of these figures is inescapable: social mobility
into the landowning group had declined in comparison to the previous
period, when almost 70 percent of estate transfers were made to new
landowners.[38]

Figure 21. Mode of Estate Acquisition by Elite Status, 1650–1719

Mode of Transfer	Old Wealth		New Wealth		Total	
	No.	Percent	No.	Percent	No.	Percent
Composición/ Denuncia	1	1			1	1
Donation	5	5			5	4
Dowry			10	25	10	8
Inheritance	37	41	1	3	38	29
Sale	47	52	29	73	76	58
Other	1	1			1	1
Total	91 (69%)	100	40 (31%)	101	131	101
Unknown					111	

Source: Appendix 3.

The personal histories of these examples of successful upward mobility show that they had served in public life in more positions than second- and later-generation landowners. Public service enhanced their prestige, reputation, and contacts, all essential to increase an outsider's chances for joining the landed elite. That both Cabeza de Vaca and Seña were immigrants is no coincidence. Second- or later-generation landowners were less visible, suggesting that such activities were less necessary to establish them socially, politically, or economically.

The biographies of these first-generation landowners reveal that they tended to acquire land later in life than established members of the landed elite.[39] Figure 22 shows that 56 percent of the first-generation landowners held at least one position before acquiring land. For example, half of the immigrants, for whom reasonably complete career profiles are available, arrived in Lambayeque in some official governmental capacity, acquired land, and then became active in local politics. Most of the others made their name and money elsewhere, invested in land in Lambayeque, and then assumed administrative responsibilities or became involved in municipal politics. Members of the established landed families often reached adulthood and began to

Figure 22. Social Origins[1] of the Landed Elite, 1650–1719

| Relative point in a person's career when land was acquired | Old Wealth | | New Wealth | | | | | |
| | | | Local-Born | | Immigrants | | Total | |
	No.	Percent	No.	Percent	No.	Percent	No.	Percent
After holding another position	17	17			14	56	31	25
Before holding another position	14	14			4	16	18	14
Held position and land simultaneously	6	6			4	16	10	8
Only held land	50	50			1	4	51	41
Unknown	13	13			2	8	15	12
Total	100 (80%)	100			25 (20%)	100	125	100
Unknown							51	

Note: [1]By acquisition of first piece of land and any occupation or position in the militia, on the cabildo, or in the bureaucracy.

Source: BIL.

participate in public life before the older members of their families died or passed on the land. This fact explains why the differences in the numbers in Figure 22 of those who held land before (fourteen, or 14 percent) or after another position (seventeen, or 17 percent) are not greater and why the numbers in these two categories are not more skewed toward those who acquired land before starting a public career as expected. Licenciado Don Francisco Palma y Vera, for instance, finished his seminary training and served as a priest for several years before his mother died and left to him and his brother the estate of San Cristóbal.[40]

It is also significant that the newcomers acquired the least expensive properties. Sixty-five percent of the estates held by first-time landowners were worth less than the average for the period (as shown in Fig. 23). The biographies of these individuals, the type of property they acquired (estancias and haciendas, some of which would later in the period be converted to sugar producers), and the date of acquisition suggest the continued importance of cattle raising as an avenue of upward social mobility.[41]

Figure 23. Value of Estates Acquired by New Wealth

Value	Estancias	Haciendas	Trapiches	Total
0–19,999	3	6	2	11
20,000–39,999	1	2	2	5
40,000–59,999				
60,000–79,999				
80,000–99,999			1	1
100,000+			1	1
Total	4	8	6	18
Unknown				28

Sources: Appendix 3 and BIL.

For outsiders, marriage into the propertied class was sometimes the only way to gain access to land. For the old local elite, marriage was a mechanism through which to co-opt important officials and bolster their own fortunes with new wealth. The acquisition of land by immigrants was connected to the individual's marriage into a local landed family in over three-fifths of all known cases. Peninsular-born Spaniards were at a premium, especially if they were of good birth, had extensive family connections, occupied an important position in Lambayeque, and had a substantial fortune. Thus, Captain Miguel de Garay y del Sol's marriage to the daughter of Francisco Tirado, Doña Ana María, undoubtedly was facilitated by the fact that he was a native of Vizcaya, Spain, the third son of Don Miguel de Garay y de la Torre, Lord (*Señor*) of the house of Garay, and that he arrived as an official in a commission headed by the Maestro de Campo Don Juan de Chavez y Mendoza, sent from Lima to review the administration of the corregidor and his lieutenants. Similar qualities in the background of General Don Bonifacio de Gastelú Pereda Eschalaz favored his marriage to a scion of the well-established Robles family. Don Bonifacio, born of a noble family in Navarre, Spain, left his considerable property and holdings behind to become King Charles II's treasurer in Peru.[42]

Newcomers found it increasingly difficult if not impossible to establish themselves because opportunities for advancement characteristic of the more socially fluid pre-1650 years had disappeared. The frontier was gone, partitioned among the haciendas and Indian communities. The bureaucracy was staffed, and no new positions were created. The positions that became vacant on the elite-dominated municipal council stayed within the family. Moreover, the few old, privileged, and powerful families, who controlled the largest and most valuable sugar estates and ranches and most of the then-productive land, had established distinguished ancestry as a criterion for elite membership. The greatest prestige value was given to the families who could claim descent from the original encomenderos of the area, probably because such descent was rare. Figure 5 shows that six generations of descendants of the encomendero of Túcume, Francisco de Samudio Mendoza, and the original founder of Saña, Captain Baltazar Rodríguez, owned estates. One property, Santiago de Miraflores, Leviche, and lands called Collazos remained in the family for five generations. In the second half of the seventeenth century, Miraflores was annexed to the trapiche of San Cristóbal, one of the single largest sugar estates in the area. The last member of the lineage to own the estate was a priest with no heirs. The owner's trusted friend and executor of his will purchased the estate after his death, thus ending the tenure of this branch of the long-lived Samudio family.

Technically, too, the Saavedra clan (shown in Fig. 13) could claim descent from the original encomenderos of the region because Doña Bernarda, the wife of Bernardo López, was the relative by marriage of an encomendero of Collique.[43] But the identification, though much recalled at family reunions, had faded somewhat from collective memory over the years and was never as strong as that made by the branch of the family that retained the family name.

Incorporated over the years into the vast Saavedra group were two families who traced their origins back to the early settlers of the area. The families founded by Cristóbal Gutiérrez Múñoz and Blas de Fragoso (shown in Fig. 13) dated from the end of the sixteenth century. Gutiérrez Múñoz's family owned land during the lifetime of four generations. The descendants of Fragoso, who established himself as a gentleman farmer by acquiring the estancia of Mamape, held land for five generations before 1719.

Diego de Rodríguez Cavanillas's family (diagrammed in Fig. 24), like most of the "old" families of the period, dated from the middle and latter years of the previous period. He and his descendants for four generations owned Cayaltí until the death of Licenciado Don Joseph Núñez de Arze, a priest with no heirs. Other members of the same branch maintained the landowning tradition by acquiring other estates in the area which they held until the middle of the eighteenth century.

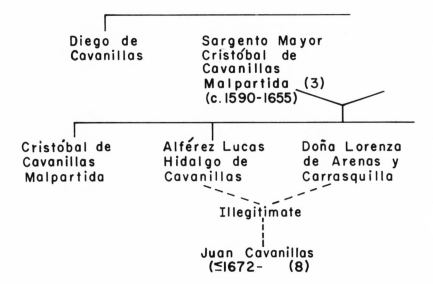

Figure 24.

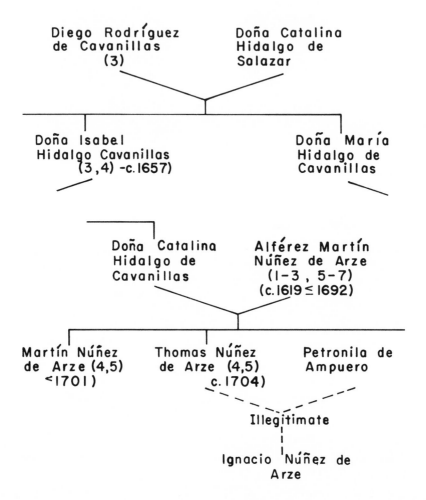

Figure 24, continued.

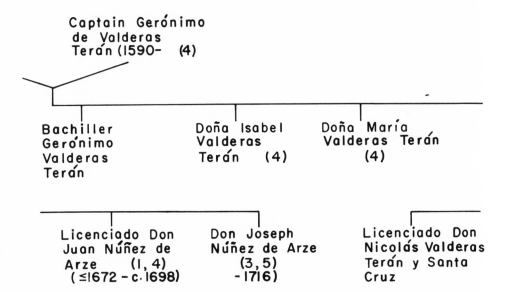

Captain Gerónimo
de Valderas
Terán (1590-   (4)

Bachiller
Gerónimo
Valderas
Terán

Doña Isabel
Valderas
Terán   (4)

Doña María
Valderas Terán
(4)

Licenciado Don
Juan Núñez de
Arze   (I, 4)
(≤1672 - c. 1698)

Don Joseph
Núñez de Arze
(3, 5)
- 1716)

Licenciado Don
Nicolás Valderas
Terán y Santa
Cruz

ESTATES

1. Calupe
2. Callanca
3. Cayaltí
4. Collús
5. Pomalca
6. Rafán
7. Samán
8. Unidentified

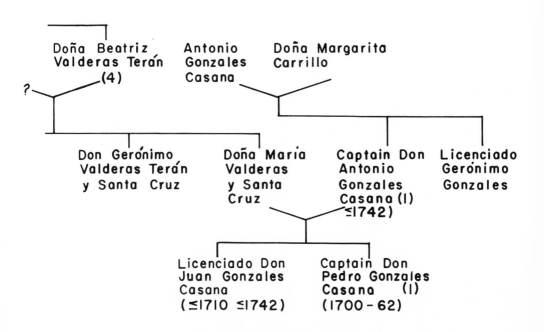

Figure 24, continued.

By then, too, this family had been linked to the Saavedra clan when Cavanillas's grandnephew married Fragoso's great granddaughter.

Examples of other prominent landed families which predate 1650 are those founded by Captain Francisco Núñez Montes, whose heirs owned San Juan for three generations and who married into the family who owned Oyotún, Cayaltí, and Cojal (which included Popán, La Candelaria and Aberru); Captain Juan Flores Osorio (see Fig. 28), whose descendants held Sárrapo for four generations; and Don Gerónimo Rodríguez, the mestizo son of the peninsular Spaniard Alonso Rodríguez and the native chieftain (*cacica*) of the Indian community of Jayanca, whose patronym was associated with La Punta, Collique, and Sipán for three generations. But his children moved to Lima and the family's presence in Lambayeque becomes obscure in the 1670s.[44]

A relatively small number of families, in contrast, were members of the landed elite for only one or two generations. Four different individuals held El Molino successively, with none owning it for even as long as a decade. The Garrosas and the Arriolas also dropped out. These families typically controlled the smallest and least capitalized estates in the area. They usually purchased the estates, but did not have the resources to maintain and expand their productive capacity and were eventually forced to sell. These sales were frequented by aspiring newcomers. The possibility of acquiring these smaller estates gave landless bureaucrats and other enterprising local inhabitants the hope of one day becoming landowners, thereby reinforcing their identification with the landed elite and their propensity to cooperate.[45]

Established elite families claimed landed status by virtue of holding one or more estates over several generations. As illustrated in Figure 13, Blas Fragoso and his heirs owned an estancia and its tina y tenería for a total of seven generations (five before 1719 and two after). The Medinas owned Santequepe and Saltrapón for five generations. In addition to this vertical tradition of land tenure, the family histories reveal a second or horizontal pattern of landholding, by which collateral members of an extended family or clan owned an estate. Descent did not always lead from father to son, but often from father to daughter and son-in-law or from father to niece or nephew.

Also, over the years, as the elite families intermarried and inbred, one functioning kinship group often held several estates concurrently. Many families evidenced both patterns of tenure simultaneously. Besides the tina y tenería, Fragoso's family held the estates of Popán, San Lorenzo, Sololipe, Collús, Sasape, and Íllimo. Likewise, Diego de

Cavanillas's heirs eventually owned Cayaltí, Collús, Calupe, Samán, Rafán, and Pomalca, among others.[46]

The formation of these large, interconnected family groups—made up of dynamic individuals who directed the agricultural development of the region, while holding positions in the bureaucracy, municipal government, and local militia as well—created the impression that the group of landowners was quite large, when in reality the number of hacendados was declining. The growth of the estates in size and productivity and the formation of the hacienda y trapiche resulted in a further concentration of property and the means of production and a corresponding reduction in the already small size of the white landowning group. In any given year, the number of hacendados was thirty or fewer. When the Jesuits united Tumán, Picsi, and Chongoyape, the number of landowners, by then largely creole, decreased by three. The number of landowners was further reduced as individuals acquired additional estates. Bachiller Don Francisco de Palma y Vera, for example, owned simultaneously San Cristóbal (which already included Leviche, Collazos, and Miraflores), Chumbenique, Oyotún, Íllimo, and Calupe. The Alférez Real Martín Núñez de Arze owned Pomalca, Cayaltí, Collús, Samán, and Calupe until his death. Pedro Gamarra y Urquiza owned San Cristóbal, Cojal, and Ucupe. Others, like Ripalda, Escurra, Seña, and Saavedra Cavero, owned two estates at the same time. This phenomenon of multiple ownership of estates reduced the number of hacendados during the thirty years between 1690 and 1719 to as few as twenty.[47]

The concentration of position and influence in these families was even greater than the patterns of land tenure and the landholders' multiple roles in society suggest, because landless members of these families held influential positions in Lambayeque and family ties were strong. Family was important to the landowners, and, because they could use kin to control the productive resources of the district, they were willing to aid even distant family members. Landowners maintained close contact with landless branches of their extended family that might not be as well off economically because relatives often held positions in the royal bureaucracy or municipal council or were competent professionals and proved an important reservoir of influence. To reciprocate for favors from their kinsmen, landowners made generous contributions to the dowries of the daughters of their "poorer" relations, invited them to social gatherings, or made them the beneficiaries of a chantry or religious trust. Compadrazgo reinforced distant kinship relations as did business, financial, and legal dealings. Relatives represented each other in legal matters, posted bond for each other, became business associates, lent each other money, and purchased office from one another to keep wealth, position, and property within the trusted circle. Regardless of relative position or landowning status, the various branches considered themselves part of one large family and cooperated with one another, using kinship as a basis on which to relate and act together to enhance the status and position of the group.[48]

Landowners, as in the past, also cooperated with others outside the family. One landowner often served as the commercial agent for one or more friends and associates. The Governor Don Juan Bonifacio de Seña, for example, purchased sugar from the brothers, Don Juan and Licenciado Don Félix Rodríguez Carrasco, the owners of La Punta, and marketed it with his own. To increase his volume, he extended credit to other sugar producers and allowed them to repay him in kind. Persons traveling to the Portobelo fair or to Lima procured imports for those who remained in Lambayeque. Transactions in which one landowner sold to another imported goods, especially slaves, frequently appear in notarial registers of the period. Landowners also guaranteed each other. Don Agustín Gerónimo de Velasco y Silva, who inherited the title of Marqués de Villablanca, bonded Captain Don Juan Gonzales Bohordo y Carranza for the purchase of seventeen slaves. The Marqués stood surety for Don Juan de la Cueva y Velasco as Saña's tithe collector in 1698 and again when de la Cueva bid on the right to collect the sales tax. De la Cueva's unexpected death and default of almost eleven thousand pesos hastened the Marqués's own impoverishment. In legal matters, landowners gave each other power of attorney to buy and sell merchandise and land, collect debts, issue wills, and represent each other before the bench.[49]

To fix and fortify their position in those few aspects of local life that they did not control, hacendados carefully cultivated close ties with persons outside their privileged circle, especially with those in key administrative positions in the province. As before, a favorite mechanism for forming such ties was for landowners to do favors to build up obligations that would make the hacendados' future requests for reciprocity impossible to refuse. Landowners, in short, used their wealth and position to keep other members of society dependent. Easily documented ties show the vast extent of this informal network: the connections between landowners and the landless extended to every level of local administration and involved many professionals and Indian officials as well. Corregidores, for example, still relied on landowners to post their bond. Bachiller Don Francisco de Palma y Vera, Don Joseph Romero de Luque, Alonso Rodríguez de Losada, Licenciado Manuel Pantoja, and Doña María Galindo y Saavedra guaranteed the Corregidor Don Luis Venegas Osorio in 1686.[50] Landowners rallied to the support of Don Tomás de Andrade y Peñaranda, the comptroller and judge of the royal treasury, when he was recalled to Lima to answer charges of fraud and malfeasance in office. The list of Andrade y Peñaranda's guarantors is a who's who of the major landowners and provincial officials of the area. As an administrator of the royal treasury, Andrade y Peñaranda had constant dealings with members of the landed elite and had done them innumerable favors, such as helping to establish religious trusts or mortgages on estates, facilitating the settlement of intestate wills, collecting taxes (allegedly at below the official rate), and, perhaps most important in the eyes of the royal bureaucrats who were trying him, providing landowners with unauthorized loans totaling thousands of pesos from the royal treasury.[51]

Landowners also guaranteed lesser officials, such as the Indian commissioner and the water judge, professionals, tax farmers, and administrators of public funds; and they used their wealth and position to help and thus obligate members of local society by financing business ventures and finding employment for both skilled and unskilled individuals.[52]

To strengthen these relationships, the landowners lent their presence to certain solemn occasions. Nonlandowners considered it an honor for hacendados to stand up at their wedding or to become the godparent of a child. Landowners and their wives accepted godparent relations to children of professionals, local officials, and Indians, thus establishing recognized relationships with mutual obligations almost tantamount to those of affinal or consanguineal kinship. Dr. Don Juan Joseph Cabero, for example, became the godfather of the corregidor General Don Francisco de la Maza Bustamante's son, Blas, in 1712. Don Pedro Norberto Gutiérrez de Ocampo became the compadre of Indian couples from Lambayeque in 1685 and again in 1688.[53]

Relations with the church grew stronger during this period, not only because such a large number of the landowners' offspring joined religious orders or became secular priests, but also because the church itself owned land and was directly dependent on the wealthy for contributions, gifts, and subsidies. Landowners continued to serve as stewards of religious brotherhoods; as lay representatives of monasteries or convents in dealings with creditors and secular courts; as trustees of special funds; and as sacristans, in return for prestige and inside information on the availability of mortgage funds.

But prosperity, now as never in the past, allowed landowners to be generous. The church benefited especially from donations from the last members of old families without direct descendants to whom to leave their fabulous wealth, accumulated sometimes over more than a century and a half. Don Francisco de Palma y Vera decided to leave his vast holdings to found a Jesuit school in Saña as a lasting monument to his line. Doña Leonor de Saavedra y Monroy, disillusioned after two childless marriages—one to a judge on the Supreme Court of Quito, who squandered thousands of her patrimony—charged the administrator of her will with founding another convent. Suaso y Ferrer built a church for the Indians of Callanca with his fortune. Such relationships fostered the attitude that what was good for the landowners was also good for the church.[54]

Equally essential to the landowners' informal network were connections to high and influential authorities outside the district. Studies in Lima gave landowners the opportunity to mix with the members of the viceregal court. A few Lambayecanos, such as Dr. Don Juan de Samudio y Villalobos y Mendoza and Dr. Juan de Saavedra Cavero, qualified and served as lawyers before the audiencia in Lima before returning to Lambayeque. The friendships and acquaintances made in Lima served them well when landowners later called on these contacts to expedite settlement of lawsuits. Other landowners had relatives who were either lawyers or judges on the royal audiencia. Marriages with viceregal authorities were encouraged. Don Joseph Barreto Aragón y Castro married the daughter of a prominent lawyer in Lima. Doña Magdalena Estrada y Hurtado, a wealthy widow, married Don Alonso de Castillo de Herrera, a judge on the audiencia in Quito. He later became the governor of Huancavelica (a highland province of Peru) and judge of the audiencia in Lima, ending his career as president of that august body.[55]

To appreciate the extent of these connections and the pervasive influence and central position of individual landowners and their families, one need only identify and enumerate the positions held by the members of one family and the relationship of these members to other important but landless figures in local society. The eight landowners making up the immediate family of Blas Fragoso (see Fig. 13) included a lawyer, a priest, a notary, and the royal accountant and treasurer of the province. Seven of the eight held positions in the militia, ranging from second lieutenant to general and field marshal. Four were active in the municipal council, serving as aldermen, magistrates, rural constables, and defender of minors. The last was commissioned by the council to retrieve the records which the last corregidor had taken with him to Lima to defend his actions against the pirate Edward David. One represented the Inquisition. They had numerous business dealings with each other and did not hesitate to give each other power of attorney. Ties with other members of the elite and with landless persons were common. They posted bond for animal raisers, majordomos, tax farmers, various corregidores and government bureaucrats; became partners in livestock raising and tanning ventures; and lent money to and found employment for friends of friends. Five of the eight were godfathers of children of Indian officials, Spanish bureaucrats, or professionals. Finally, these eight persons owned estates in Piura; tinas y tenerías in Lambayeque, Chiclayo, Motupe and Sechura; and the estates of Íllimo, Mamape, Collús, Saltur, Luya, Sasape, La Punta, Ucupe, and San Cristóbal.[56]

Similar networks could be described for each of the major families or clans; their contacts and positions multiplied. When the complex and multiple ties which bound landed individuals and families to other members of colonial society are considered, one can appreciate the control the landowners held over local life and the ready channels of communication and influence they had with other powerful individuals.

The Politics of Resource Control

Formal participation by the landowners in the municipal council, provincial administration, and the militia proved of little importance to their roles as entrepreneurs and agricultural magnates. The town council did not control what happened on the estates. The primary task of the militia was to meet external threats. Because the Spanish colonial system of administration was well established by this time, provincial administrators rarely had an opportunity to initiate or change policy which might affect estates. One of the few examples of a landowner who did use his official position to affect the implementation of governmental policy in Lambayeque to his own and his peers' benefit was General Don Bonifacio de Gastelú Pereda Eschalez, who served as the provincial treasurer. Viceregal authorities asked him for a report on the ability of the forasteros to pay increased amounts of tribute. He reported that these Indians had plenty of land with which to support themselves and that they could pay the same amount of tribute as community members. This was untrue: forasteros forfeited their right to land when they or their forefathers left their community of origin. If they did work land, it was land they rented or acquired by marrying a community member. Gastelú Pereda knew that if the forasteros' tribute was raised, they would need cash and thereby be forced to participate more actively in the money economy by producing and selling goods or by hiring themselves out more often as day laborers. Either way, the landowners as the major consumers and employers in the area would benefit.[57]

In most cases, the landowners' complex webs of personal contacts were more useful to their business concerns than their formal political power. They knew and had dealings with most if not all of the persons with money and influence in the region, and through these relationships they procured raw materials and other factors of production. Lime, for example, was supplied to the planters and tanners by one or the other of two miners who themselves were often hacendados. Landowners with established commercial connections and factors in Tierra Firme, Trujillo, and Lima obtained other raw materials, slaves, and luxury goods for themselves and for their friends and relatives. Individual landowners called on their Indian compadres to supply them with foodstuffs and lye. Landowners also received much of the surplus capital available for investment within society through their contacts with the church.

Access to cheap Indian labor depended on these ties and an understanding with the curacas. The corregidor continued to allot mitayo labor through a personal system of patronage. This explains the willingness of the planters and ranchers to bond him and to remain silent about his abuse of the Indians. The corregidor's power and importance in this respect diminished progressively during this period, however, as the use of mitayos decreased, slaves became more available, and high taxes caused Indians to flee community life.[58]

In like manner, the hacendados' ability to engage temporary Indian labor from the communities depended on personal connections with Indian officials. Landowners willingly became compadres to Indian officials because they could then call on them to recruit labor from the community for occasional work on the estates. Temporary Indian labor reduced overhead and could be acquired without large capital expenditures. Landowners, especially sugar producers, publicly acknowledged that without an adequate supply of cheap, temporary labor to supplement their slave crews they would be ruined.[59]

The politics of water also shed light on the importance of the landed elite's informal network of personal ties. The desire for the rapid increase of agricultural production put a premium on well-watered land and pastures. Planters expanded their fields to the extent that their irrigated land permitted and then sought ways to acquire more. Without water, their extensive holdings were unsuitable for cultivation. Livestock raisers also needed abundant water to increase the capacity of their soap-making and tanning facilities.

Distribution problems and the attendant scarcity at various points along the irrigation system led to several attempts to conserve water and to use the available supply more efficiently. In the months of plenty, hacendados and Indian communities alike built reservoirs to catch and hold water. These reservoirs, however, were small and generally inadequate for large-scale irrigation. To take advantage of the water that was available, they also cleaned and repaired their irrigation networks frequently to minimize loss from seepage or evaporation.[60]

Such measures, however, did not provide the quantities of water necessary to increase significantly the scale of production that some of the landowners planned. Therefore, they went to the considerable expense of opening new canals or refurbishing existing ones to tap the rivers and divert more of the water which would otherwise flow into the ocean. As noted above, land, though abandoned, retained its inherent right to a certain percentage of the water in the nearest river or canal. Landowners acquired such land and redirected the water to cultivate fields near their operations. The Alférez Real Martín Núñez de Arze, for example, might never have attempted to acquire the 150 fanegadas from the Indians of Callanca-Monsefú if the land had lacked water rights.[61]

Attempts by Spaniards to acquire additional irrigation water from the Indians sometimes assumed a much more serious and dramatic tone than Núñez de Arze's arrangement with Callanca-Monsefú. Such attempts also illustrate the landowners' success in acquiring needed resources. Water allocation for the Indian communities was sometimes literally a matter of life or death. Any change in the allotments to communities became of immediate importance and often had a profound effect on their economic well-being and survival. Over the years, a few communities had been completely deprived of their rights to irrigation water. Eten, for example, at midcentury depended on a spring for its household water needs and, lacking irrigation water, had little land under cultivation. Its landholdings served primarily as a source of firewood and poor pasturage for domestic animals.[62]

Other Indian communities had barely enough to meet their needs. As the last to receive water from the Tayme canal, Ferreñafe's position was precarious. If for some reason the water was cut off or a landowner above the community used more than his allotment, the Indians suffered. Agricultural prosperity encouraged the Spanish to usurp water, with the result that the amount of Indian land with sufficient irrigation for year-round cultivation continually declined. Indians who could not till their lands and maintain themselves abandoned the community, often to begin working as peons on the estates. The community of Jayanca particularly felt the consequences of Spanish prosperity. Only a sufficient supply of irrigation water, acquired after 1655, saved the community from extinction.[63]

The litigation records over the irrigation canal called "Tecse" illustrate the interests of Indians and Spaniards in regard to water at this time. The dispute began when the corregidor and Indian officials, at the urging of certain hacendados, agreed at a private meeting to have the mass of Indians clean, repair, and lengthen the existing canal one-half league to one league up the valley to a point near Cerro Morropillo. The Spanish misled the Indians into believing that the viceroy had initiated the project. Soon after the impending work was announced, the Indians realized that the persons interested in cleaning and lengthening the canal were those who would benefit personally, the Spanish landowners and the Indian officials of Lambayeque with land along the canal. Indians from Ferreñafe, Collique, Sinto, and Lambayeque presented petitions opposing the action to the local authorities. It is unclear who led the mass of Indians against their curacas in this unusual initiative, but the sophisticated legal jargon and the clear, well-reasoned petitions suggest outside, professional help. When local appeals brought no results, the case was transferred to the capital.[64]

There, before the audiencia, the landowners argued that the proposed work on the Tecse would be of great benefit to both the Indians and Spaniards of the Lambayeque region and to the royal treasury. They contended that (1) the extension would open up approximately four leagues of abandoned and virgin land, "all of which was level and ready to plant," by increasing the amount of irrigation water; (2) the availability of this irrigated land would halt the steady emigration of Indians to the cities and save several communities from extinction; (3)

the project would benefit the Indians by increasing the supply of corn;[65] and (4) larger agricultural output would raise the tax revenues of the crown.

The Indians of Sinto, Collique, Lambayeque, and Ferreñafe claimed, in turn, that the Spanish conspired with the Indian leaders of Lambayeque and that their main goal was to have the Indians clean and extend the Tecse for their own use. The mass of Indians, they admitted, would benefit, to a degree, because the corregidor would be forced to distribute water according to the number of tributaries in the communities, but the powerful and "untouchable" (to use the Indians' own term) hacendados would benefit disproportionately. Because the Spaniards understood the system of legal land acquisition and had access to investment capital, they would be the ones to purchase the lands made arable by the canal, thereby qualifying for most of the irrigation water. Another immediate danger was that because the new land was above the Indian communities the Spaniards would have access to the water first and take what they wanted, leaving the Indians little better off than they were. The officials in Lima recognized the truth of the Indians' assertions, and the Tecse project was not then undertaken.[66]

The landowners also used their position and personal contacts to acquire control over more property. Control of additional land continued to be the objective of the Spanish for several reasons. As noted above, acquisition of new tracts brought the right to claim extra allotments of water, which was redirected to irrigate land more convenient to an estate's existing center of operations. Land was a safe investment and an object of speculation. Land in Pátapo purchased from the crown in the visita of 1642–43 for eight hundred pesos, for example, was sold four years later for one thousand pesos, a profit of 25 percent. Land consolidation also decreased competition. Even land that was not arable was sought by landowners for pasturage. They grazed their own herds on these lands or recouped their investment by renting grazing rights to the growing number of landless persons who owned flocks. Some landowners rented marginal land on the outskirts of their estates to Indian, mestizo, or mulatto families for extra income or labor. Wresting control of land and water from the Indians was also a means of forcing them into the local labor market.[67]

The success of landowners' attempts to acquire and retain land, legally or illegally, depended on the collaboration of key people. The purchase of Indian lands, for example, still required the written approval of both the corregidor and protector as well as their sworn statements that the sale would benefit the Indians and that the lands were not needed to pay tribute. Landowners continued to secure the endorsement of these officials when they bought Indian lands: documentation from the corregidor was submitted with the titles to Lima and was essential for confirmation.[68]

Another way in which informal contacts helped landowners to procure more land was for a friend or acquaintance to alert another if possibilities for acquisition arose. The Indian commissioner Don Juan Andrés Clavijo arranged the sale of Indian lands to an acquaintance and bought land himself while he held that position. Likewise, majordomos of the religious brotherhoods often planned the rental and sale of fraternity lands for friends. While Licenciado José de Vera y Escobar was the majordomo of the Cofradía of Santa Rosa of the parochial church of Lambayeque, he rented the lands of the brotherhood to Captain Juan de Saavedra Cavero.[69]

Even acquisition of land by the censo enfiteútico, which was a perfectly legal contract, required personal influence. Alférez Real Martín Núñez de Arze acquired the lands of Nampón, Focodám, and Lonope through this device; but he had to use his personal contacts, influence, and prestige to persuade the viceroy to confirm the contract. At Núñez de Arze's request, the corregidor endorsed the sale in terms that stressed his position as an honorable and leading local citizen who was not likely to defraud the Indians. He could be trusted to pay the annual fee to the community, which needed the funds more than the land. Always stressing the potential benefit to the crown, the corregidor argued that cultivating the land would put more persons to work and generate extra tax revenues for the royal treasury; however, he failed to mention that Núñez's primary reason for the long-term lease was to acquire water rights. Núñez de Arze also retained an established lawyer in Lima to present his petitions, and he asked friends with connections at court to impress on the viceroy the utility of the project. The viceroy was reluctant to grant Núñez de Arze permission, because he knew from experience that although such contracts only gave the new "owners" usufruct rights they often served to alienate lands indefinitely and were, in essence, mock sales. The disadvantage of this type of contract from the Indians' point of view was that it often proved difficult to make the renters pay, especially when the agreement was "in perpetuity." Núñez de Arze paid the annuity until his death, but his successors stopped paying and the Indians could not get local officials to enforce their claim. Subsequent generations of Indians either forgot the terms of the contract or did not press their demands. It was not until late in the eighteenth century that the terms of the original "sale" were "rediscovered" by a lawyer involved in a bankruptcy proceeding against the owner of the estate. In the meantime, the Indians of Callanca-Monsefú had lost both the use of the land and its income.[70]

The visita of 1711–12 provided the single most important opportunity for the Spanish landowners to use their connections to legalize their claims to land and acquire additional pastures from the crown. The visitor, Don Antonio Sarmiento de Sotomayor, was the brother of General Don Juan Sarmiento de Sotomayor, the corregidor of Saña and subsequently a member of the landowning elite. How Don Antonio managed to be named visitor in Lima is unclear, but the appointment was probably facilitated by his brother's personal contacts with upper-level viceregal administrators.[71]

The extant records of the visita show how Sarmiento de Sotomayor used his power to benefit the landowners, often at the expense of the Indians. Sarmiento de Sotomayor zealously followed his instructions regarding the review and redistribution of Indian lands. He traveled from one Indian community to another, reviewing their possession and adjusting their holdings according to population. Indian officials of Lambayeque, for example, showed Sarmiento de Sotomayor the four tracts of communal property which they claimed: Culpón with an extention of 300 fanegadas; Chancay with 78 fanegadas, some of which were too sandy to be farmed; Cadape and Sopillert, with 2,752 fanegadas; and Sialupe, with 3,760 fanegadas of arable lands—a total of 6,890 fanegadas. The visitor reassigned a total of 2,167 fanegadas in Cadape and Sopillert to the mass of Indians—giving tribute-paying males 2 fanegadas each; males excused from tribute, widows, unmarried females, and boys 1 fanegada each; the cacique principal 25 fanegadas; and his lieutenant (the *segunda persona*) 12. He set aside an additional 400 fanegadas for common use. Lambayeque's legal claim was thus reduced to a mere 30 percent of what it had previously held. He declared the 4,713 surplus fanegadas vacant and announced that the property of the crown would be auctioned as public domain to the highest bidder. Likewise, he reduced Callanca-Monsefú's holdings from 1,061.5 fanegadas in Alicán, Chichipe, and Piloplo to 408 fanegadas, declaring as surplus 653.5. Sarmiento de Sotomayor found over 2,000 fanegadas of Sinto's lands vacant—including three pieces called Chin, Falen, and Supián. The Indians of Collique lost 300 fanegadas.[72]

The hacendados rejoiced. The visita, which their predecessors had so feared, had become an occasion to legalize the land occupied over the last half-century. It was probably not an unplanned coincidence that some of the land that Sarmiento de Sotomayor proclaimed vacant was the land that the Spanish had already usurped. As in the past, the hacendados had expanded onto Indian lands, undetected for years, because some of the Indian lands that were at a distance from the community were not exploited systematically. The owner of Luya, Don Miguel de Garay, began accommodating his multiplying herds on a piece of land called "Mollapuc"—legally part of Ferreñafe—and allowed the animals to water at the irrigation canal called "Terrenoles." Occasional use became a regular practice and a corral was built. Apparently, the Ferreñafanos did not notice or did not protest this usurpation immediately. Ferreñafe often rented pastures to Spaniards, and those Indians collecting firewood who saw the herds probably assumed the owner had rented grazing rights from the curaca.[73]

Sarmiento declared Mollapuc and other usurped land "vacant" and gave the landowner the occasion to legalize his possession. Sarmiento de Sotomayor disregarded a bid from the Indian community of Mochumí in favor of Garay's bid of 200 pesos. Various amounts of the rest of the land were purchased at auction by other hacendados. Licenciado Pedro Norberto Gutiérrez de Ocampo, the parish priest and vicar of Ferreñafe, legalized his possession of Falen and purchased the lands called Supían, recently declared vacant. Captain Diego de Sotomayor (a relative of the visitor?) purchased 120 fanegadas of Lambayeque's former territory. Captain Francisco López Cano and his wife, Doña Manuela Rodríguez, bought 60 fanegadas. Don Pedro de Escurra y Saravia paid 450 pesos for lands and pastures that had belonged to the community of Túcume, facilitated perhaps by a nephew who was the priest of that community. Sarmiento de Sotomayor sold other lands to the Marqués de Villablanca for 1,000 pesos.[74]

The Indians reacted in two ways. On the one hand, the Indians of Mochumí appealed to Lima and were allowed by the viceregal authorities to take possession of Mollapuc by repaying Garay his 200 pesos. The Indians of Collique petitioned Lima and eventually won a royal decree, dated 8 July 1722, restoring the community's jurisdiction to their 300 fanegadas of land. Apparently, however, in the decade or so that elapsed between their appeal and its resolution, the Indians were deprived of the use of their lands and lost interest in them. Their legal rights were upheld too late to benefit many of those who had protested. On the other hand, a few Indian officials took this opportunity to enlarge their private landholdings. Sarmiento de Sotomayor sold the cacica of Lambayeque 54 fanegadas and her brother bought another 10.[75]

It was also during this visita that a fundamental change took place in the structure of land tenure on the northern coast. For the first time, Sarmiento de Sotomayor allowed the purchase or legalization of possession of pasturage rights. Before the visita, pastures had been legally regarded as common property, or open range. The titles to estancias gave the owners legal jurisdiction to relatively small areas of land on which to build their corrals and processing facilities; over the years, however, estancieros had often established spheres of influence which gave them effective and locally recognized control over the pastures between their asientos and their outlying ring of corrals. Nevertheless, because of their legal status, these pastures had little monetary value. Numerous bills of sale dating back to the sixteenth century show that the value of an estancia was calculated solely on the basis of the number of livestock which the owner was selling. Corrals were not valuable alone and were included in bills of sale almost as an afterthought. Thus, when Gabriel de la Requera purchased eight estancias from his half-brother, Gobernador Juan Roldán Dávila, in the late sixteenth century, he paid eleven reales per head of goats and sheep. The corrals were included in the contract as incidental to the animals. In the first years of the seventeenth century, Doña Catalina de Herrera added several estancias to Luya, paying 2 pesos each for 13,500 head of sheep and goats, or a total of 27,000 pesos. About the same time, the curaca of Lambayeque sold Diego de Soria an estancia for the price of its 1,000 head of stock.[76]

The estancia, as distinguished from the livestock, began to acquire value in and of itself after the visita of 1642–43 and the building of elaborate processing facilities. The growth of the livestock industry put a premium on pastures and encouraged ranchers to patrol those they controlled in the face of growing competition. The open range, except in the very remote upper reaches and outlying edges of the valleys, progressively disappeared.[77]

The sale of pasturage rights was beneficial to both the crown and the estate owners. The alienation of pastures was another way to earn money for the royal treasury, since legally no one had clear title to the heretofore "open" ranges. The landowners were also anxious to establish their dominion legally. For a fee, Sarmiento de Sotomayor allowed landowners to legalize their possession of the pastures on land they already used and controlled.

The sale of grazing rights, however, proved to be another despoilment of the Indian communities, because Sarmiento de Sotomayor also allowed Spanish hacendados to purchase the pastures which grew on Indian lands. Sarmiento de Sotomayor, for example, sold to the community of Monsefú-Callanca for 400 pesos the 653.5 fanegadas of lands he had found over and above that which the community needed. He sold the rights to the pastures on those 653.5 fanegadas to the owner of Collús, Don Bonifacio de Gastelú, for 300 pesos. The owner of Luya purchased pasturage rights on land belonging to the Indians of Ferreñafe. The Jesuit owners of Tumán acquired the right to the pastures on the lands of Lambayeque and Chiclayo. Thus, the visita not only denied the Indians part of their land, but it also resulted in the loss of pastures and woodlands essential to their economy and subsistence.[78]

Sarmiento de Sotomayor's ties to the landowners made him sympathetic to their urgings. He stretched the law and allowed them to make blanket *composiciones* without bothering to verify their claims. Gastelú, for example, paid the crown 200 pesos to cover whatever excess lands were found within the stated boundaries of Collús in future measurements. This composición was admitted on the basis of Gastelú's "word" as an "honorable" man and without other legal proof or a new survey. Across the valley, the owner of Luya, Don Miguel de Robles y Garay, paid 100 pesos for whatever excess lands might lie within the boundaries of his estate "to avoid the cost and annoyances that subsequent title reviews and land surveys might cause." Both composiciones were confirmed in Lima by competent authorities, without verifying the boundaries. Both were granted with the condition that any excesses would "not harm third parties" and with the condition that the confirmation be null if the declarations were proven false. The records of a court case over the properties revealed just how false their declarations were. The owner of Luya, for example, exaggerated his boundaries to include all of the communal lands of Ferreñafe, most of those of Picsi, 400 fanegadas of vacant land, and the 60 fanegadas of Supián. These examples show how easily the landowners subverted officials, the visitor, and the corregidor and that the only recourse for the Indians was an uncertain appeal to higher authorities in Lima.[79]

The landowners' territorial expansion was not always at the expense of the Indians. Their desire for land sometimes pitted one planter or rancher against another, especially as prosperity faded after 1700. The real reason why Don Miguel de Robles y Garay was so anxious for Sarmiento de Sotomayor to allow him to make a blanket composición was revealed in a notarized confession made shortly after his death, some thirty years later. The statement told how at the time of the visita Don Miguel was engaged in a lawsuit against the ex-corregidor and then owner of Sicán, Don Joseph de la Parra, over the lands called Pítipo. Robles y Garay asked his friend and confidant (and the declarant), Don Pedro de Quiroga, to ask his friend, the master silversmith Estanislao Ruiz, to do him a favor. Through Quiroga, Don Miguel met and convinced Ruiz to prepare ink to match that of the titles of his estate. The ink was used to alter the titles to include the land in dispute. When Quiroga found out what Don Miguel had asked Ruiz to do, he confronted Robles y Garay. Robles y Garay insulted him, so Quiroga informed the owner of Sicán. Robles y Garay, however, asked his good friend, the notary Don Bartolomé Pérez Zavala, to authenticate the titles and declare in his favor in court. Quiroga fled to Lima for five years without testifying on behalf of de la Parra, and the judge awarded Pítipo to Robles y Garay. Quiroga made the declaration to clear his own conscience, but it was apparently recorded and forgotten in the register of the notary Pérez Zavala's successor. This example provides a final clear illustration of how important the informal network of kinship and friendship—power politics—was in colonial society to gain control over the additional local resources needed to expand and improve the estates; it also foreshadows the subsequent fragmentation of the landowning elite during the eighteenth century.[80]

Thus, the economic development of Lambayeque reinforced its social transformation. The best-connected individuals adeptly used their wealth and position to expand the scale of production, thus enlarging their economic base. Such movements had a snowball effect in that their investments paid off and allowed them to continue making money, which in turn fortified their social and political standing. The power associated with this position, and exercised through personal connections, helps to explain how landowners obtained the labor, irrigation water, and land needed to expand their estates which they could not otherwise have acquired through voluntary and legitimate channels. Although the most intense estate-building phase ended in the 1680s— and there is evidence that later generations of landowners were not as preoccupied with or as vigorous in their attempts to maximize the returns from the estates—land remained in the same families for generations. They became established as the nucleus of a creole aristocracy, whose members—given the neglect of viceregal authorities and the cooperation of local officials—became the true masters of the region in a style reminiscent of the encomenderos of the sixteenth century. Consolidation and concentration also made the elite more exclusive, since it now took much more capital and resources to gain entrance into their privileged circle than it had in the previous period. Social mobility became more difficult, but was not altogether impossible, especially during the most dynamic phases of the process. This establishment contrasts sharply with the social instability that characterized the previous period and the one that followed.[81]

PART THREE

Social Consequences of Economic Stagnation and Decline

A series of natural disasters and adverse market conditions in the first thirty years of the eighteenth century initiated a cycle of debt and bankruptcy, which ruined the estates and the old landed elite. The slow process of recovery, first visible about midcentury, encouraged priests, merchants, and public administrators, among others, gradually to acquire the land. Many of the latter arrived in the area in connection with the Bourbon reforms, designed to streamline colonial administrative machinery to make it more efficient and profitable, to reassert royal authority, and to improve the defense of the kingdom. Generous salaries, which the crown hoped would guarantee the allegiance of newly arrived peninsular administrators, allowed the highest-ranking officials to buy land. However zealously and resolutely these provincial bureaucrats proclaimed the crown's rights upon arrival, their possibilities of upward social mobility rapidly undermined official concerns as they began to identify with the landed interests. The economic and psychological distance between the two groups diminished, providing continuity between the old and new members of the elite. The other new members were not torn by such contradictory allegiances and assumed their roles easily. Although the names and faces of the landed elite changed, land tenure and the modalities of power remained largely unaltered.

7 Agricultural Crisis and Elite Transformation, 1720–1824

In contrast to the expansion and prosperity of the previous century, the 1700s, especially after 1720, were years of economic reversals. The economic about-face did not occur overnight. Hard times began about the turn of the century, but hacendados did not recognize them as such until the 1720s and 1730s. The twenty-five or thirty-year interim period was one of transition and relative stagnation. Slowdown turned into crisis following the floods of 1720 and 1728. The effort to rebuild bankrupted many landowners and their families and gave a group of persons, many of whom had made relatively modest fortunes as clerics, merchants, and bureaucrats, the opportunity to acquire gradually the estates and move into the central position of society.

Agricultural Crisis

Indications of the impending agricultural crisis appeared late in the seventeenth century with the marked decline in the price of the most important product of the region.[1] Figure 8 shows that the high sugar prices of the 1690s were ephemeral. They fell sharply thereafter and remained depressed for another forty years. The effects of the drop were somewhat mitigated by the protection against such downward fluctuations built into the haciendas y trapiches in the second half of the seventeenth century by the annexation of estancias. Ranching compensated, in part, for the decline, because the prices of livestock (as shown in Fig. 7) remained more stable.

Despite these price trends, landowners and their creditors remained cautiously optimistic and steadfastly refused to heed the omens of economic contraction. Sugar producers, overconfident and still heady from a century or more of expansion, remembered the high prices of

211

the 1690s. Most viewed the price drop as a temporary phenomenon and refused to believe that the spiral could continue. They anticipated a general reversal and upsurge, and at least a decade of high prices similar to the one at midcentury. Seasonal and annual price fluctuations, and a slow and slight rise in the price of sugar after 1705–1706, kept their hopes alive. The owners of haciendas and estancias remained confident because market conditions for their products changed little.[2]

Moreover, even at their nadir, prices appear not to have been so low that producers could not break even, especially when they received income from the sale of products other than just sugar or from pasturage rents. Expansion on the estates continued, albeit at a progressively slower pace than before. Importation of slaves and fine articles for the homes and families of the landed elite did not noticeably decline. Landowners dismissed the inability of a few to pay their accumulated debts as atypical cases.[3]

What shocked the landowners, especially the sugar producers, into recognizing the realities of the new economic order were the cumulative effects of a series of natural disasters that marked the beginning of a period of prolonged economic upset. These disasters shook their confidence and changed their optimism into pessimism as they began readily to admit hard times.

The first setback occurred in 1701 and primarily affected the haciendas y trapiches. A plague of rats and mice invaded the valleys, gnawing at the cane and decimating entire fields. At cutting time, as much as one-third of the cane proved unsuitable for processing. Because cane is a perennial crop, which can be harvested up to five times before falling yields make replanting advisable, the effects of the plague were still felt years later. Assuming a growing period of eighteen to twenty-four months between harvests, any given field was renewed only once every eight to ten years; that is, roughly 10 to 12 percent of the land in cane was replanted annually. The damage caused by the rodents required the immediate resowing of at least one-third of the cane fields, an unexpected and heavy burden on the resources of the estates. Hacienda records indicate that laborers worked two full years to replant the damaged cane fields and that near normal production resumed only when the first of this cane matured in 1704–1705.[4]

This damage paled in comparison to that caused to the estates by the floods of 1720 and 1728. Floods were not uncommon in the area. The rivers had overflowed their banks in 1578 and 1624, causing extensive damage to the irrigation network. In 1578, when native Indian labor was still abundant, the corregidor mobilized from two to three thousand Indian workers from the surrounding communities to clean and repair the canals in a matter of weeks. In 1624, the landowners reopened the ditches at their own expense, without lasting hardship.[5]

Estate owners planned on some annual water damage and geared their production cycle accordingly. They programmed their activities by holding in mind the extra labor demands needed to keep the irrigation network functional during the heavy water flow of summer and by taking precautions to guard against possible problems. In preparation for summer, administrators routinely stocked up on flour, corn, beans, and meat because swollen rivers sometimes cut off supplies from the mountains and surrounding valleys. Sugar was sent to Lima each spring to prevent spoilage and loss. Any sugar remaining on the estate was packaged or wrapped carefully to protect it from dampness. During the extraordinary summers when floods threatened, ditches were dug in the floors of buildings for drainage.[6]

Such preparations were far from sufficient to save the estates from the ravages of the Lambayeque and Saña Rivers in 1720. The rivers overflowed, drowning entire herds of livestock and destroying many of the buildings on the estates. Cayaltí was totally ruined. Sipán lost its boiling house and irrigation canal. The Canal Tayme became clogged in several places with silt and debris, leaving the community of Ferreñafe, the hacienda y trapiche of Tumán, and the estancia of Luya without irrigation water for seasons to come. In the Lambayeque and Saña Valleys, the flood uprooted most of the cane and alfalfa and ruined some pastures and algarrobo forests. The flood leveled the city of Saña: not a single house remained standing.[7]

Cleanup efforts were long and costly. Indian communities and estate owners cooperated, providing labor and supplies and draft animals, respectively, for the reconstruction of the major canals. In addition, each hacendado faced the expense of repairing the damage to his own irrigation infrastructure and other installations. The owner of Pomalca, Don Francisco de Seña, spent 14,600 pesos to clean his canals and to reconstruct and repair his offices, the laborers' residences, the boiling house, and the purifying house. Throughout this period, Seña and the other agriculturalists of the valleys had to pay wages and maintain their slaves, while food prices skyrocketed. The price of a fanega of corn, to cite just one example, increased from about two pesos to nine.[8]

The hacendados undertook these repairs under very trying circumstances. Production was at a standstill. Livestock herds had been reduced to a fraction of their former size. Milling equipment needed to be replaced. The destruction of the irrigation network deprived the estates of water. Sipán, for instance, remained without water for almost a year after the 1720 disaster, making replanting impossible. After the canals became functional, eighteen months or more elapsed before the first new cane matured and was ready to be cut. Most of the estate owners, therefore, lost over two years' income, adding to the hardships.[9]

The estates had not been totally reconditioned and were still far from having regained normal output levels when a second major flood occurred in 1728. Residents of partially rebuilt Saña abandoned it to take up residence in the Indian towns of Lambayeque and Chiclayo. Again, the estate owners were unable to produce and were forced to make significant outlays to repair and replace their production facilities.[10]

The conjuncture, then, of declining prices, three successive periods of unproductivity, and the unexpected and extraordinary expenses of rebuilding the estates left the landowners in dire economic straits and brought to an end the expansive mood of the previous era. The construction of new irrigation canals designed to bring additional land under production stopped. Owners acquired no new capital equipment to increase processing capacity. The emphasis was on rebuilding and regaining previous levels of production.

After the floods, full recovery from what most persons had hoped would be a short period of stagnation became more and more distant by the worsening cost-price squeeze. As Figure 8 shows, the price of sugar remained almost stable in the 1720s and 1730s, and then fell before enjoying an uneven resurgence at midcentury. Prices then dropped again before stabilizing at a lower level. Average sugar prices for the period were 28 percent below those of the years between 1650 and 1719. The prices of soap and hides, the principal products of the pastoral industry, were far less volatile. The price of goats and sheep rose gradually until midcentury and then dropped slightly. Soap prices remained steady until the 1760s. The gains made during the last two or three decades of the century resulted in a more than 20 percent increase in average prices for soap and cut the losses from the sale of tanned hides to a mere 2 percent for the period.[11]

Hacendados blamed competition for the low prices. Pedro Gamarra y Urquiza, a farsighted newcomer to the area, recognized a major problem of the sugar industry when he complained that "we expect the price of sugar to continue falling, because of the well-known fact that many haciendas y trapiches are being founded in these valleys, those near Lima and other parts. . . ." Lambayecan sugar producers were not the only persons to have responded to the boom conditions of the seventeenth century.[12]

Although no new large-scale sugar producing operations were established in the region after 1700, eighteenth-century sources mention small-scale sugar mills which could compete effectively with the larger estates for a certain sector of the market.The *Informaciones geográficas*, a survey report of the geography and economic state of the district written by royal bureaucrats between 1803 and 1805, declares:

> Indians have begun making sugar too, which by maintaining production at high levels, has ruined the haciendas.

The truth of the statement is corroborated by the fact that at least eight and as many as twenty-four "trapichitos," as the small counterparts of the haciendas y trapiches were called, were established on the community lands of Reque. Others were founded by both Indians and mestizos on the lands of Lambayeque and elsewhere along the coast.[13]

The word "sugar" in the above quote must not be taken literally. These rudimentary operations consisted of little more than a grinding mill, a few boiling vats, and numerous clay or wooden molds. Such small-scale operations primarily produced *chancaca* (a low-grade raw sugar sold in cake form), molasses, and alcohol. The chancaca and molasses, as relatively low-cost substitutes for refined sugar, found a growing market among the Indians, mestizos, and mulattoes, who over the years had been steadily joining the money economy. Hence, these mills were not serious competition for the bulk of hacienda y trapiche production because sugar and chancaca did not compete for the same buyers. But Spanish producers did lose part of the local market and thus were deprived of one source of income.[14]

If local competition did not increase significantly, competition from estates in other coastal valleys, especially from those closer to Lima, was substantial. By the end of the eighteenth century, sugar estates had been established in nearly every coastal valley between Lima and Lambayeque. Of forty-four estates in the valleys close to Trujillo, eighteen specialized in sugar. Katherine Coleman reports that many estate owners around the city of Trujillo switched from wheat to sugar production in an effort to recoup some of their losses due to an outbreak of wheat smut during the last decade of the seventeenth century. The

Jesuits, known for their efficient administration, owned at least thirteen large sugar estates in the valleys of Ilo, Pisco, Chincha, Rimac, Chancay, Huaura, and Santa. Nicholas Cushner provides data to show that production on these Jesuit-run estates peaked in the eighteenth century. Yields on the hacienda of Huaura topped 12,000 arrobas in the 1750s and 1760s, but production had been rising as early as 1687. The hacienda of Regis in the Chincha Valley produced 17,000 arrobas in 1759; and in the nearby Pisco Valley, sugar production on the more modest hacienda of Caucato rose three times between 1760 and 1766 to an average of more than 3,250 arrobas.[15]

Furthermore, sugar production had spread to temperate highland valleys. The temporary disruption of production and provision of the highland markets of Lambayeque, and the high prices after the 1687 earthquake, encouraged the establishment of small sugar mills in Cajamarca and Huamachuco. The coastal hacendados who had long served as their highland counterparts' commercial agents perhaps unwittingly contributed to the loss of this market by selling sugar technology to highland estate owners. The owner of Pomalca, for example, supervised the construction of a bronze sugar mill and sent it to a landowner in the northern sierra in the early 1770s; thereafter, shipments of sugar and molasses to his highland buyers ceased. The *Informaciones geográficas* for other districts in Peru mention sugar estates in the highland valleys of Abancay, Aymaraez, and Urubamba. Growing conditions in highland valleys were inferior to those on the coast, but high transportation costs protected these less efficient operations. Thus, since there is no reason to believe that aggregate demand for sugar was declining, it must be concluded that production was clearly outstripping any rise in demand which might have been due to population growth or to increased consumption.[16]

The loss of traditional Peruvian markets was certainly a heavy blow for the sugar industry of Lambayeque, but of equal or greater importance was the loss of markets outside the viceroyalty. The second half of the seventeenth century saw the sugar industry take root and grow in the Antilles. By the eighteenth century, the Antillean producers were among the most efficient and prosperous in the world. As noted above, one of the principal outlets for the sugar of the region had been the Portobelo fair. Now, Antillean producers were in a more advantageous position than Peruvian producers to supply this and other nearby markets. The suppression of the *flota* (escorted fleet of ships) system by the crown in 1740, and the subsequent disappearance of the fair, permanently and vastly reduced the shipments from Lambayeque to this northern market. After the middle of the eighteenth century, little sugar, molasses, and preserves were sent to the formerly important markets of Tierra Firme and Guayaquil.[17]

The Bourbon free-trade policies initiated in the late 1770s, and the official opening of the port of Buenos Aires, further restricted the distant markets of the region. Sugar producers believed that one reason for their continuing troubles was the large-scale, illegal importation of cheaper Brazilian sugar into the Spanish empire through this port. Lambayecan sugar could not compete and was confined for the most part to the southern markets of Lima and Chile. In some years, the glut forced the producers to dump all or part of their annual production on the local market, where prices were comparatively low.[18]

Increasing competition also accounts for the fall in the price of tanned hides. After the floods, animal raising became an immediate and logical alternative to sugar production. Herds were again growing when the loss of the important market of Portobelo forced local ranchers to switch markets. Most sent their products to Lima, where they encountered stiff competition from other established breeders on the coast as far south as Chile.[19]

While prices remained relatively stable or dropped, the costs of production rose. The average prices of raw materials, such as copper, increased by over one-third from the previous period. The cost of milling rose nearly 20 percent, as measured by the price of oxen, between 1742 and 1779. With the average price of corn up more than 100 percent and the cost of beans up some 300 percent, the cost of maintaining the labor force also rose steadily.[20]

Abnormally high demand for unskilled laborers in the 1720s and 1730s, followed by disrupted international trade and competition for skilled slaves, contributed to the related problem of labor procurement. Although the average price of an unskilled, prime-aged male slave dropped by about 10 percent from the previous period, the average price of skilled slaves rose. These trends, given the almost 30 percent drop in sugar prices, placed slaves out of the reach of all but a few producers. But even those with the liquidity to buy slaves often could not do so. Warfare and the suppression of the flota system disrupted the flow of slaves and other goods, making scarcity a problem after 1700. The rapidly developing and prosperous Antillean sugar industry provided a more readily accessible and probably more profitable alternative to slave traders than the Peruvian market. The supply of creole slaves put up for sale within the viceroyalty was also inadequate to meet demand. Producers, therefore, tended to replace only the skilled slaves needed for the milling process. Those who could not afford to purchase slaves relied increasingly on resident peons and hired labor for most tasks. The demographic recovery of the native population kept the local labor shortage within tolerable limits, but with demand outstripping supply the wages of unskilled Indian laborers rose to 2.5 and 3 reales per day in some seasons, up from the standard rate of 2 reales of the previous period. The cost of hiring slaves also increased to 2.5 to 4 reales per day between 1727 and 1812, depending on the work, the slave's skill or training, the length of employment, and whether or not the employer furnished food.[21]

Another factor that contributed to the deterioration and ruin of the estates was the tax burden. Administrative reorganization and new taxes were key elements of the Bourbon plan to make Peru and other American possessions produce revenues for Spain. A sales tax (*alcabala*) of 2 percent had been introduced in the late sixteenth century on all cash transactions, except those involving essential foodstuffs, horses, books, and goods bought by or sold to Indians. The tax rate increased to 4 percent in Lambayeque in 1639. The percentage that was actually collected, however, varied and rarely equalled the face value of the tax. The reason for this was that the crown leased the right to collect the sales tax to private individuals—in much the same way that the right to collect the tithe was rented out. Tax farmers perennially underestimated its value by as much as four to one. Because leasees paid the crown far less for the right to collect the tax than its true value, they could afford to collect proportionately less. Assuming that the landowners had grown accustomed to paying far less than the 4 percent, as one administrator complained, then the direct and systematic collection of the tax at face value by government bureaucrats was tantamount to a sharp increase in the tax rate. Then, as early as 1778, the crown raised the official rate yet another 2 percent.[22]

In addition to the general tax hikes, the crown imposed new taxes on the sugar industry. In 1746, the Viceroy Conde de Superunda (1745–61) ordered the cane growers to pay a duty on each arroba of sugar and jug (*botija*) of molasses produced. Twenty years later, the government began taxing cane alcohol at the rate of one real per jug.[23]

The cost-price squeeze and the new taxes made it increasingly difficult for the landowners, especially the sugar producers who had borrowed to rebuild after the floods, to meet their mounting financial obligations. They continued to seek loans and spend whatever income they earned to keep the estates running and to maintain their life-style. After 1720, the debt burden of the estates rose rapidly. Figure 16 indicates the degree to which various estates were mortgaged to cover debts. The debt burden of Calupe rose from about 26 percent in the 1690s to 36 percent after the plague of rodents decimated its fields—almost double that between 1715 and 1719—and another 60 percent after the first flood. The debt of Cayaltí, another hard-hit sugar estate, climbed by almost 16 points between 1706 and 1717. Some of the sharpest rises occurred in the second decade of the eighteenth century, perhaps reflecting the lingering optimism of the landowners and the fact that, because destruction was localized, credit was still plentiful. Overall, the average debt increased from 40 percent between 1650 and 1719 to almost 65 percent between 1720 and 1810. The mortgages and liens on eight estates totaled their assessed value and more.[24]

Not all the rising debt burden can be attributed to productive investment and to maintaining standards of living. Part of it represents the unpaid interest on the obras pías and capellanías established for family members during the heyday of the last period. During the years of rebuilding and underproduction, the owners could not meet their accumulating interest obligations. Interest in arrears was often imposed as another mortgage at the standard rate of 5 percent. Part of the burden of debt reflects the legal prohibition of cutting any children off from inheritance. Most parents preferred to settle heirs' claims while still alive by giving them dowries to marry or to enter a convent or monastery. Other landowners, unable or unwilling to physically partition the estates and with no other means to settle claims, established censos on their estates to guarantee heirs a lifelong source of income. A classic example was provided by the Maestro de Campo Don Joseph de Briones y Medina, who left eight heirs, including two daughters and two grandchildren, a total endowment of 24,000 pesos in his estate of La Otra Banda in the 1730s. The fact that more of the children survived to adulthood added to the problem of providing suitable endowments for all claimants; this was in contrast to the sixteenth and early seventeenth centuries, when some aging fathers gave entire estates to dower their daughters for lack of another heir. The interest on these endowments also had to be paid at an annual rate of 5 percent, whether or not the estate was productive. In this sense the natural disasters and cost-price squeeze were but catalysts that allowed the profligate spending habits and unproductive mortgages of the past to accelerate decay.[25]

Eventually, the financial condition of most landowners gave them no choice but to suspend payments on accumulating interest and loan payments. At first, creditors, especially the church, rather than press their claims went along with this unofficial moratorium and continued to lend the hacendados additional funds to meet routine operating expenses. Thereafter, the church continued to be lenient, often waiting years for repayment or accepting payment of the interest in kind. The Augustinians accepted interest in sugar, consuming part and selling the rest at a loss. The friars preferred this arrangement to default or to foreclosure proceedings. Other creditors often had no choice.[26]

Despite this tolerance, creditors eventually cut credit and foreclosed to recover what they could of their original principals. They initiated bankruptcy proceedings, usually after the death of the owner, against Chumbenique (1729), San Cristóbal (1729), Popán (1735), Cojal (1760), La Otra Banda (1762), Collús (1763), Pomalca (1775), Cayaltí (1785), Saltur (1786), and Luya (1802). When Don Francisco de Seña y Chirinos died in 1739, creditors pressured his heirs to sell Pomalca and his other property to satisfy their claims. Calupe was deeply in debt at the death of its owner, Don Antonio Gonzales Casana. Don Pedro, Don Antonio's son, had arranged in 1731 to acquire the estate after his father's death by paying him 80,000 pesos, less the value of its mortgages and legacies. Don Pedro took possession of Calupe in 1740, but his father's creditors—among whom was Don Francisco Malerva, a priest who doubled as his father's agent in Lima and who later owned Pomalca and Collús—pressed him for satisfaction. Don Pedro managed to secure financial backing and hold on to Calupe until 1756, when the estate was embargoed and placed under church administration. The immediate reason for the seizure was an epidemic of measles or smallpox which killed sixty slaves, a major financial loss that deprived Don Pedro of the means with which he had hoped to regain solvency.[27]

In other cases, owners declared themselves bankrupt to prevent sinking deeper into debt. For example, after Don Francisco de Seña's death, General Don Domingo Navarrete y Fernández, a peninsular Spaniard and ex-corregidor and chief justice of the district of Chiclayo (1734–40), and General Baltazar de Ayesta, a wealthy Limeño merchant, formed a partnership to purchase and run Pomalca. Navarrete acted as resident administrator on the estate, while Ayesta served as his factor in the capital. Together, the two invested thousands of pesos to improve the irrigation infrastructure and to replace capital equipment. The 7,000 pesos they earmarked for the purchase of slaves were never spent because of the extreme scarcity of slaves. Unable to secure the skilled labor needed for full production and, consequently, without the means to pay the accumulating interest, Navarrete decided to give up the estate. In explaining his reason for breaking his contract with Ayesta and for declaring bankruptcy, Navarrete said that Pomalca was decadent, unproductive, and unprofitable. A summary of the accounts for the years 1743 and 1750, submitted to the audiencia in the suit to terminate the partnership, showed a deficit of 6,631 pesos. Prospects for the future looked no better, leaving no alternative but to relinquish the estate.[28]

Such bankruptcies produced costly disruptions of production. Lengthy court proceedings meant church or state administration of an estate while creditors submitted documentation to substantiate their claims. Inventories and itemized assessments were taken. Judges, notaries, and various religious and secular officials had to be present and paid. The administrator of an estate under deposit earned an average of 1,000 to 1,200 pesos annually. These extra costs were added to the amount already due and deducted from the earnings of the estate or from the purchase price upon its sale.[29]

Besides the burden of extra costs, estates under deposit were mismanaged. Embargoed estates usually had a succession of administrators who disrupted the routine and functioning of the estates each time they changed jobs. Moreover, administrators did not take as good care of the property as would an owner. They usually did not invest in the estate and were lax in making needed repairs. In several cases, administrators were accused of gross mismanagement and fraud, which resulted in their personal enrichment and in the decapitalization of the property. Neither church nor government officials supervised the management with the eye for details that an owner had; so administrative corruption went undiscovered for years, too late for corrective measures to be taken or for the losses to be recouped. The available accounts show that rarely did an estate under deposit produce a profit.[30]

Delays in settling all the claims contributed to the ruin of the estates. La Otra Banda was embargoed and under "temporary" administration over twelve years. Other bankruptcy proceedings dragged on even longer. Pomalca, Collús, and Samán, for example, were embargoed after the death of Don Francisco Malerva in 1775 and not sold until 1784. Authorities did not straighten out and settle the accounts, however, until 1804.[31]

Contemporaries recognized that legal embroilments of this nature exacerbated the problems of the estates. One observer noted that

> the destruction of so many haciendas in said valley,
> whose fields are reduced to scrub and brush, has
> resulted . . . in a loss of more than one million
> pesos . . . ; not because of any defect in the land,
> but because of a lack of workers and primarily
> because of . . . the law and embargoes associated
> with bankruptcy proceedings which are
> interminable and lead to ruin.

In writing about the entire northern coast district in 1760, Miguel Feyjóo de Sosa, corregidor of Trujillo, argued that bankruptcy proceedings were not advisable for either the estates or their creditors. To the estates, foreclosure meant many years of additional costs and poor administration, while creditors risked "losing" the entire principal of a legacy. Given the poor economic conditions, he cautioned that creditors would be better advised to accept a small return on their investment, even if they were paid in kind.[32]

His remarks went unheeded. The recurrent pattern of debt, bankruptcy, deposit, and sale led to plummeting real estate values. Calupe, appraised in 1741 at 52,499 pesos, sold for 18,000 pesos in 1763. Sipán's value dropped from 25,000 pesos in 1714 to 11,000 pesos in 1752 and 8,000 pesos in 1761.[33]

Purchasers did not pay in full the price of an estate. They paid the asking price less the amount recognized as liens and mortgages. Licenciado Don Manuel Joseph de Rubiños y Andrade, for example, paid 22,847.5 pesos in cash for Cayaltí, La Candelaria, and Aberru in 1735 and recognized 30,850 pesos in obligations. Don Juan de Mata y Haro paid 5,000 pesos cash for San Cristóbal and recognized 4,000 pesos in debts in 1750. The Maestro de Campo Don Gabriel de Castañeda bought La Otra Banda for a face value of 30,000 pesos in 1755. He recognized 23,758 pesos worth of obligations and paid the difference (only 6,242 pesos) to the heirs of the former owner. As the figures show, the amount that a purchaser paid in cash at the time of a sale decreased as the debt burden increased. Even under these conditions, however, some estates were on the market for years before their sale. One official stated that "no one has bid [for Tumán] and it is unlikely that anyone will, when one considers the necessity of paying cash for the farm and the poor state in which commerce and most of the citizens are in."[34]

When the liens and mortgages exceeded the value or selling price of the estate, the former owner or his estate received nothing. The sale actually represented a transfer of the property by the creditors to another individual in return for the promise to meet the interest obligations.

Aggravating the situation further were innumerable general and estate-specific factors. Technology, for instance, remained unchanged, and the efficiency of production did not improve. Soil depletion and salination became problems, even in the fertile and well-drained upper valleys. Fire precipitated the debt-bankruptcy-deposit-sale cycle on Cayaltí. Its processing facilities burned to the ground overnight in 1739. As noted above, an epidemic killed sixty slaves on Calupe within a month's time in 1756. The dearth of slaves on the market would have made replacement difficult, even had the owner been able to afford it. Restlessness and insubordination of slaves proved a problem after midcentury on La Punta, Luya, Tumán, La Viña, and Calupe. These incidental reverses, given the economic situation, caused additional problems, hardship, drain on resources, and periods of unproductivity.[35]

The cumulative effect of these difficulties was the ruin of the estates and a general crisis for the agricultural-based export economy. Manuscripts of the period record the dilapidated conditions of the estates after the floods and show that they remained in poor repair throughout the eighteenth century. Decade after decade the estates were described in much the same terms. Seven years after the 1728 flood, the mills of Popán were still inoperative and the lands of the estate were barren. In the Lambayeque Valley proper, the estancia of Collús was described as being without livestock or slaves. A contemporary voiced considerable surprise that Calupe in 1740 was so "diminished" from what it had been a decade previously. At midcentury, San Cristóbal was badly in need of renovation, and Pomalca was described as "lost." In the 1760s Palomino was abandoned; Calupe was "very deteriorated"; and Collús was decapitalized. When Don Antonio Sánchez Navarrete acquired Tumán in 1786 it was "in a deplorable state, without implements or capital equipment." In 1787, Calupe was in worse condition than it had been in the 1760s: "now it is without workers, draft animals, implements, cane fields from which to fabricate sugar, cauldrons, tools and pastures." By the start of the nineteenth century, many estates were in various stages of ruin. La Punta was rundown and badly in need of restoration. Luya in 1803 was reported "very near its ultimate ruin." Chumbenique and La Otra Banda were both "lost." Tumán produced nothing and was described as being "in much decadence."[36]

Sugar refining never fully recovered. The accounts which Navarrete left for the decade or so that he owned Pomalca indicate the amounts of estate-generated losses. In 1741–42, Navarrete sold 872 pesos worth of sugar and collected 560 pesos from renters of pastures and various unspecified sources for a total income from Pomalca for one year of 1,432 pesos. Expenses for the purchase of draft animals and tools, maintenance of the slaves, and hired labor came to over three times that amount. During the following four months or so, he sold over 1,400 pesos worth of sugar, molasses, and preserves, while keeping his expenses at 2,245 pesos. Although he cut his losses to 845 pesos, his deficits were still more than he could afford. Similarly, the owner of Cojal recorded a loss in 1766 of 190 pesos on a total income of 1,430 pesos. Villodas reported that La Punta was unprofitable in 1789.[37]

Social Signs of Economic Contraction

The disruption of production on the estates and the crisis had far-reaching social consequences. Years of economic distress strained the financial resources of even the wealthiest members of the old landed elite. The recurrent pattern of debt, bankruptcy, deposit, and sale effectively ruined many of the landed aristocratic families, which had become firmly situated at the apogee of society during the seventeenth century, and led to their gradual replacement with a new group drawn from the ranks of a middle sector of professionals, public administrators, and merchants.

The landed families' almost total commitment to agriculture was one of the main reasons why they did not survive the crisis. Most of their assets were invested in land, capital equipment, and slaves. The landowners, some of whom represented by this time third-, fourth-, or later-generation hacendados, were accustomed to living off these investments. The events of 1701, 1720, and 1728 wiped out in a matter of days what represented years of capital accumulation and work. Now, instead of yielding income, estates cost money.

These landowners' other sources of revenue proved inadequate to rebuild the estates and maintain their life-style, which they apparently refused to alter significantly despite their economic plight. Those without known alternative occupations were the first affected. Figure 25 shows that 40 percent of the landowners belonging to the old, established families only held land; that is, there is no indication that these individuals had other occupations or were members of the militia or town council. The corresponding figure for the individuals who ac-

Figure 25. Social Origins of the Landed Elite, 1720–1824

Relative point in a person's career when land was acquired	Old Wealth		New Wealth							
			Local-born		Immigrants		Subtotal		Total	
	No.	Percent	No.	Percent	No.	Percent	No.	Percent	No.	Percent
After holding another position	40	31.0	7	21.9	41	61.2	48	48.5	88	38.6
Before holding another position	17	13.2	3	9.4	7	10.4	10	10.1	27	11.8
Held land and position simultaneously[1]	12	9.3	3	9.4	8	11.9	11	11.1	23	10.1
Subtotal	69	53.5	13	40.7	56	83.5	69	69.7	138	60.5
Only held land	52	40.3	16	50.0	9	13.4	25	25.3	77	33.8
Unknown	8	6.2	3	9.4	2	3.0	5	5.1	13	5.7
Total	129	100.0	32	100.1	67	99.9	99	100.1	228	100.0

Note: [1]The percentage difference between the men in the old wealth group and those in the locally born of the new wealth group are insignificant. The closeness of the figures may indicate a bias in the sources. Much more information was available on the group labeled "old" wealth than "new." Often the locally born do not appear in the sources until they are in a position to acquire land. Only additional research will substantiate my hunch that several more of the new members did hold some other public position or have additional sources of income (e.g., from an occupation).

Source: BIL.

quired land for the first time during this period was 25 percent. Controlling for the percentage of females in each group, the differences remain significant: 23 percent of the old and 15 percent of the new.[38]

Most of the two out of five[39] who had other professions did not engage in what appear to have been the most lucrative activities. The tradition of the gentleman farmer, which had reached its ultimate expression during the second half of the seventeenth century, and the fear of tainting their respectability prevented many from engaging actively and openly in commerce, which especially in the second half of the eighteenth century proved a very lucrative pastime for a growing number of individuals in the area (see Fig. 26). The prosperity of the previous period eliminated the need for landowners to engage in mer-

Figure 26. Known Occupations of the Landed Elite by Social Origins, 1720–1824

Primary Occupation	Old Wealth		New Wealth		Unknown		Total	
	No.	Percent	No.	Percent	No.	Percent	No.	Percent
Bureaucrats	6	9.8	19	29.7	4	18.2	29	19.7
Lawyers	11	18.0	4	6.3	0	—	15	10.2
Merchants	4	6.6	17	26.6	3	13.6	24	16.3
Priests	24	39.3	12	18.8	1	4.5	37	25.2
Financiers	13	21.3	7	10.9	4	18.2	24	16.3
Cattle raisers	2	3.3	2	3.1	5	22.7	9	6.1
Shipowners	—	—	1	1.6	1	4.5	2	1.4
Administrators	1	1.6	1	1.6	4	18.2	6	4.1
Others	—	—	1	1.6	—	—	1	0.7
Total	61	99.9	64	100.2	22	99.9	147	100.0

Source: BIL.

chandising and reinforced old prejudices against such work inherited from Spain.[40] The proscription against and disdain for being a shop-keeper characterized the members of the old landed families and un-doubtedly stopped some from opening a store or warehouse and possibly saving their fortune.

Similarly, only one-tenth held bureaucratic positions. The Bourbon reformers' reorganization of the viceregal administrative structure should have made public office more attractive for those who sought a steady source of income. One of the reformers' basic changes in the governing system was to increase salaries, fees, and stipends of royal officials in the interest of improved efficiency and maintenance of professional detachment from local pressures. It is not known whether the low level of participation of the members of the old landed elite was a function of their lack of interest; a lack of vacancies and, therefore, the oppor-tunity to serve; discrimination in recruitment in favor of peninsular Spaniards, as the general literature suggests; or a combination of the above.[41]

Instead, if inclined to pursue a career or profession at all, the sons of the old elite chose to become lawyers or to enter the priesthood. Those who could afford the training in Lima became lawyers, evidently for the prestige value of the degree because many did not practice upon their return. The sacerdotal robe also meant an education, esteem, and respect; a steady and predictable income; and opportunities, for some, to earn substantially more. However, many who finished their seminary training did not take their vows. And as with the lawyers, those who finished did not always have a benefice. Many thought it unnecessary until the destruction of the estates and subsequent economic downturn of the eighteenth century, when the unexpected loss of income from chantries and other trusts deprived many clerics, and especially those from the old landowning families who were the usual beneficiaries of such trusts, of a source of income worth hundreds and even thousands of pesos per year.

Another reason that the old families did not survive may have been that dowries and donations were no longer common mechanisms of estate transferral used to induce an outsider to marry into their circle. Dowries, almost one-tenth of the transfers of the previous period, now accounted for only about 2 percent. (See Fig. 27.) The old families thus cut off the influx of energy, new talent, and fortune that had in the past supplied dynamism and continuity to their lines.

Indeed, after the floods, land was never given as a dowry and rarely as a gift, even within the old elite. And of the six donations, most were

Figure 27. Mode of Estate Acquisition, 1720–1824

Mode	Old		New		Total	
	No.	Percent	No.	Percent	No.	Percent
Composición/ Denuncia	2	2.0	2	3.3	4	2.5
Donation	6	6.1	5	8.2	11	6.9
Dowry	—	—	2	3.3	2	1.3
Inheritance	39	39.4	3	4.9	42	26.3
Sale	43	43.4	44	72.1	87	54.4
Other	9	9.1	5	8.2	14	8.8
Total	99	100.0	61	100.0	160	100.2

Source: Appendix 3.

Note: Does not include transfers of tinas, tenerías, or transfers of estates to institutions.

not expressions of unselfish magnanimity. For example, the priest Don Matías de Villodas gave Saltur to Don Ignacio Vicente de Lara as part of the deal by which the latter purchased La Punta in 1784. Lara, in turn, gave Saltur to Dan Manuel Antonio de Quiñones when the latter bought La Punta eight months later. Figure 27 shows that, although inheritance was still an important mode of transfer, sale was the typical way in which one generation passed on an estate to another. The transfer of Calupe between the Gonzales Casanas was typical. Licenciado Don Feliciano de Ripalda inherited his share of La Punta from his mother and consolidated his ownership by purchasing the shares from her other heirs. Ripalda later donated the estate to his nephew not just to keep the property within the family, but "to repay his nephew for having exonerated him from certain sizable debts. . . ."[42]

The changing pattern of estate transfer was not the only indication that relations within the old elite were becoming more impersonal and calculating. Economic crisis and competition for control of natural resources often brought personal enmity and family feuds out into the open. The first indication of factionalism among the old families came to the fore after 1700, when Don Miguel de Robles y Garay contested Don Joseph de la Parra's claim to the lands called Pitipo. The appearance in court on separate occasions of two Saavedra Caveros against General Don Bonifacio Gastelú in a fight over irrigation water soured relations between their families for years to come. A few years later a Samudio battled Don Joseph Briones y Medina in the same court over lands. Such divisions weakened the old elite when it was challenged by the new.[43]

Although ties within the elite weakened under the strain of hard times, old families continued to foment relationships, to the extent that they could, with other groups in society. The practice of bonding corregidores continued until the intendant system was in place; but instead of one or two individuals putting up the thousands of pesos for the corregidor's bond, now twenty to thirty individuals usually contributed hundreds to raise the same sum. They served as compadres to lower-ranking public servants, professionals, and landless members of the municipal council. Volunteers served as lay spokesmen for the religious orders, representing the institutions in court, administering property, collecting rent and interest, heading religious brotherhoods, and organizing holiday festivities and celebrations. Relations with the Indians followed the familiar patterns of years past and remained a noteworthy aspect of social life. The compadrazgo relationship between landowners and Indian officials was as significant as always. But the economic circumstances of most of the old elite prevented them from maintaining as many contacts as before and limited their generosity. Domestic wax candles rather than imported, one priest at a religious celebration rather than two or more, told the story of rapidly ebbing opulence and power.[44]

Thus, when the landowners called on their traditional allies to help them reverse their fortunes or postpone bankruptcy, foreclosure, and loss, they found that their personal resource base had shrunk. Relatives, friends, and acquaintances were less able and less willing to help. Landowners called on their families as a first-order resource. Relatives joined in business deals, often using compadrazgo to reinforce kinship ties. They loaned each other money and guaranteed each other and gave each other power of attorney to collect debts, to purchase goods, to represent one another in court, and to issue legal documents. But increasingly, the social capital even within their extended families proved insufficient to solve their financial problems, and they were forced to look outside the group for economic backing and influence. Sometimes members of two or more old families pooled resources to work lands and keep their businesses afloat.[45]

Most often landowners looked beyond their group to the landless for help. Economic circumstances tended to equalize the two groups to the point where their roles were sometimes reversed, and professionals and bureaucrats were able to materially aid the landowners. Now businessmen occasionally guaranteed landowners. Don Fernando de Arze y Segovia, Don Agustín de la Daza, Don Manuel Gonzales, Don Carlos de la Toviall, and Don Miguel de Iriarte guaranteed Don Francisco Samudio de las Infantes for twenty thousand pesos to purchase Sárrapo. A similar reversal also appeared in the sponsorship roles of baptisms and marriages. The landless were copying the old and building networks.[46]

In a few cases, contacts did successfully forestall loss. Don Ignacio Vicente de Lara, for example, as a second son, could not expect to acquire the lands that had been in his family for at least six generations as long as his older brother, the firstborn Don Luis Mauro, was alive. Therefore, Don Ignacio, unwilling to study law or to join the priesthood, became one of the few members of the old elite to make his career in service to the king, eventually becoming the administrator of the Royal Monopolies of Tobacco, Playing Cards, Dice, and Liquor in the 1780s. When economic conditions threatened his older brother with loss of the family estates of Saltrapón and Santequepe, Don Ignacio, yielding to family pressure and the promise of a one-half interest in the lands, began dipping into the royal coffers under his administration to cover routine operating expenses and investments. Apparently, family pride made it more important to keep the traditional family holdings than any new acquisitions, because helping his brother meant selling part of an estate he had recently acquired on his own. Although viceregal authorities discovered his unauthorized use of royal funds before the end of the decade, he was able, with the cooperation of family and friends, to delay for twenty years the investigation, conviction for malfeasance in office, and repayment.

Technocrats found it difficult to prosecute him because he was an important person in Lambayeque, having served in the militia, as regidor and alcalde ordinario on the cabildo of Chiclayo, as provincial tax collector, and now as administrator of the crown monopolies. Two successive marriages and ties of compadrazgo linked him to other old and powerful families in the region. The notary Vásquez Meléndez was his compadre and "dependent." His brother-in-law served on the cabildo, commanded the militias in the area, and was the second most powerful bureaucrat in the region under the intendant. Therefore, local authorities, many of whom were related to him by birth or marriage or were afraid of him because of the potential power he could still exert, were reluctant to take action.

Under mounting pressure for action from central authorities, family members lent him money to reduce by half an outstanding "debt," which at one point reached nearly 14,000 pesos. He then promised authorities to pay back the balance at the rate of 500 pesos per year. In the next ten years, he met the payment only once; so the case was reopened in 1799. Then he avoided the officials for almost a year by being out of town or by feigning illness. Viceregal authorities eventually relieved him of his duties and sold his slaves at what he claimed were low prices. The unmoved viceroy answered a personal appeal with an order to collect the debt immediately and in full. Unable to meet his obligations, the proud Don Ignacio suffered the indignity of being temporarily jailed for debt by the subdelegado of Trujillo. The local magistrate Don Juan del Carmen Casos released him shortly thereafter on the rather thin excuse that no one could grade tobacco as well as he. Casos, however, to placate his superiors and to protect himself, arranged to embargo one-third of Don Ignacio's salary and the 200-peso rent that he received for his house. Authorities in Trujillo, unsatisfied with this arrangement and intent on carrying out the viceroy's commands, ordered that his house, worth 5,600 pesos, be sold. The property never changed hands because no one bid on it at the first auction; and at the second, the sole bidder offered 4,500 pesos to be paid over fifteen years, which was "unacceptable." Don Ignacio, in league with his brother and sympathetic members of the elite and the middle sector, frustrated royal intentions and in so doing was able to keep the lands in the family into the nineteenth century.[47]

The family founded by Bernardo López del Corral, diagrammed in Figure 13, was the only other family known to have survived the crisis. One branch of the family continued to own land into the nineteenth century. But this family's claim to longevity in landownership was based on the horizontal pattern of land tenure noted in the last chapter. Various branches of the same extended family owned different estates over ten generations, but no branch owned any one estate longer than four generations or a maximum of one century. The primogenitor arrived from Spain and acquired Sasape and Sodo. The fortuitous first marriage of his daughter, Doña Leonor, brought Íllimo into the family at her widowhood. Because Doña Leonor had no children of her own, she left her vast estates to a beloved niece, Doña Magdalena. Descendants of Doña Magdalena owned about thirty different estates over the next seven generations. The head of another branch, Licenciado Don Joseph Carrasco del Saz (y Soto) Bermúdez, owned Collús, Añáñala, Pomalca, and Samán. His offspring also owned Sancarranco, La Viña, Cadape, and Sialupe. His grandchildren acquired La Punta, Selenique, Íllimo, and Sasape. Some of these estates stayed within the family for another generation. Only La Punta was transferred to the next generation. Don Antonio Ramón de Peramas lost La Punta to a higher bidder. His son's claim to landed elite status rested on the purchase of Cayaltí from his father-in-law.[48]

But this family and Don Ignacio were exceptions rather than the rule. Personal influence and connections failed the old landed families when they needed them the most. Given the prevailing economic conditions, their aristocratic pretensions and their propensity to continue founding censos, the landowners' fund of power proved ineffective in getting the old elite through the crisis. In the course of the eighteenth century, all but the above two extended families, who traced their origins back to before 1650, lost their land. The landowning tradition of the family established by Diego de Cavanillas (presented in Fig. 24) continued through the Gonzales Casana branch until Don Pedro's slaves were decimated by sickness. Without labor, he could not meet his financial obligations, whereupon his creditors forced the sale of the estate. The landowning family founded by Captain Francisco Núñez Montes ended in this period with the death of Licenciado Don Eugenio León y Rivera, a priest with no direct heirs and no distant relatives with the resources or desire to purchase his property.[49]

Finally, the ennobled descendants of Captain Juan Flores Osorio (shown in Fig. 28) lost possession of La Viña and Sárrapo, which had been in the family for five generations or almost a century and a half. Don Francisco Samudio de las Infantes, the last impoverished member of the family to own the estates, was forced to sell them to Don Felipe García Alcayde de Córdova because he could not repay a 2,659 peso loan. The entire transaction, judging from the written records of the proceedings, seemed preplanned and orchestrated to force the sale. The family's financial problems began in the early 1700s, when Don Agustín Gerónimo de Velasco y Silva Manrique, Don Francisco's uncle, guaranteed the renters of the sales tax (*Real Derecho de Alcabala and Unión de Armas*), Don Juan de la Cueva and Juan de Sopeña. Cueva died unexpectedly, leaving Don Agustín indebted to the treasury for nearly 11,000 pesos. In spite of this loss and a sworn statement before a notary that he would never guarantee anyone again, Don Agustín continued as one of the most active financiers in the region. When he died, his brother-in-law, General Don Antonio Samudio de las Infantes, inherited his title, the haciendas, and his debts. Despite the noble title and his pretensions, his economic situation was precarious, especially given the state of the market for sugar. Although his name appeared in a list of the most prominent and distinguished Peruvian families in 1721, with the notation that he owned an estate and a large house, he was known as a "poor creole" and was practically a pauper compared to others with his social rank and position. The family's fortunes did not improve. Don Francisco acquired the estates burdened with mortgages and with the interest payments many years in arrears. Apparently, García Alcayde, who had been the corregidor of the province from 1756 to 1762, encouraged the creditors to foreclose. The records are filled with a sense of urgency. The public announcements of the sale were made in the space of a few days, instead of over a month's time as was customary, which suggests that the unusual speed of the sale was designed to deny Don Francisco the time to raise money to meet his obligations from other sources. García Alcayde probably used the debt to force the sale of the run-down but basically sound estates. Sárrapo and La Viña had all the elements essential to production—

over 594 fanegadas of lands and pastures and 72 slaves. The annual production of sugar was estimated at a respectable 3,000 arrobas.[50]

García Alcayde's behavior was not atypical. More often than ever before, traditional allies who were now socially mobile sided against the landowners. Corregidor Navarrete, for example, proved partial in the bankruptcy case against the Olivos family and actually facilitated foreclosure by Licenciado Phelipe Ruis Vásquez. In another instance, he persuaded the notary Don Sebastián de Polo to alter manuscripts in the bankruptcy proceedings against the owner of Chumbenique to favor a friend's claim.[51]

Such reversals of roles and the unsettling effects of the economic turnaround allowed immigrants and locally born persons of previously landless families gradually to acquire the estates during the course of the eighteenth century. By Independence, newcomers constituted nearly half (48 percent) of the landowning population, well over twice the proportion of the previous period. Of the two-thirds of these who were immigrants to the area, more than half (55 percent) came from Spain. The rest arrived from other parts of Europe, Panama, Quito, and other provinces of the Spanish domain.[52]

In contrast to the scions of the old landed families, these individuals were not necessarily born with the resources needed to acquire land. As Figure 26 shows, the 60 percent known to have exercised a profession were bureaucrats, priests, and merchants. These were the professions where the highly aspiring, socially mobile had the best chance to succeed. The Bourbons had opened the bureaucracy to talent, and peninsular-born technocrats began arriving in Lambayeque in significant numbers shortly after midcentury. The priesthood must have attracted newcomers for the same reasons as it attracted the sons of the old elite. Few chose to study law, perhaps because of the expense involved. Commerce, too, promised rewards for hardworking individuals who were skilled in shrewd dealings. It is, in fact, during this period that the merchants became conspicuous as a group in the area. In the sixteenth century most merchants located in Trujillo and itinerant peddlers served the area. For most of the seventeenth century the corregidor's *repartimiento* (forced sale of goods), the landowners' propensity to be their own local shipping agents, and their factors' willingness to supply them with goods from Panama or Lima limited commercial activities. With the end of these practices in this period, the merchants became locally influential personages in their own right, first as modest shopkeepers and by the end of the eighteenth century

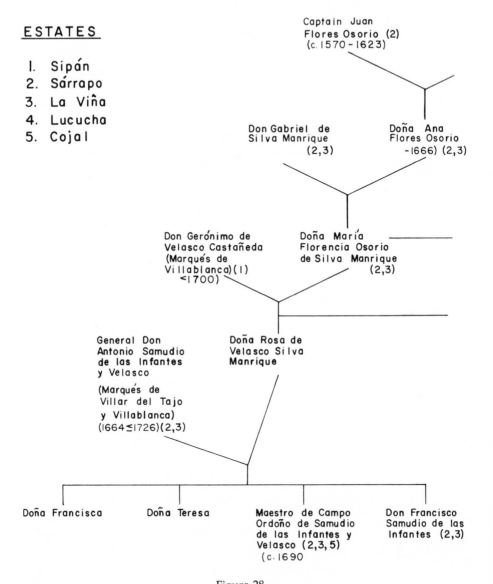

ESTATES

1. Sipán
2. Sárrapo
3. La Viña
4. Lucucha
5. Cojal

Captain Juan
Flores Osorio (2)
(c. 1570 - 1623)

Don Gabriel de
Silva Manrique
(2,3)

Doña Ana
Flores Osorio
-1666) (2,3)

Don Gerónimo de
Velasco Castañeda
(Marqués de
Villablanca) (1)
<1700)

Doña María
Florencia Osorio
de Silva Manrique
(2,3)

General Don
Antonio Samudio
de las Infantes
y Velasco

(Marqués de
Villar del Tajo
y Villablanca)
(1664≤1726)(2,3)

Doña Rosa de
Velasco Silva
Manrique

Doña Francisca

Doña Teresa

Maestro de Campo
Ordoño de Samudio
de las Infantes y
Velasco (2,3,5)
(c. 1690

Don Francisco
Samudio de las
Infantes (2,3)

Figure 28.

Doña Francisca
Dias de Sagredo
≤1656) (2,3)

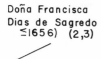

Sr. Licenciado
Don Juan de
Otalora

Doña Ana María
de Vargas

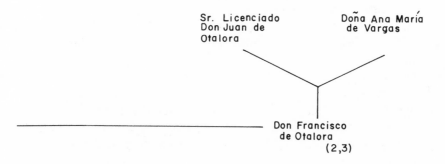

Don Francisco
de Otalora
(2,3)

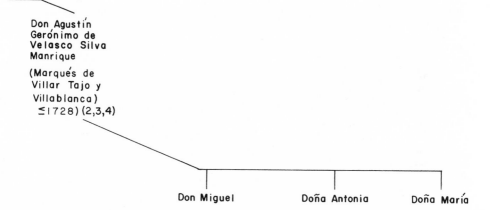

Don Agustín
Gerónimo de
Velasco Silva
Manrique

(Marqués de
Villar Tajo y
Villablanca)
≤1728) (2,3,4)

Don Miguel   Doña Antonia   Doña María

as respected and wealthy importers and exporters. Though few in number, they appear more and more frequently in the public record to bid in auctions for the right to collect the tithes, for the personal effects of the deceased, or for the indebted property of the old landed elite.[53]

They had been waiting for the opportunity to buy land. Their position and income had gained them admittance to the revitalized cabildo under the Bourbons. As the numbers in Figure 29 show, newcomers gradually equalled and eventually surpassed members of the old families in numbers on the council. Likewise, newcomers came to outnumber the old in the growing military, although they never matched the old in rank. Figure 30 shows that representatives of the old families predominated at the level of general; the new proved strongest at the rank of captain.

The newcomers' resentment had been building toward the old traditional families, who controlled the land and related resources. This was particularly true of the locally born who had experienced or had heard of the effects of the Sarmiento visita, and who had far less chance of moving into the landowning group than recent immigrants. (See Fig. 25.) From the middle of the seventeenth century until the visita of 1711–12, cattle raising had been the best opportunity for the small investor who had benefited in a peripheral way from the prosperity of the sugar industry and who had no land of his own. Costs of es-

Figure 29. Cabildo Positions by Social Origin, 1720–1824

	Old		New		Unknown		Total	
Position	No.	Percent	No.	Percent	No.	Percent	No.	Percent
Alcalde Ordinario	12	63.2	16	66.7	3	100.0	31	67.4
Regidor	4	21.1	7	29.2			11	23.9
Alcalde Provincial	1	5.3	1	4.2			2	4.3
Alférez Real	2	10.5	—	—			2	4.3
Total	19	100.1	24	100.1	3	100.0	46	99.9
		(41.3)		(52.2)		(6.5)		(100.0)

Source: BIL.

Figure 30. Positions in the Military by Social Origin, 1720–1824

Position	Old No.	Old Percent	New No.	New Percent	Unknown No.	Unknown Percent	Total No.	Total Percent
Governor/ General	10	32.3	5	13.5			15	17.2
Maestro de Campo	5	16.1	5	13.5			10	11.5
Comandante			1	2.7	1	5.3	2	2.3
Coronel	3	9.7	3	8.1	2	10.5	8	9.2
Capitán	8	25.8	15	40.5	6	31.6	29	33.3
Teniente			5	13.5	6	31.6	11	12.6
Alférez	3	9.7	2	5.4	3	15.8	8	9.2
Sargento Mayor			1	2.7			1	1.1
Ayudante	2	6.5			1	5.3	3	3.4
Total	31	100.1	37	99.9	19	100.1	87	99.8

Source: BIL.

tablishing and maintaining a herd were low, and pastures were still common. The latter fact explains why established landowners rushed to buy exclusive pasturage rights to limit production and to stymie competition as much as possible. By permitting landowners with *de facto* control of the "common" pastures to legalize their holdings, the 1712 visita had greatly restricted opportunities to invest surplus capital and had deprived the independent cattle raisers of even the most distant grazing lands. Native population recovery placed increased pressure on community pastures and limited their rental to outsiders. The lack of land, and then of pastures, left few alternatives for those with money to invest. A few continued to raise cattle on rented pastures. Some grew forage crops, grains, and vegetables on rented lands. Others became financiers or invested surplus capital in tanneries and soap-making facilities close to town, which were the first such enterprises not an integral part of a ranching enterprise and the first indication of a growing specialization of production in the agricultural sector. This trend quickened toward midcentury, after the floods made landowners more willing to rent pastures for needed income and encouraged them to allow their own herds to multiply to the point that their own soap-making facilities could not accommodate the volume of business. The revival and growth of the pastoral industry gave these newcomers the means to acquire the estates, which represented, in a sense, their vindication.[54]

But the social mobility of this group into the ranks of the landowning class did not necessarily mean that they were as wealthy then as the old landed group they displaced had once been. Local merchants suffered from the agricultural crisis. Priests saw donations and fees diminish as celebrations, baptisms, and marriages were canceled or postponed. They also suffered from the loss of the ability of the estates to pay interest on chantries and other trusts. They and the immigrants to the area were able to acquire the estates on what once might have been considered modest incomes, because, as noted above, the estates were being sold at giveaway prices and on very easy terms. So anxious were the mortgagees to close the sale on San Cristóbal in 1750 that they agreed to an interest moratorium of two years. After this period, the new owner agreed to resume the debt service at 4 percent, one point lower than the standard mortgage rate. In other cases, a new owner assumed control for the sole promise of meeting future interest payments.[55]

The newcomers' lack of liquidity and reserves conditioned their strategy for revitalizing the estates. One reason the sugar industry did not recover fully under their direction was that the landowners invested part of whatever capital they accumulated or could borrow in livestock. Competition, depressed prices, loss of markets, and low yields discouraged landowners from planting cane. Furthermore, sugar refining was a capital-intensive industry, requiring a substantial initial investment and years of work before the estates produced a profit. The floods and other problems meant that landowners were essentially starting from scratch in reestablishing the industry under very difficult circumstances, when two major factors of production—labor and capital— were expensive or unavailable. Stock raising, in contrast, required little capital or labor. Herds multiplied rapidly, and livestock could be processed easily in relatively rudimentary plants. Prices were less subject to violent fluctuations and promised more predictable returns. Sugar producers realized that although the extent of flood damage to estancias and their processing facilities was approximately the same as that to the haciendas y trapiches, the estancias resumed production faster with a smaller investment. New owners realized that the original estancieros and sugar producers with herds had made money by selling livestock on the hoof even before rebuilding their processing facilities. The new owners, therefore, maintained sugar production to the extent possible with the slaves and equipment available; but their herds, which had been a secondary concern in the seventeenth century, were allowed to grow while they rebuilt their tinas y tenerías.

Although a steady income from a source other than agriculture or evidence that a person had capital often convinced creditors that a potential buyer was capable of meeting his interest obligations, these sources of income were not always adequate to cover renewal plans and continued losses. The upwardly mobile wanted the land, because of its prestige value and because they were confident that under good administration the haciendas would once again produce a profit. But few had the ability to lose money continuously, while waiting for investments to pay off. Eventually, many were forced by debt to sell out. The lack of financial reserves among the new owners contributed to the high turnover rate of the estates during the middle and late eighteenth century.[56]

The displacement of old families by new ones meant a corresponding change in the patterns of land tenure in the valleys. The disappearance of some of the old clans ended the long tradition of continuous landholding. Short-term tenure became typical in the eighteenth century. General Don Domingo Navarrete and General Baltazar de Ayesta owned Pomalca for about a decade. Gonzales Casana's successors held Calupe only twenty-six years. The continuity of the old families and the seeming omnipotence of certain personages were broken, and consequently the reverence for and strength of tradition declined.[57]

The advance of persons of different social origins into the landowning elite also brought a corresponding change in the internal structure of the landowning class. Instead of a small number of large, interrelated, and well-integrated families who between them controlled most of the largest estates, the evolving eighteenth-century landed elite was fragmented, consisting of a number of comparatively small families.

Newcomers recognized the value of establishing personal relations in overcoming this limitation; and, as mentioned above, they were not adverse to entering into them. But the nature of intraelite cooperation had changed, and not just between old and new. Business was business even within the new group. Don Matías José de la Dehesa became indebted to Don José Joaquín de Peramas, Don Baltazar de Muro, Don

Pedro de Estela y Suazo, and several others for funds to work his land and to meet routine household expenses. Dehesa eventually relied on Estela for a sixty-peso monthly allowance to continue production. Estela refused to finance Dehesa indefinitely and eventually took over his land for debts. Such action contrasted sharply with the largesse displayed by the church in previous years.[58]

Despite ill-feelings between members of certain families, connections and, above all, common preoccupations gave members of the landed elite some basis on which to mount a united front to defend their interests against common adversaries. They had no choice but to cooperate in these unsettled times. As a group these landowners, whether old or new, were in precarious economic positions. An unexpected drop in prices or another natural disaster would mean losses that they could ill afford. They also knew that as a group they were losing control of the region to newcomers without land.[59]

The Extent of Landowners' Power

The Bourbon reforms, in trying to stimulate production and assure bureaucratic efficiency, had greatly undermined the landed elite's previously central position. It was during this period, for the first time, that royal officials with no land outnumbered the landowning bureaucrats (by almost two to one). Landowners also lost ground on the cabildo after the reformers abolished life-term seats and gave it more duties and responsibilities, making officeholding once again a serious undertaking and heightening the prestige associated with participation. Landowners continued to dominate, outnumbering the nonlandowners 44 to 28. But in contrast to the previous period, when the chances that a magistrate was landed were eight to one, now the ratio was down to two to one. Similarly, the Bourbon defense plans opened the militia to the middle and lower sectors of society and greatly increased its size. By 1780 the militia in Lambayeque was made up of fourteen companies with 1,040 men. The militia of Ferreñafe created in 1769 had two squadrons of three companies, each with a total of 540 men. Because at any one time the number of landowners remained close to 30, it is easy to understand how their relative representation fell. Even when compared to the previous period, landowners' active participation declined by almost twenty points. Apparently, as the militia lost its exclusivity, landowners became less willing to participate. After all, the militia was one activity that the landowners could avoid without major social or economic repercussions. Yet, despite their smaller numbers, the landed still outnumbered the landless at all ranks, except in the relatively low positions of alférez and sergeant.[60]

The established landowners had an ambiguous attitude toward this landless sector. On the one hand, they feared it because the landless represented a challenge to both old and new members of the propertied class. They were the aspiring elite. Some were well educated and over 10 percent had been born in Spain. A growing number of this group of over 130 individuals already grazed cattle on rented pastures or planted wheat, corn, alfalfa, beans, and tobacco on rented lands. A few had unsuccessfully bid on haciendas and were awaiting another opportunity to buy. But, on the other hand, these economic interests assured the landowners that this group, from which some of the new landed themselves had recently risen, would cooperate and be sympathetic toward their efforts to gain the resources needed to maintain and expand production. The hacendados knew that the identification of the nonlanded with themselves exceeded their jealousies. The well-being of the landless as tithe collectors, administrators of haciendas, muleteers, creditors, and suppliers was ultimately very closely linked with their own.[61]

This coincidence of interests fomented a sometimes shifting alliance between the established landowners and this middle sector, which, as in the past, allowed the former to retain and reinforce their dominance in the region and to seek advantages for their estates. As in the past, their success in depriving the Indians of land, pastures, and water depended on the connivance of the professional and bureaucratic sector.

The expansion of the livestock industry made acquisition of new lands and pastures essential. The hacendados did not have the money needed to improve and expand the irrigation infrastructure, which was the only way, given the level of eighteenth-century technology, to open additional territory to year-round grazing or cultivation. The easiest way to acquire the needed resources, then, was at the expense of the Indian communities.[62]

The power and influence of the landowners facilitated their purchase of Indian lands, despite protective legislation. Indians were forced to sell land (1) when they fell behind in their tribute payments or became indebted to individual creditors, who pressed claims for even insignificant amounts; or (2) when the Indians needed money to meet extraordinary expenses, ranging from the money needed for a funeral or baptism to legal fees for the prosecution of court cases. Time after time, the corregidor and the protector approved the sale. The texts of these sale permits followed a familiar formula after 1720. Sometimes whole sections appeared to be copied verbatim from a standardized model, suggesting that neither corregidor nor protector bothered to ascertain the true conditions of the sale, as required by law; that permission was automatic; and that the local officials simply instructed the notary to draw up the necessary papers for their signatures. The result was that many plots of community lands were sold illegally to the landowners. Purchasers included creditors and even the protectors themselves. Sometimes the corregidor or protector arranged the sales between the Indians and their friends. Don Francisco Ruvalcava purchased three pieces of land from Indians of Lambayeque after being notified of their availability by his friend, the Indians' protector. Don Pedro de Estela took advantage of a debt to take over lands from mestizo residents of Lambayeque on which he later constructed a tina y tenería. It was precisely their value as construction sites which attracted the Spanish to these relatively small plots of Indian land.[63]

The uproar over the construction of Estela's tina y tenería is a clear example of the collusion between Spanish landowners and their friends to impose their will on the less powerful inhabitants of the region. Clemente Anto and other Indians of Lambayeque, with the help of an uncommonly sympathetic protector, Don Manuel Massaredo, presented a petition to protest the building of the tina y tenería on the grounds that (1) the projected site belonged to the community and had been sold unlawfully to Estela, (2) the stench would drift over the town, and (3) the wastes would pollute the water supply. This petition touched off a long court battle.

Estela's defense left nothing to chance. He presented witnesses to counter Anto's claims. The curaca of Lambayeque, Don Eugenio Victorio Temoche, testified, for example, that Anto opposed the establishment for no other reason than a personal hatred for Estela and that the tina y tenería would be beneficial to the community because it would create additional demand for the firewood, starch, tannin, foodstuffs, and lime that Indians sold. The subdelegado Don Pedro Rafael del Castillo slandered the protector to discredit his testimony in opposition to Estela's tina and his claim of other irregularities. Castillo and other witnesses attacked Anto by defaming his character, by accusing him of being arrogant, and suggesting ulterior motives for his opposition. The subdelegado closed with a warning that if Anto was not checked he would become a leader of a tumult similar to that led by Túpac Amaru, a warning that was not unappreciated by the monitoring officials in Lima. The motivations behind the vicar Don Matías de Soto y Soraluze's defense of Estela's tina y tenería became clear when it was revealed that he had invested forty thousand pesos in the project. Other priests remained silent in order to stay on good terms with Soto y Soraluze. Four witnesses claimed that there was a need for another tina y tenería because the existing ones could not handle the present volume of business, and it took up to two years for a hide to be processed. Finally, Estela instructed Indians who owed him money to testify on his behalf. Several told the court that they signed Anto's petition against the construction without reading it or realizing what it said. Others admitted that they signed because they were relatives of the initiator of the suit, not because of an objection to the plan.

The vehemence of the attack against Anto and subsequent events lend credence to his assertion that Estela was protected by "persons who I say run [*mandan*] this place like, for example, his lordship the Subdelegado." Anto stated that to help Estela's cause Subdelegado Castillo delayed installing a new slate of community leaders for two years to keep sympathetic individuals in place.

In the final analysis, it was Estela's identity as a top political officer, large merchant and financier, and landowner that secured for him the building permit he so ardently desired. When faced with a decision which ultimately reduced the decision to "them" (Indians) or "us" (landowners), the municipal council had no trouble in deciding to grant a license. They commissioned Don Juan Romualdo de Vidaurre and Don Juan Bautista de Rivera to investigate and prepare a statement on the environmental impact of the tina y tenería. Vidaurre and Rivera reported problems with sewage and pollution, which Estela promised to correct. The other five members of the town council, which included three who might otherwise have voted no for personal reasons, approved the report and issued Don Pedro his license.[64]

In other instances, the confusion over lands and pastures enabled the landowners, with the help of local officials, to expand their estates.[65] The sale of pasturage rights on lands held and farmed by neighboring Indian communities by the visitor Sarmiento de Sotomayor in 1711–12 caused problems when the hacendados allowed their animals to graze without taking any measures to keep them out of the Indians' fields. Instances of Spanish livestock damaging the Indians' crops, once common in the sixteenth century, again became frequent as owners allowed their herds to multiply. The difference between the sixteenth and the eighteenth centuries was that in the latter period Spaniards had a legal basis on which to defend themselves against Indian complaints. Local authorities took little action to remedy the problem.

The Spaniards released their livestock in what appears to have been a premeditated and often successful campaign of harassment designed to force the Indians to abandon their lands and fields, thereby providing the landowners with the opportunity to unofficially annex vacated land to their estates and consolidate control over both pastures and lands. Without land, of course, Indians had few choices other than joining the work force of the estates. The Indians of Chiclayo, for example, had rights to five leagues of land, but in 1734 a visitor noted that most of it had been usurped by the Spaniards who controlled the pastures. The Spaniards effectively denied the Indians access to their own lands by allowing their herds to damage the Indians' fields. Don Bonifacio Gastelú (the owner of Saltur, Collús, and La Punta) occupied two leagues; Don Francisco de Seña (the owner of Pomalca and Samán) grazed goats on another league; and the priest of Chiclayo used the remaining section. The owner of Ucupe used similar tactics to discourage Indians of Mocupe from farming certain portions of their lands, allowing him to appropriate them for his own use. Appeals to the local authorities were ignored. Years of such abuses by the owners of Tumán came to a head in 1799 when the Indians of Chiclayo, armed with sticks and farm implements, rioted to dramatize their rights and the illegal possession of their lands.[66]

The Indians of Chiclayo had already rioted once over similar problems. When the Pinillos brothers bought the three estates of Pomalca, Collús, and Samán in 1784, they began charging Indians for the right to graze their domestic animals on hacienda pastures, which grew on community lands. They took one-tenth of an Indian's livestock and draft animals for what had been traditional grazing rights, restricted the number of animals the Indians could graze, and checked the collection and use of firewood. Majordomos punished infractions of these rules by confiscating tools and livestock. In addition, to demonstrate their rights to the pastures on certain lands, the Pinillos allowed hacienda oxen to graze in the Indians' fields.[67]

The riot on the main square of Chiclayo that resulted from these actions began when Indians who were gathering to go out to clean the major water main of the town began discussing the situation. Someone began shouting insults at the Pinillos. Indians threatened to kill the brothers unless they were allowed to use the pastures freely. A report on the trouble describes the disturbance thus:

> Indians armed with shovels that they were carrying
> to the communal task of cleaning the common
> irrigation ditch, at the sound of a drum, crowded
> together and two left to take possession of the
> church tower and sound [the bells] as if to
> announce a sudden and unexpected attack by an
> enemy. In a moment, over 500 angry men gathered
> in the Plaza. And their women [came] carrying
> stones and hidden knives. The mob yelled that they
> did not want the Pinillos as citizens in their Town
> and that the haciendas of Pomalca and Collús
> should be given to the Reverend Father Fray
> Antonio Mucho Trigo, the acting Provincial of the
> Seraphic Order [of Saint Francis] because they no
> longer could stand the abuses of said hacendados.

The Pinillos called on their friend, the subdelegado, to use soldiers to end the trouble and reestablish order.

The Pinillos and the subdelegado later cooperated to whitewash the incident. In the report that was forwarded to Lima describing the event, the subdelegado purposefully downgraded the seriousness of the riot. During the investigation, he influenced witnesses and encouraged them to testify falsely. The Pinillos asked a sympathetic priest to write in their behalf, saying that the riot was caused by overindulgence in alcohol and that the Indians did not have any complaints against them. Another witness the Pinillos presented to testify in their favor was a business associate who was at their tina y tenería near Chiclayo at the time that the disturbance occurred. In an attempt to ascribe some blame to others, the names of Don Teodoro Daza (discussed below), Don Pedro Cler, and Franciscan friars were mentioned as the instigators of the tumult.

The Indians of Chiclayo, in contrast, claimed that they were forced to rent pastures because much of their own land had been usurped. They said they were powerless to change the situation because of the collaboration between the Spanish landowners and the officials and because they were dependent, with a few exceptions, on native leaders who did not have their own interests at heart. The subdelegado filed their complaints instead of sending them up the administrative ladder. Their protector did not help them, either. They complained that

> we have given enough proof of all of these deeds,
> Most Excellent Lord, to Our Protector, who has not

> served us in anything because in these parts the
> only thing that counts is influence.

Notaries lost or misplaced their petitions and written proof of possession.

> Everything is confused in the courthouse of
> Lambayeque, because of the bad scribes, who take
> away from us as many manuscripts, and titles as
> we present, so that without anything with which to
> defend ourselves our cause will be lost. . . .

We know from other cases that notaries often confused titles, miscopied manuscripts, or changed the order of the documents at the request of higher officials or landowners with whom they had close ties.[68]

Both real and feigned confusion over boundary markers caused many disputes, which also gave the landowners occasion to use their position and influence to acquire lands and pastures. Land titles issued in the 1590s did not specify boundaries. Instead, they gave an individual possession of a number of fanegadas in a particular location. The first systematic land measurement and boundary specifications dated from the Meneses visita of the 1640s. At that time landmarks were chosen for their permanent and inalterable quality. Common markers included irrigation ditches, abandoned Indian shrines (huacas), and boulders; and if nothing else was available, trees, the direction of the prevailing wind, and the distance of a rifle shot were used to delineate property.

Problems arose because the markers proved arbitrary and impermanent and could be confused, moved, or destroyed. For example, irrigation canals that had been abandoned over the course of years filled up with windblown soil and sand, and disappeared without a trace. Because many irrigation canals ran parallel to each other, long-term local residents of the estates often forgot or confused the names of what had once seemed fixed and immutable markers. There was no sure way of knowing which irrigation ditch was which. Unless they were of a distinctive shape or unusual size, adobe shrines, rocks, and boulders posed the same problems of identification. Trees died and, in one case, were purposely cut down and their stumps burned. Confusion also resulted from specific instances where landowners changed the names of once commonly recognized landmarks—usually replacing Indian names with the names of Christian saints. Sometimes boundaries were moved. A bridge across the Reque River was rebuilt after a flood in another location, causing a boundary dispute years later.[69]

Defense of the Pinillos' usurpation of part of Chiclayo's lands; the usurpation by certain unnamed Spaniards of Ferreñafe's lands and pastures in 1781; and the usurpation of some eighteen hundred fanegadas of lands belonging to San Miguel de Picse (an annex of Chiclayo) by the owners of Luya, Tumán, and a man named Marcos Marra depended on the credibility of witnesses who claimed to know the boundaries. Because owners and longtime residents of the area could not always agree on which shrine, canal, or hill was which, disputes often became a matter of one person's word against another's. The community of Chiclayo based a claim to lands in 1783 on oral testimony to the effect that the closer of two parallel canals running behind the town was the one described in the titles. If this was true the Indians would gain land. Landowners often presented their tenants, workers, servants, and relatives as witnesses. The dependence of these witnesses on the landowners for their livelihood and kinship ties made their impartiality suspect. Many witnesses, at the suggestion of the litigants, deliberately lied about their ages to give their testimony more value. Almost invariably, judges, who sometimes were landowners themselves, found the testimony of the hacendados and their friends more convincing than that of their Indian counterparts, who were also handicapped by the fact that traditionally their testimony carried less weight than that of the Spaniards. Given these facts, it is not difficult to understand why the Indians almost always lost in the local courts.[70]

The same types of machinations took place in regard to water. Among the claims and counterclaims between the Indians of Lambayeque and Chiclayo over the lands called Culpón is the mention that the priest of Reque convinced Don Domingo Navarrete, the corregidor and later the owner of Pomalca and Collús, to sell him a portion of irrigation water belonging to Chiclayo for one hundred pesos. The priest wanted the additional water to increase his plantings of alfalfa, wheat, and tobacco and the amount of irrigated lands he could rent to other Spaniards, mestizos, and mulattoes. Either way, the priest benefited—from the direct sale of his produce or from the rent and primicia paid to him by the renters. The Indians could not defend themselves because the protector, Don Ordoño de Samudio de las Infantes, the son of the Marqués de Villablanca and owner of La Viña and Sárrapo, confiscated their titles.[71]

In other instances, it was the protector himself who alienated the water. In fact the Indians often worried about who occupied the position of protector and water commissioner because, in his role as their business manager and advocate, he too could sell their precious and dwindling supply. A sympathizer with the Indians' cause summarized their almost helpless predicament:

> [the protector] took away their allotments of
> irrigation water and sold them to others. The
> damage is irreparable and the appeals difficult,
> because while they address themselves to higher
> courts of law, the crops die. Even when after long
> periods of time and huge expenses they obtain
> favorable judgments, they [the authorities] make
> them useless, thus easily satisfying the Spanish
> hacendados, who because of their genius,
> education and authority can easily dominate and
> destroy the Indians, from whom for their want of
> favor and protection and misery, they have nothing
> to fear.

The Indians knew from experience that they had cause to worry on this account, because landowners had in the past conspired with their protector and others to acquire their water. The owner of Saltur, Don Bonifacio Joachín de Gastelú, made a deal with the administrator of Sipán to divert the runoff, from an irrigation ditch (which traversed the estate) called Hirpón, through a short auxiliary canal to his property. This action reduced the supply of water to the communities downstream, causing damage to their crops. They filed a written complaint in protest.

In the course of the investigation that followed, it became clear that the Indians had had possession of the water of Hirpón for at least two decades. The curaca of Callanca-Monsefú sold the water to Don Bonifacio, with the advice of and "as a result of bribes, threats and promises" from the same Don Ordoño who had refused to help the Indians of Chiclayo. The Indians claimed that

> with well-known perverseness . . . the said Don
> Ordoño became intimate friends with the said Don
> Bonifacio who now gives him board at his own
> table but restricts his freedom to consult in a
> Christian fashion to solve problems.

The Indians' lawyer was also found to be collaborating with Don Bonifacio and Don Ordoño. According to the curaca, he tricked him into signing legal papers with assurances that the community's interests would not be compromised, before he realized what the flowery legal terminology and ambiguous wording really implied. The usurpation caused such a scandal and uproar among the Indians of Reque, Monsefú, and Eten, and the Indians' rights were so clear, that the corregidor Don Pedro de Seijas had no alternative but to order Don Bonifacio's canal closed and the water restored to the Indians.[72]

Foiled in this attempt, Don Bonifacio tried to usurp part of the water from the same irrigation ditch at another point along its course. This, however, decreased the supply of water to the hacienda y trapiche of La Punta. La Punta's owner, Doña Tomasa Saavedra Cabero, a headstrong woman unafraid to defend her rights, took him to court, where a nephew and brother pleaded her case and won.[73]

A last example of the Indians' many futile attempts to defend themselves against the usurpation of the landowners is the case between the Indians of Reque and their priest over his use of their water and land. It was traditionally accepted practice in the region for priests to sow vegetables and alfalfa on community lands. The priest of Reque, Licenciado Don Matías Villodas, who also owned La Punta, abused this custom by overusing the community's water supply to irrigate his fields of sugar, corn, and wheat. He also regulated the water supply to provide power for a flour mill which he had reconstructed and restored. Villodas sent a servant to the mouth of the irrigation canal to see that no one cut off his supply. Indians were whipped if they used the water freely during the dry, winter months. The Indians complained that his excessive use of water caused extensive crop loss and that the only time there was enough water for all was during the rainy season in the mountains. Locally, the Indians could not find any justice because the subdelegado, the ecclesiastical judge of the province (who was also the priest of Saña and Villodas's superior), and other judges and officials sided with Villodas. The Indians appealed to Lima, but the ecclesiastical authorities of Trujillo intervened, claiming that they had jurisdiction. The Indians' cause was delayed repeatedly: their first set of manuscripts never arrived, and up to a year passed between hearings. Villodas's superiors eventually assigned him to another parish in the central highlands, and the abuses presumably stopped.[74]

Personal ties were not the only reasons officials did not move to help the Indians. Many took no action because they themselves were guilty of wrongdoing and misconduct. The fact that corregidores still planted fields in the region for their own benefit and profit and sold huge quantities of goods to the Indians, far beyond the legal limits of the repartimiento, kept them quiet, tolerant, and cooperative. Corregidor Navarrete had been notorious for his excessive sales of mules and wine. An administrative report written about 1760 stated:

> The corregidors' trade in this said province (without
> fear of the law or the penalties of the decree) in
> domestic and imported cloth and principally with
> liquor [is] a vice that has now been introduced to
> all the Kingdom or poison that is received through
> the hand of those who should administer justice. It
> is true that this trade will be the total ruin of the
> Provinces, because the uncorrupted representative
> of Justice converted into a merchant will be its total
> destruction. . . .

The author estimated the value of the goods sold by the corregidor to the Indians as 100,000 pesos in the past five years. In the 1780s reports estimated forced sales totaling up to 300,000 pesos. In this regard, a viceregal bureaucrat stated that Lambayeque was "very profitable to the corregidor and merited being ranked among the best [of the Kingdom]."[75]

Other officials dared not oppose the landowners' will because they personally profited from the Indians. In addition to the abuses detailed above, the protector sometimes rented out the Indians' pastures and kept the proceeds for himself, instead of depositing the money in the community treasury. Residencias that should have been the legal channel for the redress of the Indians' grievances against provincial officials on all levels were still usually mere formalities. The corregidor and his replacement, the subdelegado, routinely bribed persons to keep them quiet.[76]

If local officials were questioned about their action by suspicious viceregal authorities, they defended themselves by pleading unintentional wrongdoing. The protector of Lambayeque in a case over the exploitation of salt deposits between the Indians and a community official, the gobernador Don Norberto Guevara, defended himself against the allegation that he and the official had cooperated to get control and privately exploit the deposits by stating that he had signed a document that Guevara presented to him without reading it.

> I signed his paper without ever understanding its
> grave consequences to my parties and because I

> never expected the governor of the mass of Indians
> to ask for anything which would cause them harm
> and grave injuries.

Only afterward did he realize the intent of the document and the damages that it caused to the Indians.[77]

Contradictions to the landowners' will were few because landowners used their power to influence the selection of officials or to take collective action against those who sided with the Indians. Potentially uncooperative individuals were, with rare exceptions, co-opted or intimidated into silence. One Spanish official silenced a possible Indian troublemaker by installing him as an official of his community with the power to grant plots of land to whomever he pleased.[78]

In another case, an Indian protector resigned after at least six years of the "hatred, gossip, harassment and libel" of a landowning regidor who was using his power to acquire lands from the community of Mocupe. He stated that

> the truth is that one must have the patience of a
> Saint to tolerate his harangues just for defending
> this unhappy lot [of Indians] from his tyrannous
> extortions that greed and other private ends drive
> him [the regidor] to commit, abusing of their
> ignorance and dejection. . . . At times I cease
> pursuing some cases with heartache and remorse to
> avoid continuous confrontations and sometimes I
> continue with fear of . . . the consequences.

The landowner, according to the protector, was able to influence the panel of three judges hearing the case and to control the cabildo through his friendship with the subdelegado. The protector was later jailed for actions taken in defending the nearby community of Chérrepe.[79]

The most publicized example of the pressure that landowners could exert against an unsympathetic official is the case of Don Teodoro Daza. Daza arrived in Lambayeque to practice medicine before 1756. Within a decade his practice made him a well-known and appreciated individual among the Indians, mestizos, and certain landowners. He established close personal ties as a compadre to Indians, mixed bloods, landless bureaucrats, and hacendados alike. He also guaranteed the local notary Manuel Vásquez Meléndez and stood up at the marriage of individuals from all sectors of free society. During this time, too, he started raising livestock, renting the pastures from his compadres, the owners of Sicán. In 1782 he purchased the estate of Chumbenique and soon thereafter was appointed by the authorities in Lima as the protector of the Indians and as water commissioner.

At this point, the local establishment turned against him, probably resentful that such a person, with known sympathies for the Indians, had purchased his way into their group. The landowners used an entire session of a municipal council meeting to voice and record their objections to his appointment. Because they had no concrete evidence of wrongdoing, they based their protest on character defamation. They charged that Daza was of humble origin, a mixed blood whose name was Tiodor Ciqueña. They stated that his infidelity and otherwise immoral life-style (*"vida y costumbres malas"*) should disqualify him from holding the post (which, ironically, had traditionally been considered below the dignity of the richest landowners to accept). He was, they said, a common "barber and blood-letter" rather than a surgeon and doctor. Their only substantiated complaint was that Daza discredited other doctors in the province who charged the Indians exorbitant prices for treatment. The municipal officials concluded by predicting that Daza as protector would upset the Indians and disturb the peace of the province, a prediction with untoward connotations considering the uprising of Túpac Amaru in the south.

The landowners' complaints, however, did not have the intended effect on the viceregal authorities' original choice, especially after one member disclosed the council's premeditated plan against Daza. Officials in Lima retorted that the position of protector did not require noble birth, and that the position was given to those of Daza's class (suggesting that at least some of the council's accusations were true) "so that the Indians' rights might be served with speed and according to the law." Such persons, the reply continued, had less to worry about than "first-class citizens." The reply suggested that such people were also less self-serving. Because he had the support and recommendation from the corregidor Don Pedro Múñoz de Arjona, the four priests of Lambayeque, and the curaca and the Indians of Lambayeque, Daza was confirmed in 1784 over the objections of such well-connected and powerful individuals as Don Benito Caldas, the owner of La Viña and San Juan, alderman, and inspector of weights and measures; Don Manuel Antonio de Quiñones, the owner of La Punta, Saltur, and Pampa Grande, and an alderman and lieutenant colonel in the militia; Don Luis Mauro de Lara, an alderman, the royal standard-bearer, and owner of Santequepe and Saltrapón; Don Felipe Rivas Mateos, an alderman, captain in the infantry, and son-in-law of the discredited Dr. Don Juan Casos; Don José Andrés Gardea, a former lawyer of the royal audiencia in Lima and alderman of Lambayeque; Alférez Don Francisco Martínez de Ripalda, an alderman and former protector and water commissioner; Joseph de Rivera, an official of the royal monopolies and owner of a small plot of land; and Don Isidro de Lizarráburu, a past alderman and inspector of weights and measures.

Daza's two years in office, however, were stormy ones. He was accused of hiding crucial documents needed to prosecute a case for the Indians. As noted above, landowners blamed him for starting a riot against the owners of Pomalca and Collús. Daza was accused of collusion with the curacas and of instigating court cases among the Indians. He was continuously likened to Túpac Amaru. The charges were found to be false when some witnesses recanted and admitted that the whole smear campaign was planned and designed to discredit him.

After two years, Daza, now sixty years old, asked to be relieved of his duties on the grounds of old age and sickness. Given the troubles mentioned above, one suspects that age and health were not his real reasons. On the strength of the recommendation from his supervisor and his reputation as a good worker, Daza was appointed as the postmaster with a commission of 20 percent of receipts for the next year.[80]

Daza's case is significant because it exemplifies the pressure and power of the landowners and the attitude and proclivities of the officials in Lima. It shows how landowners, through the cabildo and their informal power network, tried to limit membership in their group. To discredit Daza would have been his ruin. His recently acquired estate would have been put on the market again. But now, in contrast to the previous period, the local landowners no longer held a monopoly of power. They were four on the cabildo—two of old families, two of new—with four nonlandowners who sat with them. Since one of the nonlandowners was the son-in-law of the physician whom Daza had discredited, they held a majority on the institution that enabled them to present a united front to Lima. This, however, was no longer sufficient to influence the technocrats of the capital who were charged with implementing the Bourbon reforms. Officials in Lima, in dismissing their objections, showed that the landowners' power was no longer sufficient to always have their own way.

This lesson was not lost on the Indians. They realized that their only recourse to the pervasive prestige, influence, and control of the landowners within the region was to appeal to higher authorities. The

Indians' experience with sympathetic officials of the visita of the 1780s[81] and with other officials who arrived in connection with the Bourbon reforms and left before becoming enmeshed in the compromising social milieu undoubtedly encouraged them to press their claims against the Spanish hacendados in appeal courts. Viceregal authorities were apt to be more impartial than provincial officials.

The community of Ferreñafe, after losing appeals to local officials, proceeded to sue the owner of Luya before the audiencia for the damages caused by his livestock while grazing in hacienda pastures on communal lands. Community officials protested that the stubble of their fields grew as a result of their hard work and with their irrigation water; therefore, the owner had no right to them. They argued as follows:

> Although the land is not the property of the
> Indians [because] his Majesty has [only] given them
> its use, it does not belong to the Spaniards [either];
> and because the pastures grow as a consequence of
> their cultivation, there is no reason for the
> hacendados to appropriate what does not
> correspond to them. . . .

The audiencia supported their claims by giving them exclusive rights to both the land and pastures in dispute. Indians thought that they had won an end to their problems; but the corregidor Don Juan de O'Kelly interpreted the order to mean that they should be given possession of all lands and pastures within a one-league radius of their town (called an "ejido"). On the rest of their land, the situation remained unchanged.

Continuing abuses and another appeal to the viceregal authorities made the audiencia settle on a compromise solution. A review of Luya's titles showed that although the owner claimed 723 fanegadas of lands he had legal title to only 170; on the remainder he owned only the rights to the pastures. Because of his long-term possession, however, the audiencia gave him legal title to the lands and pastures in question, on the condition that he keep his animals out of the pastures on Ferreñafe's other holdings. The court compensated the community with the explicit rights and exclusive possession to both the lands and pastures on a piece of land on the northern bank of the Tayme Canal. The audiencia threatened to fine any Spaniard one thousand pesos for violating their property, stipulating that the Indians could not "sell, donate or alienate the said lands, nor the pastures . . . individually or as a community, or rent them unless a Royal Judge agreed." Such appeals to Lima were not uniformly successful because even if upheld in their rights, the Indians had the problem of forcing the local officials into compliance.[82]

Although landowners' connections were not sufficient to impose their desires on viceregal authorities in Lima, they were still sufficient to win concessions. Together, old and new sugar producers cooperated to take collective action against a dictate from the viceroy in the 1740s, imposing a new tax on sugar and molasses. After rejecting the crown's plan to collect one-half peso on each unit produced, the owners offered the crown a compromise solution in 1746. They agreed to pay treasury officials 2,500 pesos per year with the condition that they be issued free licenses to transport and sell their product.[83]

The only unqualified success occurred in 1801 when at least twelve landowners took the offensive against the crown to bargain with government representatives over the commercialization and distribution of their produce. The members of the Chiclayo tobacco growers association (*gremio de cosechadores de tabaco*), the only legal producers of the leaf in the area, refused to meet their quotas and deliver their crops to the government warehouse and shipping office until they were promised a higher price. Justifying their boycott by citing the rising cost of transport and handling, they successfully forced the central authorities in Lima to raise the price from 75 to 80 pesos per 1,000 *masos* (small bundles).[84]

The ability of the owners to acquire land, pastures, and water from the Indians and to win concessions from the central government enabled them to change the organization of production on the estates and to reorient it on a regional level, thus steering the economy out of the doldrums and back toward recovery near the end of the eighteenth century. Over the years, the pastoral industry grew and eventually exceeded the sugar industry in volume and export earnings. Between 1758 and 1762 anywhere from sixty to seventy herds with an average of 850 head each were killed annually in Lambayeque. In 1766, the number of animals slaughtered passed 60,000. By the 1790s, the livestock industry had displaced the sugar industry as the major exporter of the region and had become "its principal source of wealth." Lecuanda reports that eighty herds of goats were slaughtered in eighteen tinas y tenerías with a yield of 12,000 quintales of soap and from 65,000 to 75,000 tanned hides annually. At the prices he quotes, the industry grossed between 220,625 to 236,250 pesos per year, compared to 36,000 pesos for the 16,000 arrobas of sugar exported.[85]

The new owners used stock raising to compensate for losses in the sugar sector. Navarrete, for example, used the profits from his livestock operations to offset the losses that he sustained from sugar on Pomalca. At the end of his fiscal year in March of 1743, the profits from his livestock business, although small, reduced the net losses from sugar to about 3,800 pesos. Sugar operations on Pomalca, although losing at a much lower rate, were still unprofitable in 1775–76. The owner's soap-making business, however, cleared enough to compensate. He netted over 1,800 pesos on both operations.[86]

A comparison of the biographies of the old and new owners suggests that the latter recognized sooner the possibilities of growing different crops in the region. The social ambitions which characterize upwardly mobile persons and the fact that many had reliable nonfarm sources of income may have made them more prone to risk innovation than the previous owners. Whatever the reasons, they experimented with several new crops with mixed success. Before 1800, wine, previously produced in small quantities exclusively for home consumption, began to be made on an expanded scale for the local market. Don Pablo Vélez, the owner of Calupe, for example, had "allowed the cane to be lost, in order to increase the size of his vineyard that will yield him fifty to sixty jugs of liquor." But soil and climate limited the future commercial feasibility of wine. Vines bore fruit only once every two or three years. Another hacendado tried with little success to extract lye from a wild plant which grew in the area. Others increased their product mix to include honey, fruit, indigo, cotton, rice, and tobacco. Production of the first three items was greatly reduced in favor of the last three. Lecuanda reports that cotton and rice yields in the 1790s reached 15,000 arrobas and 25,000 botijas, respectively.[87]

Tobacco, which had been grown on a small scale in the seventeenth century, took on new importance with the establishment of the crown tobacco monopoly in the 1750s.[88] The government, by restricting production and guaranteeing the growers a fixed price, encouraged them to plant on a large scale. Producers harvested and dried on the average 462,000 masos, worth more than 52,000 pesos, between 1773 and 1778. By 1785, 100,000 masos of locally produced tobacco were exported to Chile annually. In the 1790s production rose to new heights and leveled off at between 800,000 and 1 million masos per year, which were shipped from the port of Pacasmayo (to the south of Chérrepe) to Lima and

Valparaiso (Chile). Such initiatives turned a few estates into money-making enterprises before the end of the eighteenth century.[89]

That the region never fully recovered its former levels of economic prosperity—despite the increase in tobacco, rice, cotton, and livestock production—is evident from the amounts paid for the right to collect the tithes in the region. Figure 12 shows a pronounced decline in the bids after 1700.[90] But around midcentury bids rose dramatically in some cases, as in Lambayeque. The bids for Jayanca, Chiclayo, and Íllimo rose a few years later. Saña, however, proved to be the exception. It continued to drop during the same years, perhaps reflecting the almost total dominance of cane in that valley and the continued troubles of the sugar industry. What incomplete data are available, however, show sustained recovery in Chiclayo and Jayanca, which might be representative for the entire district.

The last century of colonial existence in Lambayeque, in short, was one of severe economic and social dislocation. The overextended sugar industry collapsed under the impact of continuing low prices, rising costs, a heavy debt burden, and a series of natural disasters. Because of its low capital and labor requirements, the stock-raising business grew and by the end of the century had become the principal industry of the region. The economic crisis also resulted in the ruin of the old landowners and their families and their replacement by parvenus, many of whom had come to the area in connection with the implementation of the Bourbon reforms. With their economic base seriously undermined, the personal connections of the old elite—so important in times of plenty for acquiring land, capital, water, and labor—proved insufficient to prevent their demise as a group. Despite the turnover in personnel, however, the structures of power remained unchanged. The new elite adopted the same tactics of survival as their predecessors. Their leadership position in municipal politics and in the militia helped them form alliances, sometimes with the remnants of the old elite, and sometimes with the emerging middle sector of aspiring landowners. These relationships enabled them to enhance and defend their local position and their control over the natural resources of the area from the more frequent and successful challenges of the Indians. But, as the Daza incident and the tax of 1746 compromise show, they were less successful in imposing their collective desires on central authorities and powerless to affect international market forces or the implementation of the Bourbon reforms.

8   Conclusions

The main objective of this regional-level review of land tenure in Lambayeque throughout almost three hundred years has been to assess the landowners' power—in all of its various forms—and to determine if and how it was used to affect the development of the estates. This has entailed recreating the economic history of the estates and using it as a framework or backdrop within or against which to identify the owners, assess their power, and analyze how and under what circumstances they wielded it.

The study follows the evolution of the great estate through several distinct phases: formation, growth and consolidation, prosperity, and decline. The process of estate development often followed a predictable progression, a diachronic process of development; but no one pattern prevailed. Chacras became haciendas. Some haciendas were converted into sugar mills. Other estates began as corrals and became estancias and tinas y tenerías. Some estancias remained estancias into the nineteenth century, while others evolved into haciendas y trapiches. A few estancias developed into haciendas, but they were never equipped for sugar production.

Given this change and variation, meaningful characterization of the estates has proved to be difficult. Even within the context of this single Peruvian region, "hacienda" had no one definition. Large size, a commonly accepted trait, was not an absolute, unchanging parameter. Some estates originated as land grants of forty fanega(da)s de sembradura (about thirteen of later measure), which were small in comparison to the extent of later production units, but provided more land than one settler could cultivate at once in those early years. Estates in the seventeenth and eighteenth centuries measured in the hundreds of fanegadas and were huge in comparison to the plots cultivated by an Indian. They were probably larger than the vineyards described by Robert G. Keith on the southern Peruvian coast, but smaller than the typical estate of the highlands. And they were miniscule, indeed, when compared to the estates of central and northern Mexico (described by David Brading, Charles Harris, Ida Altman, and others), which measured in the tens and hundreds of thousands of equivalent units. Large size, then, is not an exact criterion, but must remain, like the meaning of the term *hacienda* itself, specific to location and period.[1]

The almost constant and relatively rapid transformations that characterize the estates in Lambayeque also make a determination of their overall nature difficult. They were not isolated like the estates so often depicted in the general literature, but early on they were tied to important overseas markets. In this sense, even in their earliest forms as chacras and labores, the estates' organization and product mix were reflections of market forces. They differed, too, from the self-sufficient estates portrayed by François Chevalier, although their dependence on external supplies of labor, raw materials, and even rations for workers varied by period and specialization. Early estancias were more self-sufficient than later ones, which had tanning and soap-making facilities on the premises; and these were more self-contained than the sugar-producing estates. In general, however, the estates in Lambayeque were more like those described by John C. Super and Harris than those described by Chevalier, for they were seldom or never self-contained for any appreciable length of time.[2]

Labor systems were diverse, too. Owners supplemented slaves with permanent and resident Indian peons; temporarily employed and wage-earning Indians, contracted artisans, and temporary draft Indian labor. Debt peonage seems of less overall importance here than it was in areas like Oaxaca, Mexico. Over the years, a racial division of labor developed with slaves usually doing the more skilled tasks and Indians the unskilled work. The level of personal interaction between the owner or his spokesman and representative and the worker varied, too. Resident peons and slaves probably had more sustained contact than temporary wage-earners. However, even this economic relationship was tempered by the fact that temporary laborers, following ancient custom, often worked to honor a request from a person associated through kinship—whether real or fictive—or through friendship.[3]

The subject of profitability is another topic that defies facile generalizations which would hold for the entire colonial period. Although the data are far from complete for Lambayeque and probably biased slightly too low, it is apparent from the available figures and other indirect evidence that the estates made money sometimes for some—in the sixteenth century and in the second half of the seventeenth, for example. In contrast, the vast majority were clearly unprofitable for most of the eighteenth century. Nicholas P. Cushner, however, shows that the Jesuit estates—Tumán being an example in the Lambayeque area—remained profitable, at least until their expropriation by the crown in 1767. There were secular estates, like Calupe, in the area that also remained profitable long after the first bankruptcies of neighboring enterprises, which was due at least in part to their low level of mortgages and censos and undisrupted administration. Thus, even when times were bad, some estates showed a profit while others did not. In boom times, some estates made more money than others. But, as with the secular estates described by Brading, the data now on hand suggest that the periodic returns were normally relatively low, often in the range of 5 percent. Estates in Lambayeque were apparently less prosperous at a comparable stage of development than were the vineyards described by Keith; and their owners could not claim, as the Jesuits could in Mexico and Peru, that some of their estates always made a profit.[4]

Judging from these considerations—size, degree of market integration, systems of labor, and profitability—we cannot say, as some authors have attempted to do in the past, that the estate in Lambayeque was either strictly seignorial or capitalistic. Because the estates were market oriented and probably run usually with the goal of making a profit—whether owners tried to maximize returns or merely to maintain a certain level of income—the estates in Lambayeque seem to approximate more closely a capitalistic enterprise corrupted by seignorial elements, to paraphrase Magnus Mörner and Keith, rather than the other way around.[5]

To explain the change and variation noted above, one must go back to the era of the encomienda, despite the recognized fact that the estate did not directly originate from the grants of Indian labor to the first conquerors. Land did not become important to the encomenderos until their Indian subjects died or fled and the crown began to effectively regulate labor services and restrict tribute exactions. The failure of the encomienda to provide the encomenderos with an adequate supply of goods to support the growing Spanish sector of society in Lambayeque and elsewhere in Spanish America forced them to develop supplemental economic enterprises, one of which was the estate.

The early confusion between the encomienda and the hacienda is understandable because some encomenderos, like those in Mexico and Chile, began ranching and agricultural activities near their encomienda communities and in some cases on lands that had been used by Indians under their care. Of the eighty encomenderos with Indians in the area, about half (47.5 percent) are known to have eventually held land there. But only one was officially granted land within the jurisdiction of his Indian community. The others occupied vacant, abandoned land with no legal claim to it until a few years after its appropriation, when they began seeking legal title through bills of sale, grants, or confirmation.[6]

Thus, the encomienda and hacienda were two distinct institutions. Both could theoretically have their juridical origin in grants from the crown via competent local or viceregal authorities, but they were successive and not strictly contemporary phenomena, as Brading has pointed out. The connection between the two institutions was the person of the encomendero, who invested in land the capital accumulated from the work of the Indians.[7]

From this beginning, the further development of the estate and the form that it eventually acquired responded to a now familiar list of influences. Within the natural limits imposed by geography and climate, the estates grew and changed in response to effective demand, the availability of labor and investment capital, the level of technology, and governmental policy. These factors also accounted for their periods of decline. Competition and lack of markets, poor administration, lack of capital, and high levels of indebtedness—exacerbated by periodic bad harvests, floods and other natural disasters, and fire or epidemics, which decimated the labor force—also caused their ruin.

The testamentary system so detrimental to some of the estates studied by Brading in the Bajío seems to have been less so for those in Lambayeque. Heirs' claims and censos did indeed increase the debt burden of some estates and increase the frequency of their sale and the attendant disruption in administration that this implied, but rarely caused fragmentation or division. Indeed, clauses in the typical capellanía and censo foundations prohibited division of the land.[8]

There seems to have been an awareness on the part of the owners and their children of the danger inherent in direct, multiple claims on the estate. More often than not, landowners and their families made alternative arrangements when more than one heir survived childhood. In several cases one heir bought out the others to gain control. In others, all but one child were given dowries or cash advances during the lifetime of the owner in lieu of a share of the estate, which ensured that it would pass intact to one descendant, preferably the eldest son. This practice constituted the equivalent of a *mayorazgo* in an area where none were formally established.[9]

In other instances, the issue did not arise. Captain Martín Núñez de Arze, for example, owned four estates, enough to leave one each to his sons. After about 1650, when lay owners were more likely to leave more than one heir, the fact that so many priests acquired estates reduced the importance of the testamentary system as a cause for decline.

But these economic and situational conditions—which have in the past been employed to explain the evolution of the estate—cannot alone completely explain the formation, prosperity, and decline of the institution. Such factors, in combination, created the conditions for the development of the estates and as such are useful for analyzing the evolutionary process at a high level of abstraction. But, though they are necessary, these enabling conditions are insufficient to explain variations in the timing and extent of development on a regional level. Given similar conditions within the region, why did one estate develop faster than another? Why did Calupe become a hacienda y trapiche, while Collús, on its border, remained an estancia? Why did La Punta remain profitable in the middle of the eighteenth century, while most of the surrounding estates were in various stages of decay? Why was royal legislation designed to protect the Indians an effective obstacle to expansion at one site and not at another?

The answer to these questions and the key to the unexplained variance in the process of development is power, defined here in a generic sense as the capability of some members of society to take advantage of the conditions to effect agricultural development better than others. Power—in all of its various forms—implies the ability directly to make or indirectly to influence decisions and actions affecting local resources needed for agricultural development. I neither want to suggest that power is intrinsic to certain individuals, nor do I intend to underestimate or downplay the importance of the factors mentioned above. In the last analysis, they set the limits within which individuals act. Instead, I want to emphasize an important dimension of the evolutionary process at the local level that explains the variance unaccounted for by these factors alone.

This approach has necessitated my study of the landowners and the nature of their power, which have heretofore been relatively neglected topics. The depiction of the hacendado is as difficult as the characterization of the hacienda because the almost nine hundred landowners studied here exhibited elements of both a colonial version of a European lord and an entrepreneur. The description of the landowner as "feudal" or "seignorial" is accurate for some of the hacendados of Lambayeque in a qualified sense. It is probably a more accurate description for landed encomenderos, who had large extended families and numerous retainers and employees boarding in the household, than for late eighteenth-century hacendados like the Pinillos brothers, who preferred to pay cash for services and to be paid cash for access to the resources they controlled. But between these extremes and in general, a landowner's relationship with subordinates was paternalistic, probably as much because of his early socialization as because of his role as a cultural broker or intermediary between dependents and other members of Spanish society. He provided access to otherwise unattainable goods and services. By distributing favors which cost him relatively little, he built up a reserve of obligations that he used, in turn, to gain disproportionately large benefits. Such favors became a type of social currency which the businessman accumulated as an integral part of his overall management scheme and then exchanged or spent for desired goods and services, as he would do with pesos.

Such rational calculations of costs and benefits constantly showed through his paternalistic facade, suggesting that the landowner, as he existed in Lambayeque, also had some entrepreneurial or business sense. The landowner often exhibited concern for economic benefit, but as suggested above, his calculations were not always in terms of pesos and reales. If motives for acquiring estates were not always high rates of profit, for example, they often reflected other economic rationales. Speculation, discounted as a motive elsewhere in Peru, was occasionally a factor in Lambayeque, especially when investors thought the elongation of an irrigation canal (recall the Tecse canal project) or another improvement would make the property productive and valuable. Land acquisition, even when not needed immediately for cultivation, as was so often the case, was an important means to gain additional water rights, pasturage, and labor; and in so doing, competition was reduced.[10]

Similarly, the landowner's calculations included such intangibles as prestige—probably especially important for social climbers. Merchants, bureaucrats, and priests in the eighteenth century purchased estates, despite their poor condition and unprofitability, for the prestige value of land. They invested in the property in an effort to make it pay, but were unwilling or unable to sustain continued losses. Thus, while acquisition of an estate could, in the short run, confirm a social position for a new owner, it could also, in the long run, be a family's undoing. So even if traditional values were important motives for certain owners, most probably expected some return, even if modest by other standards. Few could sustain continued losses, as the number of sales and instability of ownership show in moderately good and bad times (that is, to the middle of the seventeenth century and after about 1720, respectively). Relative stability of ownership is achieved only during the boom years of extraordinary economic circumstances.[11]

The ideal may have been to become part of a group of idle rich, but typically the landowner of Lambayeque, like some of his counterparts in Mexico, was active in several economic pursuits at once. In addition to being a farmer or rancher, who controlled the administration of his estates closely and made the major decisions that affected production, he often imported raw materials and slaves, and marketed and exported products. Moreover, hacendados were lawyers, priests, notaries, wholesale and retail merchants, miners, shipowners, bureaucrats, and financiers. A hacendado's participation in municipal politics and in the militia extended his contacts and enhanced his ability to operate successfully in the locality. Only during the second half of the seventeenth century do we find a significant few who do not fit this description. These few could afford, in the short run, to lead a more leisurely and gentlemanly life, and they increasingly divorced themselves from active participation in public affairs and in the administration of the family estates.[12]

Landowners and their families formed an elite that epitomized success in this pocket of colonial society. The first were encomenderos who acquired land as the value of the encomienda declined. They set the social tone and established the aristocratic values, tradition, and customs emulated by the settlers and other members of society for years. In the late sixteenth century, landowning settlers, who could bring together the factors needed for production, displaced the encomenderos and assumed control of the frontier. Those hacendados who survived the expansion process founded the families that became the core of the entrenched landed elite of the late seventeenth century. Despite the firm establishment of certain families at the top of the regional social pyramid, the landed elite remained open to selected— wealthy, talented, well-placed, well-connected and well-born—members of the professional and bureaucratic sector of society. The prosperity of the second half of the seventeenth century allowed the hacendados to personify the encomendero ideal successfully, not only in wealth but also prestige and power. During the trying years of the eighteenth century, these landed aristocrats were replaced by a group of individuals whom they considered their social inferiors, parvenus who lacked the authority of long-standing tradition and who were relatively less wealthy. Yet, despite antagonisms, common interests could and did bind the old and new groups together to defy challenges to their elite positions.

The reconstitution of landed families negates the common belief in Peru that a few families with genealogies dating back to colonial times and especially to the conquerors themselves rule, and ruled, Peru. The Lambayequen elite was not static. Upward and downward mobility occurred constantly. Like those in certain areas of Mexico, few families maintained their elite status for more than a few generations. When they did, their claim was often based on the horizontal pattern of land tenure rather than on hereditary, direct linear descent through the male or female line. As the concentration of property proceeded, more members of the elite families were forced to seek nonagricultural professions. This contraction of the opportunity structure also implied less upward social mobility as the number of landowners declined. The frustrations of the downwardly mobile and the aspirations of the upwardly mobile undoubtedly became a reserve of potential pressure that surfaced during the wars of Independence.[13]

The examples of upward social mobility also show that position, within the predominantly white upper levels of society, was never totally ascribed rather than achieved. Wealth seems consistently more important than birth, except perhaps occasionally during the third period when birth and wealth might have been synonymous, giving certain individuals an advantage. Even then, however, the ranks of the landowning elite remained open, although opportunities for entrance were fewer than they had been previously or would be thereafter. As far as the value of peninsular birth is concerned, a consideration raised by David Szewczyk in his study of Mexico, the biographies of the landowners suggest a hierarchy of value favoring the socially mobile from Spain over those born in another part of the Spanish empire or in the area itself. Peninsular-born immigrants representing new wealth were more successful in acquiring land than others, whether they bought land or married into landowning families representing old prestige.[14]

Wealth, then, not necessarily land, seemed to determine one's position and power. Early and extraordinary service to the crown during the conquest era gained for the conquerors a grant of Indian labor which provided them with the means to accumulate fortunes, gave them automatic social prestige, and qualified them for a cabildo position. The authority implied by a seat on the municipal council, in turn, allowed the encomenderos to increase their income through price-fixing, fee collection, and the distribution of Indian labor. The combination of wealth, status, and political position set the encomenderos apart and above other members of society and put them in a favorable position to form close personal contacts among themselves and with other key individuals in the area and in the viceregal capital. This combination of factors was the basis of their ability to control the resources necessary to maintain their hegemony. But, access to capital, personal income or borrowed, was the necessary, if not the sufficient condition, for their hegemony.

The first settlers could not be described as wealthy, and certainly not aristocratic. They did not possess fortunes, but all needed capital to develop the land. They had modest holdings, as compared to their heirs and successors. Land, as suggested above, at times did not generate income or, at least, did not generate enough to cover all the expenditures of the owner, his family, and their largely culturally inspired needs. Reserves or a good credit rating were necessary to survive periodic market fluctuations and other unexpected circumstances.

But land acquisition certainly enhanced one's social position and power. Landownership—throughout most of the colonial era and regardless of whether land was granted by the king, inherited from a relative, or purchased—was associated with the richest individuals in local society. Except perhaps during the one period of stagnation, hacendados' economic power rested in part on the control of the natural resources and the means of production that land implied and the role this control gave them in the local economy.

The fact that hacienda profits could vary so greatly also suggests a tentative answer to a question posed by Mörner in his review of hacienda literature—did estates finance other activities or vice versa? We know that it usually took capital to acquire an estate for the first time or to maintain one through periodic reversals. After the flooding of the 1720s, for example, landowners who had purchased the pasturage rights to land in the visita of 1711–12 needed income and became more willing to rent grazing rights to the merchants, priests, bureaucrats, and others who rushed to start or expand their flocks. Some of these became the operators of the first independent tinas y tenerías in the region; and, indeed, although there is some indication that agriculture began a slow and uneven recovery after the middle of the eighteenth century, it was the manufacture of soap and hides that gave the region its prosperous veneer. The profits from these operations along with other income enabled some of this group to acquire the estates as the church and other creditors foreclosed on members of the old landed elite.[15]

It appears, however, that this situation was not always the rule. The late sixteenth-century estates owned by Gabriel de la Requera and Salvador Vásquez and their heirs provided enough profit, in theory, to finance other enterprises. Some profits were used to finance trips to Tierra Firme and other mercantile activities. Some went to found unproductive censos to benefit members—living and dead. Herein, then, lies one of the problems in answering Mörner's query definitively—we do not always know to what purpose such yields were put. Furthermore, the fact that a significant number of landowners had several sources of income makes it difficult to determine whether income from one activity—an estate, for example—was earmarked for a specific purpose or whether all income, regardless of source, was pooled and invested as opportunities arose. Only additional research will substantiate my hunch that the estate was both a form of consumption and a generator of income over the course of its colonial history.

Income, whether totally estate-generated or not, allowed the members of the landed elite to progress from the status of countrified settlers into cultured, educated, and well-traveled aristocrats with family trees, mansions on the main square of the town, and large staffs of domestic servants. Despite the desert heat, they dressed in fine woolens, velvets, and satin. They rode over the rutted and bumpy trails between Saña and Lambayeque and their estates in richly appointed carriages. Their life-style became the envy and the model for the rest of society and enhanced the prestige of landownership and fortunes. The respect which others accorded them is quite evident from the terms used to describe them—*don, señor,* and *caballero.* Landowners and their families became a relatively cohesive and increasingly exclusive and inbred class, which assumed its most aristocratic form in the last half of the seventeenth century. The long-lasting impression they created outlived them and clouded reality for years to come.

Wealth also gave the landowners the means and spare time to participate in the formal political process, centered in the town council. Landowners did not participate continuously. They engaged actively in local politics during the sixteenth century and again during the late eighteenth century, both periods during which important decisions concerning the social, political, and economic order were made. Positions on the town council allowed them to influence the outcome of decisions in their favor. During the seventeenth century and the first half of the eighteenth century, a period of institutional stability and inaction, landlords retired somewhat from direct political involvement, preferring to voice informal opinions on issues through friends, relatives, compadres, and business associates.

Indeed, their direct participation in the council was not always absolutely crucial to the successful administration of their rural estates. It can be argued that part of the landowners' ability to safeguard their position in society and their economic base rested on their control and domination of the municipal council in the sixteenth century; but members of the council did not indefinitely retain the power they had to make land grants and to distribute draft labor. In fact, as early as the 1550s and 1560s, the council began losing its ability to exercise direct control of natural resources to the corregidor and other royal officials. Thereafter, magistrates and aldermen could not grant land, except within the urban limits, nor could they allocate irrigation water or distribute Indian labor. Price-fixing was unimportant to the landowners because they exported most of their produce. The landowners' continuing representation on the council reflected their preoccupation with maintaining their prestige or the tradition of the family's participation in the institution. Some held seats that they inherited and served out of a sense of duty. Interest revived in the council in the late eighteenth century, not for any direct power that council seats gave them over the countryside—except indirectly, for example, to repair roads—but for the opportunity to use the institution as a forum for discussing and acting on such pressing matters as the appointment and confirmation of key bureaucrats.[16]

Landowners rarely exercised power formally and openly to affect their estates. Bureaucratic positions, despite pretentious titles, did not give them much power to affect their landholdings. Instead, they used their roles as the employers, financiers, religious patrons, and benefactors of the region to dispense favors and to aid individuals whose contact could prove helpful. The landowners, for example, took advantage of the contradictions in the governing system (that is, salaries that under the Hapsburgs were inadequate to support bureaucrats and their families in a style commensurate with their aspirations) to co-opt officials to whom the crown had entrusted the power to regulate the distribution of local resources. Bureaucrats soon became beholden to local interests, often using their formal power for the landowners' benefit and their own. Through friendship, marriage, and godparenthood, landowners guaranteed their ability to dictate policy and influence officials and other members of society. The landowners' informal relations, connections, and cooperation were more important in affecting the conduct of local affairs that touched their rural landholdings than their formal positions of power.

Such social extensions of their power explain the outcome of disputes between Spanish landowners and Indian communities and the former's ability to acquire scarce labor in the sixteenth century, necessary land and irrigation water in the seventeenth, and pasturage rights in the eighteenth. They help explain, for example, how the Alférez Real and Captain Martín Núñez de Arze was able to acquire the additional water resources he needed to turn one of his four estates into a sugar producer sooner than his neighbors. As the owner of Cayaltí, he was already familiar with sugar technology. He owned the land and had the funds for the project. He judged economic conditions to be ripe. But he had first to solve a water shortage problem. He accomplished this by using his reputation as an influential citizen and his ties to key local officials to convince a reluctant viceroy to allow him to lease, in perpetuity, 150 fanegadas of land from the Indians of Monsefú for its water allocation.

The clearest examples, however, of the difference which the individual owners made in the pace and direction of the evolution of the estates occurred during periods of disequilibrium and rapid change. In the sixteenth century, the encomenderos held the advantage over the settlers. Given the same set of circumstances, the encomenderos' control of labor and the capital accumulated from the encomienda and other business interests allowed them to mount the first molinos, establish the first tinas and tenerías, and equip the first ingenios and trapiches. Settlers were limited to small-scale food production and livestock raising because they did not have access to the necessary labor and capital. Again after 1720, the younger generations of the great landed families, accustomed to living off the income of the estates and not seriously pursuing or exercising their careers or professions, were ruined by the combination of a cost-price squeeze and a series of natural disasters. Once their economic base was destroyed, neither their political position, alternative occupations, nor personal contacts proved sufficient to prevent their gradual replacement by a new group of individuals with steady nonfarm sources of income and expanding networks of power and influence.

Power—the landowners' ability to affect decisions and actions regarding land tenure in their favor—was more complex than the analytical discussion above suggests. The landowners' dominance rested primarily on wealth; hence the economics of power, in that it made them a directing force in the local economy and gave them the means to acquire the material hallmarks and social graces of aristocrats. Wealth allowed the landowners to purchase public office and join the militia which, in turn, bolstered their social standing and authority. This made their friendship and esteem desirable to other members of society and allowed them to form connections with key persons through whom they could exert their will. The economic, political, and social aspects of their power were reinforcing and circular; each contributed to the landed elite's central and dominant position. And, in conjunction, they both affected the development of the estate and were affected by its evolution. Wealth, not land, was the basis of their position, and the necessary condition for their status and power. When the descendants of the landowning aristocrats of the late seventeenth century lost their fortunes, neither social contacts nor their seats on the town council were sufficient to maintain their hegemony.

Because the landed elite in Lambayeque was not a stable and self-perpetuating group, and because wealth, a certain level of income, or access to capital enabled merchants, bureaucrats, and priests to move up into the landowning class, a point is raised that merits reiterating: power was diffuse in this local colonial society. It was by no means concentrated exclusively in the persons of the hacendados, as has sometimes been suggested in the literature. Land implied some power, and it increased as the land became a productive and income-generating asset with the addition of capital, technology, labor, and so forth. The hacendados were powerful individually and as a group when compared to the Indians. But landowners certainly were not omnipotent even on the local level. The landowners' decisive action rested on the cooperation of their associates in the professional and bureaucratic sectors of society. There was tension at times between them; just as there were occasional instances of jealousy and rivalries, born of competition, between the great clans. Landowners suffered occasional reverses; but, at least in the local arena, their money allowed them, through most of colonial times, to establish a fragile alliance with the socially mobile who were waiting in the side lines to move into the coveted position themselves at the first sign of weakness. The available evidence suggests that the Bourbon reforms destroyed the power structure, rendering it less responsive to the established elite's demands at a time when the old families needed help the most. These realizations force us to qualify the stereotype of the hacendados and the statements to the effect that the hacienda dominated society and that land was *the,* rather than *a,* basis of power.[17]

The development of the estates and a powerful landowning class had a broadly adverse effect on the Indian communities in the area. Indians lost land, pastures, and irrigation water, their traditional sources of subsistence and independence. Over the years they became primarily suppliers of foodstuffs, raw materials, and labor. Landowners co-opted top Indian officials to guarantee the cooperation of the rest. Domination was relatively easy for the landowning Spaniard and creole because the system did not always protect the Indians as it was designed to do in theory.

From the point of view of the Indian commoners the governing structure became increasingly rigid. Written petitions and verbal protests went unheeded locally, and appeals to Lima were lengthy, expensive, and often unsuccessful. During the late eighteenth century, as their resources became less and less adequate to meet their needs, the commoners turned to violence, as did their counterparts in some parts of Mexico, to make their collective voice heard. Such armed incidents, though rare, indicate the survival—though usually muted—of a corporate strength and a growing restlessness.[18]

But the fact that Indian communities did have recourse to outside authorities demonstrates how important it is to keep this local study in perspective. Regional history used as a testing ground for certain ideas and theories must be related back to its viceregal and international contexts. In this regard, the history of Lambayeque shows the effects of its dependency on Spain. Lambayeque, as an export enclave, depended on external sources for technology and supplies. Producers themselves had little control over the marketplace. They looked to the metropolis for cultural and social norms. The local power which they wielded often so successfully during much of the colonial era rested on outside authority.

Distance from the mother country and the viceregal capital provided the system of government with local flexibility, but government policy (for example, in regard to taxes) was implemented on occasion and did affect the regional economy. The landowners best able to prevent, stall, or modify the execution of adverse policy proposals were those with personal connections in Lambayeque and Lima. But no matter how powerful they were on the local level, landowners could do little to change major policy determinations in Spain.

Finally, this regional history suggests that Peruvian history, like that of Mexico—as Altman and Lockhart's compilation shows so well—is more than generalizations of the history of the Andean mountain region, especially of the area around Cuzco, and of Lima. A number of conditions (for example, heavy and continued reliance on Indian labor, year-round cultivation based on irrigation, specialized production for export markets, and so forth) make Lambayequen estates unrepresentative of those elsewhere in Peru, even of those located in other coastal valleys. As compared to those in Lambayeque, estates described by Keith were smaller, more profitable, and more reliant for labor on slaves than Indians. They produced wine for a keenly competitive market, instead of sugar, hides, and soap for an overseas one. None of these coastal estates fits the stereotype of the classical estate of the highlands. The fact that so many of the accepted notions about Peruvian agrarian history do not hold for Lambayeque suggests that this region and others deserve more attention. Until additional regional histories are written and recognized as important, the history of Peru will remain incomplete and distorted.[19]

Appendices

Appendix 1: Value of Currencies in the Viceroyalty of Peru

Before 1555:

1 gold mark = 16 silver marks = 128 pesos (of 8 reales each), 32 maravedis = 34,848 maravedis.

1 castellano = ¹/₅₀ of a gold mark = 1 peso de oro de minas = 8 tomines. In 1689, its value was 25 reales or 850 maravedis.

1 silver mark = 8 pesos (of 8 reales), 2 maravedis = 2,178 maravedis.

After 1572:

1 silver mark (of plata corriente) = 2,250 maravedis = 5 pesos ensayados.

1 peso ensayado = 1 peso de oro de plata ensayada (as of 1586) = 8 tomines = 450 maravedis = 1.2 ducats = 13.25 reales.

1 peso ensayado de tributo (created 1592) = 12.5 reales = 425 maravedis.

1 ducado de castilla = 375 maravedis = 6 tomines = 11 reales.

1 peso de plata corriente = 9 reales = 306 maravedis = 30.906 granos.

1 peso of 8 reales = 1 patacón = 272 maravedis = 27.464 granos.

1 real = usually, 34 maravedis.

1 tomín = usually, 56 maravedis = 12 granos. The tomín's value varied proportionately with that of the peso ensayado.

Notes: Lohmann and Burzio disagree over the value of the tomín. Lohmann states that one real equals half a tomín in 1552. Burzio equates the real with the tomín. Manuel Moreyra y Paz Soldán, in *Antecedentes Españoles y el circulante durante la conquista e iniciación del virreinato* (Lima, 1941), 27, defines the peso ensayado as eight tomines. I use this definition for conversion purposes in the text. See also my note on prices in Appendix 4.

Sources: Manuel Moreyra y Paz-Soldán, *Apuntes sobre la historia de la moneda colonial en el Perú* (Lima, 1938), 14–15, 17 and 31–32; C. H. Haring, *The Spanish Empire in America* (New York, 1963), 287–88, and 290; Guillermo Lohmann Villena, "Apuntaciones sobre el curso de los precios de los artículos de primera necesidad en Lima durante el siglo XVI," *Revista histórica*, XXIX (1966), 81, 83, and 84; *Actas del Cabildo de Trujillo*, I, 242; Humberto F. Burzio, "La moneda primitiva en el Perú en el siglo XVI," *Boletín de la Academia Nacional de Historia* (Buenos Aires) XX–XXI (1947–48), 412–15; Real Academia Española, *Diccionario de la Lengua Castellana* (Madrid, 1783), 220 and 900; John Lynch, *Spain Under the Hapsburgs* (New York, 1964), i and 349; ART/Mata: 10–IV–1564; 11–IV–1564; 30–V–1565; CaO: 27–IV–1566; ANP/R: l. 7, c. 16, 1590, 4; AGI/P: l. 108, r. 7, 1562, 95; and J: 509A, [1620], 31.

Appendix 2: Weights and Measures

Almud: A unit of dry measure equal to $1/12$ of a fanega (or 4.625 liters in seventeenth-century Mexico).[1]

Arroba: A weight of 25 pounds or 11.5 kilograms.

Checo: One-sixth of a fanega = 2 almudes (for corn).

Fanega: A unit of dry measure equal to 1.5 bushels of corn (in Mexico before 1580) or 130 pounds (of flour in sixteenth-century Peru) or 6 checos (of corn).[2]

Fanegada: A unit of land measure equal to a plot 144 varas by 288 varas or 2.89 hectareas or 7.16 acres.

Fanegada or fanega de sembradura:[3]   Equals fanegadas de tierras de las antiguas = the area of land that can be planted with one fanega of seed. For corn: 3 fanegadas de sembradura = 1 fanegada. The porportions varied according to the crop and the quality of the land. This measure was still being used on the northern coast as late as 1648. Fanega de sembradura seems to be used primarily in the sixteenth century and gradually was replaced by fanegada de sembradura.

Fardo: A bale. When used to measure tobacco, a fardo equalled 125 *manojos* or handfuls (small bundles).

Legua: League or 3,000 pesos de Salmon or 5,000 varas = 4,179.5 meters or 4.2 kilometers or approximately 3 miles.

Porrón: A clay jar of no standard capacity used to measure liquids.

Quartillo: A dry unit of measure equal to one-fourth of a *celemin* or $1/48$ of a fanega.

Quintal: A hundredweight or 4 arrobas.

Sesma: One-sixth of a vara.

Vara: Unit of measure equal to 33 inches or 0.8359 meters.

Notes: ¹An almud is defined as ¹/₂ fanega in Castilla in Covarrubias, 1611, 584.

²Keith Davies defines the fanega as 2.58 bushes for colonial Arequipa. Davies, 25.

³Fanega de sembradura is defined elsewhere, as follows: in Mexico, of corn as 8.82 acres by Taylor, 241; elsewhere in Peru, as 3 fanegadas actuales by Rostworowski, 151.

Sources: ART/Mata: 2–III–1565; Paz: 14–III–1576; Robert Gordon Keith, "Origins of the Hacienda System on the Central Peruvian Coast," Ph.D. diss., Harvard University, 1969, 135; Lesley Byrd Simpson, "Exploitation of Land in Central Mexico in the Sixteenth Century," *Ibero-Americana*, XXXVI (Berkeley, 1952), 17; ANCR/Collús: [1807]; Enrique Florescano, *Precios del maíz y crisis agrícolas* (México, 1969), 144; Real Academia Española, *Diccionario de la Lengua Castellana* (Madrid, 1783), 780; AGI/E: 511A, 1648, 40v; AL: 100, [1646], 30; *La Unión*, 11–V–1959, 1; ACMS/1778; Keith A. Davies, "The Rural Domain of the City of Arequipa, 1540–1665" (Ph.D. diss., University of Connecticut, Storrs, 1974); Sebastián de Covarrubias, *Tesoro de la lengua Castellana o Española* (Barcelona, 1943) [for 1611], 584; William B. Taylor, *Landlord and Peasant in Colonial Oaxaca* (Stanford, 1972), 241; ANP/TP: c. 634 cited by María Rostworowski de Diez Canseco, "Mercaderes del valle de Chincha en la época prehispánica: Un documento y unos comentarios," *Revista Española de Antropologia Americana*, V (Madrid, 1970), 151; and ANCR/ 1729.

Appendix 3: Chronology of Landownership

Appendix 3: Chronology of Landownership

Date	Owner	Mode of Acquisition	Area (in fanegadas*) [1]	Total Population [2]	Price/ Value [3]	Value of Mortgages
CALUPE						
pre-1599	Maestro de Campo Juan Rodríguez Vejete	purchase			6,700	
1599	Alonso de Paz	confirmed	30		225 [4]	
pre-1611	Juan de Salinas		Fellupe	4 mitayos		none
1611	Bachiller Manuel Fernández	purchase	100 (Fellupe)	4 mitayos		
pre-1628	Francisco Ruiz Vejarano	purchase		4 mitayos		none
1628	Cristóbal Gutiérrez Muñoz, Esteban Alonso	transferred from Francisco Ruiz Vejarano	133 (Fellupe added ca. 1616)			
1643	Cristóbal Gutiérrez Muñoz	purchased half from his partner	433		6,700	

Date	Name	Transaction		Slaves/Mitayos	Value	
1644	Doña María Luisa Rivadeneyra y Villavicencio, Don Nicolás Gutiérrez de Villavicencio	inheritance from husband and father, confirmed	433		1,080[4]	
1645	Manuel Carvallo	purchased from Doña María Luisa Rivadeneyra and son	433	9-11 mitayos, 13 slaves (in 1647)	12,000+	none
pre-1672	Antonio Vedón de Sanabria	purchased from Carvallo				
n.d.	Captain Juan de Urrutia Gallardo					
pre-1692	Captain Martín Núñez de Arze	purchased from Urrutia Gallardo		46 slaves		1,000
1693	Bachiller Don Francisco de Palma y Vera	purchased from Núñez de Arze		49 slaves	63-68,000	17,350
1694	Jesuits	donation from Palma y Vera	500	52 slaves, 9-10 mitayos	67,000	
1704	Captain Nicolás de Urrutia Gallardo	purchased from Jesuits	433	50 slaves	55,000	20,000

Appendix 3, continued.

Date	Owner	Mode of Acquisition	Area (in fanegadas*)[1]	Total Population[2]	Price/Value[3]	Value of Mortgages
1715	Don Bartolomé Pérez Zavala	purchased in auction of estate of Urrutia Gallardo		100 slaves	41,000	30,000
1719	Captain Antonio Gonzales Casana	purchased from Pérez Zavala	433	52 slaves,5 117 slaves, mitayos	58,500	41,100, 67,300 after 1720 flood)
1731, 1741	Don Pedro Gonzales Casana	purchased from his father, Antonio; took possession	434	83 slaves 74 slaves (in 1744)	80,000, (52,499 in 1741)	30,000, 37,358 (in 1741)
1757	church administered			24 slaves (in 1756)		
1763	Licenciado Rafael Vélez	purchased from estate of Gonzales Casana	433	30 slaves	18,000 (14,136)	
1789	Don Pedro Vélez	inherited from father; purchased from other heirs	563	slaves	(65,205)	13,556

CALLANCA (not including Focodan, Lonope and Nampón)

| 1628 | Esteban Alonso, Francisco de Acosta | | | | | |

Date	Owner	Notes		
pre-1672	Don Bartolomé Vásquez de Saavedra			
ca. 1672	Licenciado Don Rafael Suazo	purchased from heirs of Vasquez de Saavedra		2,000
ca. 1679	Captain Don Luis de Briones de Quintanilla	inherited from Licenciado Rafael Suazo	(12,000)	2,000
1694	Licenciado Don Juan de Requena y Ulloa	special purchase from Briones y Quintanilla		
ca. 1694	General Don Pedro de Escurra y Saravia			
1726	priests of Reque			
CANCHACHALA				
ca. 1610	Doña Juana de Asturizaga	Juan Domínguez Corzo gave it to her for debt (included various estancias)	18,075	
n.d.	convent	donation from Doña Juana		
ca. 1721	General Francisco de Seña			
1748	Captain Don Joseph Roxas			

Appendix 3, continued.

Date	Owner	Mode of Acquisition	Area (in fanegadas*)[1]	Total Population[2]	Price/Value[3]	Value of Mortgages
1788	Don Gabriel de Roxas					
CANDELARIA						
pre-1609	Cristóbal Pérez					
pre-1609	Fernando de Obregón, Juan de Obregón	purchased from the estate of Pérez				2,250
1612	Juan de Obregón, Doña Estefania de Vargas, Fernando de Obregón					2,250
1618	Fernando de Obregón	purchased in auction of goods of Juan de Obregón	(San Lorenzo added prior to 1643)	26 slaves (in 1627)		5,795 (1627 Candelaria), 7,373 (in 1643)
1666	Francisco Ruiz Vejarano, María Suárez Gordillo			8 slaves (1668)		

ca. 1668	heirs of Ruiz Vejarano, Suárez Gordillo	inheritance	13 slaves 7 peons	12,754	8,541
pre-1696	Juan Bautista Cabeza de Vaca				
pre-1696	Doña María Gómez de San Mar	inherited from husband			
pre-1699	Francisco de Villalobos				
1728	Licenciado Don Juan de León y Rivera	purchased from Villalobos	69 (joined Cayaltí)	5,000	3,375
ca. 1735	Licenciado Manuel Joseph Rubiños y Andrade	purchased from: León y Rivera	120 slaves (incl. Cayaltí)	53,569[6]	30,850[6]

(Added to Cayaltí, ca. 1752)

CAYALTI (sometimes with Candelaria, Popán and San Juan)

pre-1622	Vicente Gonzales Serrano				
1622	Alférez Alonso Meléndez de Estrada	purchase	20 slaves	20,500	1,125

Appendix 3, continued.

Date	Owner	Mode of Acquisition	Area (in fanegadas*)[1]	Total Population[2]	Price Value[3]	Value of Mortgages
1624	Alferez Cristobal de Cavanillas Malpartida and Diego Cavanillas	purchased from Gonzales when Melendez failed to make the payments			20,500	
ca. 1655	Doña Isabel Hidalgo de Cavanillas	inherited from her husband Cristobal de Cavanillas Malpartida				
ca. 1657	Captain Martin Nuñez de Arze	purchase				4,373
1694	Don Martin Nuñez de Arze (Jr.)	inherited from father		19 slaves		
1704	Licenciado Don Jose Nuñez de Arze	inherited from brother	130	54 slaves		13,625 (1705) 21,625 (1706)
1717	Licenciado Don Juan de Leon Rivera Cabeza de Vaca	purchased from estate of Nuñez	155	58 slaves	28,000	26,071

pre-1732	Licenciado José de Torres y Villavicencio	purchase	230 slaves[5]		
pre-1735	Licenciado Don Manuel Joseph de Rubiños y Andrade	purchased from estate of León y Rivera	50 slaves	53,698[6]	30,850[6]
1752	Licenciado Don Juan José López Collado	purchased from Rubiños y Andrade	60 slaves	40,745	40,745+
1785	Don Pedro Fernández de la Cotera	purchased in auction	48 slaves (1791)	13,500 (56,036 in 1791)	
1801	Doña Agueda Rosa Durán	inherited from her husband, Fernández de la Cotera			

COJAL

pre-1600	Diego de Soria		2 mitayos
pre-1600	Gregorio de Robles		2 mitayos
1598	Alonso Flores		2 mitayos
1621	Pedro Flores		2 mitayos

Appendix 3, continued.

Date	Owner	Mode of Acquisition	Area (in fanegadas*)[1]	Total Population[2]	Price[3] Value	Value of Mortgages
ca. 1633	Captain Juan Vasquez de Saavedra	purchased in auction from estate of Pedro Flores		68 slaves, 4 females, 15 males 17 mitayos		600
1645	Captain Lucas Arias de Saavedra					8,687
pre-1655	Don Pedro de Vargas Oteo and Doña Ana María Gutierrez de Espinosa			60 slaves, mitayos		12,000
pre-1684	Don Juan Vasquez de Saavedra, Licenciado Don Bartolome Vasquez de Saavedra					
pre-1697	Doña Ana María Vasquez de Saavedra, Licenciado Don Bartolome Vasquez de Saavedra					

Date	Owner	Notes	Labor		
1697	Don Pedro de Gamarra	purchased from previous owners		48,000	
1722	Don Eugenio de León y Rivera			22,000	
ca. 1730	Maestro de Campo Don Ordoño de Samudio de las Infantas				
1732	Licenciado Don Juan León y Rivera	purchased from estate of Samudio de las Infantas		22,000	
pre-1743	Don Pedro de Arbulú		14 slaves (1756)		
1775	Don Francisco Aljovín	purchased from Don Pedro Juan Sanz		12,700	5,500

COLLIQUE

Date	Owner	Notes	Labor		
ca. 1561	Luis de Atienza				
1602	Juan Rodríguez de Fuentes		8 mitayos		
pre-1621	Juan Rodríguez de Fuentes, Juan García Meléndez				4,500

Appendix 3, continued.

Date	Owner	Mode of Acquisition	Area (in fanegadas*)[1]	Total Population[2]	Price/Value[3]	Value of Mortgages
1621	Alonso de Cuebas, Juan Bautista Moreno	purchased from previous owners	100	19 mitayos, 7 slaves		5,625
pre-1686	Gerónimo Rodríguez	purchase			14,675	
1686	Doña María Carrasco Escudero Vda. de Rodríguez	inherited from husband		12 mitayos		
pre-1693	Don Félix Rodríguez					
1693	Don Pedro de Escurra y Saravia	purchased from Rodríguez		mitayos		6,325
1700	Don Juan de Rodríguez					

COLLÚS

pre-1596	community of Callanca	

1596	Francisco Sesudo	confirmed	1	169^4
1596	Juan Romero	confirmed	2 (Añáñala)	
1596	Juan Fragoso	confirmed	12	33^4
1596	Alonso de Paz	confirmed		113^4
1608	Juan Rodríguez Vejete			
n.d.	Moises Escurra Cortes			
n.d.	Torcuato Pasco Portocarrero			
1611	Dimitre Dexio, Manuel de Saa			
1628	Esteban Alonso, Francisco de Acosta			
pre-1638	Licenciado Don Joseph Carrasco del Saz, Captain Gerónimo de Valderas Terán			
1638	Captain Gerónimo de Valderas Terán	Acosta gave Valderas his half in return for a fixed annuity to the Monastery of San Francisco		none

Appendix 3, continued.

Date	Owner	Mode of Acquisition	Area (in fanegadas*)[1]	Total Population[2]	Price/Value[3]	Value of Mortgages
pre-1645	Licenciado Don Juan Vargas Orejón		200			none
ca. 1645	Don Gerónimo de Valderas Terán and María Hidalgo Cavanillas	purchased, inherited 25 fanegadas from Padre Vargas Orejón				7,000 (1635)
n.d.	Doñas Isabel, Beatriz and María Valderas Terán	inherited from parents				
1668	Don Martín Núñez de Arze	purchased from the Valderas Terans		22 mitayos	(40,000 in 1672)	13,000
1676	Don Martín Núñez de Arze	censo reservativo from the Indians of Monsefú	150		1,000	
1692	Don Juan Núñez de Arze	inherited from father				
n.d.	Captain Juan de Rosales	purchased from Núñez de Arze				
n.d.	Don Juan Núñez de Arze	repossessed estate after Rosales's death				

Year	Owner	Transaction				
n.d.	Licenciado Don Tomás Núñez de Arze	purchased from his brother			9,500+	
1699	Captain Juan de Salazar	purchased estate from Núñez de Arze		mitayos	25,000	8,860
1705	Captain Don Baltazar de Robles Jiménez	purchased from Salazar		mitayos, 1 slave	25,000	14,260
1706	Captain Don Baltazar de Robles Jiménez	purchased Filtum from Captain Nicolás de Urrutia Gallardo	40		1,500	
1711	Captain Don Baltazar de Robles Jiménez	confirmed	623.5	40 slaves	200[4]	15,185
1727	María Robles y Garay and Bonifacio Gastelú Pereda Echalaz	dowry		40 slaves, Indians	(50,000)	15,185
1735	Don Leonardo de Lara Terán de los Rios	purchased from General Bonifacio de Gastelú y Pereda			41,000[7]	24,585
1738	Don Leonardo de Lara and General Bonifacio Gastelú	split estate: Lara gets Collús, Gastelú keeps Saltur			25,690	18,260

Appendix 3, continued.

Date	Owner	Mode of Acquisition	Area (in fanegadas*)[1]	Total Population[2]	Price/Value[3]	Value of Mortgages
pre-1754	heirs of Lara	inheritance		6 slaves	(11,650 in 1765)	
pre-1754	Don Juan Fructuoso de Tejada	purchased in auction of Lara's estate				
1754	Don Gabriel de Castañeda	Tejada declared he bought Collús for Castañeda				
1768	Presbítero Francisco Malerva	bought in auction			10,000	8,000
1784	Juan Alejo Martínez de Pinillos and Juan José Martínez de Pinillos	purchased as part of Malerva's estate			9,000	
CORBACHO						
pre-1617	Francisco Fernández Corbacho					4,725

pre–1641	Captain Fernando de Arze			slaves		
pre–1643	Manuel de Arze	confirmed	71–73		2,205[4]	
1653	Captain Juan Fernández Dávila, Captain Don Joseph de Vera y Soto	owned half		3 mitayos		
1656–68	Captain Don Andrés de Olea y Mantilla					2,000
pre–1690				17 slaves	(33,100)	
pre–1702	Doña Juana Petronila de Olea y Mantilla					
1702	Don Diego Sánchez purchased from estate (Cortez de los Ríos) of Doña Juana				3,000	3,000

CHARCAPE

pre–1642	Captain Domingo Ruiz, Captain Lucas Arias de Saavedra and Captain Juan Vásquez de Saavedra

Appendix 3, continued.

Date	Owner	Mode of Acquisition	Area (in fanegadas*)[1]	Total Population[2]	Price/Value[3]	Value of Mortgages
pre-1643	Don Francisco de Samudio					
1645	Don Agustín de Castro	purchased from Samudio				
1674	Captain Juan Bautista de Cabeza de Vaca	purchased from Samudio				
n.d.	Juan Bautista de Meneses					
n.d.	Don Baltazar de Moncada y Cháves	purchased from estate of Meneses				
pre-1720	Doña Petronila Garate					none
1742	Don Pedro Francisco López Garate		(included Chafán, Faclo)			
1754	Don Pedro Manuel de Issassi	purchase		11 slaves	4,000	

Date	Owner	Notes		Slaves		
n.d.	Don Juan Ignacio de Otaequi	Issassi gave estate to him in payment of debt				
1781	Don Edubigio Paredes	given in payment of debt by Otaequi	130	28 slaves (in 1807)	12,000	

SAN CRISTÓBAL

Date	Owner	Notes		Slaves		
1636	Cristóbal Gutiérrez Muñoz					
pre-1670	Sargento Mayor Don Nicolas Gutiérrez de Villavicencio					
1666	Doña Francisca de Vera y Soto					
pre-1670	Bachiller Don Francisco de Palma Vera y Soto and Bachiller Don Diego de Palma Vera y Soto	purchased from goods of their mother	(included Santiago de Miraflores, Leviche and Collazos)	80 slaves	30,000 (60,000)	9,236
1677	Jesuits	donation to found school from the previous owners				
1693	Bachiller Don Francisco de Palma Vera y Soto	repossessed estate		60 slaves		22,375

Appendix 3, continued.

Date	Owner	Mode of Acquisition	Area (in fanegadas*)[1]	Total Population[2]	Price/Value[3]	Value of Mortgages
1696	Maestro de Campo Pedro de Gamarra y Urquisa	purchased from estate of Palma Vera y Soto		80 slaves, 2 mitayos	(100,000)	24,375
1708	General Don Joseph Sarmiento de Sotomayor or Doña Ana María Vásquez de Saavedra			85 slaves[5]		
ca. 1711	Doña Juana de Estrada					
pre–1729	Maestro de Campo Don Juan Fernández de Bulnes					4,000
1750	Don Juan de Mata y Haro	purchase		13 slaves	9,000	4,000
1764–65	Don Manuel de Casanoba					
n.d.	Licenciado Don Domingo Aljovín	purchased from Don Joseph de Casanoba, Don Miguel de Bosillo		140+ slaves		

Date	Name	Notes			
ca. 1789	Don Francisco Aljovín				

CHONGOYAPE

Date	Name	Notes			
pre–1702	Don Manuel Mateos de la Calle, Leonor Gilas	confirmed			
pre–1702	Antonio, Bernardo and Gonzalo Pantoja				
1704	Antonio Pantoja	purchased rights of other two brothers			
pre–1707	Antonio Pantoja, Petrona de la Cruz de la Calle de Gregorio Javier de Vargas				
1707	General Don Juan Sarmiento de Sotomayor y de los Rios	purchased from Pantoja			
1709	Jesuits	purchased from Sarmiento de Sotomayor to annex to Tumán			9,900
ca. 1766	Don Tomás de Veléz	purchase	16 slaves	7,000	2,700

Appendix 3, continued.

Date	Owner	Mode of Acquisition	Area (in fanegadas*)[1]	Total Population[2]	Price/Value[3]	Value of Mortgages
1781	Doña María Ana Darroch y Moreno	purchased in auction with Tumán	300		5,000	
n.d.	Don Francisco de Villapol y Soraluze					
CHUMBENIQUE						
pre-1638	Martín de Navarrete					
pre-1642	Captain Juan Vásquez de Saavedra			20 slaves		
pre-1692	Licenciado Francisco de Palma y Vera					
pre-1692	Captain Juan de Gamarra	purchased from Bachiller Francisco de Palma y Vera				
pre-1692	Captain Joseph de Gamarra	inherited from Captain Juan de Gamarra				

Year	Name	Description	Quantity	Amount	
1692	Maestro de Campo Don Juan Bautista y Vizcarrondo y Aldape	purchased from Palma	100 slaves	96,000	26,000
1704	Don Manuel de Andonaegui		111 slaves[5]		
1729	Licenciado Don Francisco Bracamonte Dávila y del Campo	purchased in auction of Andonaegui's goods		48,000	
1735	Don Dalmacio de Losada	purchased from Bracamonte	42 slaves, Indians	48,000	
1745	Don Felipe Coronel y Basán	purchased in auction	20 slaves	20,000 (cash)	
ca. 1756	Don Nicolás Barrueta				
ca. 1756	Doña Teresa de la Banda		38 slaves		
ca. 1782	Don Teodoro Daza				
ca. 1796	Doña Teresa de la Banda		38 slaves		
ca. 1796	Presbítero José de los Santos Niño Ladrón de Guevara	purchase			

Appendix 3, continued.

ÍLLIMO

Date	Owner	Mode of Acquisition	Area (in fanegadas*) [1]	Total Population [2]	Price/Value [3]	Value of Mortgages
ca. 1643	General Don Nicolás Fernández de Villavicencio and Juana Carrasco					
pre-1663	Doña Leonor de Saavedra			6-7 slaves		
pre-1663	Licenciado Don Gerónimo Ortiz de Sapata	dowry of Doña Leonor de Saavedra				
ca. 1689	Licenciado Don Alonso Pardo del Castillo					
pre-1693	Bachiller Francisco de Palma y Vera					
1693	Jesuits					
1711-12	Comisario General Don José de la Parra					

Date	Holder	Acquisition	Holdings	Mitayos	Value
1713	Don Matías de Ripalda	purchase			
pre-1719	General Don Pedro Escurra y Saravia				4,000

ISO (ISCO)

Date	Holder	Acquisition	Holdings	Mitayos	Value
n.d.	Manuel Carvallo			mitayos	
1585	Juan Gonzales Cornejo		(associated with Tecapa)	7 mitayos	
n.d.	Convento de Nuestra Señora de Guadalupe	purchased from Gonzales Cornejo			
1591	Antonio Corso	purchased from Convento	20	13 mitayos	1,800
1595	Antonio Fernández			none	none
ca. 1595	Sancho Casco	purchase	45		1,250[4]
pre-1602	Captain Juan Martínez Palomino, Inés de Loranca				
pre-1602	Luis Delgado, Fulgencia Santillán	purchase			
1602	Juan Romero de Arnedo, Juan Rodríguez Vejete	purchased from Delgado			

Appendix 3, continued.

Date	Owner	Mode of Acquisition	Area (in fanegadas*)[1]	Total Population[2]	Price/Value[3]	Value of Mortgages
1608	Simón de Farinas	purchased from Romero				
1609	Simón de Farinas	purchased from Rodríguez Vejete				
1607	Lope de Castro, Cristóbal Sánchez	purchased from Delgado, Fulgencia Santillán		15 mitayos	3,544	788
1610	Cristóbal Sánchez	purchased from Castro				
1614	Alonso García de las Cañas	purchased from estate of Farinas				
1617	Martín de Navarrete	purchased from García de las Cañas				
1643	Hernán Sánchez Maraver		460			
JANQUE						
pre-1611	Juan Domínguez Corso		(includes Jotoro)		(11,094)	
1611	Doña Juana de Asturizaga	Domínguez gave it to her for debt				

Date	Owner/Buyer	Transaction	Notes	No.	Slaves	Value
n.d.	Convent	donation from Doña Juana				
pre-1698	General Don Juan Bonifacio de Seña					
1698	Captain Lázaro de Arrasque	purchased from Seña				
ca. 1721	General Francisco de Seña					
1742	Hypólito de Seña	purchased from estate of Don Francisco	(includes Paltaraca, Macuchima, Mallacola, Muchumí)			10,150 (2,400 cash)
pre-1758	Licenciado Don Luis de la Rosa	purchase				3,750 (cash)
1780	Don Joseph Ramírez de Arellano					
1788	Brothers of Don Pedro Villalobos y Ramírez					

SAN JUAN BAUTISTA

Date	Owner/Buyer	Transaction	Notes	No.	Slaves	Value
pre-1635	Francisco Núñez Montes			40	24 slaves (30,000)	2,000 (in 1635), 5,675 (in 1638)

Appendix 3, continued.

Date	Owner	Mode of Acquisition	Area (in fanegadas*)[1]	Total Population[2]	Price/Value[3]	Value of Mortgages
ca. 1656	Doña Antonia Ventura Montes de Inoxossa and Captain Andrés de Olea y Mantilla					8,060
ca. 1689	Doña Juana Petronila de Olea y Mantilla	inherited from her father, Andrés				
1702	Fray Alonso de Horna y Estrada	purchased in auction of Olea y Mantilla's goods		42 slaves	43,000	26,400+
1706	Doña Magdalena de Estrada y Hurtado	purchased in auction of Horna's goods			57,500	
ca. 1711	Doña Juana de Estrada					
pre-1721	Governador Don Félix de Estrada					
ca. 1721	Doña Luisa de Castañeda	inherited from her husband				

1725	Licenciado Don Casimiro de Estrada	purchased in auction	92	36 slaves	(20,615)
1739	Félix José de Estrada y Castañeda	purchased from Doña Luisa de Castañeda		4 slaves	14,000 (cash)
pre-1771	Don Benito Caldas				
1771	Licenciado Don Domingo Alprin	purchased from Caldas			5,200 (cash)
1785	Don Pedro Fernández de la Cotera		111		
ca. 1789	Don Marzelino Sosa				
LEVICHE					
1570–1595	Antonio Fernández	occupation (1570), confirmed (1595)		peons	169[4]
pre-1630	Alonso Fernández Mellado	dowry of wife, Catalina de los Rios		3 mitayos	none
pre-1670	Miguel Refolio				
1670	heirs of Miguel Refolio (including Juan de Quintea)	inheritance, dowry		4 mitayos	

Appendix 3, continued.

Date	Owner	Mode of Acquisition	Area (in fanegadas*)[1]	Total Population[2]	Price/ Value[3]	Value of Mortgages
pre-1695	Bachiller Don Francisco de Palma y Vera			1 slave		
pre-1727	Marqués de Villar de Tajo y de Villablanca					
1727	heirs of Marqués de Villar de Tajo y de Villablanca	inheritance				
ca. 1758	Don Luis de Lara			74 slaves, 33 Indians		
(becomes part of La Viña)						
SAN LORENZO, EL REAL						
pre-1579	Salvador Vásquez		50	slaves	13,235	2,809
pre-1579	Diego de Segovia	purchased from Vásquez				2,809
ca. 1593	Lorenzo de Samudio Mendoza	purchased from Segovia	120		5,850	

Date	Name	Acquisition		
ca. 1617	Doña Juana de Toledo Vda. de Samudio	inherited from husband	1,463	
ca. 1626	Don Francisco Samudio y Mendoza	inherited from mother	3,000	
ca. 1643	Fernando de Obregón		11,325	
pre-1663	Alférez José Herrera		1,350	
pre-1663	Doña Magdalena de Sepúlveda Vda. de Herrera			
ca. 1663	Captain Juan Bautista Cabeza de Vaca	purchased from Doña Magdalena de Sepúlveda	3,039	
pre-1682	Doña María Gómez de San Mar Vda. de Cabeza de Vaca	inherited from husband		
1696	Maestro de Campo Don Juan Bautista Viscarrondo y Aldape	purchased from Gómez		34,000
pre-1699	Francisco de Villalobos			

Appendix 3, continued.

Date	Owner	Mode of Acquisition	Area (in fanegadas*)[1]	Total Population[2]	Price/Value[3]	Value of Mortgages
pre-1708	Tomás de Mallorga					
1728	Licenciado Don Casimiro de Estrada	auction of Villalobos's rights to estate		14 slaves	15,000	15,000
1751	Don Pedro Pichardo	purchased in auction			2,000	2,000
1755	Don Juan Manuel de Mata y Haro	transfer from Pichardo			2,000	2,000
LUYA						
1590	Hernán García			1 Spaniard, 2 yanaconas, 4 mitayos		
1590	Juan Salguero			2 "persons," 6 mitayos		
1596	Hernán García Rincón	confirmed	(included Carcarleche, Manchancap, and Molep)		130[4]	

Date	Holder	Transaction			
pre-1608	Juan de Buissa Sanabria				
1608	Doña Catalina de Herrera	purchased from Buissa	(Mamape)	mitayos	
pre-1613	Dr. Don Gaspar de Herrera				
1613	Don Alvarado Noreña Figueroa	purchased half from Dr. Herrera			
1619	Juan de Samudio Mendoza	purchased half from Dr. Herrera			none
pre-1663	Maestro de Campo Juan García Garrosa		(80 in Tulipe)		
pre-1663	Captain Miguel de Garay	purchased from García Garrosa			
ca. 1682	Dr. Pedro Francisco Gutiérrez de Ocampo				
n.d.	Dr. Don Juan de Samudio Villa-lobos Mendoza	purchased Tulipe from estate of García Garrosa			
pre-1687	Doña Leonor de Bracamonte Dávila	purchased rights from her children	(included 9 estancias)	13.5 mitayos[9]	12,000

Appendix 3, continued.

Date	Owner	Mode of Acquisition	Area (in fanegadas*)[1]	Total Population[2]	Price/Value[3]	Value of Mortgages
1692	Don Domingo de Villalobos Samudio Bracamonte	purchased from his mother, Doña Leonor de Bracamonte	90	6 mitayos, 12 slaves	12,000	4,000
1698	Don Baltazar de Robles y Jiménez	Villalobos gave Robles half the estate to settle a debt	90	13 mitayos, 12 slaves	12,000	4,000
1712	Don Miguel de Robles Garay	purchased from his father, Don Baltazar de Robles Jiménez		4 slaves, Indians	34,305	12,000
1712	Licenciado Don Norberto Gutiérrez de Ocampo	confirmed	(Falen, Supian)		120–160[4]	
1721	Captain Miguel Robles y Garay	purchased Supian and Falen from Licenciado Don Pedro Norberto Gutiérrez de Ocampo	60	15 slaves		
1725	Captain Miguel de Robles y Garay	purchased an orchard from the Cofradía de la Purísima Concepción	20		200	

Year	Owner	Transaction		Slaves		
1728	Captain Miguel de Robles y Garay	confirmed	57.5		115^4	17,900
1732	Captain Miguel de Robles y Garay	purchased cane fields called "Chacarilla" from Licenciado Pedro Norberto Gutiérrez's estate	(included Pitipo)	7 slaves		1,000
1745	Dr. Don José Laso de Mogrovejo y Escandón	purchased from estate of Robles y Garay		20 slaves	23,000 (33,305 in 1744; 108,000 in 1767)	15,000 (19,000 in 1766)
ca. 1775	Dr. Francisco Martínez de Tamayo	inherited from Laso Mogrovejo				
ca. 1782	Don Luis de Guzmán	inherited from Martínez de Tamayo				
pre-1782	José Ignacio Iturregui	purchased at auction				
pre-1782	Don Pedro Fernández de la Cotera		623			
ca. 1789	Don Baltazar Muro					
ca. 1804	José Gerónimo Vivar					

Appendix 3, continued.

Date	Owner	Mode of Acquisition	Area (in fanegadas*)[1]	Total Population[2]	Price/Value[3]	Value of Mortgages
ca. 1804	Don Pedro Estela					1,850
MAMAPE						
pre-1608	Roque Zejuela y Traña					
pre-1608	Roque de Zejuela (nephew of Roque Zejuela y Traña)					
pre-1608	Juan de Buissa Sanabria					
1608	Doña Catalina de Herrera	purchased from Buissa Sanabria	(included Luya)	mitayos		
pre-1609	Andrés Delgado					
1609	Gaspar Fragoso					
(see Luya)						
SANTIAGO DE MIRAFLORES						
ca. 1560s	Baltazar Rodríguez	grant				

Date	Owner	Notes		Labor	Value
ca. 1624	Baltazar de Rodríguez and Diego de Vera	Rodríguez inherited from father	32	6 slaves	2,000
1625	Deigo de Vera	partner's heirs give him half the estate to settle accounts	32		
ca. 1734	Licenciado Casimiro de Estrada				
(see San Cristóbal)					

EL MOLINO

Date	Owner	Notes		Labor	Value
pre-1605	Don Juan Bautista Indo (Governador del pueblo de Chiclayo)				
ca. 1605	Diego de Cavanillas	purchased in auction from estate of Indo			2,610
pre-1611	Diego Fernandez de Ugarte	purchased from Cavanillas		mitayos	
1611	Blas de León	purchased from Ugarte			none
1620	Hernando de Espinosa Beltranilla	dowry of daughter of Blas de León		1 slave, 6 mitayos	none

Appendix 3, continued.

Date	Owner	Mode of Acquisition	Area (in fanegadas*)[1]	Total Population[2]	Price/Value[3]	Value of Mortgages
1636	Roque García de Zejuela	purchased from estate of Espinosa			3,500	none
ca. 1641	Bernave Rentero	purchased from Zejuela, confirmed	11	1 slave, 1 mitayo	4,700, 110[4]	none
ca. 1655	Antonio de Suárez y Figueroa y Refolio	purchased from Rentero	15	1 slave, 1 mitayo	4,100	1,200
pre-1688	Doña Elena de Vera y Soto de Antonio de Suárez y Figueroa					
1688	Captain Juan Fernández de Escalante	purchased from heirs of Suárez y Figueroa	20	1 mitayo	4,000	1,500
ca. 1700	Doña María Suárez Vda. de Fernández Pardo					
ca. 1700	Diego López Collado	purchased from estate of Doña María Suárez				

Date	Owner	Transaction	Extent	Labor		
ca. 1700	Alférez Fernando Vela y Arze					
1702	Doña Ana Suárez de Figueroa Vda. del Captaín Juan Fernández de Escalante	inheritance from husband, repossessed				
1702	Alférez Don Baltazar de Guinea	purchased from Doña Ana Suárez de Figueroa	20		5,700	1,200
pre-1749	Doña María Guinea					
pre-1749	Alférez Don Pedro de Guinea					
1768	Don Juan de Guinea	inherited from sister and Pedro Guinea	40	12 slaves, peons	(4,357 in 1754)	4,000
ca. 1768	Convento de San Francisco		(estate fragmented)			
1768	Don Francisco Malerva	purchased dominio útil[8] from Don Juan de Guinea				1,500
1770	Don Fernando Pantoja	purchased from estate of Doña María de Guinea			1,500 (land only)	3,600
1770	Don Joseph Barreto de Castro	purchased dominio útil from Malerva			1,200	1,200

Appendix 3, continued.

Date	Owner	Mode of Acquisition	Area (in fanegadas*)[1]	Total Population[2]	Price/Value[3]	Value of Mortgages
ca. 1779	Don Luis Sánchez		53.5		(1,337.5 land only)	
1780	Don Joseph Lorenzo Lusquinas	purchased dominio útil from Convento de San Francisco			1,200	
ca. 1782	Doña Francisca Seña Vda. de Don Fernando Pantoja					
MOLOTÚN						
n.d.	Cristóbal Ruiz, Juan Ruiz	inheritance				
ca. 1604	Cristóbal Ruiz, Juan Ruiz, Diego de Villasana			7 mitayos		
1606	Diego Fernández de Ugarte, Juan Ruiz	Diego purchased half in auction of Cristóbal Ruiz's estate				
ca. 1606	Juan Ruiz	transfer from Ugarte		7 mitayos		

Date	Owner(s)	Transaction	No.		Price
n.d.	Cristóbal Ruiz, Gerónimo de Monteza	Monteza purchased half from Juan Ruiz	6	2 slaves, 7 mitayos	none
n.d.	Juan de Aspilaga, Juan Ruiz	Aspilaga purchased half from Monteza, Juan Ruiz inherited half from Cristóbal			1,750
1606	Juan Ruiz, Diego Fernández de Ugarte	Ugarte bought half from estate of Cristóbal Ruiz			
1606	Juan de Aspilaga	purchased from Ugarte	40	2 slaves, 7 mitayos	5,000
pre-1608	Juan Ruiz	purchased half from Aspilaga			1,750
pre-1639	Captain Juan de Olivos	purchased from Amaro Gonzales			

SAN NICOLÁS

Date	Owner(s)	Transaction	No.		Price
1643	Alférez Lino Martínez	confirmed	35	97 slaves[5]	767[4,10]
pre-1688	Don Pedro de Vargas Oteo				

(1700, became part of Popán)

Appendix 3, continued.

Date	Owner	Mode of Acquisition	Area (in fanegadas*)[1]	Total Population[2]	Price/Value[3]	Value of Mortgages
LA OTRA BANDA						
ca. 1603	Antonio Fernández					
pre-1635	Juan Fernández de Ávila, Br. Blas Fernández de Ávila		(included Culcoque)	4 shepherds		
ca. 1642		confirmed	137			
pre-1677	Captain Domingo de Arriola					600
pre-1677	Juan de Garro, María de Aguilar					
ca. 1678	María de Aguilar Vda. del Captain Juan de Garro					
ca. 1678	Licenciado Manuel Pantoja	purchased from the previous owner		18 slaves	(30,000 in 1685)	11,500
ca. 1678	Licenciado Juan Barzeló and Licenciado Manuel Pantoja	Barzeló purchased half from Pantoja		1 yanacona, slaves		

Date	Owner	Method	Slaves	Value	Value
pre-1694	Licenciado Manuel Pantoja				
ca. 1694	Governador Don Santos Gil de la Torre	purchased in auction from Pantoja's estate	47 slaves		
1707	Captain Don Luis de Briones y Medina and General Don José de Briones y Medina	purchased in auction of Gil's estate	330 slaves[5]	43,000	24,000
1735	Don Luis de Briones y Medina		slaves	(100,000 in 1739)	29,200 (in 1739)
1755	Maestro de Campo Don Gabriel de Castañeda	purchased in auction of Briones y Medina's goods	130 slaves	30,000	23,758
1761			140 slaves	(106,000)	
ca. 1773	Don Luis Mauro de Lara y Briones	inheritance from his great uncle			
pre-1785	Don Teodoro Daza	purchase			
pre-1785	Sor Isabel de Briones	awarded possession as relative of former owners			12,000

Appendix 3, continued.

Date	Owner	Mode of Acquisition	Area (in fanegadas*)[1]	Total Population[2]	Price/ Value[3]	Value of Mortgages
1781	Don Domingo Castañeda y Lara	transferred to Don Domingo by Sor Isabel				
1785	Don Andrés Rivas y Lupianes	transferred by Don Domingo Castañeda y Lara		43 slaves		12,000
1810	Doña Gregoria Monroy					
OYOTÚN						
pre-1602	Luis Delgado, Fulgencia de Santillán		160			788
1602	Juan Romero de Arnedo, Juan Rodríguez Vejete	purchased from Delgado		7 mitayos	4,968	none
1607	Juan Romero de Arnedo	purchased from Vejete		8 mitayos		
1608-09	Simón Farinas	purchased from Juan Romero de Arnedo		7 mitayos	3,781	none
1614	Alonso García de las Cañas	purchased from estate of Farinas		mitayos		

1617	Martín de Navarrete	purchased from Alonso García de Cañas	400			
n.d.	Don Francisco Tantaxarxa, Doña Beatriz Escobar					
n.d.	heirs of Tantaxarxa and Doña Beatriz and Don Melchior Escobar	inheritance from parents				
1613	Doña Andrea de Escobar de Pedro de León	bought one-quarter of estate from Don Melchior de Escobar	100		300	none
1619	Juan Fernández Dávila	purchased one-quarter of estate from Doña Andrea			300	none
1648	Pedro de León		375	14 slaves	(14–15,000)	2,000
1655	Licenciado Domingo Vásquez confirmed		101		100[4]	
n.d.	Manuel Carvallo	purchased from Licenciado Alonso de Navarrete Godoy		mitayos		
n.d.	Don Pedro de Gamarra			mitayos		
1660	Comisario Manuel de Saa	purchase			14,000	2,000

Appendix 3, continued.

Date	Owner	Mode of Acquisition	Area (in fanegadas*)[1]	Total Population[2]	Price/Value[3]	Value of Mortgages
1660	Juan León, Pedro Matías de León	granted possession as relatives of previous owners			14,000	2,000
1660	Captain Don Joseph Barreto de Castro, María Alfonsa de León	purchased half from the Leones, received 50 fanegadas as a dowry	50		14,000	
1670	Alférez Don Cristóbal de León Rivera, Captain Don Joseph Barreto de Castro	Don Cristóbal buys half from Barreto de Castro		6 slaves, peons	4,500	1,500
pre-1688	Doña Inés Cabeza de Vaca Vda. del Ayudante Don Cristóbal de León y Rivera					
1688	Bachiller Don Francisco de Palma y Vera	purchased from Doña Inés Cabeza de Vaca		11 slaves, 74 Indians		6,000

pre-1695	Maestro de Campo Don Juan Bautista de Vizcarrondo y Aldape	purchased from previous owner		21 slaves[5]	9,000	4,000
pre-1730	Captain Francisco López Cano		9	14 slaves		
pre-1747	Licenciado Don Toribio de la Torre Saldaña					
pre-1747	Alférez Pedro de Vargas	purchased from Torre Saldaña				
1747	Maestro de Campo Don Phelipe Coronel y Basán	purchased from Vargas			2,000	2,000
1750	Doña Josepha de Núñez y Boy Carrillo Vda. de Coronel y Basán	purchase				
pre-1753	Captain Don Juan de Desa					
pre-1753	Don Antonio de Desa	inherited from his brother, Don Juan				
1753	Don Antonio Bellido	purchased from Don Antonio de Desa			2,200	2,000

Appendix 3, continued.

Date	Owner	Mode of Acquisition	Area (in fanegadas*)[1]	Total Population[2]	Price/Value[3]	Value of Mortgages
1756	Don Nicolás Barrueta	purchased from Don Antonio Bellido			2,200	2,000
1756	Maestro de Campo Don Gabriel de Castañeda y Velasco	purchased from Don Antonio Bellido			2,200	2,000
1768	Don Manuel Gómez de Silva					
1783	Agustín Peralta	purchased from Don Gabriel de Castañeda y Velasco			3,200	2,000
ca. 1783	Don Pedro de Quiñones Barreto de Castro					
PÁTAPO						
1643	Dr. Gerónimo de Villalobos	confirmed	10		100[4]	
1650	Antonio Suárez Refolio Figueroa					

Date	Name			
1665	Don Antonio de Orduña Vidaurre			
ca. 1683	Dr. Pedro Francisco Gutiérrez de Ocampo			
ca. 1692	Doña Leonor de Bracamonte Dávila	10		
1717	Captain Don Pedro Norberto Gutiérrez de Ocampo			
1751	Doña María Clemencia Luz	(included Cuculí)		
1782	Don Manuel Tomás de Larraondo	80 (included Tulipe)	2,000	
ca. 1789	Josefa Larraondo y Risco de Morales de Aramburu	inherited from father		
1812	Don Pedro de Estela			

PICSI

Date	Name			
1540s	Pedro de Barbarán	mitayos		
1570s	Alonso de Mingolla		none	6 yanaconas, 1 Spaniard, 8 mitayos, 20 Indians

Appendix 3, continued.

Date	Owner	Mode of Acquisition	Area (in fanegadas*) [1]	Total Population [2]	Price/ Value [3]	Value of Mortgages
pre-1619	Captain Melchior de Osorno		70	12 yanaconas, 31 women, 15 children, 100 souls (1624)		3,160
1637	Doña Juana de Carvajal y Collazos Vda. de Osorno	inherited from husband		29 Indians		
ca. 1643	Captain Luis de Collazos	inherited from sister				
1645	Jesuits	donated by Doña Juana de Carvajal		29 mitayos, 24 yanaconas, and their families		3,160

(added to Tumán)

POMALCA

1560-70	Pedro de Olmos					
1574	Pedro de Barbarán					
pre-1584	Alonso Flores					

Date	Name	Transaction		Mita		
1593	Fransicso Martín			2 mitayos, 1 yanacona		
1596	Andrés Martín Pizarro	confirmed				
pre-1608	Juan Rodríguez Vejete					
1608	Juan de Oliver de Hoces	purchased from Rodríguez Vejete				
n.d.	Licenciado Joseph Escarral					
n.d.	Juan de Arriola	purchased from Escarral				
pre-1642	Doña Claudia del Villar					
ca. 1642	Licenciado Don Joseph de Carrasco de Saz	purchased from Doña Claudia del Villar	10 (included Samán)			
pre-1649	Sebastián Gonzales	purchased from Arriola				2,250
1649	Presbítero Don Antonio Suárez de Figueroa y Refolio	purchased from Gonzales	5	7 mitayos	4,750	2,250

Appendix 3, continued.

Date	Owner	Mode of Acquisition	Area (in fanegadas*)[1]	Total Population[2]	Price Value[3]	Value of Mortgages
pre-1672	Alférez Real Captain Martín Núñez de Arze		50	mitayos		
1692	Captain Martín Núñez de Arze (Jr.)	inherited from father	19 slaves (between Cayaltí and Pomalca)			
1695	Licenciado Don Tomás Núñez de Arze, Don Joseph Núñez de Arze	each inherited half from brother		21 slaves		7,250
1699, 1702	Governador Don Juan Bonifacio de Seña	purchased half from Don Tomás, and half from Don Joseph	400+	7 mitayos, 19 slaves	15,325 (half)	7,500
1709	Don Francisco de Seña Chirinos	purchased from father	203-213	slaves		
1717	Captain Don Francisco de Seña Chirinos	purchased Alcarleche from Jesuits	325-335	153 slaves[5]	450	
1734	Don Pedro de Saavedra y Chica	purchase				

Year	Owner	Transaction		Slaves		
1739	Fray Félix Seña	repurchased from Don Pedro and heirs of father				6,500
1742	General Don Domingo Navarrete	purchased in auction of Seña's estate		72 slaves	40,000	25,000
1743	Don Domingo Navarrete and Don Baltazar de Ayesta	formed a partnership		72 slaves		25,000
1754	church administered			36 slaves	(30,220)	
1758	Doña Francisca Leal Rayo	purchased in auction		38 slaves	24,000	20,000
1768	Don Francisco de Malerva	purchased in auction when Leal Rayo could not meet payments		53 slaves (in 1780)	20,000	
1784	Don Juan Alexo and Don José Martínez de Pinillos	purchased in auction of Malerva's goods	902 (Samán and Collús sold with Pomalca)	23,150	13,688	

POPÁN

n.d.	Licenciado Francisco de los Olivos, Gaspar de Miranda					

Appendix 3, continued.

Date	Owner	Mode of Acquisition	Area (in fanegadas*)[1]	Total Population[2]	Price/Value[3]	Value of Mortgages
n.d.	Alonso de Buitrago	purchased from Olivos and Miranda				
ca. 1590	Baltazar Fernández Delgadillo, Francisco de Saavedra	purchased from Buitrago				
ca. 1617	Baltazar Fernández Sánchez and Francisco Sánchez Fernández	inherited part from Saavedra			(30,000)	4,000
1627	Alférez Luis Martínez	purchased half from Sánchez			22,000	
1627	Alférez Mayor Baltazar Fernández Sánchez Delgadillo	purchased half from Sánchez		slaves	22,000 (50,000)	11,000 (ca. 1630)
pre-1635	Francisco Núñez Montes		40	24 slaves		
ca. 1635	Captain Juan Fernández Dávila					
1643	Manuel de Arco	confirmed	73			

Date	Owner	Transaction	Slaves	Value	Value
1666	Licenciado Don Juan Fernández de Cabrera				
pre-1685	Doña Magdalena de Sepúlveda				
1685	Don Pedro de Valdivia	purchased from Sepúlveda	18 slaves	11,000 (24,600 in 1685)	9,000
pre-1695	Doña Isabel Basán Herredia y Caravajal de Don Alonso Carrillo	purchased from Valdivia	17 slaves	(30,000 in 1694)	
1700	Marqués de Villablanca	purchased from Carrillo	24 slaves	41,000	9,100
1702	Captain Don Alonso Carrillo		slaves		9,100
pre-1704	Licenciado Don Joseph Zeteno	purchased from estate of Carrillo			
ca. 1705	Licenciado Don Gregorio Gonzales Bohordo y Carranza	purchased from Zeteno			
pre-1732	Licenciado Don Joseph de Torres y Villavicencio		75 slaves[5] (in 1720)		

Appendix 3, continued.

Date	Owner	Mode of Acquisition	Area (in fanegadas*)[1]	Total Population[2]	Price/Value[3]	Value of Mortgages
pre-1732	Don Juan León de Rivera		300	14 slaves		9,098
1735	Licenciado Don Manuel Joseph de Rubiños y Andrade	purchased from estate of León y Rivera			53,698[6]	30,850[6]
ca. 1785	Don Pedro Fernández de la Cotera					

LA PUNTA

Date	Owner	Mode of Acquisition	Area (in fanegadas*)[1]	Total Population[2]	Price/Value[3]	Value of Mortgages
n.d.	Doña Leonor de Valdez					
1658	Captain Domingo de Arriola					2,100
n.d.	Juan de Arriola	inherited from his father				
pre-1681	Gerónimo Rodríguez	purchased from estate of Juan de Arriola		40 slaves, mitayos	ca. 15,000	
ca. 1681	Don Juan and Licenciado Félix Rodríguez	inherited from father			24,000	7,000

Year	Owner	Transaction	Notes	Slaves		
1692	Don Juan Rodríguez and Don Jacinto Samudio y Bracamonte	Licenciado Félix Rodríguez donated his half of the estate to Don Jacinto with conditions		33 slaves		10,500
1692	Don Juan and Licenciado Félix Rodríguez	Samudio returned half the estate to the original owner				10,500 (in 1694)
1697	Licenciado Félix Rodríguez	purchased half from brother	(includes Pampa Grande and Pucalá)	28 slaves	13,000	
1711	María Rodríguez Carrasco de Espinosa	purchased in auction	433			
1714	Don Bartolomé de Robles y Garay	purchased in public auction		471 slaves[5]		
1724	Captain Matías Martínez de Ripalda	purchased from Robles y Garay				
1728	Doña Tomasa de Saavedra Vda. de Ripalda	inherited from husband		104 slaves (in 1741–50) 111 slaves (in 1756)	60,000	20,000
1764	Licenciado Feliciano de Ripalda	inherited part and purchased part from his mother's other heirs			60,000	20,000

Appendix 3, continued.

Date	Owner	Mode of Acquisition	Area (in fanegadas*)[1]	Total Population[2]	Price/Value[3]	Value of Mortgages
1778	Licenciado Matías Villodas	given to him by his uncle in payment for debts		104 slaves	43,000	43,000
1784	Don Ignacio Vicente de Lara	purchased from Villodas			58,000	42,000
1784	Captain Manuel Antonio de Quiñones	purchased from Lara		110 slaves	58,000	43,000
1789	Don Tomás García de la Banda	given possession as relative of former owners		100+ slaves	58,000	42,000
1802	Don Manuel Antonio Quiñones	repossessed after deposit of three years in lawsuit against de la Banda			(42,833)	
1803	Juan Joseph García de la Banda			60+ slaves	(42,833)	
1814	Don Mauricio Arbulú	purchased in public auction			25,000 (17,052 in 1808)	

RACO

pre-1592	Juan Roldán Dávila		11 mitayos
1592	Gabriel de la Requera	purchased from Roldán	
1592	heirs of Gabriel de la Requera		
1598	Don Antonio Cabero de Balderravano	dowry of Doña Mariana de Ulloa Rivera	

RAFÁN

1643	Alferez Lino Martínez	confirmed	4.5
n.d.	Sargento Mayor Bernardo López de Aragón		
n.d.	Convento de Las Mercedes	donated by López de Aragón	
ca. 1676	Captain Don Pedro Vargas Oteo	purchased the usufruct rights for three lives	

Appendix 3, continued.

Date	Owner	Mode of Acquisition	Area (in fanegadas*)[1]	Total Population[2]	Price/Value[3]	Value of Mortgages
ca. 1676	Captain Martín Núñez de Arze and Captain Don Pedro Vargas Oteo			47 slaves[5]		
1688	Don Pedro de Gamarra					
n.d.	Doña Juana de Estrada	confirmed				
pre-1721	Don Félix de Estrada Hurtado					300
1721	Cabildo de Saña	purchased usufruct from Convent				4,000
n.d.	Don Pedro de Quiñones Barreto de Castro	held usufruct				
pre-1726	Doña Juana, Doña Magdalena and Don Félix Estrada y Hurtado					

ca. 1739	Maestro de Campo Don Félix de Estrada			
ca. 1748	Captain Don Francisco Durán			
1752	Don Juan Joseph López de Carvajal	purchased usufruct for three lives	110 per year	2,200
1767	Don Sebastián de Sosa	purchased usufruct	86.5 per year	1,730
ca. 1789	Don Marcelino Sosa			
ca. 1804	Don Agustín de Piedra			
1809	Widow of Piedra			
1817	Don José Leonardo Ortiz	purchased usufruct rights		

SALTRAPÓN

n.d.	Juan Fernández de Ávila, the elder	purchase	mitayos	2,000
n.d.	Juan Fernández de Ávila, the younger	inherited from father		

Appendix 3, continued.

Date	Owner	Mode of Acquisition	Area (in fanegadas*)[1]	Total Population[2]	Price/Value[3]	Value of Mortgages
ca. 1635	Juan de Arriola	purchased from Fernández		13 mitayos		
1638	Juan Medina Dávila	transferred from Arriola	200	8 mitayos		
1667	Doña Ana María Medina Cortez					
pre-1735	Don Joseph de Briones y Medina					
1735	heirs of Briones y Medina	inheritance	(includes half of Santequepe and La Otra Banda)			
1785	Don Luis Mauro and Don Ignacio Vicente de Lara					
1821	Don Ramón Navarrete					

SALTUR (Sometimes with La Punta and Pampa Grande)

ca. 1575	Francisco de Saavedra					
1597	Alonso de Bustrago	confirmed	100			
1640	Alonso Mateos de los Hijuelos		133			
ca. 1711	Captain Baltazar Robles Jiménez		300			
ca. 1711	Doña María Robles y Garay, Don Bonifacio Gastelú y Pereda	dowry				
1735	Don Leonardo de Lara Terán	purchased from Gastelú			41,000[7]	6,325
1738	General Don Bonifacio Gastelú	repossessed Saltur, Lara kept Collús	133	slaves, peons		
1747	Licenciado Don Bonifacio Gastelú y Robles	purchased from his father	133	30 slaves, 3 Indians and families	30,775	9,614
1752	monastery of Santo Domingo	Gastelú gave the monastery the dominio directo, but retained dominio util[8]	(included Pampa Grande)			

Appendix 3, continued.

Date	Owner	Mode of Acquisition	Area (in fanegadas*)[1]	Total Population[2]	Price[3] Value	Value of Mortgages
1764	Licenciado Feliciano de Ripalda	purchased usufruct from Gastelú			8,000	6,500
1778	Licenciado Matías Villodas	Ripalda donated the estate to Villodas	(included Pampa Grande)			6,500
1784	Don Ignacio Vicente de Lara	Villodas donated estate to Lara				
1784	Don Manuel Antonio de Quiñones	Lara gavie it to him			(9,000)	8,500
1808	Doña Jacoba Rubio y Medina Vda. de Quiñones	inherited from her husband				
1817	Ramón Navarrete y Robles	purchased usufruct rights for 84 years			280 per year	7,000

SAMÁN

1596	Andrés Martín Pizarro	confirmed	1		68[4]	

Date	Owner	Acquisition		Labor	
ca. 1608	Juan de Olivos de Hoces	purchased from Andrés Martín Pizarro			
ca. 1608	Luis de Arias de Saavedra				
ca. 1642	Licenciado Don Joseph Carrasco de Saz	purchase	10		
ca. 1681	Don Martín Núñez de Arze				
n.d.	Luis de Atienza, Juana Farías	purchase			
pre-1698	Alférez Manuel de Atienza	inherited from parents			
1698	Governador Don Juan Bonifacio de Seña	purchased from Atienza	1	mitayos, slaves	400
ca. 1709	Francisco Arias de Mendoza				none
n.d.	Governador Don Bonifacio de Seña	purchased Salitral from Arias de Mendoza		30 slaves (in 1699)	
1709	General Don Francisco de Seña Pichardo	purchased from his father (included Alcarlech)			300

Appendix 3, continued.

Date	Owner	Mode of Acquisition	Area (in fanegadas*)[1]	Total Population[2]	Price Value[3]	Value of Mortgages
1742	General Domingo Navarrete	purchased from estate of Seña	(united with Pomalca)			
(see Pomalca)						
SANCARRANCO (sometimes with La Viña)						
n.d.	Don Fernando de Arze					
pre-1634	Maestro Francisco Díaz de Morales	purchased from Arze		9 mitayos		none
1634	Mateo Bermejo	purchased from Díaz de Morales			6,690	
pre-1682	Captain Juan Martínez de la Serda					
ca. 1683	Doña Juana María de Velez Layseca y Alvarado	inherited from husband Martínez				

Date	Owner	Transaction	Notes	Slaves/Indians	
1683	Captain Don Juan Saavedra Cabero	purchased from Doña Juana		11 slaves, Indians	
ca. 1711	Doña Gregoria Carrasco de Saz Vda. de Saavedra		(included La Viña)	24 slaves, mitayos	4,000
pre–1746	Dr. Don Juan Joseph de Saavedra Cabero	inherited from parents			
pre–1769	Don Joseph Joaquín de Irigoyen y Mayora			20 slaves, 35 Indians	
1769	Doña Nicolasa Ripalda	"followed" Irigoyen		11 slaves	
1769	Licenciado Don Matías Villodas	transferred from Doña Nicolasa		7 slaves	
ca. 1790	Don Miguel Paredes	purchased			
1798	Presbítero Don Lorenzo Paredes				
1800	Don José Gregorio Vidaurre				
1810	Don Juan Romualdo de Vidaurre		(included Sonolipe)		

Appendix 3, continued.

Date	Owner	Mode of Acquisition	Area (in fanegadas*)[1]	Total Population[2]	Price/Value[3]	Value of Mortgages
1830	Manuel Salado					
SANGANA (sometimes including Tangasca, Mochumí, El Viejo, and Miraflores)						
pre-1603	Don Lorenzo de Ulloa Rivera					
pre-1733	Governador Don Francisco de Soto y Aliciato, Doña Teresa de Soraluze y Escurra			peons		
ca. 1733	Licenciado Don Matías de Soto y Soraluze	inherited from parents				
1752	Don Joseph Ramírez de Arellano	purchased from Soto			17,000	10,250
1788	Don Pedro Villalobos y Ramírez			6 peons and families		
1810	Don Diego Laso					

SANTEQUEPE (sometimes with Saltrapón)

				peons	169[4]	1,200
1570–1595	Juan Fernández Dávila	confirmed				
1614	Juan Alonso de Salinas					
pre-1638	Juan Fernández de Ávila, the younger					
1638	Captain Juan Medina Dávila	purchased from Fernández	231	21 mitayos	21,200	1,200
1667	Doña Ana María Dávila	purchase	(included Saltrapón)	18 mitayos	18,000	
pre-1694	Licenciado Manuel de Pantoja					
1694	Captain Don Luis de Briones Quintanilla					
ca. 1711	Don Joseph and Luis de Briones y Medina	purchased from mother				
1785	Don Luis Mauro de Lara	owned half				

Appendix 3, continued.

Date	Owner	Mode of Acquisition	Area (in fanegadas*)[1]	Total Population[2]	Price Value[3]	Value of Mortgages
1799	Don Ignacio Vicente de Lara	bought out heirs				
SÁRRAPO						
1566	Pedro de Tineo	grant from municipal council	92–96			
1595	Juan de Tineo, the younger	inheritance from father, confirmation	360		112.5[4]	
1595	Sancho Casco	confirmed	405	4 mitayos	1,367[4]	
ca. 1595	Inés de Loranca Vda. de Casco	inherited from her husband		2 mitayos		
ca. 1595	Juan Martínez Palomino	inherited from his wife Inés		mitayos		
n.d.	Diego Rodríguez de Vargas, Clara Palomino					
pre-1597	Luis Delgado, Fulgencia Santillán	purchased hlaf from Palomino and Loranca		15 mitayos		

n.d.	Roque de Saldaña	purchased part from Martínez Palomino	200	4 mitayos		
1602	Juan de Oliver	purchased part from Saldaña	100	16 mitayos	1,112	none
pre-1607	Agustín Calderón	purchased part from previous owners	30			
1607	Lope de Castro, Cristóbal Sánchez	purchased part from Delgado y Santillán		16 mitayos	3,544	788
1610	Cristóbal Sánchez	purchased his partner's half			2,700	788
1619	Cristóbal Sánchez	bought lands from Juan de Tineo			220	
1620	Gaspar Gutiérrez Muñoz	purchased from Sánchez		16 mitayos		
1627	Cristóbal Gutiérrez Muñoz, Hernán Sánchez Maraver	purchased from Gaspar Gutiérrez Muñoz		8 mityaos		
1643	Hernán Sánchez Maraver	confirmed	460		915[4]	
n.d.	Juan Flores Osorio and Doña Francisca Díaz Sagredo		(La Viña)			

Appendix 3, continued.

Date	Owner	Mode of Acquisition	Area (in fanegadas*)[1]	Total Population[2]	Price Value[3]	Value of Mortgages
n.d.	Doña Ana Flores Osorio and Don Gabriel de Silva Manrique own half, Doña María Florencia Osorio de Silva Manrique owns half	donated by Doña Francisca as the dowry of her daughter and granddaughter	(La Viña)			
ca. 1666	Doña Margarita Sánchez de Maraver y Villavicencio		360	6 mitayos		800
1678	Joseph de Torres y Villavicencio	inheritance from mother		6 mitayos		
1679	Doña María Galindo y Saavedra			6 mitayos		
1692	Doña Inés de Escobar and Licenciado Don Luis Romero Ramírez	inherited from Doña María				4,000

Date	Name	Transaction		Slaves		
1694	Licenciado Don Luis Romero and Don Antonio Domínguez de Moncada					4,000
1695	Captain Don Antonio Domínguez de Moncada	purchased half from his partner		slaves	(73,500)	35,000
1708	Don Agustín de Velasco y Silva, Marqués de Villablanca	purchased part from Domínguez de Moncada		380 slaves[5]	3,500 in cash	
pre-1727	Don Ordoño de Samudio	inherited from the Marqués Samudio				
pre-1757	Don Antonio de las Infantes Marqués del Villar Tajo	inherited from the Marqués de Villablanca				
1759	Don Francisco de Samudio de las Infantas	purchased in sale of estate for debts		15 slaves	34,000	
1759	Don Felipe García Alcayde de Córdova	assumed ownership when Samudio could not repay a loan of 2,659 pesos	460	72 slaves		
1765	Don Manuel de Casanova y Valcarcel			39 slaves		

Appendix 3, continued.

Date	Owner	Mode of Acquisition	Area (in fanegadas*)[1]	Total Population[2]	Price/Value[3]	Value of Mortgages
ca. 1778	Don Joseph Rudecindo de Casanova y Encalada	inherited from Don Manuel de Casanova				
ca. 1778	Don Benito Antonio Caldas	donation from Rudecindo de Casanova				
1804	Captain Vicente de Lafora y Tudela					
SASAPE						
pre-1592	Governador Juan Roldán Dávila					
pre-1592	Gabriel de la Requera	purchased from his half-brother				
1592	heirs of Gabriel de la Requera	inheritance				
1595	Doña Mariana de Ulloa	inherited from her daughter		4 mitayos		

ca. 1615	Juan Domínguez Corso		
ca. 1615	Bernardo López	purchased from Juan Domínguez	
ca. 1615	Doña Juana de Asturizaga	purchased from Juan Domínguez	
1650	Juan de Olivos	purchased	30,000
pre-1663	Leonor de Saavedra y Monroy Vda. de Olivos	inherited from husband	36.5 mitayos[9]
1668	Magdalena de Estrada y Saavedra	inherited from her aunt, Leonor de Saavedra y Monroy	7 slaves peons
ca. 1714	Doña Gabriela de Castillo de Herrera y Estrada	inherited from her mother	
1702	Don Pedro de Escurra y Saravia		
1713	Don Matías de Ripalda	purchase	
1781	Licenciado Don Juan Francisco de Castañeda		

Appendix 3, continued.

Date	Owner	Mode of Acquisition	Area (in fanegadas*)[1]	Total Population[2]	Price/Value[3]	Value of Mortgages
SIALUPE						
pre-1680	Don Melchior Huycop					
1680	Doña Francisca, Don Andrés, Doña Lucía, Doña María, and Don Valentín Siarsa Huycop	inherited from father				
n.d.	Dr. Don Juan Joseph Saavedra Cabero (a fifth); Doña Barbola, Doña María and Doña Ángela Huycop (two-fifths); Don Tomás Huycop (two-fifths)	Saavedra purchased a fifth from Doña Francsica; Doñas Barbola, María and Ángela inherited two-fifths from Don Andrés and Doña Lucía; Doña Lucía acquired a fifth from Doña María and then sold it to Don Tomás; Don Tomás purchased the other fifth from Don Valentín				

Date	Owner	Notes			
ca. 1711	Doña Gregoria Carrasco Vda. de Saavedra (a fifth); Don Tomás Huycop (two-fifths); Doñas Barbola, María and Ángela Huycop (two-fifths)	Doña Gregoria inherited from her husband; these owners paid 200 pesos to legalize their tenure in the visita	115		
n.d.	Don Feliciano Martínez de Ripalda	inherited from parents			
pre-1781	Dr. Don Joseph Joachín de Irigoyen y Mayora	inherited from Martínez de Ripalda			
1781	Don José Manuel Villodas			2,181	
pre-1803	Don Eugenio Victorio Temoche		none		
1803	Captain Don Joseph Damaso Temoche	inherited from father	150	3,750	

SICÁN

Date	Owner	Notes			
1597	Francisco de Barbarán	confirmed			2,500

Appendix 3, continued.

Date	Owner	Mode of Acquisition	Area (in fanegadas*)[1]	Total Population[2]	Price/Value[3]	Value of Mortgages
pre-1612	Don Juan de Barbarán	inherited from uncle				
1612	Alonso de Villavicencio	purchase				
pre-1711	Don Joseph de la Parra			slaves, mitayos, peons		
1724	Don Juan Fernández Bulnes	purchase		11 slaves	30,250	27,125
ca. 1742	Captain Don Juan Sanz de Vidaurre					
ca. 1751	Doña Juana de la Parra y Guzmán			2 slaves		
ca. 1758	Don Francisco de Aguilar and Doña María Luisa de Vidaurre Vda. de Larrainsa	inherited from Doña Juana		11 slaves, 3 peons		

Date	Owner	Transaction			
1778	Dr. Don José Andrés Delgado	purchased from Doña María Luisa	2 slaves	5,084	5,000
1782	Don Pedro Fernández de la Cotera	purchased from heirs of Doña Juana de la Parra y Vidaurre		40,100	25,000
1806	Familia Delgado				
SIPÁN					
1640	Andrés de la Torre	confirmed		480[4]	
pre-1673	Alférez Juan de Ortega Cayos				
1673	Captain Don Juan Ruiz de la Llana	purchased from Ortega	mitayos, slaves	10,000	5,000
1674	Don Gerónimo de Velasco y Castañeda	purchased from Ruiz de la Llana	mitayos, slaves	14,000	5,000
1678	Captain Don Juan Gonzales Bohordo y Carranza				
pre-1693	Licenciado Don Félix de Rodríguez 11				

Appendix 3, continued.

Date	Owner	Mode of Acquisition	Area (in fanegadas *)[1]	Total Population[2]	Price/Value[3]	Value of Mortgages
1693	Don Pedro de Escurra	purchased from Rodríguez				
1694	Doña Ana Rodríguez de Castro			30 slaves	(30,000)	12,000
ca. 1699	Captain Don Juan Gonzales Bohordo y Carranza and heirs of Doña Juana Gonzales de Carranza and Governador Don Joseph de Munar y Hontaneda	they claimed ownership of a sixth of the estate		19 slaves		
ca. 1708	Licenciado Don Félix Rodríguez					
1714	Captain Gregorio Gómez de Arguellas	inherited from Rodríguez	100		(25,000)	
1715	Antonio Viduarre			91 slaves[5]	12,000	

Date	Owner	Method	Notes	Slaves		
1725	Francisco de Pro León and Valentín de Aguilar	purchase		14 slaves		
pre-1746	Francisco Pimentel y Sotomayor	purchase		18 slaves		
ca. 1746	Don Joseph and Antonio Pimentel y Sotomayor	inherited from father				
1752	Don Bonifacio de Gastelú y Robles	purchased from Don Joseph and Don Antonio			11,000	9,000
1752	monastery of Santo Domingo	Gastelú gave the Dominicans the dominio directo				
1755	Pedro Gastelú	purchased the dominio útil from Gastelú y Robles		11 slaves	11,100	9,000
1761	Doña Antonia Berrú Vda. de Gastelú	inherited from husband		11 slaves	(7,603)	9,000
1761	Joseph Aniseto de Samudio	purchased in auction			8,000	9,000
1761	Don Pedro de Rivas y Lupianes	purchased as a relative of previous owners			8,000	9,000

Appendix 3, continued.

Date	Owner	Mode of Acquisition	Area (in fanegadas*)[1]	Total Population[2]	Price[3] Value	Value of Mortgages
1784	Don Manuel Antonio Quiñones					
ca. 1797	Don Miguel de la Torre y Sánchez					
TULIPE						
ca. 1584	Andrés Martín Pizarro					
n.d.	Doña Leonor de Bracamonte					
n.d.	Dr. Domingo de Villalobos Samudio y Bracamonte	purchased from his mother				
1643	Alférez Manuel de Arze	confirmed	80		800[4]	
1647	Tomás Gonzales de la Torre	purchased from Arze		yanaconas	1,000	

Date	Holder	Notes			Indians
1656	Juan de Luzón	purchased from de la Torre	1,000		
1663	Maestro de Campo Juan García de Garrosa	purchased from Luzón	none		
1664	Dr. Don Juan de Samudio y Mendoza	purchased from García de Garrosa	2,000		
1677	Dona Catalina de la Torre y Leyva	won court case against Dr. Don Juan de Samudio Mendoza by proving that Luzón did not legally own the land			

(See Pátapo)

<u>TUMÁN</u>

Date	Holder	Notes			Indians
pre-1574	Pedro de Barbarán				Indians
1590	Juan Venenciano				1 Spaniard, 7 people, 4 mitayos
1590[12]	Francisco Sesudo				1 Spaniard, 4 people, 4 mitayos
pre-1593	Don Francisco Llontop, cacique of Callanca			60	1 Spaniard, 1 married yanacona, 4 mitayos

Appendix 3, continued.

Date	Owner	Mode of Acquisition	Area (in fanegadas*)[1]	Total Population[2]	Price/Value[3]	Value of Mortgages
ca. 1593	Juan Romero Arnedo	purchased from Llontop	60			
ca. 1591	Andrés Martín Pizarro	confirmed				
n.d.	Doña Catalina de Toledo					
pre-1610	Dr. Gaspar de Herrera Escobedo					
1610	Melchior Osorno	purchased from Herrera	(estancia Chumán)		6,000	
n.d.	Padre Francisco Pacho de Bustamante	acquired it from his brother, M. Osorno				
n.d.	Manuel de Saa, Demítre Dexío		(estancia Lloteque)			
n.d.	Juan Rodríguez de Fuentes	purchased from Saa and Dexío	60			
1610	Melchior Osorno	traded lands with Rodríguez de Fuentes	60			

Date	Owner	Means of acquisition					
n.d.	Doña Juana de Carvajal y Collazos Vda. de Osorno	inherited from her husband			29 Indians		
ca. 1680	Jesuits	donated by Doña Juana	(includes Chongoyape)		4 slaves, 29 slaves (1724), 170 slaves (ca. 1700)	(86,750)	
1767	crown	expropriated Jesuit holdings after their expulsion			180 slaves	(110,000)	5,000
1776	Don Miguel O'Phelan	purchased from Crown		453	peons	(110,921)	
1777	Doña María Ana Daroch y Moreno Vda. de O'Phelan	inherited from husband				75,000 65,000 (81,951)	58,000[13] 57,986
1786	Don Antonio Sánchez Navarrete	acquired from Daroch who could not meet the payments			103 slaves	73,067	57,986
1792	Sargento Mayor José Antonio Muñecas y la Guarda	purchased from the government				80,000	
1803	Rosalía Rodríguez y Carazas Vda. de Muñecas	inherited from husband		580	slaves	(81,886) (in 1812)	

Appendix 3, continued.

Date	Owner	Mode of Acquisition	Area (in fanegadas*)[1]	Total Population[2]	Price/Value[3]	Value of Mortgages
UCUPE						
1566	Captain Juan Delgadillo	grant	50			
1567	Antonio Fernández	purchased from Delgadillo	50	peons, mitayos	169	
1595	Luis Fernández	inherited from father		peons, 2 mitayos		
1609	Simón Farinas	from Fernández		7 mitayos		
pre-1613	Tomás de Ayala, Mencía de Escobar					
1613	Damian de Bustamante	purchased from Ayala and wife	100		230	none
1614	Alonso García de las Cañas	purchased from Farinas's estate	(included Isco)	12 mitayos	3,000	
1617	Martín de Navarrete, García Martín Fajardo	purchased from Las Cañas and Gerónima Vernal, his wife	(includes part of Chumbenique)	16 mitayos	8,250	

Date	Owner	Transaction		Labor		
n.d.	Doña Juana Muñoz de Godoy Vda. de Navarrete					
1638	Br. Martín de Navarrete Godoy	purchased from mother, Doña Juana		16 mitayos	9,390	1,200
pre-1649	Br. Alonso de Navarrete Godoy	purchased from brother		16 mitayos	13,300	
1649	Manuel Carvallo	purchased from Navarrete Godoy		16 mitayos, 4 slaves	14,300	8,000
1667	Antonio Segundo Carvallo	inherited from father				
1670	Captain Don Juan Ruiz de la Llana Alvarado	purchased from goods of Carvallo		slaves		
1675	Don Pedro de Gamarra	purchased in auction		181 slaves,[5] mitayos	19,000	
ca. 1694	Don Miguel Joseph Muñoz	transferred by Gamarra (rental?)	47 (includes Isco and parts of Oyotún)	mitayos		
1705	Don Luis and Don Joseph de Briones	purchased from Gamarra	(includes Colo)	2 slaves, 3 mitayos	20,000	11,115

Appendix 3, continued.

Date	Owner	Mode of Acquisition	Area (in fanegadas*)[1]	Total Population[2]	Price/Value[3]	Value of Mortgages
ca. 1711	Don Luis de Briones	split estate with brother				
1715	Don Juan Sulueta					
1735	Don Antonio de Urrutia y Aldape	from Don Luis Briones	(included Santequepe)	31 slaves, 26 peons and families		
1789	Don Gerónimo Lamas					
1793	Don Antonio Ramón Jaramillo	purchased in auction	(included Santequepe)	slaves, peons	7,450 (9,000)	9,000

SAN LORENZO DE VALLE HERMOSO (or PALOMINO)

Date	Owner	Mode of Acquisition	Area (in fanegadas*)[1]	Total Population[2]	Price/Value[3]	Value of Mortgages
pre-1625	Diego de Villasana					
pre-1627	Doña Magdalena Gutiérrez Vda. de Villasana	inherited from husband				
pre-1627	Manuel and Francisco Rodríguez Surita	inherited from mother and stepfather, Francisco Rodríguez Surita				

1632	Diego de Mestanza and Juan de Contreras		
1643	Alférez Lino Martínez	confirmed	40
pre-1685	Doña Catalina Arias de Saavedra		
ca. 1685	Captain Don Pedro de Vargas Oteo	purchased in auction of estate of Doña Catalina	
ca. 1694	Don Francisco de Vargas Oteo	inherited from his father	60 slaves
ca. 1711	Doña Juana de Estrada Hurtado		
pre-1721	Governador Don Félix de Estrada		
ca. 1721	Licenciado Don Juan García Galisteo	purchased as part of Estrada's estate	
1721	Licenciado Don Eugenio de León y Rivera	purchased in auction of García Galisteo's goods	
pre-1738	Licenciado Don Casimiro de Estrada	purchased at auction	14 slaves

Appendix 3, continued.

Date	Owner	Mode of Acquisition	Area (in fanegadas*)[1]	Total Population[2]	Price[3] Value[3]	Value of Mortgages
1738	Doña Luisa de Castañeda	inherited from husband				
1747	Licenciado Don Luis de Palomares y Córdova			slaves		
ca. 1760	Don Juan Joseph López Collado			14 slaves, 4 free blacks		

*In most cases it was impossible to determine whether these figures were fanegadas or fanegadas de sembradura.

Notes:

[1] Only selected large estates are included. The estates not included (for lack of sufficient information) are: Aguapuquio [Janque], Añáfiala [Collús], Aranjes, Cadape, Calasnique, Calera, Calu, Callach, Camacho, Capote, Cárcamo [Samán], Carliche [Luya], Colo [Ucupe], Collique [La Punta], Conchucos [Luya], Coscupián [Collús], Cosquepón, Cuchipunid [Janque], Cullcoque [Otra Banda], Culpón, Cumbil, Cupián [Luya], Chacarilla de Balera, Chafán [Charcape], Chalpen [Luya], Chillancape, Chillatambo [Luya], Chocotocupe [Collique], Chucupe, Chullamcap, Chumán [Tumán], Chusa, Chuscol [Luya], Faclo [Charcape], Falen [Luya], Fanupe, Faya, Filtún [Collús], Focodán [Collús], Follup or Fellupe [Calupe], Gegipo [Collús], Imanasa [Collique], Jotero or Jotoro, Juncap [Sancarranco], Laleche [Sárrapo?], Laquipampa [Janque], Llamencap, Lonope [Collús], Lulincap, Lusincapo [Collús], Lloteque [Tumán], Macuchima [Janque], Machancap [Luya], Mallacola [Janque], Mocsec, Mollip [Sárrapo?], Morrop [Sárrapo?], Nampón [Collús], San Nicolás, Oscute [Íllimo], Palfaraca [Janque], Nudán [Luya], Orda, Pampa Grande, Pantoja, Pitipo [Luya], Penso, Pochos, Polpón, Pomap, El Potrero, Pucalá, Rampón [Collús], Rincop, Salcante, Salitral de Samape, Selinique [Íllimo], Sodo [Íllimo],

Solcupe, Sonconsech, Sonolipe, Sontocap, Susián, Tejada, Terrán, Transecanán, and Usan [Sancarranco]. The names enclosed in brackets are the estates to which the first-named properties were eventually annexed.

[2]The population figures do not always accurately indicate the size of the Indian and free colored population resident on the estates. The figures show a marked decrease in numbers and the eventual disappearance of Indian laborers. Slaves, however, as shown above, did not displace other types of labor; the technically free population of the estates undoubtedly grew. The population figures and lack thereof reflect, instead, legislation which prohibited the inclusion of Indians in land transfers. See, ANP/DI: 1. 39, c. 820, 1737, II-5; and AAT/C: 1704; and T: 1717.

[3]Figures enclosed in parentheses refer to the assessed or approximate value of the estates as opposed to the market price of the property. All prices are in pesos of 8 reales each.

[4]Amount paid for composiciones.

[5]These figures are taken from the manuscript written by Justo Modesto Rubiños y Andrade in 1782. They refer to the slave population before the flood of 1720. The figures are invariably too high.

[6]The figures refer to Popán, Cayaltí, Candelaria, and Aberru.

[7]This figure included both Collús and Saltur.

[8]See Chapter 3, note 31 for the definitions of these terms.

[9]One mitayo served half a year.

[10]Included Balde Hermosa, Rafán, and San Nicolás.

Appendix 3, continued.

Notes, continued.

[11] Sipán and Collique may have been part of the same estate at this date.

[12] At this time, there were two estates called Tumán. They were probably two separate corral complexes in the place called Tumán by the Indians.

[13] This mortgage money was earmarked to pay off the Jesuits.

Sources:

CALUPE: ANCR/[1645]; 1674; 1716; 1720, 4-7v; 1744; and 1763, 184; HS: 1674; Vázquez: 1793; Polo: 12-IX-1751; and 22-I-1747; BP/1632, No. 280-87, 1616; and 2817, 1756, 3; AAT/1697; T: 1697; 1703, 13v-14, 23-63; 1704, 6v, 13-18, 40v-41; 1743; 1757, 57v and 218; and 1758, 24v-25, 65v, 270v; C: 1766, 55; AAL/AT: 23-V, 1703; 2-III, 1632, 229; and 26-V, 1719, 3 and 12; BNP/C2995, 1789; ANP/RA: 1. 282, c. 1072, 1695; and 1. 283, c. 2511, 1789, 1v; TP: 1. 23, c. 611, 1783; and 1. 23, c. 613, 1787, 93; TH: 1. 18, c. 164, 1791; and 1. 21, c. 131, 1805, 65v, 76v-77; AGI/AL: 1387, 1789; Justo Modesto Rubiños y Andrade, "Un manuscrito interesante: Successión cronológica ... de los curas de Pacora y Mórrope en la Provincia de Lambayeque ... [1782]," Revista histórica, X, No. 3 (1936), 347 and 354; and AFA/1. 1, c. 15; c. 19, 195; and c. 20.

CALLANCAS: ANCR/1716; and 1726; Rivera: 20-VIII-1694, 338v-89; and 25-VIII-1694, 390; AAL/AT: 2-III, 1632, 213v and 229; 15b-II, 1678, 223 and 226; ART/IC: 30-VII-1798; and AAT/C: 1663; and T: ca. 1803.

CANCHACHALÁ: ANP/RA: 1. 37, c. 136, 1615, 231; AAT/C: 1734, 64; AGI/AL: 148, 7v; ANCR/Polo: 23-XII-1748; and ART/IO: 13-II-1788.

CANDELARIA: ANCR/Candelaria: 1668; 1614, 391–92; 1617; 1668; 1724; and 1730; ASFL/Reg. 9, No. 2, Ms. 22, 4–XII–1618; ANP/Aguas: 1. 2, 3–3–3–1, 1666, 3v–4v; ACMS/1735, 4½15v; AAT/C: 1796; AFA/Cayaltí: 5v; and J. W. Ibáñez, Informe: Acompaña prueba instrumental y pericial fotográfica. Deduce la falsedad de piezas que indica (Chiclayo, 1920), 89.

CAYALTI: AAT/C: 1721, 8; 1732, 10; 1764, 2v; 1792; 1796; and 1802, 8 and 17–19; Curatos: 1746; ACMS/17–II–1637, 684; and 1735, 4 and 15v; BP/2817, 1756, 2; ANCR/1617; Rivera: 1–X–1694; 15–VIII–1704; 26–X–1706; 1730; 8–VI–1748; and Polo: 1753; AGI/AL: 1417, n.d.; and 1387, 1789; ANP/Aguas: 1. 2, 3–3–3–1, 1666, 3v; and TH: 1. 18, c. 164, 1791; AC/Sipán: 1828; AAL/AT: 27–VI, 1721, 9–10; Ibáñez, 89; Rubiños y Andrade, 354; Jorge Zevallos Quiñones, "Lambayeque en el siglo XVIII," Revista del Instituto Peruano de Investigaciones Genealógicas, II (junio 1947), 88; ART/IC: 8–VIII–1805; and CoO: 25–VIII–1702, 149–49v; AFA/Cayaltí: 5 and 19v; Teodoro Rivera-Ayllón, Lambayeque: Sol, flores y leyendas (Chiclayo, 1976), 63.

COJAL: ANCR/Rentero: 2–IV–1670; Rivera: 18–XII–1684; HS: 1692; Lino: 5–VIII–1730; Cojal: 1733; 1748, 3; and Melendez: 29–XI–1775; ANP/RA: 1. 44, 1619, 30, 44, and 61v; 1. 56, c. 216, 1622, 12; and Aguas: 1. 2, c. 3–3–3–1, 1666, 3; APF/1744; and LF: 1633; AAT/1772, 11; C: 1663, 3–3v, 12, 17v–18, 20v, and 24; 1665; T: 1667; 1704; and 1708; ACMS/1642, 6v and 25; 1766; and 1773, 1–3v; BP/2817, 1756, 3; Ibáñez, 89–91; ART/ID: 28–V–1802; AFA/1. 1, c. 12, 1655; and BM/Add. 17588, No. 5, 46v.

COLLIQUE: ANP/RA: 1. 44, 1619, 53v; and Portalanza: 1–VIII–1769; ART/Reyes: 1561; AAL/AT: 1–III, 1608, 20; ANCR/Rivera: 11–VII–1686, 60; 25–VIII–1694; and 26–II–1700, 372v–74; and AAT/C: 1773.

COLLUS: AAT/T: 1789, 3v, 5, 19, 19v, 21v, 35v, 61v–62, 114v, 116v, and 137v; [1676], 5–7, 43v and 71; 1704, 5–7v; 1717, 18v; 1777, 3, 21, 45, 96; 1795, 5 and 53v; and 1803, 1; and C: 1704; AAL/AT: 1–III, 1608, 20; and 2–III, 1632, 229; AGI/AL: 1387, 1789; ART/Palacios: 16–I–1611; and IC: 11–XII–1787; ANCR/Collus: 1643; 1716; and 1787–88; Rivera: 31–VII–1698; VM: 22–VII–1775; Lino: 23–XII–1732; and Polo: 4–XII–1753; BAH/9–26–1, 9; and 9–4763, 1707; ANP/Torres Campo: 26–VI–1728; TH: 1. 21, c. 131, 1805; LC: 1789; 1792; 1793; 1801–06; 1808; and 1821; BP/2817, 1756, 5v; ACI/Monsefú: P 110–5345, 63; and Rubiños y Andrade, 354.

CORBACHO: AAT/C: 1617, 318; and 1668; and T: 1738, 36v; ACMS/1642, 36v; ANP/RA: 1. 120, c. 431, 1642, 26v–27 and 42; and 1. 194, 1676, 131–33; ANCR/SG: 21–VIII–1653, 382–v; Rentero: 22–VI–1670; 2–IV–1670; Rivera: 31–VIII–1694; 1702, 295v and 323–30; and 1706; and A: 1–III–1656.

Appendix 3, continued.

SAN CRISTÓBAL: ANCR/Polo: 1729, 2,4 and 97v; 1752; 14-I-1747; and 17-I-1747; Rentero: 2-IV-1670; and Rivera: 2-VIII-1686; 16-IV-1686; 11-XI-1694; 4-II-1700; 3-XII-1700; 2-XII-1704; ANP/Aguas: 1. 2, 3-3-3-1, 1666, 3; Títulos: 1. 2, c. 71, 1678; Jaraba: 1750, 397v-401v; LC: 1789-90; 1792-93; and 1810; ACMS/1678, 2v-3v; AAT/C: 1706; T: 1697; 1708, 58-58v; and 1739, 155; and Curatos: 1746; CVU/8; AAL/AT: 23-v, 1703, 41-42; BP/2817, 1756, 2-3; ART/CoD: 8-III-1770; and ID: 28-V-1802; and AGI/AL: 1387, 1787.

CHARCAPE: ACMS/1642, 38; ANCR/Rivera: 1?-XII-1674; Dapelo: 20-X-1807; and 1735; ART/IC: 16-II-1785, 283v and 291v; ART/S: 1693; BP/2817; AGI/AL: 1417; and 1387; and ANP/LC: 1789; 1790; 1801-08; 1810; 1815; and 1821.

CHONGOYAPE: ANP/T: 917, 1772, 7v; and Núñez Porras: 1713, 65-70; Pablo Macera Dall'Orso, "Feudalismo colonial americano: el caso de las haciendas peruanas," *Acta historica*, XXXV (Szeged, Hungary, 1971), 12; ART/I: 22-II-1785; AAT/C: 1766, 61-62; and J. Walter Saenz, *Racarrumí* (Lima, 1975), 41-42 and 46.

CHUMBENIQUE: ACMS/1642, 10-11; and 1729-30, 95v; ANCR/1729, 58v, 496v-97, 502, 507v-08, 523-23v, 544, 551-52, 635-36, 648, 655-56v, 660, 662, and 666v; 1730; Rivera: 2?-XII-1704; [Calupe]: 1704, 35; and Lino: 9-IX-1730; and 18-III-1734; AAT/T: 1697; 1708, 13v; 1697; 1704, 35; 1708, 13v; and 1758, 11; ID: 28-V-1802; and C: 1746; AGI/AL: 1387, 1781; ANP/SG: 1782-92, 13v and 60v; CVI/8, 1703; AAL/AT: 23-v, 1703, 3-4v; 26-v, 1719, 3; Rubiños y Andrade, 354; Macera, "Feudalismo," 10; idem. and Felipe Marquez Abanto, "Informaciones geográficas del Perú colonial," *Revista del Archivo Nacional del Peru*, XXVIII, No. 1-2 (1964), 47; and AFA/ 1. 1, c. 7; and Cayaltí, 16v.

ÍLLIMO: AAL/AT: 19-VIII, 1689; 23-v, 1703, 49 and 50v; AAT/D: 1680, 2v; and T: 1697; BAH/9-26-1, 9-4763, 1707, 26v; ANCR/1714; and Prieto: 7-XII-1712; ART/SR: 1718; ACMS/1729-30, 95v; ANP/RA: 1. 309, c. 2803, 1792; and BNP/B357, 1668, 7 and 26v; and C2259, 1769.

ISCO: AFA/1. 1, c. 19, 13v, 14v, 20-23, 34v-39, 104-05v, 122-24, and 166-66v; and c. 3; ART/CoO: 19-IV-1591; ANP/RA: 1. 44, 1619, 101-01v; and ANCR/1595.

JANQUE: ANP/RA: 1. 37, c. 136, 1615, 210v; AGI/AL: 148, 7v; and C: 1864, 1757–58; AAT/T: 1742, 150; 1747–48, 100–00v; 1717, 64; 1746, 359; and C: 1734, 64; ANCR/VM: 17–X–1780; and ART/IO: 13–II–1788.

SAN JUAN: ANCR/1617; 1702; 1703; and 1706; A: 1–III–1656; HS: 1692; 1617; Polo: 15–I–1747; and 17–I–1747; and Rivera: 18–IX–1707; and 27–IX–1707; AAT/C: 1668, 23; T: 1739, 131v, 140–42, 152v, and 188v; 1738, 3–45; 1746; 1758, 69v–71; and Curatos: 1746; ANP/Moreno: 17–V–1771; and LC: 1789; and AGI/AL: 1387, 1789; and ART/Concha: 1785, 21v and 34.

LEVICHE: ANCR/M: III–1633; Rentero: 7–VI–1670; and 1727; and Gamarra: 1678; BP/2817, 1756, 3; and AFA/ 1. 1, c. 2, 6.

SAN LORENZO, EL REAL: ANCR/1617; Lino: 5–I–1734; and 18–III–1734; and CV: 10–I–1755; ACMS/1754, 2; APF/1744; and LF: 1633; AAT/Curatos: 1746; T: 1697; and 1708, 5v and 58; ANP/Aguas: 1. 2, 3–3–3–1, 1666, 3v; ART/CoJ: 4–VIII–1598; and 16–VIII–1604; and CoC: 1–X–1600; and 28–II–1598.

LUYA: BNP/B871, 1627, 4v; and C2195, 1756, 103; AAT/T: 1619; and 1744, 6, 32v, 170 and 322; Causas: 1737; V: 1783; D: 1795; and C: 1818; ANP/PL: 10–IX–1692; and 30–X–1692; DI: 1. 12, c. 295, 1756–58; LC: 1789; 1792; 1793; 1801; 1804; 1806; 1808; 1810; 1815; and 1821; I: 1. 1, 22–II–1785; RA: 1. 194, 1676, 112v and 157v; and 1. 302, c. 2711, 1791, 147v; RA–Criminal: 1. 24, c. 225, 1819; and DI: 1. 19, c. 483, 1793, 12, 23, 26v, 39, 40v–46, 50v and 51v; ART/Álvarez: 1676; CaO: 3–XII–1799; ID: 17–IV–1811, III, 39v–40; and IO: 1–IV–1788; ACMS/1747; BAH/9–26–1, 9–4763, 1707, 26v; OCIL/1970, 31–33; ASFL/Reg. 9, No. 2, Ms. 26, 1647; and Ms. 27, 1760; ANCR/1763, 25 and 149; Rivera: 12–I–1685; Lino: 30–IV–1722; Polo: 10–VII–1742; 29–X–1751; Rentero: 20–VIII–1654; and Luya: 1779, 149; BNP/C2195, 1756, 103; BP/2817, 1756, 6; BNS/Ms. 19262, 1785, 123–24; AGI/AL: 1387, 1789; and Comisión del Departamento de Lambayeque, Informe de la Asesoría Técnica (Lima, 1947), 83. territorial y política del Estatuto y Redemarcación Territorial. Ley 10553, La demarcación

MAMAPE: AAT/C: 1706; and 1835, 22–23 and 69v; and T: 1744, 322; and ANP/RA: 1. 194, 1676, 157v.

SANTIAGO DE MIRAFLORES: ANCR/Soto: 13–VIII–1625, 330; and Polo: 23–VII–1753; and AAL/AT: 23–v, 1703, 50; and AAT/T: 1697; and 1739, 155 and 204.

EL MOLINO: ANP/RA: 1. 194, 1676, 112v; and 1. 148, c. 1222, 1763, 2, 6 and 49; BP/2817, 1756, 5v–6v; ANCR/ 1787–88, 88v; Rentero: 20–VIII–1654; CV: 2–XII–1754; and Vásquez: 19–VII–1771; and 28–I–1780; ART/Vázquez: 1771, 165; and 1779; and CoÁguas: 26–IV–1768.

Appendix 3, continued.

MOLOTÚN: ANP/RA: 1, 24, c. 82, 1609, 1-3, 37-39, 49-50v, 77-78, 81-82v, 105, 107-07v, 136v-37 and 149; BNP/B357, 1668, 229; AC/1820; La Unión: 16-V-1959, 1; and AGI/AL: 1786, 1789.

SAN NICOLÁS: AGI/AL: 278; AFA/1. 1, c. 18; and Cayaltí: 29; ART/CaO: 4-II-1780; Macera, "Feudalismo," 10; and Ibanez, 13.

LA OTRA BANDA: ANCR/1732; Gamarra: 1678; Rivera: 26-I-1692, 392v; 10-VIII-1694; 14-VIII-1694; 31-VIII-1694; and 24-V-1708; Polo: 22-VII-1742; 16-I-1747; 23-XI-1748; and 23-VII-1753; CV: 13-XII-1756; Lino: 19-III-1734; VM: 14-I-1771; and 16-II-1785; AAT/Causas: 1664; 1763, 2; T: 1697; C: 1742; and [Collús]: 1777, 32v; ACMS/1773, 1; ASFL/Reg. 7, No. 2, Ms. 10, 1766; and Reg. 7, Ms. 12, 1761; AGI/AL: 1387, 1789; Rubiños y Andrade, 354; Macera and Márquez, "Informaciones," 47; and Macera, "Feudalismo," 10; AAL/AT: 1-I, 1603, 8; AFA/1. 1, c. 8; c. 18; and 1. 2, c. 17, 4-4v; AKT/ID: 28-V-1802; and ANP/LC: 1789-93; 1801-06; 1808; and 1810.

OYOTÚN: ACMS/V-1698; Rubiños y Andrade, 354; AAT/T: 1697; Zevallos Quiñones, I, 144 and II, 101; and ANCR/Rentero: 15-IX-1670; Lino: 25-I-1730; Polo: 20-V-1747; CV: 25-IV-1753; 24-I-1756; and 1-VIII-1756; VM: 28-VI-1768; 30-VII-1783; and 1803; AFA/1. 1, c. 20; c. 19, 20-20v and 166-85; c. 3; c. 4, 1613; c. 12; and c. 18; BNP/B1034, 6-45, 89-92, 107-09, 127v and 154; and B1133, 1684, 3-5v.

PÁTAPO: Demarcación, 95; ANP/RA: 1. 194, 1676; DI: 1, 19, c. 483, 1793, 37-40; PL: 30-X-1698; and 10-IX-1692; LC: 1789; 1792-93; 1806; 1810; 1815; and 1821; ANCR/1645; and 1803; Collús: 1643; Polo: 27-VII-1742; and 7-XI-1742; and VM: 25-V-1792; Rentero: 20-VIII-1658; Rivera: 12-I-1685; Lino: 5-VI-1717; and CV: 27-XI-1752; AAT/T: 1758, 133v; and 1762; C: 1706, 7; and 1793-1818; Causas: 1739; Censuras: 1789; and D: 1795; APL/LF: 1633; ART/Álvarez: 1676; CoCE: 15-V-1676; IO: 1-IV-1788; and IAG: 14-I-1812; AGI/AL: 100 [1646], 30-31; and 1387, 1789; BNP/B871, 1627; and AFA/1. 1, c. 19.

PICSI: BNP/A157, 128v-31; B871, 1627, 1, 3, 13, 18, and 79; and B1737, 1669, 22; ANP/DI: 1. 4, c. 72, 1622, 101v; RA: 1. 35, c. 192, 1598; and Histórico: 1075, 1790, 45v; ASFL/Reg. 9, No. 2, Ms. 26, 1647, 44, 45, 58 and 115; ASDL/C: Libro I, No. 12, 102-06v; and Libro II, No. 25, 394-96v; ART/Palacios: 18-VIII-1610; and VB: 1786, 46; ANCR/Collús: 1643, 151v; Lino: 20-VII-1723; and Polo: 2-VI-1747; and ACMS/1723.

POMALCA: AAT/[1740?], 44; and [1742], 35v; D: 1588, 39; T: 1742, 102; 1744, 34, 112v, and 215; 1747-48, 82; 1750, 2v; 1775; 1776, 53 and 100; 1779; 1789, 19, 61v-62, 105, 125 and 142; C: [1740], 28; and 1750; ANCR/[1645]; Collús: 1643, 65v and 157v; Rivera: 1-X-1694; 27-III-1704; and 1716; Polo: 6-III-1748; and 21-I-1747; and Meléndez: 19-VI-1775; and 20-VIII-1775; AAL/AT: 1-III, 1608, 20; ANP/TP: 1. 23, c. 611, 1783, 12; RA: 1. 283, c. 2511, 1789, 4, 5, 34 and 215; TH: 1. 21, c. 131, 1805, 51v and 77-77v; LC: 1789; 1792; 1793; 1801-06; 1808; and 1821; AGI/AL: 1387, 1789; Domingo Angulo, "Diario de la segunda visita pastoral que hizo de su arquidiócesis el Ilustrísimo Señor Don Toribio Alfonso de Mogrovejo . . . 1593," Revista del Archivo Nacional del Perú, I (1920), 237; Rubiños y Andrade, 354; BNP/A157; AFA/1. 1, c. 19; ART/CoAguas: 26-IV-1768, 171v; and IE: 13-XI-1815; and BM/Add. 17588, No. 5, 47v.

POPAN: AAT/C: 1617, 318, 327v-28v; 1619; 1668, 23; 1670, 356-57 and 389v-90; 1674; 1750, 34; T: 1704, 31; 1708, 5v; and 1753, 43; ACMS/1642; 19-VII-1698, 541v; and 1735, 1, 4 and 5; ANP/Aguas: 1. 2, 3-3-3-1, 1666, 3v; and RA: 1. 194, 1676, 14-15, and 131-33; LC: 1790; ANCR/1702, 331v; Sánchez: 21-VIII-1653, 382-82v; A: 18-III-1656, 301v-02; Rivera: 20-III-1685; 31-VIII-1694; and 23-IX-1694, 415-16v; and Pardo: 5-IV-1632; and 20-III-1632; AGI/AL: 1387, 1789; and E: 511A, 1648, 5v-6v; Rubiños y Andrade, 354; Ibáñez, 8, 13 and 89-90; ART/CoO: 25-VIII-1702, 121, 136-37, 146-46v, and 149v-50v; S: 1693; CoAG: 28-VI-1740; and Concha: 1785, 21v; and AFA/Cayaltí: 7.

LA PUNTA: AAT/T: 1697, 3, 7v, and 15v-16v; and 1708, 13; C: 1739, 6v; and 1817, 18; and Causas: 1789, 123; ANCR/1711, 3; 1761; 1803, 20v, 63, 97-98, 106, 125, 153-55, 197 and 203; Rivera: 22-I-1692; 9-IX-1692; 9-VII-1694; 26-II-1700; 20-XII-1704; and 21-V-1707; Polo: 20-V-1747; and 25-VI-1742; and Rentero: 14-IV-1670; AFA/Cayaltí, AGI/AL: 1387, 1789; ANP/TH: 1. 13, c. 134, 1802; 1. 22, c. 198, 1784, 8v, 69v-75v and 123v; 1. 23, c. 611, 1783, 21v; 1. 28, c. 261, 1789, 13, 19v and 22v; 1. 18, c. 164, 1791, 123v and 179; 1. 13, c. 124, 1802, 5-6, 44 and 63; Portalanza: 1-VIII-1769; RA: 1. 103, c. 873, 1746; 1. 313, c. 2841, 1792, 67v; 1. 363, c. 3325, 1798, 5v-8; and 1. 9, c. 97, 1801, 8v, 22, 25-26, 48v and 143v; LC: 1808, 38v; 1810; and 1815; BP/2817, 1756, 3; Rubiños y Andrade, 354; Ibáñez, 9 and 63-64; and ART/IC: 8-VIII-1808; and IE: 13-XI-1815.

RACO: ART/Mata: 1596; and 1598; and CoO: 2-V-1598; and Angulo, 230-31.

RAFÁN: AGI/AL: 278, n.d.; and 1387, 1789; ACMS/1676, 6; ANCR/Rivera: 11-VII-1694, 367v-68; Lino: 4-II-1730; 1739; Polo: 11-IX-1748; CV: 15-VIII-1752; VM: 25-IX-1767; Rubiños y Andrade, 354; Zevallos Quiñones, II, 101; AFA/1. 1, c. 18, 1v; 1. 2, c. 2, 3v-4; San Luis: 171, 185, 191, 194 and 200; and ANP/Meléndez: 20-I-1721; and 5-III-1721; and LC: 1789; 1801-08; and 1810.

Appendix 3, continued.

SALTRAPÓN: AFA/1. 1, c. 8, 3; c. 10; c. 16, 1667; and c. 18; 1. 2, c. 15, 7v; and c. 17; AAL/AT: 37-I, 1794, 28; ANP/LC: 1790; 1810; 1815; and 1821; and AGI/AL: 1387, 1789.

SALTUR: ART/CoO: 22-I-1578; and IT: 25-VI-1790; AAT/T: 1708, 10; 1753, 43v; and 1789, 36-36v; AFA/Cayaltí: 5v; ASFL/Reg. 7, No. 2, Ms. 12, 1739; ANP/RA: 1. 103, c. 873, 1746, 1, 7v and 115; 1. 363, c. 3325, 1798, 7v-8 and 56; and 1. 9, c. 97, 1801, 5-6, 10 and 40; TH: 1. 22, c. 198, 1784, 7v, 66 and 104v; and SG: 1782-92, II, 7v-8; ANCR/1744, 1748; and 1803; Polo: 25-VI-1742; and 11-VIII-1751; PG and S: 1796; VM: 20-VI-1787, 8; CV: 3-IV-1755; and 24-IV-1755; AGI/E: 511A, 1648, 5v-6v; and C: 1864, 1722; and BP/2817, 1756, 3.

SAMÁN: ANCR/1645; and Rivera: 31-VII-1698; ANP/RA: 1. 148, c. 1222, 1763, 17v-19, 33 and 38v; and 1. 283, c. 2511, 1789, 2v, 79 and 136; and TH: 1. 21, c. 131, 1805, 12v; and AAT/T: 1747-48, 62 and 83-85; and 1776, 100.

SANCARRANCO Y LA VIÑA: ANCR/Lino: 25-I-1723; Rivera: 30-VIII-1698; Polo: 30-IV-1751; VM: 31-I-1769; 30-I-1769; and 28-XI-1769; BP/2817, 1756, 3; ANP/RA: 1. 123, c. 443, 1642, 106-20v; LC: 1789; 1790; 1792; 1793; 1800-06; and 1810; Zevallos Quinones, II, 67; AGI/E: 534A, 27; ART/RH-Manual: 1-V-1746; ID: 17-IV-1811; and IT: 25-I-1790; and 25-VI-1790, 31v; and ACMS/1722; and 1829-30.

SANGANA: ART/Mata: 26-II-1603; LC: 1789; 1792; 1793; 1801; and 1810; and IO: 13-II-1788; ANCR/Álvarez: 23-V-1663; Lino: 30-XII-1733; and 25-VIII-1730; and CV: 14-VIII-1752; ANP/TH: 1. 13, c. 124, 1802, 44; and AGI/AL: 1387, 1789.

SANTEQUEPE: ANCR/Rivera: 17-VII-1694; 12-VIII-1694; and 31-VIII-1694, 400; ACMS/1698, 6-6v; AAL/AT: 37-I, 1794, 4-6v, 13, 17-17v and 28v; AFA/Mocupe: 7; 1. 1, c. 2; c. 8, 3; c. 10; c. 16; c. 18, 3, 15v and 17v; c. 19; and c. 20; 1. 2, c. 2, 3v-4; c. 7, 1797; c. 15; and c. 17, 1802, 1v; AGI/AL: 100 [1646], 17-17v; and ART/CoC: 21-I-1712; and RHC: 17-IV-1809.

SÁRRAPO: ANCR/1680; 1716; Soto: 15-VII-1625; M: V-1633, 102; Gamarra: 8-VII-1678; Rivera: 21-I-1692; 3-I-1695; 4-II-1704; and 13-V-1708; HS: 1607; Rentero: 10-IV-1670; and CV: 31-X-1755; 1727; and 1795; AAT/Curatos: 1746, 13-13v; ACMS/1637, 653v-57v; 25-IX-1637; 1633; 31-VIII-1637; and 8-IX-1637; and 1722, 7v-8, 12, 14v, 17, 26v-28, 32, 36-39 and 42-48v; BP/2817, 1756, 3 and 7; AGI/AL: 1387, 1789; ANP/RA: 1。44, 1619, 68, 97v-99v, 104-05 and 118-19v; LC: 1789; 1790; 1792; 1793; 1810; 1815; and 1821; Rubiños y Andrade, 324; Macera and Márquez, "Informaciones," 47; AFA/1. 1, c. 19; ART/CoD: 8-III-1770; and AAL/ AT: 25-XIV, 1715, 53.

SASAPE: ANCR/1714; 1719; and 1763; and Álvarez: 9-III-1663; ART/Mata: 1596; and 1598; Rentero: 15-XI-1679; 17-II-1679; and 18-III-1670; IAG: 16-X-1793, 64; and IO: 19-VIII-1785; ACMS/1813, 22v and 26; APF/1744; ANP/RA: 1。37, c. 136, 1615, 231v; and SR: [1719]; BAH/9-1-26, 9-4763, 1707, 26v; Interview with Don Agusto Castillo Muro Sime, 1971; Zevallos Quiñones, I, 132; and BNP/B357: 1668, 7, 29, 32v, 159-60 and 218。

SIALUPE: ANCR/Polo: 29-X-1751; 1763, 161; and 1803; ACMS/1813, 20v, 26, 46, 54-56 and 65v; and ART/CoC: 15-I-1781.

SICÁN: Enrique Brüning, Estudios monográficos del Departamento de Lambayeque (Chiclayo, 1923), III, 71; Augusto D。 León Barandiarán, Mitos, leyendas y tradiciones Lambayecanas (n。p。 (Lima?), n。d。 (1938?)), 208-10 and 228; ACMS/1829-30; ANCR/Polo: 12-III-1751; 1-II-1751; 22-I-1754; and 20-VI-1756; VM: 4-V-1781; 1763, 2, 5, 12-12v, 25 and 71; Prieto: 5-X-1712; and Polo: 6-VIII-1742; BNP/C2195, 1756, 63v-66; and C2259, 1759, 6v-7v, 10v and 28-34; AAT/T: 1744, 156v; AGI/AL: 1387, 1789; ANP/RA: 1。309, c。2803, 1792; LC: 1790; DI: 1。19, c。483, 1793, 12v; and RA-Criminal: 1。14, c。153, 1751, 6v; and BP/2817, 1756, 7; ART/IO: 18-I-1800; and Concha: 1785, 37。

SIPÁN: ANCR/1673; 1709; 1720, 5-7, 17 and 32; 1761; 1796; 1827-28; Rivera: 31-VIII-1674; 25-VIII-1694; 20-X-1694, 441-43; 28-III-1704; 27-V-1704; 29-XI-1704; and 18-IX-1706; HS: VI-1678; Polo: 17-I-1747; CV: 3-IV-1755; VM: 25-XI-1783; Luya: 1779; and AC/1828; and Memorandum, 1920, 8; AAL/T: 1789, 92; and [1751], 38 and 46; AAT/Curatos: 1746, 7-9; ANP/PL: 3-X-1752, 82-85; Ibáñez, 102; Macera, "Feudalismo," 10; Rubiños y Andrade, 354; AGI/E: 511A, 1648, 5v-6v; and ART/Álvarez: 1676; CoCE: 15-V-1676; and CoO: 25-VIII-1702.

TULIPE: AAT/D: 1588, 31v; ANP/RA: 1。194, 1676, 9, 75v-78, 82, 91, 102, 107, 112v, 114v-15, 132, 135-37, 152, 154-58v, 182-87v, 192 and 204-05; AGI/E: 511A; and ANCR/Álvarez: 3-IX-1663.

Appendix 3, continued.

TUMAN: ASFL/Reg. 9, No. 2, Ms. 26, 1647; BNP/A157, 4v-5, 99v-100; and B871, 1627; ANP/T: 1. 106, 1767, 10; Histórico: 1075, 1790, 13, 45v and 106; and 1. 21, c. 5, 1819, 9; RA: 1. 302, c. 2711, 1791, 147v; and TH: 1. 21, c. 131, 1805, 50v; SG: 1782-92; and LC: 1810; AAT/D: 1680, 2; and 1795; ANCR/1777; and 1803; Collús: 1643; and Tumán: 1782-83; and 1812; ART/IT: 1-VIII-1786; 12-VIII-1789; and 7-I-1790; Palacios: 17-VIII-1610; and 26-II-1611; I: 1. 1, 22-II-1785; Rentero: 1804; CoT: 20-XI-1782; VB: 1786, 41, 46v and 91; and Dapelo: 1804; and Angulo, "Diario . . . de visita . . . 1593," 237.

UCUPE: APF/1744; and LF: 1633; AAT/H: 1794, 2; and T: 1738; ANCR/1735; and Rentero: 17-VI-1670; BP/ 2817, 1756, 3; AGI/AL: 1387, 1789; and 1412; ANP/RA-Criminal: 1. 14, c. 153, 1751, 1; and LC: 1792; 1793; and 1810; AAL/AT: 37-I, 1794, 1 and 15; and Rubiños y Andrade, 355; AFA/1. 1, c. 1-4, c. 7, c. 11-13, c. 15-20; and 1. 2, c. 1-4, c. 8, c. 10-13, and c. 16-18; Manuel Burga, "San Jacinto de Ucupe," Análisis, Nos. 2-3 (1977), 187, 190 and 192-93; ART/CoC: 21-I-1712; IAG: 12-III-1802; CoT: 13-IX-1784; IT: 14-XII-1785; and IO: 21-VII-1796; Barandiarán, 247-48; and BM/Add. 17588, No. 5, 48v.

VALDE HERMOSA (or PALOMINO): ANCR/[1645]; and 1690; Soto: 17-VII-1625; Pardo: 1632; Rivera: 16-X-1686; 11-VII-1694; 7-VIII-1694; 21-I-1700; and 1-IV-1700; CV: 2-IV-1754; and Polo: 16-I-1747; ASFL/Reg. 7, No. 2, Ms. 7, 1694; AGI/AL: 278, n.d.; AAT/C: 1734; T: 1739, 131v and 188v; 1738; 1743, 93; and 1746, 333; BP/ 2817, 1756, 3; BAH/9-26-1, 9-4763, 1707; and AFA/1. 2, c. 2; c. 3; and c. 10.

Appendix 4: Methodology

At various stages in the research and writing of this study, decisions had to be made regarding analysis and methodology. Assumptions, definitions, and comments on the quality and abundance of the primary sources have been incorporated wherever possible into the text or footnotes. In the following paragraphs, I discuss methodological decisions and the handling of data I deemed to cumbersome to be included above.

Determining the factors that affected the development of large-scale agriculture in Lambayeque involved: (1) analyzing and describing the evolution of the agrarian structure of the region in terms of its economic and demographic history; (2) explaining how decisions regarding land use, water use, and labor distribution were made; (3) determining the extent to which hacienda owners participated in making these decisions; (4) identifying the bases of their power and influence; and (5) assessing the impact of these decisions on actual tenure relations.

To keep the discussion of the estate in perspective—because the hacienda did not develop in a vacuum, but in direct competition for scarce resources with the Indian communities in the area—the analysis included both institutions and the forces conditioning their development. Information from colonial manuscript sources was used to establish the basic chronology of landownership (presented in Appendix 3) for each of the major estates. The chronology includes the names of owners, the dates and circumstances of land acquisition, the sale price or assessed value of the property, the amount of the recognized liens and mortgages on an estate, and its area and population figures. Details on the organization and operation of the various estates—use of natural resources, technology, labor regime, and management—which add form and life to the chronology were incorporated into the text. The history of the Indian communities is recounted in terms of demographic fluctuations and changes in land tenure and control over water, providing a background against which to gauge the development of the estates. Other factors which affected the evolution of both the estates and the Indian communities include local geography and climate, effective demand for products and accessibility of markets, the availability of labor and capital, and government policy.

These variables in different combinations accounted for changes in the two institutions and in the regional agrarian structure, that is, changes in (1) the function and productivity of the communities, (2) the organization and scale of production of the estates, (3) the relative proportion of the local natural resources controlled by the two, and (4) the interdependence that developed between communities and estates over the years. From the histories of the estates and the communities, general economic trends and a basic periodization of the agricultural development of the region were defined.

The periodization, admittedly, is based more on the economic history of the estates than on the history of the Indian communities. The origins of the large estate were traced back to the chacras and labores of the sixteenth century. During a second period (1595–1649), the estates assumed—through land concentration and the organization of large-scale production—the characteristic physiognomy that they retained for the rest of their colonial existence. The third period (1650–1719) was one of expansion, intensification of production, and prosperity. The last, from 1720 to Independence, was characterized by visible stagnation and eventual ruin.

The social and economic characteristics of local economic development were used to divide the nearly three centuries covered in the study into four periods; the years 1594 and 1595 end the first and begin the second periods, respectively, because they were the dates of the first visita de la tierra, which clarified and established on a legal rather than a *de facto* basis the land tenure of the area. Those years also marked the end of the encomendero dominance of the region; after those dates only a few encomenderos continued to own land in Lambayeque, and none lived there permanently. The years 1649 and 1650 were midpoints of a single 130-year expansive epoch. The sharp rise of sugar prices in these years provided a natural break between an era characterized generally by the growth of estancias, haciendas, and trapiches, and an era characterized by the spread of sugar monoculture and windfall profits. The year 1720, the date of a devastating flood which almost completely destroyed the processing facilities on both the sugar estates and the ranches, marked the beginning of a period of renewed interest in animal raising. After 1720 the mentality of the landowners changed from one of optimism and expansion to one of pessimism and survival.

The best example of the leads and lags and continuity between one period and another, and the difficulty of defining periods with the choice of a single year, was the selection of 1720 as the start of the fourth and final period. I considered four other dates. The earliest, 1686, was the date of the pirate Edward David's attack and plundering of Saña. I rejected this date because he and his men did not destroy the rural estates. In the next year an earthquake caused severe physical damage up and down the coast and apparently so upset the chemical balance of the soil that wheat would no longer grow. While this caused major cropping changes in other valleys, it had little effect in Lamba-yeque. Most of the estates had already been converted to sugar pro-duction, and wheat was no longer a major cash crop. The year 1701, the date of the plague of rodents which reduced production by one-third, was not used because the estates and their owners remained solvent. The plague caused considerable grumbling among the owners, but it did not actually cause any bankruptcies and was seen by most as one of the periodic "bad years" in agriculture. The year 1728, the date of the second major flood, was too late. The inundation of 1720 had already brought widespread destruction; plunged the previously money-making estates deeply into debt which, given the market con-ditions, they could not afford; and confirmed the fears of prolonged depression of the landowners and the Spanish population in general.

The economic history of the region and this periodization served as the framework for the aggregate analysis of the landowning popula-tion. I collected biographical information (for example, date of birth and death, year of land acquisitions, place of birth, date(s) of mar-riage(s), number and type of other occupations, level of education, extent of participation in the militia and on the town council) on per-sons of known Spanish or mestizo ancestry who appeared by name in the primary sources reviewed. The data were recorded by individual on index cards, and these were subsequently separated into four groups: (1) landowners; (2) landless persons who held at least one position in the provincial administrative hierarchy, held a leadership position in the local militia, or held a post in the municipal council; (3) merchants; and (4) others.[1]

There is no way to gauge the completeness of this population sample before 1670 because no census for the non-Indian population of the district was found. The only indication of the completeness of the sample is a listing by a local historian, Dr. Jorge Zevallos Quiñones, of upper-class families in the eighteenth century, with some references back to approximately 1650. Of the 216 families he names, I identified all but 45 (20.8 percent). Because Zevallos Quiñones does not explicitly state the criteria that he used for inclusion or reveal his sources, I have no idea of how far down on the social scale he goes. Judging from the approximate dates of arrival in the area, I suspect that most of the family names I could not identify were those of persons who came to Lambayeque in connection with the Bourbon reforms late in the eighteenth century and remained to become prominent after the wars of Independence. Bullón, Barandiarán, and Laca, for example, are three patronyms which do not appear in the records used for this study, but members of these families became important public officials and landowners in the nineteenth century.

Given the types of documents used in the study, one probable bias of the sample is toward an overrepresentation of the wealthiest, most active, and powerful individuals in the first three groups, people who had the resources and connections to pursue vigorously their interest and who left written records of their activities. Members of the lower classes imputed the prestige and reputation of the most active landowners in public affairs to less active and visible ones. Because, in the mass mind, landowners were more or less of the same status, prestige, and power, they were all treated with roughly equal deference by the nonelite members of society. I am confident, therefore, that the analysis and conclusions based on the sample are sound.

Because my purpose was to correlate the social and economic histories of Lambayeque, I divided the hacendado population into four mutually exclusive groups by the year that an individual acquired his first piece of property to coincide with the four periods of economic history. I chose to divide the landowning population by this date rather than by date of birth or death, for example, because landownership was the defining characteristic of the population and, therefore, this information, however approximate, was recorded for every individual. Categorization by this date alone proved unsatisfactory in one respect: it did not take into consideration the quality of the datum. Landowners who were assigned to a group based on the date of their will, listing their property holdings and establishing them as a landholder, had obviously held the land before that time. Youngsters who acquired land before the age of majority did not assume active administration until they were older. Accordingly, the records of the landowners who acquired land within five years of the limits of each period were reviewed individually to determine whether or not they merited inclusion in the previous or the following group. The individual was assigned to the period in which he had spent most of his active (public and adult) life.

The results of this categorization of the landowning population are as follows:

Figure 31. Landowning Population by Period

| | No. of Landowners | | | | | |
| | Males | | Females | | Total | |
Period	No.	Percent	No.	Percent	No.	Percent
Conquest to 1594:						
Encomenderos	34	4.7	4	2.8	38	4.4
Other Encomenderos	32	4.5	10	6.9	42	4.9
Landholders	90	12.6	2	1.4	92	10.7
1595–1649	179	25.0	35	24.3	214	24.9
1650–1719	129	18.0	47	32.6	176	20.5
1720–1824	252	35.2	46	31.9	298	34.7
Total	716	100.0	144	99.9	860	100.1

Personal data on the individuals in each group were of two types and were analyzed in two different ways. Biographical data, such as date and place of birth, date and place of death, date(s) of marriage(s), level of education, occupation(s), years an individual held political positions, and rank(s) in the local militia, were coded for analysis by computer. Computer analysis gave me such aggregate statistics as the number and percentage of the individuals in any group who participated in the town council during a period, and the number and percentage of the individuals by place of birth, highest level of education, and so forth. In addition, the computer provided me with individual career profiles, listing by date (from first to last), military and political positions, occupations, and acquisition of land.[2]

The sources also revealed the names of relatives, business associates, and friends with whom to establish and understand informal power relations. Affinal and consanguineal kinship relationships were used to make genealogies. The extended family included up to three generations as well as first and second cousins. More distant relatives were not included unless explicitly recognized as part of the functional family in the primary sources. Compadres, business associates, and friends were diagramed in like manner and superimposed on family trees to show the potential extent of an individual's indirect network of influence.

The file of the nonlandowners (persons who held at least one position in the provincial administrative hierarchy, held a leadership position in the local militia, or held a post in the municipal council) was divided to correspond to the four periods by the date the individual held his first position. If a person's public career began in 1594 or before, he was placed in Group 1; if an individual's career began between 1595 and 1649, he was placed in Group 2; and so forth. Merchants were divided in the same manner by the first year of their known commercial activity. Each group of nonlandowners was referred to as the professional and bureaucratic sector or group in local society. These individuals alone cannot be considered completely representative of the landless but influential and powerful group in Lambayecan society because neither priests nor women joined the militia, participated in the municipal council, or held bureaucratic position. Priests were influential as makers of public opinion and in other capacities, and women exerted influence through charitable, church-related activities and compadrazgo. Because the number of influential clerics and women is relatively small, I consider the conclusions based on comparisons of landowners and nonlandowners in public life as valid and indicative of general trends.

As important to an understanding of the history of this region as identifying the landowners was determining how decisions affecting tenure relations were made and the extent to which the hacendados participated. This entailed the attempt to understand the roles and respective jurisdictions of the members of the town council and the provincial administrators. Once the key decision-making positions were identified, I determined how many landowners served in these posts during each period. The frequencies that landowners held specific positions on the town council or in the provincial bureaucracy were tabulated and compared to the frequencies for the corresponding group of landless, with the results indicating the landowners' relative political and administrative strength.[3]

A study of specific instances of decision making revealed that direct participation by the landowners provided only a partial explanation of their local hegemony. The identification of the landless individuals who made or implemented decisions in terms of their kinship, compadrazgo, and business and legal relations with the landowners helped determine the motivations and aided in understanding the actions of individuals and their significance in the context of a specific dispute over the natural resources of the area. Such identification also showed the extent of the landowners' ability to indirectly influence decisions as well as the importance of the informal aspects of power relations.

The hacendados' overall position in society as compared to other social groups was gauged by assessing the success that they or their political spokesman had in deciding issues related to land tenure to their advantage. The effects of these decisions were established by comparing the socioeconomic facts of hacienda life before and after the decisions for evidence of change.

Assumptions, Definitions and Conventions

Landowners. I included all individuals who were known to *own* land for one year or longer and who were not holding the land as members of Indian communities. Men given land as part of a dowry were counted as landowners because they took over active administration, despite the fact that their wives theoretically retained ownership. These women were also included if they took an active role in the administration or sale of the estate.

Racial terminology. I used the racial terms employed by the individuals I studied. Accordingly, *Spaniard* and *Indian* serve as generic terms throughout the text and as synonyms for "estate owners" and "member of indigenous communities," respectively. No attempt was made to identify in a systematic way the percentage of individuals who may have been of mixed parentage in either group, because the terms have both racial and cultural connotations. An individual's racial designation depended partly on his life-style, occupation, and social group identification and partly on ancestry and physical appearance. In general, "Spaniard" included both peninsular-born and American-born (creole) individuals. When an individual's status in this regard was known and was relevant to the analysis, he was so identified in the text. "Slave" and "black" were used interchangably; I substituted the currently fashionable term "black" for "negro," except in direct quotes.

Currency. The many different types of currency used during the colonial era in Peru are presented in Appendix 1. To avoid confusion and facilitate comparisons, all prices, values, wages, and salaries, unless specifically stated otherwise, were converted into pesos of eight reales each. Peso amounts were rounded to the nearest whole, unless the fraction proved to be important to the analysis. Peso amounts were not expressed in constant terms. But care was taken to convert sixteenth-century pesos (corrientes or ensayados) to pesos of eight reales each, according to the following conversion factors.

Prices. With very few exceptions, prices plotted in the charts reflect the wholesale value of a commodity. The exceptions are prices taken from Guillermo Lohmann Villena's article on prices in sixteenth-century Lima. He did not make a systematic distinction between wholesale and retail prices; some of his figures were obviously retail, while others were wholesale. The use of retail prices (for sugar, for example) ex-

Figure 32. Monetary Conversion Factors, Sixteenth Century

Year	Conversion Factor (in percent)	Pesos Ensayados[1]	Pesos Corrientes[1]
1532	8.9	490.0	410.0
1559–60	13.0	508.5	391.5
1562	20.0	540.0	360.0
1564	18.0	531.0	369.0
1566	28.0	576.0	324.0
1570–74	20.0	540.0	360.0
1578	25.0	562.5	337.5
(early 1580s)	32.0	594.0	341.0
1586	36.0	612.0	288.0
1587	40.0	630.0	270.0
1591	42.6	641.5	258.5
1598	42.5	641.25	258.75
1598	43.0	643.5	256.5

[1]In maravedis

Sources: ART/CoO: 1–VIII–1587, 31–I–1598, 8–VIII–1587, 13–VII–1570, 18–I–1574; CoAG: 27–XI–1586; CoJ: 4–VIII–1598; LC: 21–V–1559, 24–X–1560; Mata: 11–VI–1564; and AGI/P: 97, r. 4, [1562], 18; and J: 455, 1898.

aggerated the differences of prices in Lima and Lambayeque in the sixteenth century. The only other retail prices included in the study were the quoted prices of basic foodstuffs purchased locally in small quantities (for example, corn, chickpeas, beans, oil, and so forth); the fact that the prices were retail is apparent from the text and the graphs. Because prices are missing for so many years, the plots on the graphs should be considered suggestive of general trends.

Occupational structure. Most of the occupational terminology in the text is self-explanatory. A few terms, however, need clarification.

> *Occupation:*   Work by which an individual earned money or profession—whether or not practiced.
>
> *Bureaucrat:*   Refers to any provincial administrator, regardless of how the individual acquired the position. Most of the positions were salaried or gave the individual the right to collect fees; in this sense, bureaucratic posts were occupations, not political positions.
>
> *Politician:*   A member of the town council, regardless of whether or not the position was remunerative.

High-level bureaucratic positions include: accountant, treasurer, corregidor, lieutenant corregidor, comptroller (*factor*), intendant (*intendente*), chief judge, and governor. They had provincial-wide responsibilities. Low-level bureaucratic positions include: judge, water commissioner and judge of cattle brands, and protector of Indians. These were usually short-term positions (a matter of years rather than for life, as some of the upper-level positions were) and were limited to one municipal district or Indian community; these positions implied more specific responsibilities and smaller incomes than higher-level positions. If one individual held more than one bureaucratic position simultaneously, he was placed in the category of the highest position.

Several problems were encountered in the analysis of occupations and career patterns which limited the number of valid generalizations and comparisons that could be made between one period and another. One problem was the changing relative importance of an occupation in terms of status and remuneration. For example, estate administration in the sixteenth century was a means by which some individuals—for example, the first nonencomendero settlers of the Lambayeque valleys—became estancieros and moved into the landowning class. During the seventeenth century, estate administration was placed in the hands of majordomos, who were of lower socioeconomic status than former administrators. Estate administration as a respectable profession disappeared until the eighteenth century, when it again became acceptable. The same is true of the tithe collector. In the sixteenth century the renter of the tithes (if other than an encomendero) was his own collector, and in this sense the position was an occupation. For the encomenderos of the sixteenth century and the landowners of the seventeenth century, tithe collecting was an opportunity to invest surplus capital; employees collected the tithe. In the eighteenth century the tithe became another tax administered directly by the crown, and the individual opportunities for this speculative investment disappeared.

Another problem was the significance of political participation. My conception of "political" implies that the professional, career politician did not exist. Motivations for sitting on the municipal council and the manner of recruitment changed between the sixteenth and the eighteenth centuries. For most of the sixteenth century, members were either appointed by a viceregal authority outside the district or elected by their peers for one-year terms, and positions were usually unsalaried. Encomenderos and landowners participated for the power and prestige value of the positions. Because the central bureaucracy was still in a formative stage, council members had *de facto* control over some aspects of provincial administration. In the seventeenth century, when the provincial hierarchy of crown officials became fully established and began to function, landowners purchased seats on the council for their prestige value rather than for the inherent power to affect rural conditions. The remuneration of the positions was probably not a strong motivation to participate because it was small in comparison to the profits from agrobusiness. In the eighteenth century, some individuals held office as a means of supplementing their incomes and increasing their power and visibility.

Social mobility. An underlying assumption of this study is that individuals aspired to become landowners.

Genealogies. The genealogies included in the text are not meant to be complete family trees, but are designed to show the key relationships between families and patterns of land tenure and capital accumulation.

Sources. On the estate, see Susan and Douglas Horton, "Sources for the Investigation of Peruvian Agrarian History," Land Tenure Center Paper No. 84 (Madison, Wis., February 1973); Susan Ramírez-Horton,

"The Sugar Estates of the Lambayeque Valley, 1670–1800: A Contribution to Peruvian Agrarian History," Land Tenure Center Research Paper No. 97 (Madison, Wis., November 1973), 57–60; and Susan Ramírez-Horton, "Sources for the Study of Peruvian Hacienda History," *Research Guide to Andean History,* ed. John TePaske (Durham, 1981), 273–83.

Biographical information on the landowners and their families was gathered at the same time from many of the same manuscript sources reviewed for details on the estates. Of these, capellanía records deserve special mention because, aside from the valuable information they contain on estate mortgages and liens, many often include entire family genealogies. Priests applying for the annual income from these legacies had to prove that they qualified as a beneficiary, for example, that they were the nearest male relative to the founder, and so forth. Many traced their ancestry back several generations to establish their claim. One must realize, however, that in their effort to demonstrate their rights to the stipend family trees were sometimes inaccurately presented. Genealogies should be cross-checked with other sources when two or more persons claimed the same stipend or when the cases dated from the eighteenth century, a period in which the money was more crucial to the economic well-being of the claimant.

However, hacienda documents, with the exception of the capellanía records, provide little more than incidental information on the landowners. Far richer in personal data on the landowners were *probanzas* (or *hojas*) *de servicios y méritos,* minutes of town council meetings, parish registers of baptisms and marriages, and the legal documents bound together in notarial registers.

Probanzas de servicios are the records from court hearings in the sixteenth or early seventeenth centuries on the noble origins or extraordinary services performed for the king by encomenderos and early settlers. They were made to establish a person's or family's claim to a special grant from the king: for a coat of arms, an encomienda, or other pension. The probanzas include information on the military exploits of one or more generations of a family and incidental information about their assets and wealth.

The minutes of the town council meetings provide a record of an individual's formal participation in politics and his stand on various issues. Reference is also made to an individual's military rank.

Parish registers are a rich source of information on kinship and friendship ties. Baptismal entries typically include the date, the name of the child, his age or date of birth, his racial classification (Spaniard, Indian, mestizo, pardo, and so forth), the names of his parents, the father's title or rank, the names of his godparents, and any specially invited witnesses. Representative of the baptismal entries in the parish registers of Lambayeque is the one for Doña Josepha María, baptized at the age of two months and four days. She was the daughter of Captain Don Manuel Antonio Vigil de Quiñones y Sagardia, who was at the time the Indian protector and water commissioner of Lambayeque, and his wife, Doña Jacoba Rúbio de Medina y Bucaro. Don Ignacio Vicente de Lara, the comptroller of the royal tobacco monopoly, and Doña Margarita Rubio de Medina y Bucaro, the sister of Doña Jacoba, were the godparents of the child and became compadres of Quiñones y Sagardia. Invited witnesses included Don Miguel de Otermin, the accountant of the government monopolies of tobacco, gunpowder, playing cards, and dice; Don Antonio Albo, a lieutenant colonel in the militia of Mórrope; Don Luis Mauro de Lara, a lifelong alderman, chief of police, and brother to the godfather; and Don Joseph Vásquez Meléndez, the notary.[4]

Marriage entries record the date; name of the bride and groom; their respective places of birth; the names and identities of the couple's parents; and the names, rank, position, or title of the witnesses. The first of two representative entries of marriages is one for the son of the curaca of Lambayeque and the daughter of Don Francisco Minollulli and Doña Francisca Barbola Uycop. Juan de Saavedra Cabero, a rich and respected landowner, and his wife, Doña Gregoria Carrasco, stood up at the wedding. The other is dated over a century later and involves only Spaniards. Don Joseph Andrés Delgado, the legitimate son of Spaniards and himself born in Spain and, then, a leading citizen of Lambayeque, married Doña Clara Fernández de la Cotera. She was born in Lambayeque, the legitimate daughter of the provincial representative of the Inquisition, Don Pedro Fernández de la Cotera, and his wife, Doña Agueda Durán. Among the distinguished witnesses were the royal standard-bearer of the town council (Alférez Real) and heir to the estate of Sicán, Don Juan Romualdo de Vidaurre y de la Parra, and a close relative of an ex-corregidor of the province, Captain Don Joseph Antonio de Oteyza.[5]

Finally, notarial registers contain contracts and agreements, which include many details of a personal and biographical nature. Dowries, for example, besides naming the individuals and other family members directly involved, list the value of items that a bride brought to a marriage and often also indicate the approximate worth of a groom's estate. Sales contracts and powers of attorney document personal relationships between individuals. Wills list a person's assets at death, his heirs, and other members of his family.

Footnote Abbreviations. I conducted research in the archives of Spain, Germany, Peru, and the United States.[6] A list of the archives, sections, and *legajos* (bundles) or years follows. The format differs by archives, but in most cases it is a variation on the following form: Archive/Section: Document identification numbers, year(s), *folio* (page) numbers.

Archivo Arzobispal de Lima (AAL):
   Apelaciones de Trujillo (AT)
Archivo Arzobispal de Trujillo (AAT):
   Capellanías (C)
   Causas
   Censuras
   Cossio Villegas (CV)
   Curatos
   Diezmos (D)
   Hospital (H)
   Testamentos (T)
   Visita (V)
Archivo de Comunidades Indígenas—Lima (ACI):
   Monsefú: P 110–5354
Archivo Castillo Muro Sime—Lambayeque (ACMS)
Archivo del Complejo Agro-industrial Cayaltí (AC):
   Sipán
Archivo del Fuero Agrario, formerly Archivo Rural de Lima (AFA):
   Cayaltí
Archivo General de las Indias—Seville, Spain (AGI):
   Audiencia de Lima (AL)
   Contaduria (C)
   Escribanía de Camara (E)
   Escudos
   Indiferente General (IG)
   Justicia (J)
   Patronato (P)
   Residencia (R)
Archivo del Museo Naval—Madrid (AMN):
   Manuscritos (Ms.)
   Malaspina

Archivo Notarial Carlos Rivadeneira—Lambayeque (ANCR):
Álvarez
Arriola (A)
Candelaria
Cojal
Collús
Cossio Villegas (CV)
Gamarra
Gómez
Gómez Guevara (GG)
Herrera
Hojas Sueltas (HS)
Lambayeque
Lino
Luya
Mendoza (M)
Pampa Grande and Saltur (PG and S)
Pardo
Pérez Zavala (PZ)
Polo
Prieto de Zúñiga (Prieto)
Rentero
Rivera
Sánchez
Sipán
Soto
Tumán
Vásquez Meléndez (VM)
Archivo Nacional del Perú—Lima (ANP):
Águas
Derecho Indígena (DI)
Geneologia (G)
Gremial
Histórico
Jaraba
Libros de Cuentas (LC)
Meléndez
Moreno
Núñez Porras
Pérez Landero (PL)

Portalanza
Real Audiencia (RA)
Real Audiencia–Criminal (RA–Criminal)
Residencia (R)
Superior Gobierno (SG)
San Ramón (SR)
Temporalidades (T)
Terrán
Tierras de Comunidades (TC)
Tierras y Haciendas (TH)
Títulos
Títulos de Propriedad (TP)
Torres Campo
Tributos
Archivo Parrochial de Ferreñafe (APF):
Libro de Fábrica (LF)
Archivo Parrochial de Lambayeque (APL):
Registro de Bautismo (B)
Registro de Matrimonio (M)
Archivo Regional de Trujillo, now Archivo Departamental de La
Libertad (ART):
Álvarez
Cabildo, Compulsa (CaC)
Cabildo, Ordinario (CaO)
Compulsa (C)
Concha
Corregimiento, Águas (CoÁguas)
Corregimiento, Asuntos de Gobierno (CoAG)
Corregimiento, Compulsa (CoC)
Corregimiento, Causas Eclesiásticas
Corregimiento, Diezmos (D)
Corregimiento, Justicia (CoJ)
Corregimiento, Juzgado Varios (CoJV)
Corregimiento, Ordinario (CoO)
Corregimiento, Pedimento (CoP)
Corregimiento, Residencia (CoR)
Corregimiento, Temporalidades (CoT)
Cortijo Quero (CQ)
Dapelo
Eclesiástica (E)

Intendencia (I)
Intendencia, Asuntos de Gobierno (IAG)
Intendencia, Compulsa (IC)
Intendencia, Ordinaria (IO)
Intendencia, Diezmos (ID)
Intendencia, Eclesiástica (IE)
Intendencia, Temporalidades (IT)
Jiménez
Loose
López de Cordova (LC)
Martínez de Escobar (Escobar)
Mata
Muñoz Ternero (MT)
Obregón (O)
Palacios
Paz
Real Hacienda (RH)
Real Hacienda, Asuntos de Gobierno (RHAG)
Real Hacienda, Compulsa (RHC)
Real Hacienda, Ordinaria (RHO)
Rentero
Reyes
Ríos
Salinas
San Ramón (SR)
Superior Gobierno (SG)
Títulos de Saña
Valdez
Vásquez
Vega
Vega Basán
Archivo de Santo Domingo de Lima (ASDL):
  Capellanías
Archivo de San Francisco de Lima (ASFL):
  Registros (Reg.)
Biblioteca de la Academia Real de Historia—Madrid (BAH):
  Mata Linares
  Muñoz
  Salazar y Castro (SC)
Biblioteca Nacional del Perú—Lima (BNP)

Biblioteca Nacional de España—Madrid (BNS):
   Manuscritos (Ms.)
Biblioteca del Palacio Real de Madrid (BP)
Biblioteca de la Universidad de Sevilla, Colección Risco (BUSR)
British Museum—London (BM)
Brüning Collection—Hamburg, Germany (BCH)
Colección Vargas Ugarte—Lima (CVU)
Newberry Library—Chicago, Illinois (NL):
   Ayer Collection
Oficina de las Comunidades Indígenas de Lambayeque (OCIL):
   Reque

Notes

1. Individuals are assumed to be landless until proven otherwise.

2. The data will be deposited in the files of the Data and Program Library Service and are available now to any interested scholar from the author.

3. I did not use any index of formal political power because the sources did not provide complete or even partial lists of the persons who held seats on the town council or served as provincial administrators. Also, informal power proved as significant as formal power in understanding decisions and events.

4. APL/B: XII 20–V–1780.

5. APL/M: I 18–V–1698; and VII 21–I–1790. Trusted friends and business associates.

6. I also received documents on Peru in microfilm from the British Museum in London.

Notes

Chapter 1

1. Some of the best known of these pioneers (and their work) are: José María Ots Capdequí, *España en América: Las instituciones coloniales* (Bogotá, 1952); idem, *El régimen de la tierra en la América Española durante el período colonial* (Ciudad Trujillo, Santo Domingo, 1946); Silvio Zavala, *La encomienda indiana* (México, 1935); Jaime Vicens Vives, *Historia social y económica de España y América* (Barcelona, 1957–59); and Frank Tannenbaum, *Ten Keys to Latin America* (New York, 1963).

2. On Mexico see: Lesley Byrd Simpson, *Many Mexicos* (Berkeley, 1941), 260–64; idem, "Exploitation of Land in Central Mexico in the Sixteenth Century," *Ibero-Americana,* XXXVI (Berkeley, 1952), 17; Nathan L. Whetten, *Rural Mexico* (Chicago, 1948), 75 and 90–99; George M. McBride, *The Land Systems of Mexico* (New York, 1923), 25–38; François Chevalier, "The North Mexican Hacienda," in Archibald R. Lewis and Thomas F. McGann, eds., *The New World Looks at Its History* (Austin, 1963), 95–101; Arnold Bauer, "The Church and Spanish American Agrarian Structure: 1765–1865," *The Americas,* XXVIII, No. 1 (July 1971), 78; and Jan Bazant, *Cinco haciendas Mexicanas* (México, 1975), especially 7–34 and 73–83. On Peru see: Louis C. Faron, "From *Encomienda* to *Hacienda* in Chancay Valley, Peru: 1533–1600," *Ethnohistory,* XIII, Nos. 3–4 (1966), 156–71; and idem, "A History of Agricultural Production and Local Organization in the Chancay Valley, Peru," in J. H. Steward, ed., *Contemporary Change in Traditional Societies,* III (Urbana, 1967), 237 and 248. On Chile see: Jean Borde and Mario Góngora, *Evolución de la propiedad rural en el Valle de Puangue,* 2 vols. (Santiago, 1956), 58 and 62. Nonetheless, *hacienda* is a convenient word and will be used here as a generic term for "large estate" wherever appropriate. When reference is made to a specific type or variation, original Spanish terms will be preferred as a way of respecting original concepts and definitions and as a means of transmitting to the reader a feeling for the times.

3. Duvon Corbitt, "*Mercedes* and *Realengos:* A Survey of the Public Land

System in Cuba," *Hispanic American Historical Review*, XIX, No. 3 (August 1939), 265; Borde and Góngora, 30 and 88; AAT/Causas: 1570; Isabel Gonzalez Sánchez, *Haciendas y ranchos de Tlaxcala en 1712* (México, 1969), 9–15; Chevalier, *Land and Society in Colonial Mexico* (Berkeley, 1963), 66, 70, 75, 88, 105, 135, and 137; and David A. Brading, *Miners and Merchants in Bourbon Mexico, 1763–1810* (Cambridge, 1971), 16 and 230. More detailed descriptions and discussions of these types and their variations can be found in: AAT/Causas: 1664; Faron, *"Encomienda to Hacienda,"* 169; Enrique Florescano, "Colonización, ocupación del suelo y 'frontera' en el norte de Nueva España, 1521–1750," in Álvaro Jara, ed., *Tierras nuevas* (México, 1969), 62; Pablo Macera Dall'Orso, *Instrucciones para el manejo de las haciendas Jesuitas del Perú (Siglos 17–18)* (Lima, 1966), 18; Gonzalez Sánchez, ed., "La retención por deudas y los traslados de trabajadores tlaquehuales o alquilados en las haciendas, como sustitución de los repartimientos de indios durante el siglo 18," *Anales del Instituto Nacional de Antropología e Historia*, XIX, No. 48 (1966); Robert G. Keith, "Origins of the Hacienda System on the Central Peruvian Coast" (Ph.D. diss., Harvard University, 1969), 3, 70, 75, 88, 105, 119, and 155; McBride, 84; Carlos Meléndez, "Los orígenes de la propiedad territorial en el valle central de Costa Rica durante el siglo 16," *Revista de la Universidad de Costa Rica*, XXVII, Sem. 2 (diciembre 1969), 58; William B. Taylor, *Landlord and Peasant in Colonial Oaxaca* (Stanford, 1972), 5, 15, 47, 122, 126–27, 136, and 392; James Lockhart, "Introduction," in Ida Altman and Lockhart, eds., *Provinces of Early Mexico* (Los Angeles, 1976), 25; Brading, *Haciendas and Ranchos in the Mexican Bajío* (New York, 1978); Florescano, 64–65; and ART/CoO: 19–IV–1591; and 9–X–1591.

4. Or the ways in which factors such as land, labor, capital, etc., are combined in the production process.

5. Chevalier, *Land and Society*, 42 and 167; Taylor, *Landlord and Peasant*, 122. See also his "Landed Society in New Spain: A View from the South," *Hispanic American Historical Review*, LIV, No. 3 (August 1974), 408. Brading, 13; idem, *Bajío*; McBride, 25–29; and Fernando Suárez de Castro, *Estructuras agrárias en la América Latina* (San José, 1965), 76; Charles H. Harris, III, *A Mexican Family Empire* (Austin, 1975) for Mexico. Faron, "History," 232, 244, and 248; Henry Favre, "Evolución y situación de las haciendas en la región de Huancavelica," in idem, Claude Collin Delavaud, José Matos Mar, *La hacienda en el Perú* (Lima, 1967), 237; Keith, *"Encomienda, Hacienda* and *Corregimiento* in Spanish America: A Structural Analysis," *Hispanic American Historical Review*, LI, No. 3 (August 1971), 432 and 437; idem, "Origins," 37, 41, and 47; and Matos Mar, "Las haciendas del valle de Chancay," in Favre, et al., 284–85 and 326–33, for Peru. Borde and Góngora, 58–62, for Chile.

6. Sidney M. Greenfield, "An Alternative Sociological Model for the Analysis of Brazilian Agriculture" (Latin American Center Discussion Paper No. 14, University of Wisconsin, Milwaukee, 28 September 1968), 7; Susan Ramírez-Horton, "The Sugar Estates of Lambayeque Valley, 1670–1800: A Contribution

to Peruvian Agrarian History" (Master's thesis, University of Wisconsin, Madison, 1973); Ward Barrett, *The Sugar Hacienda of the Marqueses del Valle* (Minneapolis, 1970); idem, "Morelos and Its Sugar Industry in the Late Eighteenth Century," in Altman and Lockhart; Herman W. Konrad, *A Jesuit Hacienda in Colonial Mexico* (Stanford, 1980); Nicholas P. Cushner, *Lords of the Land* (Albany, 1980). Throughout the text I use Tierra Firme interchangeably with Panama.

7. Grant of Indian labor. See Chapter 2.

8. Magnus Mörner, "The Spanish American Hacienda: A Survey of Recent Research and Debate," *Hispanic American Historical Review*, LIII, No. 2 (May 1973), 183–216.

9. Such as the work of Silvio Zavala and José María Ots Capdequí.

10. Taylor, *Landlord and Peasant*, 128; and Harris, *The Sánchez Navarros: A Socio-economic Study of a Coahuilan Latifundio, 1846–53* (Chicago, 1964).

11. Murdo MacLeod, *Spanish Central America: A Socioeconomic History, 1520–1720* (Berkeley, 1973), 288–302; Chevalier, *Land and Society*, 189–91; and Brading, 13.

12. Brading is one who recognizes the need. He states, "The pattern of landownership reflected the balance of political power within society. But that is a theme which demands another book." Brading, *Bajío*, 217.

13. Lockhart, "*Encomienda* and *Hacienda:* The Evolution of the Great Estates in the Spanish Indies," *Hispanic American Historical Review*, XLIX, No. 3 (August 1969), 417.

14. Encomenderos were individuals granted Indians in trust and are discussed in detail in Chapter 2.

15. On the landed elite see: Borde and Góngora, 20–21; Keith, "Origins," 130, 155, 235, and 318; idem, *Conquest and Agrarian Change* (Cambridge, 1976); Brading, 103 and 215; and Chevalier, *Land and Society*, 125, 140–50, 188, and 258. Also see: Raymond E. Crist, *The Cauca Valley, Colombia: Land Tenure and Land Use* (Gainesville, 1952), 14–15; Florescano, *Estructuras y problemas agrarios de México (1500–1821)* (México, 1971), 163–64; idem, *Precios del maíz y crísis agrícolas en México (1708–1810)* (México, 1969), 196; Simpson, *Many Mexicos*, 257–62; Tannenbaum, 90; Whetten, 100–101; Taylor, *Landlord and Peasant*, 192; Lockhart, "*Encomienda* and *Hacienda*," 422–23; idem, "The Evolution of the Great Estate," in Helen Delpar, ed., *The Borzoi Reader in Latin American History* (New York, 1972), 74; Peter Boyd Bowman, "A Spanish Soldier's Estate in Northern Mexico (1642)," *Hispanic American Historical Review*, LIII, No. 1 (February 1973), 95–105; and John M. Tutino, "Provincial Spaniards, Indian Towns and Haciendas: Interrelated Agrarian Sectors in the Valleys of Mexico and Toluca, 1750–1810," in Altman and Lockhart, 178.

16. On the powerful hacendado see: Matos Mar, 321; Jacques Lambert, *Latin America: Social Structures and Political Institutions* (Berkeley, 1967), 74; Harris, *Sánchez Navarros*, 5, 15, and 97; Chevalier, *Land and Society*, 172; Hector Martínez, "Evolución de la propiedad territorial en el Perú," *Revista de economía y agri-*

cultura, I, No. 2 (1963–64), 104; Macera Dall'Orso, "Feudalismo colonial americano: El caso de las haciendas Peruanas," *Acta Histórica,* XXXV (Szeged, Hungary, 1971), 12; McBride, 41; Brading, 244 and 303; Tannenbaum, especially 90; Keith, "Origins," 130 and 312; Taylor, *Landlord and Peasant,* 74 and 158–62; and Florescano, "Colonización," 59–70. On land as the basis for political power see Clarence Haring, *The Spanish Empire in America* (New York, 1963), 241; Chevalier, *Land and Society,* 176; Harris, *Sánchez Navarros,* 24 and 97; and William B. Taylor, "Town and Country in the Valley of Oaxaca, 1750–1812," in Altman and Lockhart, 73. Taylor shows that not all landowners were wealthy men.

17. Power, in the generic sense, is defined as the ability to influence and change the outcome of a decision or action. It may take an economic form, such as a bribe, the ability to give someone a loan, a guarantee, or a job. Political power may be *formal*—implying direct participation in a decision-making body, such as the municipal council or possession of bureaucratic office. Political power can also be *informal.* Influence, exerted through family, friends, and business associates, is an example of the latter. Adding to the leverage of a landowner might be social power, prestige, or reputation, which seems especially effective when dealing with persons of lower social and economic status. I have tried to make references to the different forms of power as specific as possible in the text. When the word appears alone it is used in the broad, generic sense. For a theoretical discussion of power, see: Robert A. Dahl, *Modern Political Analysis* (Englewood Cliffs, N.J., 1963), especially Chapter 5; and Talcott Parsons, "On the Concept of Political Power," *Proceedings of the American Philosophical Society,* CVII, No. 3 (June 1963), especially 232–44.

18. Lockhart suggests the need to document the connection in his article, *"Encomienda* and *Hacienda,"* 419.

19. André Gunder Frank, *Lumpen-bourgeoisie, Lumpen-development* (New York, 1972), 27; Chevalier, *Land and Society,* 89, 97, 122–23, 143, 165, 176, 223, and 230–31; Lockhart, *"Encomienda* and *Hacienda,"* 419; idem, "Evolution," 71; Keith, "Origins," 230 and 312; Taylor, *Landlord and Peasant,* 159–60; Harris, *Sánchez Navarros,* 97; William P. Glade, *The Latin American Economies* (New York, 1969), 61; and John C. Super, "The Agricultural Near North: Querétaro in the Seventeenth Century," in Altman and Lockhart, 245; Taylor, "Town and Country," in Altman and Lockhart, 73; and Altman, "A Family and Region in the Northern Fringe Lands: The Marqueses de Aguayo of Nuevo León and Coahuila," in Altman and Lockhart, 255.

20. Taylor, "Town and Country," 73; P. J. Bakewell, "Zacatecas: An Economic and Social Outline of a Silver Mining District, 1547–1700," in Altman and Lockhart, 223; Harris, *Empire,* 18, 75, 119, 125–26, and 136; Leslie Lewis, "In Mexico City's Shadow: Some Aspects of Economic Activity and Social Processes in Texcoco, 1570–1620," in Altman and Lockhart, 128; and Konrad, 6, 7, 33, 67, and 156.

21. Keith; Manuel Burga, *De la encomienda a la hacienda capitalista* (Lima, 1976); Cushner, 4; and Macera Dall'Orso, "Feudalismo," 12.

22. Juan Friede, *El indio en lucha por la tierra* (Bogotá, 1944); Taylor, *Landlord and Peasant*, especially 197 and 201; idem, "Landed Society," 395–96; and Bazant, 11, 14, 18, and 21. William Foote Whyte and Giorgio Alberti reject the notion of the passive peasant in twentieth-century rural Peru. See their book, *Power, Politics and Progress: Social Change in Rural Peru* (New York, 1976), especially page 243.

23. Paul Kosok, *Life, Land and Water in Ancient Peru* (New York, 1965), 147.

24. The need for a systematic institutional history of the estate is noted by Lockhart, *"Encomienda* and *Hacienda,"* 416.

25. The contents of the extant documentation make it impossible to do a parallel study of the leaders of the Indian communities.

Part One

1. Or in George Foster's terms "a culture of conquest." See Foster, *Culture and Conquest* (Chicago, 1960), especially Chapter 2.

Chapter 2

1. The men who arrived in Peru with Pizarro and with Almagro, according to James Lockhart, were of very similar backgrounds. He states, "Shortly after Cajamarca a new group of around 200 men under Almagro arrived in Peru, apparently of much the same social composition as the first contingent [under Pizarro]." He also notes that many of the founders of Trujillo had arrived with Almagro and settled in Trujillo. Among those I identified were: Alonso Carrasco, Alonso de Ávila (or Dávila), Lope de Ayala, Blas de Atienza, Diego de Mora, and Francisco de Fuentes. The first four were rewarded with encomiendas in Lambayeque; the last two received encomiendas in other areas of the Trujillo district. James Lockhart, *Spanish Peru* (Madison, 1968), 14; idem, *Men of Cajamarca* (Austin, 1972), 38 and 62; Manuel de Mendíburu, *Diccionario histórico biográfico del Perú*, II (Lima, 1878), 303; and ibid., III, 377–83. Among the few who had property in Spain, indicating a somewhat more secure socioeconomic background, was Juan de Barbarán, the encomendero of Lambayeque. See his will in Domingo Angulo, "Cartulario de los conquistadores del Perú: El Capitán Juan de Barbarán," *Revista del Archivo Nacional del Perú*, IV, No. 2 (1926), 187–206, especially page 196.

2. See Appendix 1 for equivalencies.

3. See Appendix 2 for equivalencies.

4. Angulo, 187–206; Lockhart, *Men of Cajamarca*, 98–99; Cristóbal Espejo, "La carestía de la vida en el siglo XVI y medios de abaratería," *Revista de archivos, bibliotecas y museos*, XVI, Nos. 1–3 (Madrid, enero-marzo 1920), 43–44; Earl J. Hamilton, "American Treasure and Andalusian Prices," *Journal of Economic and Business History*, I, No. 1 (November 1928), 19–20; idem, "Wages and Subsistence on Spanish Treasure Ships, 1503–1660," *Journal of Political Economy*, No. 37 (August 1929), 443; and idem, *American Treasure and the Price Revolution in*

Spain, 1501–1650 (New York, 1970), especially Appendices 3 and 7. They were probably richer than they ever dreamed possible, not only when compared to the remuneration of workers and professionals in Spain, but also considering that in Mexico the governor and captain general of Yucatan earned 250,000 maravedis (or about 925 pesos of eight reales) in 1526. See Enrique Florescano, *Origen y desarrollo de los problemas agrarios de México (1500–1821)* (México, 1976), 27.

5. Guillermo Lohmann Villena, "Apuntaciones sobre el curso de los precios de los artículos de primera necesidad en Lima durante el siglo XVI," *Revista histórica*, XXIX (Lima, 1966), 89, 91, 97, and 99. Lohmann quotes prices in Lima. His information is of limited value because he does not consistently identify the types of pesos (e.g., ensayados, corrientes, etc.) used in the transactions which were the sources of his price data. See also: Rolando Mellafe, "Frontera agraria: El caso del Virreinato Peruano en el siglo XVI," in Álvaro Jara, ed., *Tierras nuevas* (México, 1969), 23. Mellafe's price data are in pesos de plata corriente. I have converted them to pesos of eight reales each for the sake of consistency and to facilitate comparison with the figures in the preceding paragraph.

6. Manuel Vicente Villarán, *Apuntes sobre la realidad social de los indígenas del Perú ante las leyes de Indias* (Lima, 1964), 28–29; and Lockhart, *Spanish Peru*, 21.

7. Centro de Estudios de Historia Eclesiástica del Perú, *Monografía de la Diócesis de Trujillo*, I (Trujillo, 1930), 35–36 (hereafter cited as *Monografía de Trujillo*); AGI/AL: 201, 1633; and Marco A. Cabero, "El Corregimiento de Saña y el problema histórico de la fundación de Trujillo," *Revista histórica*, I, No. 4 (Lima, 1906), 512–13.

8. Cabero, "Saña," 345, 372 and 509–12; idem, "El Capitán Juan Delgadillo, Encomendero de Saña," *Revista histórica*, II, Trim. 1 (1907), 96–97 and 99; idem, "El conquistador Don Juan Roldán de Ávila," *Revista histórica*, III, No. 1 (1908), 116; idem, "En la época de la conquista," *La Industria*, 31–X–1971, 8; ART/Mata: 1560; AGI/E: 502a (1607–11), 39v; AL: 201, 1633; P: 1. 108, r. 7, 1562, 40–41; BAH/Muñoz: A–92, 1540, 67; ML: t. 82, 1548, 138v; t. 96, 22; and Rubén Vargas Ugarte, "La fecha de la fundación de Trujillo," *Revista histórica*, X, No. 2 (1936), 234. Note that the "Patronato" source reports that Jequetepeque was granted on 3–III–1535; Cabero states the date was 8–XI–1536.

9. Pizarro's founding act (considered by most Peruvian historians as the second founding of Trujillo) and the list of vecinos are published in *Actas del Cabildo de Trujillo, 1549–60*, I (Lima, 1969), 391–94. Hereafter cited as *ACT*. See also *Monografía de Trujillo*, I, 7–23, 30–33, and 38–39. Those who were not named vecinos were known as residents (*residentes*) or inhabitants (*moradores*). James Lockhart's collective biography of Pizarro's original force of fighting men at Cajamarca shows that, in general, they were not career soldiers. Lockhart considers the word soldier to be a distortion. See Lockhart, *Spanish Peru*, 14 and 137–39.

10. AGI/P: 185, r. 24, 1541, 62; *ACT,* I, 82 and 296; and Darius Othaniel Blaisdell, "Aspects of Life in Lima in the Sixteenth Century" (Master's thesis, University of Texas, 1956), 83.

11. The local notary earned about eighty pesos per year in 1550.

12. The approximate nature of the 1548 figures cannot be overemphasized. Only after more research has been carried out to chronicle more exactly the development of the market can these figures be more precisely evaluated. Robert G. Keith, personal communication, February 1981.

13. ART/Mata: 1592; CoO: 1559, 31v–2; CaO: 1557–66; AGI/P: 97, r. 4, [1569], 16v–17v; and BCH/1555.

14. Angulo, 191–206, especially 197–98 and 200; and BNP/A157, 132. In evaluating his accounts, I used 1 castellano = 696.96 maravedis and 1 peso de oro de minas = 497 maravedis. I did not count his income from Spain.

15. Ibid., 191–206; AGI/P: 116, r. 3, no. 2, 7; J: 420, 1574, I, 48v, 79, 80v and 83; ART/CoO: 13–VII–1570, 101; and Lockhart, *Spanish Peru,* 189.

16. All were encomenderos, except the notary. The notary was present at all sessions, but not considered a member. Later, the position of treasurer became a bureaucratic appointment. See Vargas Ugarte, 234–35; Angulo, 205; Alberto Larco Herrera, *Anales de cabildo. Ordenanzas de la Ciudad de Trujillo (3 setiembre 1555)* (Lima, n.d.), 7 and 8; *ACT,* I and II; ART/Mata: 1569 and 1580; Vega: 1582; and Ríos: 1579.

17. *ACT,* I.

18. There were two types of vecinos in Trujillo at this time. Encomenderos were known as *vecinos-feudatarios* and nonencomenderos were called *vecinos-ciudadanos.*

19. *ACT,* I, 1–7 and 264.

20. Ibid.; and BAH/A–109, 1540.

21. AGI/P: 185, r. 24, 1541, 52.

22. *ACT,* 1–7 and 264.

23. AGI/P: 185, r. 24, 1541, 52; ART/Salinas: 18–VIII–1539; Mata: 30–IX–1562; Luis Arroyo, *Los Franciscanos y la fundación de Chiclayo* (Lima, 1956), 67; José Pablo Capitán A., "421 aniversario de [la] fundación de Ferreñafe," *La Industria* (Chiclayo), 13–XII–1971, 2; ART/CoO: 19–X–1568; and LC: 29–VII–1561; and Spain, *Recopilación de leyes de los Reynos de las Indias,* II (Madrid, 1681), ley 23, tit. III, lib. VI, 201. Hereafter cited as RLI.

24. BAH/Muñoz: A–109, No. 1046, 4–VI–1540, 112; ART/Salinas: 18–VIII–1539; and Roberto Levillier, ed., *Gobernantes del Perú,* I (Madrid, 1921), 20–25.

25. BAH/9–4664, 1549, 23v–24; ART/Mata: 24–X–1563; 30–I–1564; LC: 22–X–1562; *ACT,* I, 198; and BNP/A310, 32.

26. Letter from Fray Domingo de Santo Tomás to His Majesty, 1 julio 1550, in Emilio Lissón y Chavez, *La iglesia de España en el Perú,* I, No. 4 (Sevilla, 1943), 190–206.

27. Arlene Eisen, "The Indians in Colonial Spanish America," in Magali

Sarfatti, *Spanish Bureaucratic-Patrimonialism in America* (Berkeley, 1966), 106; AGI/ J: 454–62, 1570–74, especially 461 and 857 on the cruelty and power of Don Juan curaca of Collique; Karen Spalding, "El kuraca y el comercio colonial," in *De indio a campesino* (Lima, 1974), 31–60; Felipe Guamán Poma de Ayala, *Nueva corónica y buen gobierno (1615)* (Paris, 1936), 897–98; and AGI/P: l. 189, r. 11, 1566.

28. AGI/J: 457, 1145v; Santo Tomás in Lissón y Chavez, 192; María Rostworowski de Diez Canseco, *Curacas y sucesiones, Costa norte* (Lima, 1961), 104–6; and Nathan Wachtel, *The Vision of the Vanquished* (New York, 1977), 115.

29. John Hemming, *The Conquest of the Incas* (New York, 1970), 28; Poma de Ayala, 114 and 944; Henry F. Dobyns, "An Outline of Andean Epidemic History to 1720," *Bulletin of the History of Medicine*, XXXVII, No. 6 (1963), 493–515; Rostworowski, "Mercaderes del Valle de Chincha en la época prehispánica," *Revista Española de antropología americana*, V (Madrid, 1970), 135–77; Miguel Acosta Saignes, "Los pochteca," *Acta antropológica*, I, No. 1 (México, 1945), 1–62; Anne Chapman, "Port of Trade Enclaves in Aztec and Maya Civilizations," in Karl Polanyi, ed., *Trade and Market in the Early Empires* (Glencoe, 1957), 115–53; John H. Rowe, "The Kingdom of Chimor," *Acta americana*, VI, Nos. 1 and 2 (Washington, enero-junio 1948), 53; Santo Tomás in Lissón y Chavez, 191; ART/Paz: 1576; and CoR: 30–VI–1576; *ACT*, I, 261–62; BNS/R14986; Pedro de Cieza de León, *The Incas* (Norman, 1959), 319; Cabero, "Don Juan Roldán de Ávila," 116; ANP/R: l. 22, c. 57, 845–46; and Susan Ramírez-Horton, "Land Tenure and the Economics of Power in Colonial Peru," Ph.D. diss., University of Wisconsin-Madison, 1977, Appendix I.

30. AGI/P: 185, r. 24, 1541, 51; J: 461, 870; AL: 32, 11–V–1589; BAH/Muñoz: A–92, 1540, 18; ART/CoO: 13–VIII–1570, 243; 15–I–1571; Sebastián de la Gama, "Visita hecha en el valle de Jayanca [Trujillo]," *Historia y cultura*, VIII (Lima, 1974), 215–28. Epidemics in the early 1570s, 1589, and 1596 decimated the native population in the Lambayeque region.

31. They became known as *forasteros*, literally "strangers," and were considered and treated as a disparate group of individuals without ties to a community or curaca.

32. *ACT*, I, 261; and Spalding.

33. The position of the *corregidor* (or district governor) had not yet been created. Villarán, 59–60; and AGI/P: 185, r. 24, 1541, 51–62.

34. The town of Chiclayo formed around the site of this monastery. ART/ Mata: 24–V–1588, 67–70; LC: 1560; BAH/Muñoz: A–92, 1540, 18; and AGI/P: 185, r. 24, 1541, 53–62.

35. ART/Mata: 14–V–1562; and AGI/P: 97, r. 4, iv; Escudos: No. 62.

Chapter 3

1. The Law of Succession decreed 26 May 1536 for all the Indies and specifically for Peru in Valladolid on 7 September 1537 gave an encomendero

irrevocable possession of the Indians for two lives—his own and that of one heir. Manuel Vicente Villarán, *Apuntes sobre la realidad social de los indígenas del Perú ante las leyes de Indias* (Lima, 1964), 37–39.

2. Woodrow W. Borah, *Early Colonial Trade and Navigation between Mexico and Peru* (Berkeley, 1954), 20.

3. Santo Tomás, in Emilio Lissón y Chavez, *La iglesia de España en el Perú*, 6 vols. (Sevilla, 1943–46), I, No. 4, 192–93 and II, No. 2, 63–65.

4. Ibid., I, No. 4, 192–93; AGI/P: 185, r. 24, 1541, 51; J: 457, 722; AL: 100, [1646], 30; and BAH/9–4664, 1549, 23v–24. Tribute is for one year unless otherwise specified. Note that the tribute obligations of the Indians were specified as sowing a given area. This is consistent with the Indian conception of measurement. Plots of land were measured according to the amount of seed needed to plant the plot, not by a standard unit of measure. The first Spanish land grants were made in these units, called *fanega(da)s de sembradura*. Three fanegadas de sembradura de maíz (of corn) = 1 fanegada of 144 varas by 288 varas. They were still in use in the visita of 1641–42 discussed in Chapter 5. See: AGI/ E: 511a, 1648, 40v; and Darius Othaniel Blaisdell, "Aspects of Life in Lima in the Sixteenth Century" (Master's thesis, University of Texas, 1956), 65.

5. ART/MT: 1574; and AGI/J: 457, 846v. The regulation and tasas did not mean that they were enforced or entirely obeyed by the encomenderos immediately. Some evidence exists that encomenderos continued to exact more than the legally specified tribute at least until the mid-1560s. BAH/SC: N–33, 276.

6. See the sources of Figure 2; AGI/J: 420, 1574, I, 117; and ART/Mata: 14–V–1562. It seems likely that the income to encomenderos from some encomiendas peaked earlier than 1559. Without more data, however, a definitive statement in this regard cannot be made.

7. "I obey, but will not comply." This was an excuse used by Spanish authorities to delay implementation of a decree. They recognized the authority of the king to decree the law, but refused to enforce it because it did not fit local circumstances. See John Leddy Phelan, "Authority and Flexibility in the Spanish Imperial Bureaucracy," *Administrative Science Quarterly*, V, No. 1 (June 1960), 47–65.

8. Marco A. Cabero, "El Capitán Juan Delgadillo, Encomendero de Saña," *Revista histórica*, II, Trim. 1 (1907), 93; AGI/P: l. 148, r. 1, no. 1, 3; *ACT*, I, 139–40; and Augusto D. León Barandiarán, *Mitos, leyendas y tradiciones Lambayecanas* (Lima [?], 1938 [?]), 260–61.

9. Paul B. Ganster, in a paper entitled "Aspects of Indian-Spanish Relations in the Moche Valley, Peru, during the Colonial Period" (presented at the Annual Meeting of the American Society for Ethnohistory, St. Paul, Minn., October 1974), reports that the mita required the service of one-sixth of the Indians of Moche. They worked six months at a time as agricultural laborers or as shepherds. In the seventeenth century, the standard length of service of mitayos

engaged in agricultural labor was two months on the coast. ART/CoAG: 20–VII–1607; and AGI/AL 100, [1646], 12.

10. Discussed below.

11. C. H. Haring, *The Spanish Empire in America* (New York, 1963), 59. In Lambayeque, able-bodied males were required to pay tribute between seventeen and forty-seven years of age. Elsewhere, Indians paid tribute from the age of eighteen to fifty. BAH/SC: N–33, 18–IX–1568, 108–9; and *ACT*, I, 139–40.

12. *ACT*, I, 261 and 296–98; and Guillermo Lohmann Villena, "Apuntaciones sobre el curso de los precios de los artículos de primera necesidad en Lima durante el siglo XVI," *Revista histórica*, XXIX (1966), 82. Indians before 1550, and in places throughout the decade, were given food and clothing for their labor, following ancient Indian tradition. The growing scarcity of labor pushed the wages of mitayos to 3/4 of a tomín and a ration of corn per day by 1563. Three years later, shepherds received 6 tomines per month and a fanega of corn. ART/LC: 21–IV–1559; *ACT*, II, 6; Alejandro O. Araujo, "Reseña histórica de Saña," typescript (Eten, Perú), 29–XI–1957, 14; and Domingo Angulo, "Fundación y población de la Villa de Zaña," *Revista del Archivo nacional del Perú*, I, No. 2 (mayo-agosto 1920), 297.

13. The encomenderos themselves distributed mitayos when they served as alcaldes or as lieutenants of the corregidor. *ACT*, I, 38.

14. AGI/J: 420, 1574, I, 117 and 151v–52; P: 97, r. 4 [1569], 4v–10 and 15–15v; and ART/CoO, 13–VII–1570. Some of the rich merchants who began to lend money to the encomenderos included Diego de Angulo, Guillermo Daniel, and Alonso Zofre. ART/Mata: 5–VIII–1562; 10–V–1565; and 31–VII–1563; and CoC: 22–I–1560.

15. Centro de Estudios de Historia Eclesiástica, *Monografía de la Diócesis de Trujillo*, I (Trujillo, 1930), 9; Blaisdell, 83; Cabero, "El Corregimiento de Saña y el problema histórico de la fundación de Trujillo," *Revista histórica*, I, No. 4 (1906), 345; *ACT*, I, 5, 11, 29, 75–96, 135, and 264; ibid., II, 3–6; ibid., III, 74; ART/Mata: 4–XI–1562; 1564; Juan López de Velasco, *Geografía y descripción universal de las Indias* (Madrid, 1971), 238; Borah, 45 and 57; and ART/CaO: 1557–66. Profits on the export of wheat to Tierra Firme averaged almost ten pesos per fanega of 130 pounds each. If the exporter invested these profits in merchandise for sale in Peru, he could expect to double his money in four years.

16. Borah, 11, 16, 17, 42, 45, and 57; *ACT*, I, 176 and 326.

17. Lohmann Villena, 91–92; 98–99; *ACT*, I, 285; Borah, 47 and 43; AGI/P: 185, r. 24, 1541, 51; BAH/Muñoz: A–92, 1540, 18; ART/Álvarez: 5–IV–1543 and 10–IV–1543; James Lockhart, *Men of Cajamarca* (Austin, 1972), 238; Angulo, 199; and Rolando Mellafe, "Frontera agraria: El caso del Virreinato Peruano en el siglo XVI," in Álvaro Jara, ed., *Tierras nuevas* (México, 1969), 23.

18. Angulo, 198; AGI/J: 420, 1574, I, 99v; and ART/Álvarez: 30–IV–1543, 34. The statement on the cost of shepherds' labor is based on the price of sheep

in 1561 (i.e., twelve tomines per head). The cost of the ration of corn was calculated at two tomines per fanega. Wages are those cited above, and it is assumed an Indian worked twelve months per year.

19. ART/Salinas: 18–VIII–1539; Reyes: 1561; LC: 21–IV–1559; *ACT,* I, 261–62; AGI/J: 420, 1574, I, 101; 455, 1684v; 457, 1253; and 461, 923v; and Sebastián de la Gama, "Visita hecha en el valle de Jayanca [Trujillo]," *Historia y cultura* VIII (Lima, 1974), 223. Encomenderos left a few animals in their Indians' care before they became interested in building corrals and seeking formal title to land.

20. ART/LC: 22–X–1561; and CoO: 30–1–154 _ .

21. The document did not specify whether the persons were Indians or Spaniards. BAH/ML: t. 21, 191–92. The Cabildo recognized this prohibition and did not make land grants on pasture lands. *ACT,* I, 80.

22. AGI/AL: 121, 1566, 5; P: 185, r. 24, 1541, 75; *Recopilación de leyes de los reynos de las Indias (RLI),* ley 19, tit. 9, lib. 6, 231v; and BAH/ML: t. 97, 1541, 181; and t. 21, 191–92.

23. *ACT,* I, 21–22 and II, 3–4; and AGI/J: 458, 1840v.

24. BAH/Muñoz: A–109, 1540, 164; ART/LC: 22–X–1561; AAT/Causas: 1570; and Appendix 3.

25. ART/Ríos: 1579; Mata: 1565; Vega: 1567; MT: 1578; LC: 1559; 10–X–1561; 16–V–1564; BNP/B871, 1627; and AAT/Causas: 1570.

26. This pattern is also noted by Charles Gibson in Mexico. See his classic study, *The Aztecs under Spanish Rule* (Stanford, 1964), 288. For Lambayeque, see ANCR/1586–1611; and AGI/J: 461, 1443–43v.

27. ART/Mata: 1586; 24–X–1563; 1565; 30–IX–1562; and CoAG: 30–IX–1567; *ACT,* II, 16–17; AGI/P: 108, r. 7, 1562, 48v; AL: 28B; and J: 460, 429v; Robert Gordon Keith, "Origins of the Hacienda System on the Central Peruvian Coast" (Ph.D. diss., Harvard University, 1969), 233; and Angulo, "Zaña," 296.

28. Borah, 9–10 and 99–100; and Lockhart, *Spanish Peru* (Madison, 1968), 22; and Keith, *Conquest and Agrarian Change* (Cambridge, 1976), 51–52 and 81–85.

29. Lockhart's research shows that by the 1560s encomiendas were extremely difficult to get. Lockhart, 16–18; *ACT,* I, 352; ibid., II, 277–78; and Borah, 99–100.

30. BAH/ML: t. 97, 1534, 131.

31. *Dominio directo* (dominion, ultimate control, and disposition) as opposed to *dominio útil* (usufruct or use).

32. AGI/AL: 101, 1642; and Carlos Valdez de la Torre, *Evolución de las comunidades indígenas* (Lima, 1921), 50–51.

33. RLI: ley 5, tit. 12, lib. 6, 242. The cédula was first signed in 1532 and reiterated in law 7 of 1588. César A. Ugarte, "Los antecedentes históricos del régimen agrario Peruano," *Revista universitaria,* I, No. 2 (1923), 368–74; BAH/ML: t. 97, 1535, 133–35; and Lissón y Chavez, 1536, 76. The prohibition against donating lands to the church was unevenly observed in later years.

34. See note 4.

35. ART/LC: 1564; *ACT,* I, 11, 177 and 202–3; and Keith, "Origins," 153. Perhaps a better way to translate "labrador pobre" to convey the disdain with which the encomenderos uttered the phrase would be "poor whites."

36. *ACT,* I, 11, 37, 67, 77, 82, 95, 98, 186–87, 264, and 298–99.

37. BCH/1555; *ACT,* I, II, and III. This contrasts with the findings of Lockhart, i.e., that the cabildo granted land to the encomenderos within the jurisdiction of their Indian communities. Lockhart, *Spanish Peru,* 22.

38. By this time, there were three separate categories of city dwellers: the vecino-feudatarios, or encomenderos; the vecino-ciudadanos, or citizens with lots and houses who were not encomenderos; and residentes (*habitantes* or *moradores*), or residents of the city who did not own property. Each term designates a separate socioeconomic group.

39. For example, see on the brothers Ortiz: ART/Mata: n.d. [V–1563]; 9–XII–1562; 14–X–1563; and 13–II–1564; CoP: 15–IX–1562; and *ACT,* I, 202.

40. Arlene Eisen, "The Indians in Colonial Spanish America," in Magali Sarfatti, *Spanish Bureaucratic-Patrimonialism in America* (Berkeley, 1966), 108.

41. Cabero, "Saña," 501; and *ACT,* I, 48–50, 59, and 371.

42. Ibid., I, 353, 358, and 359; and ART/Vega: 1567.

43. *ACT,* I, 230, 278, and 338.

44. Ibid., 371; and II, 38 and 39.

45. The *defensor de bienes de difuntos* received a 10 percent commission in 1542. The decree prohibiting councilmen from engaging in trade was not strictly observed. Angulo, 205; Blaisdell, 16; Sarfatti, 76–77; Peter Marzahl, "The Cabildo of Popayán in the Seventeenth Century: The Emergence of a Creole Elite" (Ph.D. diss., University of Wisconsin, 1970), 1–3 and 66; *ACT,* I, 11; and II, 169; and Alberto Larco Herrera, *Anales de Cabildo* (Lima, 1917), 6, 8, and 9.

46. *ACT,* I, 1, 3, 65, 75, 82–83, 98, 139, and 187.

47. *ACT,* I, 181; and AGI/P: 97, r. 4, [1569], 20v–21.

48. ART/MT: 1567. Note the definition of "family" in Appendix 4.

49. ART/LC: 1559; Paz: 1568; MT: 1569; Cabero, I, No. 4, 496; *ACT,* I, 47, 59, 75, 118, 168, 173–74, 325, 361, 364, and 374; and ibid., II, 40, 69 and 324–36.

50. *ACT,* I, 302; ART/LC: 1561; and Mata: 1565 and 1572.

51. ART/Vega: 1567.

Chapter 4

1. Domingo Angulo, "Fundación y población de la villa de Zaña," *Revista del Archivo Nacional del Perú,* I, No. 2 (mayo-agosto 1920), 281; ART/CoR: 30–VI–1576; and Alejando O. Araujo, "Reseña histórica de Saña," typescript (Eten, Perú, 29–XI–1957), 13.

2. ART/CoO: 28–II–1591.

3. These were fanegas de sembradura de maíz. ART/Mata: 29–II–1564. See, also, note 4, Chapter 3.

4. Criminal cases could be appealed before the corregidor of Trujillo or the

real audiencia in Lima. Appeals of civil suits involving less than one hundred pesos were heard by the entire cabildo; cases involving one hundred pesos to five hundred pesos were decided before the corregidor of Trujillo. Any case involving more than five hundred pesos could be appealed before the royal audiencia. Angulo, 283–99.

5. *Actas del Cabildo de Trujillo, 1549–60,* I (Lima, 1969), 3, 43, 131, 157, 159, 180, 202, 239, 258, 275, and 311; II, 30 and 46. Hereafter cited as *ACT.* Angulo, 285 and 302; and ART/Mata: 23–XI–1561; 22–XI–1563; and 29–I–1564.

6. Angulo, 286 and 294; and *ACT,* I, 131, 311, and 319–21.

7. ART/LC: 1560 and 1564; and Mata: n.d. [1563].

8. Angulo, 285, 294, and 295; *ACT,* II, 98; Fray Reginaldo de Lizárraga (1604), quoted in Teodoro Rivero-Ayllón, *Lambayeque: sol, flores y leyendas* (Chiclayo, 1976), 29.

9. Simón Pérez de Torres (1586) quoted in Rivero-Ayllón, 29.

10. ANP/RA: l. 33, 1592; and l. 30, c. 166, 1563, 13; and AGI/J: 462, 1774 and 1775v.

11. Angulo, "Diario de la segunda visita pastoral que hizo de su arquidiócesis el Ilustrísimo Señor Don Toribio Alfonso de Mogrovejo Arzobispo de Los Reyes," *Revista del Archivo Nacional del Perú,* 1, No. 2 (mayo-agosto 1920), 229; ANP/R: l. 3, c. 7, 1582, 98v; and BP/1278, 77, 79v, and 82v. The price of a slave is an average for unskilled males between fifteen and forty-five years of age in the years 1565 and 1591. See: BNP/A157, 133v; ART/1574; CoO: 15–I–1583; 3–II–1586; 22–I–1578; and Mata: 20–IV–1565; 8–VI–1565; and 1593.

12. ART/Paz: 1576, 20; MT: 1578, 128v; Vega: 1567; Mata: 13–VII–1570, 141; BNP/A157, 100; AGI/J: 458, 2167; 462, 1776v; and Marcos Jiménez de la Espada, ed., *Relaciones geográficas de Indias,* II (Madrid, 1885), 223.

13. Angulo, "Zaña," 285 and 294; *ACT,* I, 216; II, 1, 13, 15, 46, 58, 74, 157, 201, 215, and 259; and III, 1 and 164; ART/Mata: 14–X–1563; 29–II–1564; 17–II–1565; 22–II–1565; 16–III–1565; 29–X–1565; and CoO: 12–VI–1566.

14. ART/Mata: 3–XI–1584; 1584 [*sic,* 1583], 224v; Paz: 16–I–1576; MT: 1573 [1587]; Vega: 1585 [*sic*]; CoO: 26–IV–1569; 22 and 26–VIII–1572; AGI/AL: 15, 1633; J: 460, 3650; and *ACT,* II, 154, 212, 283, and 316. In the 1560s the position of *fiel executor* (inspector of weights and measures) was added to the cabildo. This official visited stores, warehouses, the slaughterhouse, and anywhere else where merchandise was sold to check the accuracy of the weights and measures. He also was responsible for maintaining the quality of products and enforcing price controls. For these services each retailer and wholesaler paid him a fee and, undoubtedly, bribes for overlooking infractions. This source of revenue probably could not compare with the yearly income from an encomienda, but it and the prestige of the office were substantial enough to make it worth the encomendero's time.

15. ART/Mata: 3–XI–1584; 2–X–1590, 492; LC: 30–XII–1561; MT: 1578; *ACT,* I, 65, 75, and 158; AGI/P: 97, r. 4, [1569]; J: 455, 1705; ANP/DI: l. 24, c. 638,

1597; RA: 1. 35, c. 192, 1598; Nathan L. Whetten, *Rural Mexico* (Chicago, 1948), 95; and Helen Phipps, *Some Aspects of the Agrarian Question in Mexico: A Historical Study* (Austin, 1925); and Spain, *Recopilación de leyes de los Reynos de las Indias*, I (Madrid, 1681), leyes 1, 2, 12, and 13, tit. 16, lib. 1. Hereafter cited as *RLI*. C. H. Haring, in *The Spanish Empire in America* (New York, 1963), 14, writes that the tithe was a tenth of all *net* profits. The wording of the royal decree of Ferdinand and Isabella, dated 1501, suggests that the tithe was a tenth of the *gross* production.

16. To document Gonzales's financial empire, see: ART/Vega: 1573 and 1587; Mata: 14–V–1562; 11–VI–1565; n.d. [VII–1564]; 24–I–1565; and 1569; CoO: 24–I–1562; 4–II–1562; 30–XII–1562; 28–VII–1563; 31–VII–1563; 10–I–1565; 5–VII–1565; 6–XII–1567; 7–VIII–1568; 22–VIII–1570; 13–VII–1573; 26–VIII–1573; 15–I–1583; MT: 1573; 1574; and [1587]; and BNP/A157: 1v, 33v–43, 99–102, 106, 110v, and 132v.

17. ART/Vega: 1582; and CoO: 13–VII–1570, 119v.

18. ART/Mata: 1586; and 24–V–1586, 67–70.

19. ART/Mata: 1565; 5–IX–1562; CoO: 26–IX–1561; 30–I–1564; CaO: 29–III–1588; Ríos: 1579; Vega: 1567; BNP/A310, 1584; AGI/J: 457, 912v; and AAT/Causas: 1570, 7.

20. ART/Vega: 1573; and Mata: 1572.

21. ASFL/Reg. 9, No. 2, Ms. 8, 1591; and Ms. 11, 1590; ANP/DI: 1. 8, c. 169, 1693–96; R: 1. 3, c. 7, 1582; RA: 1. 35, c. 192, 1598, 22v and 74; AGI/AL: 474; AAT/Causas: 1570, 1, 7, and 9v; and ART/Mata: 1596; MT: 1578; CoAG: 20–VII–1607; and Vega: 1567. There is no documentary evidence that debt was used to keep workers on the estates at this time.

22. Centro de Estudios de Historia Eclesiástica del Perú, *Monografía de la Diócesis de Trujillo*, II (Trujillo, 1931), 71–72; BNP/C2817, 1756, 7. These upper and lower age limits were almost meaningless because Indians rarely knew their ages. Spaniards estimated an Indian's age by physical appearance. See BAH/SC: N–33, 1569, 108–9.

23. AGI/P: 185, r. 24, 1541; J: 456, 419; 459, 2842, and 3062; 461, 928v; Luis Arroyo, *Los Franciscanos y la fundación de Chiclayo* (Lima, 1956), 34; Susan Ramírez-Horton, "Chérrepe en 1572: Un análisis de la visita general del Virrey Francisco de Toledo," *Historia y cultura*, XI (Lima, 1978), 79–121; and Marco A. Cabero, "El Capitán Juan Delgadillo, encomendero de Saña," *Revista histórica*, II, Trim. I (1907), 94.

24. Carlos Valdez de la Torre, *Evolución de las comunidades indígenas* (Lima, 1921), 67 and 76, cites a law of Philip II, dated 1573; *RLI*, II, leyes 8 and 9, tit. 3, lib. 6, 199; and BAH/ML: t. 97, n.d. [1568], 52 and 334. Philip issued a royal decree in 1568 declaring that vacant lands automatically became the property of the crown. He reserved the right to distribute them for himself and his successors.

25. Before the visita the Indians of Chérrepe lived in three villages: the

community center of Chérrepe on the coast, populated mainly by fishermen; another settlement of farmers near the site of the monastery of Nuestra Señora de Guadalupe; and the town of Ñoquique (Nonquique, Noqui, Ñoquiq) composed of both fishermen and farmers. BNP/A310, 1584.

26. Ibid., 31v–33.

27. The date of the Indians' petition (27 January 1572) is another indication of the careful planning done by the Spanish prior to the actual reducción (23 October 1572). BNP/A310, 1584, 31v and 34; ART/Mata: 27–I–1572; and CoR: 30–VI–1576.

28. ANP/RA: l. 283, c. 2511, 1789, 8; and Víctor Arenas Pérez and Héctor E. Carmona, *Anuario de Lambayeque* (Chiclayo, 1947), 505.

29. Joseph A. Tosi, Jr., *Zonas de vida natural en el Perú* (n.p., 1960), 14–19; Pedro de Cieza de León, *The Incas* (Norman, 1959), 319; and BAH/9–4664, 1549, 23v–24v.

30. Felipe Guamán Poma de Ayala, *Nueva corónica y buen gobierno (1615)* (Paris, 1936), 951.

31. Paul Kosok, *Life, Land and Water in Ancient Peru* (New York, 1965), 151; AGI/J: 461, 929 and 1395v. Further south, in Ica, where the viceregal officials felt the Indians were in danger of losing the water they needed, they seem to have followed a consistent policy of preventing Spaniards from acquiring land at the head of irrigation ditches. At Lima, Toledo prohibited Spaniards from irrigating at night. Such policies may also have applied to the Lambayeque region, although the written complaints in local archives suggest uneven implementation this far north. Personal communication, Robert G. Keith, 17 February 1981.

32. Bernabé Cobo, *Historia del Nuevo Mundo* (Madrid, 1956), 92–95.

33. Antonine Tibesar, *Franciscan Beginnings in Colonial Peru* (Washington, D.C., 1953), 50; Martín Fernández de Navarrete, ed., *Colección de documentos inéditos para la historia de España*, XXVI (Madrid, 1842–1895), 104; Thomas R. Ford, *Man and Land in Peru* (Gainesville, 1955), 134; César A. Ugarte, "Los antecedentes históricos del régimen agrario Peruano," *Revista universitaria*, I, No. 2 (1923), 377–91; and Louis C. Faron, "A History of Agricultural Production and Local Organization in the Chancay Valley, Peru," in Julian H. Steward, ed., *Contemporary Change in Traditional Societies*, III (Urbana, 1967), 243; and AGI/J: 455, 1148.

34. BNP/A310, 1584, 43; Angulo, "Diario," 239; and ACMS/1698. For the Chicama Valley, see: AGI/J: 457, 1147–48. Keith reports that in the Chancay Valley large tracts of former Indian lands were sold at auction following the reducciones. See Robert G. Keith, "Origins of the Hacienda System on the Central Peruvian Coast" (Ph.D. diss., Harvard University, 1969).

35. Marco A. Cabero, "El Corregimiento de Saña y el problema histórico de la fundación de Trujillo," *Revista histórica*, I, No. 4 (1906), 501–2; AAT/T: (1676); (Calupe): 1697; and 1708, 73 and 91; C: n.d., 10; Causas: 1737; ANCR/Rivera:

11–II–1700, 346; Polo: 1742; Collús: 1643; AGI/AL: 201, 1633; and ART/CoO: 27–VII–1580; and 30–IX–1582.

36. ART/LC: 22–X–1561; CaO: 1–IV–1558; Mata: 4–V–1565; CoO: 13–VII–1570, 141; 29–III–1588; MT: 1578; AGI/P: 185, r. 24, 1541, 52; J: 457, 758v and 912v; ASFL/Reg. 9, No. 2, Ms. 26, 1647, 45; and ANP/RA: l. 35, c. 192, 1598.

37. BNP/A157, 133v; B871, 1627, 50; ART/Mata: 1566; and *ACT,* II, 343.

38. AAT/D: 1588, 9, 28, 31v, and 34.

39. BNP/A538, 1580, 226, and 227v; and B871, 1627, 3, 51, and 87; ANP/RA: l. 27, c. 95, 1610; l. 35, c. 192, 1598, 2, 15v, 28v, 54v, 74, 92v, and 115; l. 37, c. 136, 1615; ART/Mata: 1565; 31–I–1566; 29–VII–1584; and 1586; O: 1592; MT: 1574; and 1578, 92; Paz: 1576; *ACT,* II, 343; III, 15; Angulo, "Diario," 228; ASFL/Reg. 9, No. 2, Ms. 26, 1647, 43, 45, and 48; and ANCR/Álvarez: 9–III–1663.

40. ANP/RA: l. 27, c. 95, 1610, especially 11, 13v, and 101v; l. 22, c. 74, 1608; RA–Criminal: l. 37, c. 136, 1615; and ART/MT: 1578.

41. ART/Mata: 1580; and 1596; O: 1591, 143v–44; AAT/D: 1588, 35v, 38 and 41v; and *ACT,* I, 87.

42. *ACT,* I, 161 and 164; ART/Mata: 24–VII–1585; and *RLI,* II, ley 20, tit. 3, lib. 4, 200v; ley 19, tit. 9, lib. 6, 231v; and ley 12, tit. 12, lib. 4, 103v.

43. ART/Mata: 1596, especially 79v. It is difficult to be more precise because the accounts are incomplete and part of the larger record of the settlement of the estate of the deceased owner. The fact that double-entry bookkeeping is not used adds to the confusion.

44. Ibid.; Jiménez: II, 223; and ART/CoO: 30–IX–1582.

45. ART/Ríos: 1579; Mata: 1565; and 1585; CoO: 8–VIII–1587; and O: 1592; and ASFL/Reg. 9, No. 2, MS 8, 1591.

46. *ACT,* I, 285.

47. On the exploitation of the Indians by the Spaniards, see: Juan Comas, "Historical Reality and the Detractors of Father Las Casas," in Juan Friede and Benjamin Keen, eds., *Bartolomé de las Casas in History* (DeKalb, Ill., 1971), 495; Bartolomé de las Casas, "The Brevíssima Relación," in Francis A. MacNutt, *Bartholomew de las Casas* (New York, 1909), especially 313–17 and 394–99; and AGI/AL: 32, 26–XII–1590. For the law prohibiting Indian service in the sugar processing works, see: *RLI,* ley 8, tit. 13, lib. 6, 250v; and BAH/ML: t. 98, 18.

48. ART/CoO: 8–VIII–1587; 7–IV–1592; CoAG: 8–II–1595; CoJ: 4–VIII–1598; and Mata: 1588; and AGI/J: 455, 1684v.

49. Madelaine G. D. Evans reports that sugar was still being imported from Mexico in the late 1560s. See her Ph.D. dissertation, "The Landed Aristocracy in Peru, 1600–1680" (University College, London, 1972), 144.

50. ART/Vega: 1582: CaO: 8–VIII–1562; CoO: 31–X–1580; and CoJ: 16–VIII–1604. The 15,000-peso figure may be a bit exaggerated. It would have been in Vásquez's interest to overstate this figure, since he was trying to justify his request for mortgage money and assure the creditors that he was a safe risk. It is not known whether the 9,925-peso figure is gross or net income per year.

51. ART/O: 1592.

52. ART/Paz: 2–X–1576; and 2–XI–1576; MT: 1578; Mata: 26–X–1565; 24–VII–1585; 15–IX–1590; CoO: 22–I–1578, 6v–8v; and Vega: 1567; ANP/RA: l. 33, 1592, 3–4v, 8v–9, and 11; BCH/1555; Appendix 3; and Demetrio Ramos Pérez, *Trigo Chileno, navieros del Callao y hacendados limeños entre la crisis agrícola del siglo XVII y la comercial de la primera mitad del XVIII* (Madrid, 1967), 215–17 and 224. His research indicates an early and flourishing trade along the Peruvian coast. Flour was exchanged for wood in Guayaquil. Sugar was exported to Tierra Firme, a major market for coastal produce.

The figures in the text represent those chacras and ingenios known to exist as separate entities. The molinos that operated on the premises of the ingenios are not counted separately. The number of functioning tinas y tenerías is not known.

53. Poma de Ayala, 944. For local complaints, see: ASFL/Reg. 9, No. 2, Ms. 26, 1647; AGI/AL: 270, 481, and 589; J: 461, 1443v, 1554, 1559, and 1580v; *ACT*, II, 3; ART/Ríos: 1582; Mata: 1580; CoO: 30–X–1582; and 1597; and AFA/ l. 1, c. 2.

54. The first corregidor de indios of whom we have notice was Francisco Cárdenas in 1566–67. *ACT*, II, 147; Don Martín Enríquez, "Relación hecha por el Virrey Don Martín Enríquez de los oficios que se proveen en la gobernación de los reinos y provincias del Perú (1583)," in Roberto Levillier, *Gobernantes del Perú: Cartas y papeles (Siglo XVI)* (Madrid, 1921), IX, 203; Arlene Eisen, "The Indians in Colonial Spanish America," in Magali Sarfatti, *Spanish Bureaucratic-Patrimonialism in America* (Berkeley, 1966), 108; *ACT*, I, 249; and II, 147; AAT/Causas: 1570; ANP/R: 1. 3, c. 7, 1582, 133; ART/Vega: 1587; and AGI/AL: 464, 1583. In the seventeenth century the same person might assume both positions at once. Also see: Keith, *"Encomienda, Hacienda* and *Corregimiento* in Spanish America: A Structural Analysis," *Hispanic American Historical Review,* LI, No. 3 (August 1971), 431–46.

55. Valdez de la Torre, 63; Pablo Macera Dall'Orso, "Feudalismo colonial americano: el caso de las haciendas peruanas," *Acta histórica,* XXXV (Szeged, Hungary, 1971), 7; *ACT,* I, 353; and III, 11; and ART/O: 1591, 144v–145; and 1609.

56. ART/Mata: 1580; CoO: 27–VII–1580; and ANP/R: l. 3, c. 7, 1582, 101–3.

57. ASFL/Reg. 9, No. 2, Ms. 11, 1590; and Ms. 2; Emilio Lissón y Chavez, *La iglesia de España en el Perú* (Sevilla, 1943–46), 16–II–1590, 538; ART/CoAG: 24–XII–1582; CoR: 30–VI–1576; ANP/R: l. 3, c. 7, 1582, 99v–107; and AGI/J: 457, 1151–v; 460, 365v; and 461, 1430v.

58. *ACT,* II, 146; and III, 15; ANP/R: l. 2, c. 5, 1582, 27v–28; and ART/Vega: 1587.

59. *ACT,* II, 266.

60. ART/MT: 1578; *ACT,* III, 11–13; and ANP/R: l. 3, c. 7, 1582, 135.

61. AAT/Causas: 1570.

62. Ibid.; AGI/AL: 273, 1576, 361–63; C: 1785; J: 457, 850v; *ACT,* II, 14–16; BNP/A534, 1580; ART/Ríos: 1582; and C: 18–I–1574; and ASFL/Reg. 9, No. 2, Ms. 26, 1647.

63. AGI/E: 534A; and ART/Paz: 1576. My findings contrast with those of such authors as Haring and Gibson who stress the functional aspects of residencias. See: C. H. Haring, *The Spanish Empire in America* (New York, 1963), 12, and 138–42; and Charles Gibson, *Spain in America* (New York, 1966), 100. The residencias of 1576 and 1582 were still partially functional. Thereafter, the contradictions inherent in the system began to weaken the institution. One noteworthy exception in the mid-seventeenth century was the residencia of Don Pedro de Meneses, a judge of the royal audiencia, sent to the north to review land titles. The abuses he committed were so blatant and the persons implicated so well placed that the resulting scandal forced authorities to examine more vigorously his exercise of power. This eventually brought limited redress to the Indian communities. The Meneses visita is discussed in more detail in the next chapter. Madelaine Evans reports the same contradictions in the institution as it functioned in the Lima and Ica areas. See her dissertation, especially p. 286 (cited in note 49, above).

64. See Juan Friede, *El indio en lucha por la tierra, historia de los resguardos del macizo central colombiano* (Bogotá, 1944); and ART/CoR: 30–VI–1576.

65. ART/LC: 1562; MT: 1573 [*sic,* 1587]; and Vega: 1573.

66. ART/CoR: 30–VI–1576, 10v, 18, and 33.

67. *ACT,* II, 8–10, 47–48, 98, 104, 128, 227, 256, and 346; *RLI,* II, 230–31 (lib. 6, tit. 9, leyes 10, 14, and 15); AGI/J: 455, 1317v–18, and 1329v; and Katherine Coleman, "Provincial Urban Problems: Trujillo, Peru, 1600–1784," in D. J. Robinson, *Social Fabric and Spatial Structure in Colonial Latin America* (Ann Arbor, 1979), 379.

68. *ACT,* I, 276–77 and 371–72; and ibid., II, 139.

69. ART/O: 1592; Mata: Registros 1586–87; 1588; 1592; and 1603; MT: 1573 [*sic,* 1587]; Vega: 1573; CoO: 13–VII–1570; and Ríos: 1579; and "Indice General de los papeles del Consejo de Indias," in *Colección de documentos inéditos relativos al descubrimiento,* Segunda Serie, XVI (1924), 42; Jiménez de la Espada, Appendix 1, t. II, iv and 223; AGI/AL: 28B; and Coleman, 383.

70. Angulo, "Zaña," 285–86, 294, and 299; ANP/DI: l. 24, c. 684, 1606; and RA: l. 35, c. 192, 1598, 38; ART/Mata: 1572; and 1603; and Ríos: 1579. Settlers did not necessarily buy an entire property intact. Several, for example, bought pieces of land from Salvador Vásquez. See: Cabero, "Juan Delgadillo," 94. Only twelve of thirty-three individuals who sat on the cabildo during this period were not identified as landholders or directly related to a landholder.

Chapter 5

1. Pedro Flores, el viejo, is a good example of a settler who made a modest fortune and moved to Los Reyes. See ART/CoR: 30–VI–1576.

2. Frederick P. Bowser, *The African Slave in Colonial Peru, 1524–1650* (Stanford, 1974), 75; Peter Boyd-Bowman, "La procedencia de los españoles de América," *Historia Mexicana*, XVIII, No. 1 (México, 1967), 50; and Virgilio Roel Pineda, *Historia social y económica de la colonia* (Lima, 1970), 169–73.

3. Figures 6 and 8. On Venezuelan wheat imports to Tierra Firme between 1570 and the middle of the seventeenth century, see Robert J. Ferry, "Cacao and Kindred, Transformations of Economy and Society in Colonial Caracas" (Ph.D. diss., University of Minnesota, 1980), especially pp. 13 and 38.

4. For hogs and tallow: ART/CoO: 21–IV–1559; 22–I–1560; 6–XII–1560; 30–I– 1564; 22–I–1578; 15–I–1583; 4–IV–1573; LC: 1560; and 11–VII–1564; CaO: 1562; Paz: 1–VI–1576; Mata: VI–1564; CoR: 30–VI–1576; 22–I–1578; CoAG: 24–XII– 1582; Palacios: 29–X–1610; ANP/RA: l. 35, c. 192, 1598, 2; l. 24, c. 82, 1609, 22, 24, 27v–28v, 136–37 and 153; l. 27, c. 95, 1610, 6v, 13v, 41, 47v, and 49; AGI/J: 461, 1221; BNP/A157, 121 and 130–30v; Guillermo Lohmann Villena, "Apuntaciones sobre el curso de los precios de los artículos de primera necesidad en Lima durante el siglo XVI," *Revista histórica*, XXIX (1966), 98; and Woodrow W. Borah, *Early Colonial Trade and Navigation between Mexico and Peru* (Berkeley, 1954), 47–49. For goats, see Figure 7 and Jean Borde and Mario Góngora, *Evolución de la propiedad rural en el Valle de Puangue*, 2 vols. (Santiago, 1956), 39. For leather (*cordovanes*): ART/CoO: 24–I–1596, 71; and 19–I–1616; Palacios: 16– XII–1610; O: 1592; Mata: 2–X–1590; and 8–I–1590; and ANP/RA: l. 22, c. 74, 1608, 26. For soap, see Figure 9. On the dispute between pig raisers and other ranchers and agriculturalists see: ANP/RA: l. 27, c. 95, 1610, 1–3 and 29. One shepherd could guard 600 sheep or 200 goats or 200 pigs, if over half a league from the nearest cultivated land. Droves of 25 to 50 pigs near cultivated fields required one or two swineherds to contain them. As agriculture expanded, a decree, dated 1578, establishing these ratios was more strictly enforced. It is instructive to note that the Indians had for years been complaining about the damage to their crops done by the pigs. No action was taken until the Spanish and creoles complained. Their protests were understandable considering the size of their investment and production. Sheep and goat raisers alone paid 6,000 pesos per year in sales tax in the first decade of the seventeenth century, which at the average price of 1 peso to 1¹/₂ pesos per head at 2 percent meant that herds were upwards of 200,000. (Data presented in Chapter 7 make this figure seem unrealistically high.) In the valley of Jayanca alone from 10,000 to 20,000 head were sacrificed each year. Grain production was estimated at 100,000 fanegadas annually. See also, ART/Paz: 30–X–1576; David E. Vassberg, "Concerning Pigs, the Pizarros, and the Agro-Pastoral Background of the Conquerors of Peru," *Latin American Research Review*, XIII, No. 3 (1978), 52; and BP/ 1632, No. 263–67, 1616.

5. For syrup and preserves: ART/MT: 1598; LC: 28–IV–1559; CoO: 22–I–1578; CoAG: 17–II–1593; Mata: 19–VI–1602; CoJV: 6–XI–1612; and 15–V–1642; and Ríos: 1579; Borah, 48; *ACT*, I, 285–87; and AGI/J: 461, 1232v. For oxen: ART/O:

1602; LC: 24–X–1560; CoAG: 20–VII–1607; and CoO: 22–I–1560. For copper: ART/Mata: 1596; and ANCR/1680.

6. AFA/l. 1, c. 8.

7. Emilio Lissón y Chavez, *La iglesia de España en el Perú*, No. 9 (Sevilla, 1943–46), 608; BP/1632, No. 263–67, 1616; ANP/RA: l. 44, 1619, 119; ANCR/M: III–1633; ACMS/1642; BNS/2734, 1648, 85; Interview with Don Agusto Castillo Muro Sime, 1971; and AFA/l. 1, c. 8.

8. BAH/ML: t. 97, 1591, 679–84; AGI/AL: 101, 1640s; David Weeks, "The Agrarian System of the Spanish American Colonies," *Journal of Land and Public Utility Economics*, XXIII, No. 2 (May 1947), 164–65.

9. A royal decree of 1593 empowered García Hurtado de Mendoza (the first Marqués de Cañete) to review land titles. His commissioners took over and finished the reviews that in some districts had been started on an informal basis by the corregidores. See Fred Broner, "Tramitación legislativa bajo Olivares: La redacción de los arbitrios de 1631," *Revista de Indias*, Nos. 165–66 (1981), especially pp. 418–22.

10. For example, they were granted by a town council that did not have the authority to do so or were for less land than the amount presently held.

11. For example, they were bills of sale from Indians, etc.

12. BAH/ML: t. 97, 1589, 660; 1591, 66; 1592, 49–52; 1598, 768; and 1679–86; AGI/AL: 132, [1593–95]; Carlos Valdez de la Torre, *Evolución de las comunidades indígenas* (Lima, 1921), 88.

13. AGI/AL: 32, 25–IV–1588. In 1592 a royal decree provided that titles issued by cabildos were valid, until the council was specifically prohibited from making land grants. See: BAH/ML: t. 97, 49.

14. AGI/AL: 32, 27–V–1592; Rolando Mellafe, "Frontera agraria: El caso del virreinato peruano en el siglo XVI," in Álvaro Jara, ed., *Tierras nuevas* (México, 1969), 39; and BAH/ML: t. 97, 1589, 654; and 1591, 66.

15. ANP/TP: l. 23, c. 613, 1787, 94.

16. ART/Mata: 1596; ANCR/[1645]; ASFL/Reg. 9, No. 2, Ms. 26, 1647; ANP/TH: l. 21, c. 131, 1805, 501; Valdez de la Torre; 86–87; and François Chevalier, *Land and Society in Colonial Mexico* (Berkeley, 1963), 88–90, for Mexico. The continued existence of common pastures and the fact that boundaries were not delineated in Lambayeque make it appear that the hacienda system was less developed than further to the south. Robert G. Keith, personal communication, 18 February 1981.

17. AGI/AL: 132, [1593–95].

18. AAT/T: 1667, 40v; 1776, 100; C: 1617, 318; 1619; 1706, 8v; 1802; ANCR/1614, 391–92; 1617; 1730; Soto: 13–VIII–1625; ASFL/Reg. 9, No. 2, Ms. 22, 1614; and Ms. 26, 1647, 55; ASDL/C: Libro I, No. 12, 106v; and Libro II, No. 25, 394–96v; BNP/B871, 1627, 13; ANP/RA: l. 44, 1619, 97v, 99, 104, 118v–19; APF/LF: 1633; and ACMS/31–VIII–1637, 698v; 1637, 653v–57v; and 1754, 2.

19. Mitayos earned 1¼ reales per day as chacareros (field hands) for 48 days at a time in 1607, compared to 1½ reales per day paid to day laborers working

in construction. Resident peons earned 15 to 20 pesos per year, plus some combination of food, land, seed, agricultural equipment, oxen, and clothing in 1607 and up to 50 pesos, food, clothing, and medicine in 1649. See ART/ CoAG: 20–VII–1607; Valdez: 8–V–1649; Oscar Malca Olguín, "Ordenanzas para corregidores del XIII Virrey . . . 1624," *Revista del Archivo Nacional del Perú*, XIX, No. 1 (1955), 170; and Jorge Zevallos Quiñones, "Don Luis de Velasco y los corregidores," *Revista del Archivo Nacional del Perú*, XVII, No. 2 (1953), 130 and 137. Another problem for landowners was that, by law, Indians could not work in the processing facilities of sugar mills. Mitayos discussed in official records were sent to work in the cane fields. BAH/ML: t. 98, 15.

20. The effective rate of tribute was much higher (sometimes up to 20 pesos) than the official, because community members had to pay for those who were on the lists, even though some had died or fled since the last census. See AGI/ J: 455, 1626; and ANP/DI: l. 4, c. 72, 1622, 138, 139v, and 170.

21. Bowser, 18–21, 110, and 116; Antonio Vázquez de Espinosa, *Compendio y descripción de las Indias Occidentales* (Madrid, 1969), 458–69; AGI/AL: 167, 1646, III, 19v; AAL/AT: 2–III, 1632; Lissón y Chavez, No. 10, 738–39; BAH/ML: t. 98, 132.

22. Bowser, 116 and 121.

23. ART/CoAG: 20–VII–1607; and ART/Valdez: 8–V–1649; and Manuel Burga, *De la encomienda a la hacienda capitalista* (Lima, 1976), 192. There is no documentary evidence to suggest debt as a means of retaining labor during this period.

24. Lockhart, *Spanish Peru* (Madison, 1968), 172, 178–79, 183, 188, and 202– 3; Bowser, 11, 69, 71, 74, 94, and 137; BNP/A157, 133v; ART/Loose: 1574; LC: 30–XII–1561; MT: 1598; Mata: 1593; and XII–1562; CoO: 15–I–1583; 3–II–1586; 31–I–1598; 16–VI–1642; Jiménez: 10–VI–1597; ANCR/Soto: 1625; and Pardo: 1632; ACMS/2–IX–1637; 6–IX–1637; and 1637, 718; and ANP/RA: l. 24, c. 82, 1609, 41v–42, and 132–33; and l. 120, c. 431, 1642, 188v–89.

25. Domingo Angulo, "Diario de la segunda visita pastoral que hizo de su arquidiócesis el Ilustrísimo Señor Don Toribio Alfonso de Mogrovejo . . . en el año 1593," *Revista del Archivo Nacional del Perú*, I, No. 2 (mayo-agosto 1920), 237; BNP/B871, 1627; ANCR/1614, 391–92; 1617; [1645]; Collús: 1643; and 1730; ASFL/Reg. 9, No. 2, Ms. 22, 1614; Ms. 26, 1647; AAT/T: 1776, 100; C: 1617, 318 and 327v–28v; 1764; and 1802; and ACMS/1642.

26. ANCR/Collús: 1643; ASFL/Reg. 9, No. 2, Ms. 26, 1647, 44; AAT/C: 1706; and 1835; T: 1667; 1795, 53v; and 1803; and ACMS/1642.

27. BNP/B871, 1627, 13 and 103v; ASDL/C: Libro I, No. 12, 106v; and Libro II, No. 25, 394v–96v; ACMS/1642; and AAT/T: 1667, 40v–50. Not all the debt increase, of course, can be automatically attributed to productive investment.

28. ACMS/1754, 2; ANCR/1617; AAT/C: 1617, 318, 327v–28v; and 1802. See also Appendix 3 for figures for the estates of San Lorenzo, San Juan, and Oyotún.

29. In my Master's thesis I erroneously reported that Fellupe was incor-

porated after 1670. See Susan Ramírez-Horton, "The Sugar Estates of the Lambayeque Valley," 1670–1800: A Contribution to Peruvian Agrarian History" (Master's thesis, University of Wisconsin, 1973), 22. Also see AAT/T: 1744.

30. ASFL/Reg. 9, No. 2, Ms. 22, 1614; ANCR/1617; and [1645]; AGI/AL: 278, n.d.; AAT/C: 1802, 7v–8; ACMS/1642; and Appendix 3.

31. BP/1632, No. 280–87, 1616; ANCR/[1645]; AAL/AT: 2–III, 1632, 229; AAT/T: 1697; BNP/C2995, 1789; ANP/RA: l. 283, c. 2511, 1789, 1v.

32. ANP/RA: l. 35, c. 192, 1598; BNP/B781, 1627, 1 and 3; ANCR/Collús: 1643, 151v; ASFL/Reg. 9, No. 2, Ms. 26, 1647, 44 and 55; ASDL/C: Libro II, No. 25, 394–96v.

33. ACMS/1642.

34. ACMS/1642; ANCR/Pardo: 15–III–1632.

35. BNP/C2995, 1789 or ANCR/[1645], 71. Calupe was a sugar producing estate at the time, but because it included annexed estancias, its sphere of influence was much greater than its 433 fanegadas.

36. The population figures are probably low because, given the fact that Cojal produced sugar, it would not have been prudent to list Indian residents for fear of raising suspicions that they were engaged in dangerous occupations. A 1609 royal decree prohibited "selling" Indian residents with the land. By 1647, therefore, Indian population figures were usually not listed in inventories and court proceedings. See: ANCR/1744 and Appendix 3.

37. BNP/B871, 1627; ASFL/Reg. 9, No. 2, Ms. 26, 1647, 63.

38. ASFL/Reg. 9, No. 2, Ms. 22, 1614; ANCR/1617; and 1730; ACMS/1637, 653v–57v; 31–VIII–1637; 1642; AAT/C: 1668; and 1802, 8.

39. Only one bankruptcy is known during this period. See ART/CoO: 1–X–1600.

40. Known descendants of the encomenderos constituted 5.1 percent of the landowners of the period. When possible descendants are included, the percentage rises to 8.4 percent. Very few of these were still local landowners by the middle of the period under discussion. Madelaine G. D. Evans notes the same trend for central Peru. See her Ph.D. dissertation, "The Landed Aristocracy in Peru: 1600–80" (University College, London, 1972), especially 31.

41. The information now available is not adequate to permit speculation on the relative amounts of private versus borrowed capital that was being invested in the estates. Source: Biographical Index: Landowners [BIL].

42. ANP/RA: l. 33, 1592, 3–4v, 8v and 11. This statement is based on the fact that wages and salaries of workers remained stable, while landowners were generally making more money.

43. ART/ME: 1609; and ANCR/M: IV–1633.

44. ACMS/1642, 1–34.

45. Male landowners numbered 179. Barandiarán estimates the number of priests in the area in the late sixteenth century at 24. Augusto D. León Barandiarán, *Mitos, leyendas y tradiciones Lambayecanas* (n.p. [Lima ?], n.d. [1938 ?]), 291.

46. ANP/RA: l. 35, c. 192, 1598, 22v; l. 44, 1619, 53v–54; AAL/AT: 1–III, 1608,

20; ANCR/1643 and 1645; BNP/B871, 1627, 1 and 79–80; ASFL/Reg. 9, No. 2, Ms. 26, 1647. For other instances of rentals see: ANCR/M: III–1633; and ACMS/ 1637, 653v–57v.

47. BIL. In Trujillo, the cabildo licensed the retail sale and set prices of sugar and soap. It is not known whether this practice was followed in Saña, but even if it was, local retail sales would have accounted for a small fraction of the total trade. ART/CoAG: 3–XI–1615 and 8–II–1616. Cabildo seats had been sold since 1595. See: AGI/AL: 133, 1597; and "Indice general de los papeles del Consejo de Indias," in *Colección de documentos inéditos relativos al descubrimiento*, Segunda Serie, XVI (Madrid, 1924), 42.

48. AMN/Ms. 317, seventeenth century, 81v; and BIL.

49. AAL/AT: 1–III, 1608, 483v; and 5–III, 1644, 91; ANP/RA: l. 44, 1619, 81; and ASFL/Reg. 7, No. 2, Ms. 3, 1619; and Ms. 2, 5–IX–1628.

50. The way a person acquired his first estate, from whom he acquired it, his patronym and family history, his place of birth, and his father's identity were the factors I considered in determining whether or not a person was a member of one group or another. Information on place of birth was too sporadic to be used alone.

51. These ratios are based only on those known to have been both land-owners and either bureaucrats or notaries. AGI/AL: 117, 1629; IG: 1660, 1640s and E: 1188, 1637; ANCR/M: 9–II–1633, 42 and III–1633, 73v; Collús: 1643, 142; ACMS/22–IX–1637, 689v and 1642; María Rostworowski de Diez Canseco, *Curacas y sucesiones: Costa Norte* (Lima, 1961), 13; and BIL.

52. The term refers primarily to the Spanish sector of the population.

53. AGI/AL: 165, 1627; and AAT/C: Cayaltí, 1802, 17.

54. BP/1632, No. 280–87, 1616; "Índice general," 42; ANCR/Collús: 1643, 170; M: IV–1633; AAT/C: 1663, 23; ANP/RA: l. 194, 1676, 75v, 134 and 146v; TP: l. 5, c. 149, 1653; DI: l. 6, c. 122, 1649, 53, 96–97 and 119; l. 19, c. 483, 1793, 39v; ART/ME: 1609; Mata: 1600; CoO: 13–VII–1570; and AGI/P: 109, r. 10, 3v–10v.

55. ANCR/1617, 317; ART/Paz: 1576; and ANP/RA: l. 194, 1676, 3. See also note 40.

56. See Appendix 3. Recorded interest rates on all investment capital varied from 7.14 percent, which appears to be the "prime" rate given to the most credit-worthy, to 17 percent early in the period. The standard seems to have been 10 percent. Rates on commercial capital were generally higher. Mortgage rates eventually fell to 5 percent in 1614 and remained stable until the second half of the eighteenth century. ART/Escobar: 1–VII–1617; Mata: 1592; 24–V– 1588; 24–XI–1565; and ANP/RA: l. 33, 1592; and l. 120, c. 431, 1642, 2–2v and 34v; and Robert G. Keith, *Conquest and Agrarian Change* (Cambridge, 1976), 101.

57. AAL/AT: 1–III; 1608, 6; ART/ME: 1629; ANCR/Collús: 1643, 155; Arriola: 28–IX–1656, 220; AGI/AL: 100 [1646], 56; E: 1190, n.d.; ANP/RA: l. 27, c. 95, 1610, 1v, 4, 6–7; and l. 194, 1676, 107; and AFA/l. 1, c. 13, 10v.

58. ANCR/1614, 336; and 1643, 149; *RLI*, t. 1, lib. II, tit. 20, ley 22; and ART/ IC: 20–II–1786.

59. ANCR/1614, 375–79v; and Soto: 15–VII–1625.

60. Zevallos Quiñones, "Lambayeque en el siglo XVIII," *Revista del Instituto Peruano de Investigaciones Genealógicas,* III (Lima, noviembre 1948), 104; ART/ ME: 1609; CoAguás: 26–IV–1768, 41; ANCR/Soto: (–VII–1625; and 13–VIII–1625; Guillermo Lohmann Villena, *Informaciones genealógicas de peruanos seguidas ante el Santo Oficio* (n.p., 1957), 193; ANP/RA: l. 56, c. 216, 1622, 89; SG: l. 6, c. 90, 1682; AAT/C: 1663, 28; ACMS/1642. These marriages appear to have been a means of tapping additional sources of revenue and keeping the land within a family. If so, these alliances help explain the notable lack of bankruptcies during the period.

61. ANCR/Soto: 12–VII–1625; M: IV–1633; A: 25–I–1656; and AAT/T: 1795, 49v–50. Compadrazgo is a relationship between the parents and godparents (*compadres*) of a child. In colonial Peru, it established quasi-kinship ties between the two couples and implied a recognized, unwritten agreement of mutual aid between them.

62. ASFL/Reg. 9, No. 2, Ms. 22, 4–XII–1618; ANCR/Collús: 1643, 141 and 174; A: 28–IX–1656, 220v; and Pardo: 11–VIII–1631; ANP/RA: l. 44, 1619, 29v and 31; and ACMS/22–IX–1637, 689v; and 1642, 33v.

63. The available evidence suggests that in any given year the number of nonlandowning bureaucrats, merchants, and priests was smaller or, at most, roughly equal to the number of landowners. Priests earned stipends of 185 to 1,275 pesos per year at the end of the sixteenth century. Majordomos earned an average of 200 pesos per year plus food and lodging. The doorman (portero) of the cabildo earned 50 pesos per year. The provincial treasurer earned 1,000 ducados or 1,375 pesos de 8 (approximately the same average salary as the corregidor) in 1614–15. A minor bureaucrat, such as a *protector de indios* (defender of Indians), in contrast, earned 150 pesos per year. See: Angulo, 230–39; ART/CoO: 24–I–1596; Palacios: 23–XIII–1610; Lissón y Chavez, 1598, 218–19; AGI/J: 509A, [1620], 159; Vásquez, 506; BNS/Ms. 3048, 106v.

64. ANP/RA: l. 35, c. 192, 1598, 46; ANCR/Soto: 23–VII–1625; and ART/ Álvarez: 15–VI–1658.

65. ANCR/Soto: 12–VII–1625.

66. ACMS/1642.

67. APL/B: I, 7–VIII–1622; 22–IX–1622; 29–IX–1653; and ANCR/1614, 483v.

68. AAL/AT: 2–III, 1632, 33; ANP/RA: l. 194, 1676, 134 and 146v; ANCR/ Álvarez: 9–III–1663; interview with Agusto Castillo Muro Sime, 1971; and ART/ S: 1638.

69. ANP/RA: l. 44, 1619, 7–7v and 53v; and AGI/IG: 1660, 1640s; ART/CoAG: 2–VI–1605; and AFA/l. 1, c. 19, 140–57v and l. 2, c. 1.

70. ANP/RA: l. 44, 1619, 5, 102, and 158; DI: l. 4, c. 72, 1622, 93v; AAL/AT: 2–III, 1632, 108; ASFL/Reg. 9, No. 2, Ms. 26, 1647, 61–62; AGI/AL: 7, 17–IV– 1646; 100, 1648, 34v; P: 148, No. 1, r. 1 [1598]; and BNS/Ms. 2933, n.d.; Ms. 2939, 107; and Ms. 3048, 163; BP/1632, No. 280–87; Vásquez, 506–7; and Zevallos Quiñones, "Don Luis de Velasco y los corregidores," *Revista del Archivo Nacional*

del Perú, XVII, No. 2 (1953), 128. Evans cites an administrative document (AGI/E: 511A, 1642) which indicates that petitions for office ranked the corregimiento of Saña after the governorship of Chile, the presidency of New Granada, and the corregimientos of Potosí or Cuzco. See p. 279. The salaries of corregidores are as follows.

Year	Salary	Notes
1605	3,300	
1613	1,365	
1614–16	1,650	Lambayeque
1614–15	1,325	Chiclayo
1629	3,000	Lambayeque and Chiclayo, combined
1640	1,000	Saña

71. AGI/AL: 1417, n.d.; AAL/AT: 2–III, 1632, 108–9 and 164; and ANP/DI: l. 4, c. 72, 1622, 32v, 102v–3v; l. 6, c. 122, 1649, 28v–29; and R: l. 22, c. 57, 1611, 124 and 133v.

72. AGI/AL: 100 [1646], 24.

73. Shane Hunt, "The Economics of Haciendas and Plantations in Latin America" (Research Program in Economic Development, Discussion Paper No. 29, Princeton University, October 1972), 42.

74. AGI/AL: 32, 25–IV–1588; and ANP/RA: l. 194, 1676, 91; l. 22, c. 57, 1611, 85, 96v–7, 124, 167; and AFA/Mocupe, 14.

75. BP/1632, No. 280–87, 1616; and ANP/DI: l. 6, c. 122, 1649, 30 and 39–39v.

76. ANP/DI: l. 4, c. 72, 1622, 30v–35; RA: l. 22, c. 57, 1611, 124; l. 27, c. 95, 1610, 24; AGI/AL: 100, [1646], 30 and 33v; E: 511A, 1648, 7; ART/CoAG: 20–VII–1607. The cabildo elected or named the water commissioner until 1638, when the viceroy began appointing him. See: ART/S: 1638.

77. ANP/RA: l. 194, 1676, 91v and 141v.

78. Ibid., 142; *Actas del Cabildo de Trujillo, 1598–1604,* III (Lima, 1969), 158; and Felipe Guamán Poma de Ayala, *Nueva corónica y buen gobierno* [1615] (Paris, 1936), 900.

79. ANP/RA: l. 44, 1619, 109v; Histórico: 1075, 1790, 45v; DI: l. 4, c. 72, 1622, 30v and 133; ART/CoAG: 9–IX–1583; and Valdez de la Torre, 81.

80. ANP/DI: l. 6, c. 122, 1649, 64–65v; and AGI/IG: 1660, 1640s.

81. BAH/ML: t. 97, n.d., 48–54 and 334; and t. 99, 1631, 15–16; and 1642, 198; and 9–9–2, 1664, 497; ANCR [1645]; AGI/AL: 54, Carta No. 74, 30–V–1648; AL: 100, [1646], 33v; ANP/DI: l. 6, c. 122, 1649, 57v; and Valdez de la Torre, 88.

82. AGI/AL: 277, n.d. [1642], 5–6.

83. AGI/AL: 51, No. 21, 20–V–1643; and 101, n.d.

84. Ibid.

85. ANCR/[1645].

86. See Appendix 3. One source suggests that Meneses accepted an official fee in the name of Su Majestad and accepted another "fee," read "bribe," for himself. The latter "fees" were estimated to total one-third of the sum sent to the royal coffers. See: AGI/AL: 277, n.d. [1642], 5–6; and ANP/RA, l. 24, c. 82, 1609, 31.

87. ANP/RA: l. 194, 1676, 138–39.

88. AGI/IG: 1660, 1640s; and AL: 100 [1646], 32 and 101, 24–V–1654; ANP/RA: l. 194, 1676. Meneses justified not measuring lands called "Laleche" for the same reasons.

89. ASFL/Reg. 9, No. 2, Ms. 26, 1647, 114.

90. He probably acquired it by virtue of a contract called a *censo enfiteútico*, by which a person acquired the usufruct rights and the original owner retained dominion. See Francisco García Calderón, *Diccionario de la legislación Peruana*, I (Paris, 1879), 380–87.

91. AAL/AT: 2–III, 1632, 237–39; AGI/AL: 100, [1646]; and 167, 1648, 39 and 42.

92. ANP/DI: l. 6, c. 122, 1649; BNP/B871, 1627; BAH/ML: t. 97, 51; AGI/AL: 278 [1648]. Despite these proceedings, evidence of guilt, and irregularities, Meneses was eventually absolved and acquitted posthumously. See AGI/IG: 1660, 1640s.

93. AGI/AL: 100 [1646], 6–7 and 33v; 101, n.d.; 51, No. 21, 20–V–1643, 1; E: 511A, 1648, 19v, 28v, and 32v; ANP/DI: l. 6, c. 122, 1649, 94; RA: l. 194, 1676, 139; and *La Unión*, 12–V–1959, 6–7; 16–V–1959, 1; and note 84.

94. AGI/AL: 100, n.d.; E: 511A, 1648, I, 14v and II, 10–12; RA: l. 194, 1676, 134, and 146v; and ANCR/1643, 170.

95. AGI/AL: 100, [1646], 1, 3, 19, 68–68v; 101, I, 1654; 167, 1648, 2 and 176v; E: 511A, 1648, 26v; and *La Unión*, 12–V–1959, 1 and 3; 16–V–1959, 1; 20–V–1959, 1; and note 90.

96. AGI/AL: 167, 1648, 2v–4.

97. ANP/DI: l. 6, c. 122, 1649, 36; and APF/LF: 1633.

98. ASFL/Reg. 9, No. 2, Ms. 24, 28–VI–1643; ANP/DI: l. 6, c. 122, 1649, 23v–26 and 30v; R: l. 22, c. 57, 1611, 115v, and 190v; and AGI/AL: 100 [1646], 30–33v. Once arable lands that were then without water and, therefore, unusable were estimated to be over 25,000 fanegadas de sembradura in this district alone. For Chicama, see: ART/CoAG: 20–VII–1607.

99. In 1593, for example, the priests of Ferreñafe, Íllimo, Túcume, Mochumí, Lambayeque, and Reque earned 662 pesos and received provisions of food-stuffs. The priest of Callanca-Monsefú collected 1,164 pesos and provisions. See Angulo, 230–38. See also note 62.

100. BAH/9–9–2, 1664, 506; and AFA/l. 1, c. 10.

Chapter 6

1. The weighted average of local wholesale sugar prices declined about one-third from the previous period. This is not indicative of a slump, because, as shown below, most of the landowners sold their produce in Lima or Tierra Firme, where prices were higher, and because costs of inputs fell more than these prices. See Figure 8.

2. Figures 7 and 9; BNP/B357, 1668, 66–66v, 80v–82v, 95, 103v, 142v–46, 182v, 199–203, and 274; and ANCR/Rivera: 2–VIII–1698.

3. ANP/RA: l. 33, 1592; l. 173, 1668; ACMS/1–IX–1637; and 1642; ART/Mata: 8–I–1590; 1596; CoAG: 20–VII–1607; ANCR/1680; and IX–1707; Collús: 1643, 131v and 137v; Rivera: IX–1707; and X–1707; AAL/AT: 2–III, 1632, 213; AAT/T: 1717; *ACT:* III, 196; AGI/AL: 165, 1627, 15 and 100; and 1644; ACMS/I–IX–1637; and BNP/B1737, 1669, 3v.

4. Appendix 3.

5. ANCR/A: 28–IX–1656, 220v–22v; Rivera: II–VIII–1686; Candelaria: 1668; BAH/9–9–2, 1664, 509; ART/SR: 1718, 33v; Appendix 3; and Nicholas P. Cushner, *Lords of the Land: Sugar, Wine and Jesuit Estates of Coastal Peru, 1600–1767* (Albany, 1980), 82.

6. AAT/C: 1663, 3v; BNP/B357, 1668, 29, 73, 205–6, and 303v; AFA/l. 1, c. 10; and Appendix 3.

7. ANP/Tributos: l. 2, c. 25, 1734; and BNP/B357, 1668, 144.

8. ANCR/M: 2–V–1633; 1719; ACMS/15–IX–1637, 674v; 1813, 95v–98v; and AAT/1664; C: 1664, 6; ART/CoAG: 17–IV–1671, 1v–2; SG: 13–X–1661; and Rentero: 30–I–1679; ANP/RA: l. 194, 1676, 112–13; AFA/l. 1, c. 13; and BNP/B357, 1668, 70v–71, 96, 248, and 409.

9. Some Indians had community lands but rented them out and worked on the estates. Others began working for extra cash, became indebted to the landowner, and remained.

10. BAH/9–9–2, 1664, 507; ANP/DI: l. 39, c. 820, 1737, 2v and 8v; ANCR/ 1787–88, 47 and 50v; and Lino: 23–XII–1722. I do not have enough information on debt peonage to be able to judge how widespread it was in the area.

11. AAT/T: 1708, 14v; and 1766, 51v–52; BNP/B357, 1668, 215–15v and 405; B1034, 188–89; ANCR/Candelaria: 1668; and ART/CoO: 25–VIII–1702, 130 and 150. Cushner believes that slaves were, in the long run, more economical than wage earners (p. 82). This may be true for the Jesuit estates he studied, but awaits verification for others.

12. ACMS/1642; ANCR/Álvarez: 9–III–1663; ANP/Terrán: 645, 1728; and BNP/ B357, 1668, 198–99, 206, 211, and 213; and B1034, 188–89.

13. ANCR/HS: VI–1678; and Rivera: IX–1686. The shopkeepers to whom I make reference here operated small, retail outlets. They were few in number and most had meager assets as compared to the hacendados. See: AGI/E: l.

1190; l. 534A, 28 and 88; AL: 167 [1648]; AAL/AT: 9–V, 1656–57, 147; and ACMS/ 1637.

14. ANCR/Rivera: 1–X–1706; AAL/AT: 27–VI, 1721, 9–10; AAT/C: 1721, 8; and 1802, 8, and T: 1757, 63; and Appendix 3. Apparently, the prohibition against sugar estates within six leagues of Lima had been revoked or was no longer enforced. Don Gerónimo de Velasco y Castañeda sought a 4,000-peso mortgage to construct buildings, plant more cane, and buy other equipment to turn the hacienda of Sipán into a trapiche in the 1670s. See ANCR/HS: VI–1678.

15. ANCR/1645; and 1720; AAT/T: 1697, 210; 1703; 1704; and 1766; Appendix 3; AAL/AT: 26–V, 1719, 35; and AFA/l. 1, c. 20.

16. José María Ots Capdequí, *España en América: las instituciones coloniales* (Bogotá, 1952), 43; AAT/T: 1676; and 1697; and C: 1773, 2; and ANP/RA: l. 283, c. 2511, 1789, 5.

17. Pablo Macera Dall'Orso, *Instrucciones para el manejo de las haciendas Jesuitas del Perú (Siglos XVII–XVIII)* (Lima, 1966), 33–34; and Appendix 3.

18. AAT/C: 1750; and ANP/RA: l. 283, c. 2511, 1789, 79.

19. Recall that in the previous period the estate encompassed three-and-a-half square leagues. Four square leagues is approximately five times the area represented by 433 fanegadas.

20. See below.

21. AAT/T: 1697, 215 and 219; 1704, 36; and 1758, 218; ANP/Aguás: l. 2, 3–3-3-1, 1666, 3; and J. Walter Sáenz, *Racarrumi* (Lima, 1975), 41.

22. BNP/B357, 1668; B1737, 1669, 27; and ANP/RA: l. 194, 1675, 79v.

23. AAL/AT: 15B–IX, 1678, iv; Jorge Juan and Antonio de Ulloa, *A Voyage to South America* (London, 1772), II, 95; Oscar Febres Villarroel, "La crisis agrícola del Perú en el último tercio del siglo XVIII," *Revista histórica*, XXVII (1964), 102 and 119; ANP/RA: l. 148, c. 1222, 1763, 70; ART/Vásquez: 1771; and 1779; S: 1693; ANCR/1673; BNS/MS. 3024, 1659; BNP/B357, 1668, 266v; and AGI/AL: 576, as cited by Katherine Coleman, "Provincial Urban Problems: Trujillo, Peru, 1600–1784," in David J. Robinson, *Social Fabric and Spatial Structure in Colonial Latin America* (Ann Arbor, 1979), 385. Some of the wheat and flour exported from Lambayeque then and later originated in the mountains, in districts such as Guancabamba. A few estates that had been transformed into sugar producers still had molinos functioning on a sporadic basis during this period.

24. AAT/T: 1704, 3v; D: 1680, 1v; Domingo Angulo, "Fundación y población de la Villa de Zaña," *Revista del Archivo Nacional del Perú*, I, No. 2 (Lima, 1920), 281.

25. ACMS/1666; ANP/Águas: l. 2, 3–3-3-1, 1666, 3v; RA: l. 194, 1676, 76v; ANCR/1714, 2; and Rivera: 11–VII–1686, 60; APF/1744; AAT/T: 1772; and AAL/ AT: 37–I, 1794, 13.

26. Not counting payments for composiciones and not counting payments for territorial acquisitions to the main estate. Average of 37 transactions between 1595 and 1649 is 11,042. Average of 59 transactions between 1650 and

1719 is 28,971. See Appendix 3. The averages may be a bit high, given the greater amount of documentation on the larger and more capitalized estates.

27. Palma y Vera's silver service weighed 77 marcos. AAT/T: 1697.

28. Defined as able to sign his name.

29. ANCR/Rivera: 31–XII–1699, 313–19; VII–1704, 439v; 6–XII–1704, 511; and 20–XII–1704; and Prieto: 10–XII–1712; ACMS/20–VII–1698; and AAT/C: 1818, 7.

30. AAT/C: 1734, 1v.

31. ANCR/Rentero: 2–VII–1654; 15–VII–1654; and 10–I–1670; Álvarez: 7–V–1663; 12–VI–1663; 27–VII–1663; 11–VIII–1663; and 30–VIII–1663; and Prieto: 27–X–1712; BNP/B357, 1668, 145, 200–200v and 209; BNS/Ms. 3024, 1656, 13v; AGI/AL: 304, 1698; and C: 1864, 1722; ACMS/1723; and Stanley J. Stein, "Bureaucracy and Business in the Spanish Empire, 1759–1804: Failure of a Bourbon Reform in Mexico and Peru," *Hispanic American Historical Review*, LXI, No. 1 (February 1981), 2–28. The salaries of the best-paid bureaucrats were much higher than those listed here. The highest paid official, the corregidor, earned over 1,650 pesos per year, plus fees for his services and profits from his commercial dealings with the Indians. The provincial treasurer earned fifteen reales per day.

32. Social prejudice against merchants is evident from the fact that in 1551 the town council of Trujillo discussed a petition which suggested that to maintain the quality and prestige of being a vecino, no *"regatón"* (regrater or, popularly translated, haggler or huckster; a derogatory word for retailer) be granted that status and its privileges. In 1569 a royal decree from the king ordered that

> the persons that are to be appointed as treasury officials
> should be intelligent and competent ("habiles y
> suficientes") persons and not merchants or traders . . .

As a result, Francisco de Villalobos was replaced as comptroller (*factor y veedor*) by Francisco de Samudio Mendoza. In this period the town council received another royal decree regarding the sale of wheat and other foodstuffs to retailers, who were again identified by the disparaging term of huckster. *Actas del Cabildo de Trujillo, 1549–1560,* 11 for 9–I–1551; II; 168–69 for 5–IV–1569 and III: 27 for 17–X–1598. Although in the seventeenth century prejudices apparently softened, a rich merchant's economic position could still be inconsistent with his social status.

33. BIL. Twenty-six landowners served on the cabildo during this period. ANCR/Rivera: 2–I–1704.

34. James M. Lockhart, *Spanish Peru, 1532–1560* (Madison, 1968), 153–54; and BIL. The exact figure is 67 percent of 104 landowners joined the militia, not including 22 priests. Women used the term *doña* as early as the sixteenth century.

35. ANCR/1617; and 1668; Rivera: 8–X–1674, 350; and 1–XII–1674, 369–69v;

ART/Rentero: 1670; AGI/E: 1192, 1680; and 534A, 13 and 326; AAL/AT: 18–IV, 1682, 1–2; AAT/T: 1697; and APF/1744.

36. ART/Álvarez: 7–III–1684; and 10–IV–1684; ANP/DI: l. 8, c. 169, 1693–96, 8v–9; ANCR/Rivera: 7–VIII–1694; AAT/T: 1697, 203v, and 1742, 150; Jorge Zeva- llos Quiñones, "Lambayeque en el Siglo XVIII," *Revista del Instituto Peruano de Investigaciones Genealógicas*, III (November 1948), 94.

37. BIL.

38. See note 50, Chapter 5. Old wealth indicates families (as defined in Appendix 4) in which at least one member owns land. Thus, if an uncle sells land to a previously landless nephew, the transaction would be counted as a transaction under "old wealth." If a locally born bureaucrat, from a family with no known land, acquires land, the transaction would be counted under "new wealth." These concepts, therefore, probably underestimate the strength of "new wealth," especially in periods of greatest social flux (e.g., 1595–1649 and 1720–1824), but are appropriate given the quality of the data on hand.

39. Not in terms of age, but in terms of positions held before and after their first land acquisition.

40. AAT/T: 1697; and Figure 5.

41. One of the reasons so many are unknown in the figure is that most estancias were acquired early before they became part of a larger property and before the ownership of the pastures was legalized in the visita of 1711–12, discussed below.

42. AGI/E: 534A, 523; Zevallos Quiñones, I: 146 and 148; and ANP/RA: l. 103, c. 873, 1746, 113.

43. This last relationship is not shown in the figure.

44. ACMS/1654–1765; ANCR/1702, 297v–99; Álvarez: 27–VII–1663; and Ri- vera: 11–VII–1686, 60; AAT/C: 1668; and ANP/RA: l. 194, 1676, 9.

45. Zevallos Quiñones, I, 114–15; and ACMS/V–1698.

46. I use the term *family* as it was used in colonial times. Today such extended families are called *clans.* See Appendix 4.

47. Appendix 3.

48. ANCR/Rivera: 8–I–1692; 11–VIII–1694; 5–II–1700; 2–I–1704; 26–V–1704; V–1708; 14–V–1710; and 10–XII–1712; APL/B: V, V–1705; AAT/C: 1734; and 1818, 12v; and T: 1740; BNP/C4379, 1736, 6v; AGI/AL: 453, 1717; and Appendix 3.

49. ANCR/1673; Rivera: 31–XIII–1674; 21–I–1692; 22–I–1692, 388v–89; 10–VIII– 1694, 346v; 11–VIII–1694; 27–VIII–1694, 394v; 28–III–1700; 31–III–1700; 22–XII– 1702; 29–IV–1704 and 20–XII–1704; Gamarra: VIII–1678; and ACMS/1722.

50. Five out of six guarantors were landowners.

51. ANCR/1690; Rivera: 26–I–1692; 3–XII–1694; 3–I–1695; 3–II–1700, 338v; 2– IV–1700; 21–IV–1700; 6–XII–1704; and Lino: 14–VIII–1723; AGI/E: 534A, 72–72v; and AAL/AT: 27–VI, 1721, 63.

52. ANCR/A: 29–IX–1656; Rivera: 6–XII–1692; 2–IV–1700; 21–IV–1700; 31–III– 1704; and 2–X–1707; AGI/E:534A; and AAT/T: 1743, 63v.

53. APL/B: II, 23–VIII–1693; V, 7–XI–1716; 28–XII–1716; 10–V–1715; 1685; 1688; 3–IV–1712; M: I, 18–V–1698; ANCR/Rivera: 9–I–1700.

54. AAL/AT: 5–III, 1644, 32; AGI/E: 534A, 243v; AAT/T: 1697; and ACMS/2–VII–1698.

55. Zevallos Quiñones, I, 132; ANP/RA: l. 194, 1676, 3 and 200; ANCR/1680; AAL/AT: 19–III, 1689; and AAT/T: 1743.

56. APL/B: I, 2–VIII–1662; and 21–XI–1666; II, 13–II–1695; and 8–VI–1698; III, 26–XI–1695; V, 10–VIII–1697; and 10–V–1715; ANCR/Álvarez: 23–IX–1663; Gamarra: VIII–1678; Rivera: 29–VIII–1686, 78; 22–IV–1694, 256v; 17–VII–1694; 25–VIII–1694, 390; 29–I–1700, 365v; 3–II–1700, 338v–41; 21–V–1707; Lino: 3–I–1717; 14–VIII–1723; and 25–XI–1730; Polo: 25–VI–1742; 1690; and 1719; ANP/RA: l. 173, 1668, 921; l. 103, c. 873, 1746, 1 and 8; SG: l. 8, c. 147, 1729; and SR: (1719); ACMS/1676, 84 and 17; and V–1698; AAT/T: 1697; 1703; 1704; 1717; 1740; 1746, 681; 1789; C: 1845, 9v; D: 1720; AGI/E: 534A, 523; and AL: 453, 1717; APF/1744; and Zevallos Quiñones, III, 105.

57. ANCR/1766 for 1675; ASFL/Reg. 9, No. 2, Ms. 24, (1721); ANP/Tributos: l. 2, c. 25, 1734, 2 and 5–5v; and OCIL/Reque, 40v–41v and 45.

58. The unofficial tax rate was three times the official, because Indians in the community had to pay for those absent since the last census, which might have been twenty years earlier. This worked against the Indians until the demographic recovery began. ART/RH,C: 10–V–1698; and AGI/E: 534A, 1675, 696v–99.

59. ANCR/Rivera: 1–X–1694.

60. BNP/B1737, 1669, 31v.

61. AAT/T: 1795, 5, 36v and 45; and 1717 for an example of land sold with the right to one-third of the water of a given irrigation ditch.

62. Eten eventually received a modest allotment from the community of Reque. ANCR/1787–88, 110v.

63. AGI/E: 534A, 239; and BNP/B1737, 1669, 34v.

64. Ibid., 42.

65. The Spaniards did not point out that greater supplies of corn would probably lower its unit price, hurting the Indians as the chief suppliers of corn and benefiting the Spaniards as consumers.

66. BNP/B1737, 1669.

67. ANP/RA: l. 194, 1676, 107, 112v, and 114v–15.

68. ANP/DI: l. 17, c. 417, 1786, 3v–4; ANCR/1787–88, 149 and 153; and AAT/T: 1795, 6.

69. AAT/T: 1676; ACMS/20–VII–1698; ANCR/1787–88, 63v; and Lino: 22–III–1723; and ANP/RA: l. 148, c. 1222, 1763 for 1653.

70. AAT/1784; T: 1795; and H: 1803, 13v–29.

71. ANCR/1740; and Saenz, 41.

72. ANCR/1756, 6v; and 1808, 12v; and Collús: 1807; ANP/TP: l. 23, c. 611, 1783, 37 (according to this document Lambayeque had a total of 7,022 fane-

gadas); DI: l. 19, c. 483, 1793, 47; ACMS/1813, 9v–13 and 14–16; ACI/Monsefú: P 110–5345, 57; and Comisión del Estatuto y Redemarcación Territorial. Ley 10553, *La demarcación territorial y política del Departamento de Lambayeque, Informe de la asesoria técnica* (Lima, 1947), 96 and 101. (Hereafter cited as *La demarcación.*)

73. ANP/RA: l. 194, 1676, 99v; BNP/C2195, 1756, 3v, and 35–35v; ANP/DI: l. 19, c. 483, 1793, 47; and *La demarcación,* 100.

74. AGI/IG: 1692; BAH/9–26–1, 9–4763, 1707, 24v and 26v; ANCR/Lino: II–1730; BNP/C2195, 1756, 2; ACMS/1813; and *La demarcación,* 90.

75. ANCR/1740, 45–45v and 52; and BNP/C2195, 1756, 3.

76. ART/Mata: 1596; and 1598; ANP/RA: l. 44, 1619, 109v; l. 283, c. 2511, 1789, 5v and 8; AAT/T: 1744; and Appendix 3.

77. BNP/B357, 1668, 206.

78. BAH/9–9–2, 1664, 490; 9–26–1; 9–4763, 1707, 9, and 24v–25v; ACI/Monsefáu; P 110–5345, 57 and 67; OCIL/Reque: 86v; ANCR/1787–88, 45v; Tumán: 1782–83; Collús: 1807; and Lambayeque: 1766; ANP/TP: l. 23, c. 613, 1787, 94; RA: l. 283, c. 2511, 1789, 7v–8; DI: l. 19, c. 483, 1793, 21; and *La demarcación,* 96.

79. BAH/9–26–1; 9–4763, 1707, 25; AGI/IG: 1662; ANCR/1763; ANP/TP: l. 23, c. 613, 1787; RA: l. 283, c. 2511, 1789, 8v; DI: l. 19, c. 483, 1793, 25v–26; and *La demarcación,* 90.

80. ANCR/Polo: 6–VIII–1742; and AAT/T: 1744, 156v.

81. ART/CoC: 9–X–1702.

Part Three

Chapter 7

1. Oscar Febres Villarroel, Virgilio Roel Pineda, and J. R. Fisher date the start of the agricultural crisis on the Peruvian coast with the earthquake of 1687, which made much of the land unsuitable for wheat production. The earthquake damaged the irrigation infrastructure in the Lambayeque region, but did not seriously affect agricultural production because wheat was no longer a principal crop. In Lambayeque, prices began to fall in the last years of the seventeenth century, but the social effects of the economic situation did not begin to appear until after the flood of 1720. Therefore, 1720 seems a more accurate date with which to begin a new period than 1687 for the Lambayeque valleys. Oscar Febres Villarroel, "La crisis agrícola del Perú en el último tercio del siglo XVIII," *Revista histórica,* XXVII (1964), 102; Virgilio Roel Pineda, *Historia social y económica de la colonia* (Lima, 1970), 170; and J. R. Fisher, *Government and Society in Colonial Peru: The Intendant System, 1784–1814* (London, 1970), 128. Also, see the discussion of my periodization in Appendix 4.

2. The customs duties collected by the provincial treasurer also show that imports were substantially higher in the 1720s than they were in the 1730s and 1740s. See AGI/C: 1864, 1722; 1821, 1729–67; AL: 1386; and Figures 7 and 8.

3. For example, AAT/T: 1697, 18.

4. AAL/AT: 28–X, 1706. Note the miniboom in sugar prices in the area (Figure 8) caused by this reversal.

5. AAT/T: 1795; and BNP/A538, 1580, 220.

6. Pablo Macera Dall'Orso, *Instrucciones para el manejo de las haciendas Jesuitas del Perú (Siglos XVII–XVIII)* (Lima, 1966), 78–85.

7. AAT/C: 1796; T: 1747–48; and Causas: 1737; ANCR/Sipán: 1719; and 1720, 7; Luya: 1779; Macera, 82–84; Justo Modesto Rubiños y Andrade, "Un manuscrito interesante: Sucesión cronológica de los curas de Mórrope y Pacora en la Provincia de Lambayeque . . . (1782)," *Revista histórica*, X, No. 3 (1936), 319 and 347; and Fernando Silva Santisteban, "Las ruinas de Saña," *La Prensa*, Magazine Section, 4 October 1971, 20–21.

8. AAT/Causas: 1737; and T: 1742, 158; ANCR/1719; Sipán: 1720, 7 and 32; and Pablo Macera Dall'Orso and Felipe Márquez Abanto, "Informaciones geográficas del Perú colonial," *Revista del Archivo Nacional del Perú*, XXVIII, Nos. 1–2 (1964), 182.

9. ANCR/Sipán: 1720, 32.

10. The seat of the town council of Saña was moved to Lambayeque. Years passed before the move was officially recognized. ANCR/1617; and AAT/Curatos: 1746, for a description of the ruin of San Lorenzo, el Real.

11. AAT/T: 1758, 51v.

12. AAT/T: 1704.

13. ANP/SG: 1782–92, 10; LC: 1800, 22–23; AAT/Causas: 1789, 8–24; BCH/ [1788]; and 1789; ART/ID: 6–VI–1815, 1v; ANCR/Lino: 3–VIII–1722; and Macera and Márquez, 42.

14. ANP/Gremial: 1743–50; RA: l. 283, c. 2511, 1789, 56; and ART/ID: 6–VI–1815, 22–24v.

15. Macera, 8–9; and Macera and Márquez, 148–49; Carlos Malpica and Gustavo Espinoza, *El problema de la tierra* (Lima, 1970), 162; Katherine Coleman, "Provincial Urban Problems: Trujillo, Peru, 1600–1784," in D. J. Robinson, *Social Fabric and Spatial Structure in Colonial Latin America* (Ann Arbor, 1979), 385; and Nicholas P. Cushner, *Lords of the Land* (Albany, 1980), 117 and 122–224.

16. Macera and Márquez, 146–203; AAT/T: 1777, 144; and 1779, 132, 135, 147 and 172; and Fisher, 123.

17. Jorge Juan and Antonio de Ulloa, *A Voyage to South America* (London, 1772), I, 127 and 193; Macera and Márquez, 42; ANP/T: l. 106, 1767, 115v, 196; José Ignacio de Lecuanda "Descripción del partido de Saña o Lambayeque," in Manuel A. Fuentes, ed., *Biblioteca Peruana de historia, ciencias y literatura*, II (Lima, 1861), 267; and Manuel Pardo, "El Partido de Saña o Lambayeque en el siglo pasado," in Jacinto López, *Manuel Pardo* (Lima, 1947), 281 and 283–85. For information on the rise of Caribbean sugar production and the effect of this competition on the production of Lambayeque and other regions see: Stuart B. Schwartz, *Sovereignty and Society in Colonial Brazil* (Berkeley, 1973), especially 243–44; Rae Flory and David Grant Smith, "Bahian Merchants and Planters in the Seventeenth and Early Eighteenth Centuries," *Hispanic American*

Historical Review, LVII, No. 4 (1978), 571–94; Robert J. Ferry, "Cacao and Kindred, Transformation of Economy and Society in Colonial Caracas," Ph.D. diss., University of Minnesota, Minneapolis (1980), 55 and 87–88.

18. C. H. Haring, *The Spanish Empire in America* (New York, 1963), 320; Fisher, 15–16 and 128; Malpica and Espinoza, 163; BNS/Ms. 19671, 145v; ANCR/Polo: 1753; and AAT/T: 1758, 124. Some Brazilian sugar undoubtedly entered the La Plata region clandestinely before Buenos Aires became an open port. The volume of this illicit trade, however, was probably relatively small and inadequate to supply the entire market. See also, Louisa Schell Hoberman, "Merchants in Seventeenth-Century Mexico City: A Preliminary Portrait," *Hispanic American Historical Review,* LVII, No. 3 (1977), 489. Ferry also mentions the slave-labor shortage in eighteenth-century Caracas. Ferry, 230 and 255.

19. Juan and Ulloa, I, 229; Mario Góngora, *Encomenderos y estancieros* (Santiago de Chile, 1970), 107–8; and Arnold J. Bauer, *Chilean Rural Society* (New York, 1975), 13.

20. ACMS/1766; ANP/DI: l. 15, c. 349, 1773; Gremial: 1743–50; T: l. 106, 1767, 117; BNP/B1737, 1669, 9v and 17v; and AAT/T: 1717; 1742; 1743; 36v and 307–8; 1763; and 1779, 203v.

21. AAT/1742; [1742], 7; T: 1742, 18–19; 1743, 100; 1744, 104 and 112; 1757, 75v; 1758, 108v and 321; 1779, 195v–97; and Causas: 1789, 4, 6, 52v–53 and 63; ANCR/1727; and 1752; Polo: 1752–53; ACMS/ 1736; ANP/TH: l. 13, c. 124, 1802, 63v; DI: l. 23, c. 675, 1809, 23; Tierras: l. 5, c. 37, 1811–19, 18; ART/CoAguas: 26–IV–1768; Fisher, 149; and Manuel A. Fuentes, ed., *Memorias de los virreyes que han gobernado el Perú,* IV (Paris, 1859), 135 and 140.

22. Ibid.; Fisher, 149; AAT/T: 1742; [1742], 7; 1757, 75v; 1794–95, 78; BNS/Ms. 2933, n.d., 285; ANP/T: 1770–76; ACMS/1806; AGI/AL: 1386; and ANCR/Rivera: 6–XII–1704.

23. ANCR/Polo: 14–I–1747; 24–I–1747; and César A. Ugarte, *Bosquejo de la historia económica del Perú* (Lima, 1926), 46.

24. The eight estates with mortgages and liens over their value were Calupe (after 1720), San Lorenzo (1728 and 1751), Oyotún (1747), Sipán (1763), Ucupe (1793), El Molino (1770), Cayaltí (1752), and La Punta (1778). See also Appendix 3. Two exceptions to the general trend are Cayaltí and Luya. The debt of the former dropped significantly, and the average debt of the latter remained about stable.

25. Robert G. Keith, Personal communication, 18 February 1981: ANCR/Herrera: 9–III–1734; 4–XII–1733; Polo: 1752–53; and AAT/T: 1743; and C: 1756.

26. AAT/[1742]; ANP/SG: 1782–92, II–7 and 8; ACMS/1735, 5; Fisher, 150–5; and ANCR/Polo: 14–IV–1742.

27. ACMS/1735, 5; and 1773, 1; BP/2817, 1756, 3; AAT/1785; Causas: 1763, iv; [T], 1777, 59v; T: 1743, 130v; 1757, 45–45v and 74v; and 1766; ANP/SG: 1782–92, II–8; TH: l. 24, c. 225, 1819, 4; and RA: l. 283, c. 2511, 1789, 90.

28. ANP/Gremial: 1743–50, 103; and AAT/1742, 7–7v.

29. AAT/T: n.d.; and ANP/T: l. 106, 1767.

30. AAT/T: 1742; 1743, 40v and 46; and 1744, 112v–14v; and ANP/Gremial: 1743–50.

31. See, for example, the records of the estate of Chumbenique: ANCR/1729, especially 502v, 511v, 517v, 518, 543, 555v, and 654v; AAT/Causas: 1774; T: 1779; and AGI/AL: 1387, 1789.

32. AAT/T: 1758; BP/2817, 4; and Miguel Feyjóo de Sosa, *Relación descriptiva de la ciudad y provincia de Trujillo del Perú* (Madrid, 1763), 77–78.

33. ANCR/Sipán: 1720; and 1761, 42; ANP/Terrán: 496, 3–X–1752, 81v; and AAT/T: 1743, 57v; 1750, 2v and 85; and 1758, 217.

34. ANP/Histórica: 1075, 1790, 91; and Jaraba: 1750, 397v–400v; ACMS/1735, 4–5; and ASFL/Reg. 7, No. 2, Ms. 10, 1761.

35. AAT/C: 1742; and T: 1747–48; and 1757, 45v; ANP/TH: l. 18, c. 164, 1791; l. 28, c. 261, 1789; RA: l. 9, c. 97, 1801; and l. 313, c. 2841, 1792, 68v; BNS/Ms. 19262, 1785; and ART/Dapelo: 1804.

36. ACMS/1735, 1v; BP/2817, 1756, 3 and 5v; AAT/[1740]; T: 1757, 57v; and 1789, 21v; Curatos: 1746; ANP/Jaraba: 1750, 397v–401v; RA–Criminal: l. 9, c. 97, 1801, 22; and l. 24, c. 225, 1819; and RA: l. 283, c. 2511, 1789; l. 363, c. 3325, 1798, 5v; ANCR/Collús: 1763; ART/VB: 1786, 8v; RH,AG: 24–IX–1817; and Macera and Márquez, 47.

37. AAT/T: 1742; Causas: 1789, 8v; and BP/2817, 1756, 3.

38. Included in the last percentage are eight locally born women (25 percent of the total locally born group) and two female immigrants (3 percent of the total immigrant group).

39. This percentage is the number of individuals with a career from the old established families (see Figure 26) divided by the total number of males known to be from these families.

40. See note 32, Chapter 6.

41. The basic annual salary of the contador was 1,350 pesos from 1724 to 1770. The corregidor made 2,810 in 1770. Subdelegados presumably earned more. AGI/C: 1864, 1722; and AL: 1068; and 1417; BAH/ML: t. 25, 1770, 66; Mark A. Burkholder, *The Politics of a Colonial Career* (Albuquerque, 1980), esp. 22–29 and 104–7; and idem, "From Creole to *Peninsular:* The Transformation of the Audiencia of Lima," *Hispanic American Historical Review,* LII, No. 3 (August 1972), 395–415.

42. ANP/SG: 1782–92, II, 7v; TH: l. 22, c. 198, 1784; l. 28, c. 261, 1789, 116; RA: l. 9, c. 97, 1801, 25v; and ANCR/PZ: 3–III–1727.

43. ANCR/1717. For another example, see AFA/l. 1, c. 18, 7–9.

44. AAT/T: 1779, 67v.

45. ANCR/1720; [1803], 63v; Polo: 25–VI–1742; and 7–X–1742; Rivera: 12–XIII–1694, 394v; Lino: 9–IX–1730; and 27–VI–1742; APL/B: XI, 16–VI–1748; and XIX, 28–VIII–1796; ANP/RA: l. 103, c. 873, 1746, 41; l. 148, c. 1222, 1763, 33; l. 302, c. 2711, 1791, 79v; Gremial: 1743–50, 47; SG: 1782–92, 34; ART/Dapelo: 13–X–1804; BNP/C2259, 1759, 7; and AAT/T: 1775, 88–91.

46. ANP/TH: l. 22, c. 198, 1784, 75; l. 28, c. 261, 1789, 11; ACMS/1722, 23–

25v and 36; APL/B: VII, 6–IV–1756; and XX, 3–I–1802; ANCR/Lino: 13–III–1734; ART/RH,O: 2–VI–1783, 40–40v; VB: 1790; and AAT/Causas: 1790.

47. ART/RHC: 17–IV–1809; IO: 29–IV–1794, 1, 8v and 10–14v; ANP/IC: 1800, 38v–39; DI: l. 19, c. 483, 1793, 2; TH: l. 22, c. 198, 1784, 4; G: l. 2, c. 63, 1812, 43v; ANCR/VM: 31–X–1775; APL/B: XI, 4–I–1767; and Jorge Zevallos Quiñones, "Lambayeque en el siglo XVIII," *Revista del Instituto Peruano de Investigaciones Genealógicas*, II (1947), 56.

48. Claims of landed status seemed to ignore how the estates were transferred or whether or not descent was consanguineal or affinal. As the sample genealogies presented here will attest, direct or indirect descent did not seem to make a difference. What mattered was the ability to claim that the family had owned land over the past *n* number of generations, the higher the better. Had landed status required a stricter definition of descent, claims would have been much less pretentious.

49. There is no indication as to whether or not debt would have forced him to sell if he had not died.

50. Conde Bertrando del Balzo, ed., "Familias nobles y destacadas del Perú en los informes secretos de un virrey napolitano, 1715–25," *Revista del Instituto Peruano de Investigaciones Genealógicas*, XIV (Lima, 1965), 109; ANCR/Rivera: 28–III–1700; 6–XII–1704; 1–X–1706; XI–1706; BP/2817, 1756, 1v and 3; ACMS/1722, 12–13, 17, 24v, 27v–28, and 36–39; AGI/C: 1864, 1722; BNP/C2195, 1756, 8; AAT/T: 1757, 48 and 75; and ANP/DI: l. 17, c. 410, 1784, 1.

51. ACMS/1736, 33–35; and ANCR/1729, 497v.

52. The dichotomy between creole and peninsular is not meaningful in this context. ANCR/GG: 8–III–1756; Polo: 16–II–1748; ACMS/1766; ART/ID: 17–IV–1811, 17v and 22v; CoAG: 28–IV–1768, 1; and AAT/D: 1680; and 1695, 21.

53. AGI/J: 461, 1259–59v; BNP/A157, 2; ANP/R: l. 22, c. 57, 1611, 83v and 197; TC: l. 5, c. 37, 1811–19, 15; ANCR/Pardo: 2–IV–1632; 29–III–1632; Rivera: 18–XII–1684; Herrera: 27–VII–1730; Gómez: 23–VI–1804; ART/ID: 27–VII–1805; 2–III–1804; and Zevallos Quiñones, I, 123.

54. Examples of nonlandowners renting pastures include the carrier and Alférez de Milicias Don Juan José Arenas; the regidor and major importer and exporter Sargento Mayor Don Juan del Carmen Casos; the notary Don Domingo Cossío Morante; the Indian commissioner and Captain Don Francisco Rodríguez Durán; the royal tax collector and exporter Lorenzo Tufino y Estrada, among others. ANCR/1817, 3v, 19–20; 1803; Herrera: 4–IX–1722; and 1739; 1787–88, 8; ANP/DI: l. 23, c. 675, 1809, 6; AAT/T: 1779, 95v; AFA/l. 2, c. 9, 1737; and Zevallos Quiñones, III, 107.

55. ART/C: 1785, 17, 48v and 69–70. Priests received an average basic stipend of 800 pesos in 1730; 650 pesos in 1756; 600 pesos in 1770; and 722 pesos in 1780. They also collected fees for baptisms, marriages, burials, Masses, and celebrations and were given *primicias* (first fruits). Fees for burials ranged from

9 reales for a "menor" to 4 pesos and 6 reales for a "mayor." Priests collected 1.5 to 2.25 pesos for Masses. Indians gave the church half a peso each for primicias. Some priests earned as much as 800 pesos from trusts and pious works. One source estimates that a priest with a stipend of 625 pesos really earned 1,400 pesos annually in a small, poor parish such as Monsefú; and those receiving 800 pesos often took in 2,000 pesos in Lambayeque. A parish such as Ferreñafé could yield the priest 3,075 pesos above his basic stipend of 725 pesos. See: BP/2817, 1756, 2–7; BAH/ML: t. 25, 1770, 66; ANP/Tributos: l. 3, c. 51, 1780, 6v–7v; Gremial: 1743–50; ANCR/Lino: 14–X–1730; ART/E: 3–X–1814; IO: 18–I–1800; 25–VI–1796, 7v; and 12–III–1814; AAT/Curatos: 1746; V: 1782; and T: 1758, 99.

56. The data are too fragmentary to allow direct comparison of the net worth of the immigrants and the locally born, upwardly mobile with representatives of the old landed families. This conclusion is based on the value of the estates, the degree of property concentration, the length of tenure, and other assets of the two groups. For examples of the net worth of upwardly mobile individuals, see: ACMS/1736, 1–57v for Pedro Francisco de la Oliva and ANP/Taboada: 13–VIII–1706 for Captain Don Juan de Urrutia Gallardo. BAH/ML: t. 25, 1770, 60; t. 80, n.d.; ANP/Jaraba: 1750, 397v–401v; AAT/Curatos: 1746; and ANCR/Sipán: 1761, 42 and 67.

57. Appendix 3.

58. ACMS/1811; ANP/RA: l. 103, c. 873, 1746; and ANCR/Polo: 25–VI–1742; and 1803.

59. The Lambayeque River overflowed its banks in 1791, but caused little damage.

60. ANCR/1729, 654v; BNP/D10034, [1801]; APL/B: VII, 1–IV–1756; and VIII, 13–XI–1746; and BAH/ML: t. 88, 1792, 327 and 336. Another source, dated ca. 1784, lists the militia establishment of Lambayeque as four battalions of infantry with 1,944 persons; nine squadrons of cavalry with 1,080 persons and four squadrons of *"dragones"* (?) with 480 persons. BAH/ML: t. 25, n.d., 109.

61. ANCR/1726; 1817, 3v and 21; Tumán: 1782–83; and 1790; VM: 6–VI–1788; and Lino: 9–IX–1730; AAT/T: 1738, 45; 1779, 95v; D: 1795, 37v–38; ANP/RA: l. 148, c. 1222, 1763, 25–26; l. 38, c. 390, 1804; Tierras: l. 5, c. 37, 1811–19, 1–2, 7v, II–18; TH: l. 13, c. 124, 1802; ACMS/1722, 2v–23; ART/ID: 10–IX–1799; and 16–IX–1817.

62. ANP/DI: l. 23, c. 675, 1809, 9v; and Tributos: l. 2, c. 25, 1734, 3.

63. ANP/TP: l. 23, c. 611, 1783, 42v–43 and 50; ANCR/1733; 1756; 1787–88, 1 and 165v; Lino: 14–VIII–1723; and II–1730; Polo: 20–VIII–1742; and CV: 11–VI–1756.

64. ANP/DI: l. 19, c. 504, 1795, 38–39v, 44, 76, 80, 86v, 103, 107, and 145–45v; and RA: l. 302, c. 2711, 1791, 20v.

65. The distinction between pastures and lands also served as the basis for

suits between Spanish landowners. See, for example, the records of the court case between the owners of Pomalca and Collús and the owner of Calupe: ANP/RA: l. 283, c. 2511, 1789, 14.

66. AGI/AL: 459, 1723; ANP/Tributos: l. 2, c. 25, 1734, 4–5v; BNP/C3684, 1799, 1–1v and 4v; and ANCR/Tumán: 1782–83.

67. ART/I: 22–II–1785.

68. ANP/SG: 1782–92, 7–8, 10v–12, 22, 25v, 28, 31v, 38, and 48v; and DI: l. 17, c. 410, 1784, 2 and 7.

69. ANCR/1766; PG and S: 1796; and [1807]; ANP/TH: l. 21, c. 131, 1805, 5v, 48 and 54; RA: l. 283, c. 2511, 1789, 22v, 54, and 79; and l. 148, c. 1222, 1763, 73v; and ART/CoC: 15–I–1781.

70. ANCR/1801, 1v; Tumán: 1782–83; 1787, 77v and 88; OCIL/1970, 47 and 86; ANP/TH: l. 21, c. 131, 1805, 80 and 88v; RA: l. 148, c. 1222, 1763; l. 283, c. 2511, 1789, 55v and 68; l. 302, c. 2711, 1791, 103; and AGI/E: 511A, 1648, 32v. Traditionally, the testimony of one Spaniard was considered equivalent to that of six Indians.

71. AAT/Curatos: 1746; and ANCR/1740, 74.

72. ANCR/1748, 1–11.

73. See, for example, ANP/RA: l. 51, c. 334, 1725; l. 103, c. 873, 1746; l. 283, c. 2511, 1789, 5v; and ANCR/1817.

74. AAT/Causas: 1789, 1, 3v, 55v, 59v, 30, 32 and 81.

75. AMN/Malaspina: t. 120, 121; BAH/ML: t. 25, n.d., 81v; AGI/AL: 791, (1718–95); and 1417, 1761–62; ANCR/1752; BP/2817, 1756, 6v and 7; and ANP/TC: l. 5, c. 37, 1811–19, II, 43v.

76. ANP/DI: l. 15, c. 346, 1772, 4v; SG: 1782–92, 22; BNP/C2778, 1781; ART/I,AG: 22–II–1784; and ANCR/Polo: 24–X–1747.

77. ANP/RA: l. 302, c. 2711, 1791, 145–47v.

78. APL/B: VIII, 23–VII–1758; and 4–XI–1759; IX, 1762; X, 1756; XII, 1768; XIV, 1766; M: III, 6–IX–1766; IV, 10–I–1789; VII, 13–III–1773; and 3–III–1778; BNP/C2259, 1759, 34; AGI/AL: 1417, (1770); ANP/SG: 1782–92, 19, 31v–34, 53v–58v, 60v–62; and II, 17; DI: l. 17, c. 410, 1784, 1–13; RA: l. 302, c. 2711, 1791, 77v and 86v; and ANCR/1765.

79. ART/I,AG: 12–III–1802.

80. ANP/DI: l. 17, c. 410, 1784, 8; and RA: l. 302, c. 2711, 1791, 77v–86v.

81. The visita of 1787–88, although not completely without abuses, restored the Indians' faith in the power and justice of the king and his representatives in Lima. The visitor reapportioned both land and water resources to accommodate the growing Indian population. BAH/ML: t. 112, 280v–83; ANCR/1787–88, 184v to end; ANP/DI: l. 19, c. 483, 1793, 5; and AGI/IG: 1662, [1778].

82. ANP/TP: l. 23, c. 611, 1783; DI: l. 19, c. 483, 1793, 3v, 21–22, 30v, 52v–53; OCIL/1970, 6 and 19 for 1781; *La demarcación*, 62–63, 74 and 78; *RLI*: Libro 6, Título 3, ley 20; Carmelo Viñas y Mey, "La sociedad americana y el acceso a la propiedad rural," *Revista internacional de sociología*, I, No. 1 (1943), 103. For

other examples, see: ART/IO: 18–X–1788; I: 22–II–1785; and ANCR/1756.

83. ANCR/Polo: 24–I–1747.

84. ANP/TH: l. 18, c. 164, 1791, 281; and ART/RH,AG: 24–IX–1817. The king issued an order in Aranjuez on 12 April 1788 setting up a monopoly of tanned hides sold in Lima. Noble and important hacendados obliged the king to revoke the decree. Details are too sketchy to determine whether landowners of Lambayeque were involved in this action. Therefore, I have omitted it from the text. See BAH/ML: t. 114, 41 for more details.

In another instance, a Bourbon visitor in 1784 reported on the "unhappy state" of the province and proposed a reduction of mortgage rates from 5 percent to 3. Almost ten years passed, however, before the estate owners in Trujillo and Lambayeque and church officials backed the proposal. Another twenty-three years passed before the restored monarch issued the decree in 1816. It was received in Trujillo fourteen months later, too late to make a meaningful difference to the fortunes of the colonial economy. Again, because details are lacking, I preferred not to use the example in the text.

85. Lecuanda, 241 and 265; Pardo, 284; BP/2817, 1756, 6v; BAH/9–4756, 1766; Cosme Bueno, *Geografía del Perú virreinal, Siglo XVIII* (Lima, 1951), 52–53; ACMS/1766; and AGI/AL: 996, 1780, 8. These figures suggest that the 100,000 figure reported in the early seventeenth century is exaggerated.

86. AAT/T: 1742; 1776, 28; and 1779.

87. Cotton was also grown by the Indians; therefore, the figure does not represent that produced by the estates alone. ANP/LC: 1794, 22–23; ART/I,AG: 14–I–1812; BNP/C: 2259, 1759, 34; and AAT/D: 1795.

88. The tobacco monopoly was created in Lima in 1752. The next year it was announced in Trujillo, but the laws regulating its operation were not published until 1759. Therefore, its introduction must date from the 1760s. The regional office with twenty-three employees was functioning in Lambayeque in 1780. Haring, 275; Ugarte, 46; Guillermo Céspedes del Castillo, "La renta del tabaco en el virreinato del Perú," *Revista histórica*, XXI (1954), 153; and Fuentes, *Memorias de los virreyes*, II, 241, 246 and 327; and V, 267–68.

89. AAT/T: 1758, 61v; and ANP/LC: 291, 1773–78.

90. ART/CoD: 8–III–1770, 2.

Chapter 8

1. David A. Brading, *Haciendas and Ranchos in the Mexican Bajío, León, 1700–1860* (New York, 1978), 17 and 24; Charles H. Harris, III, *The Sánchez Navarros: A Socio-economic Study of a Coahuilan Latifundio, 1846–53* (Chicago, 1964), 7; Ida Altman, "A Family and Region in the Northern Fringe Lands: The Marqueses de Aguayo of Nuevo León and Coahuila," in Ida Altman and James Lockhart, eds., *Provinces of Early Mexico* (Los Angeles, 1976), 260; and Henry Favre, "Evolución y situación de las haciendas en la región de Huancavelica," in Favre,

Claude Collin Delavaud, and José Matos Mar, *La hacienda en el Perú* (Lima, 1967), 237.

2. Francois Chevalier, *Land and Society in Colonial Mexico* (Berkeley, 1963), 310–11; John C. Super, "The Agricultural Near North: Querétaro in the Seventeenth Century," in Altman and Lockhart, 235; and Harris, 44.

3. William B. Taylor, *Landlord and Peasant in Colonial Oaxaca* (Stanford, 1972), 199. The relative absence of debt peons on the labor scene may also be due to a bias in the sources.

4. Nicholas P. Cushner, *Lords of the Land* (Albany, 1980), especially 114–25; Taylor, 111–63, especially 114 and 162; Robert G. Keith, *Conquest and Agrarian Change: The Emergence of the Hacienda System on the Peruvian Coast* (Cambridge, 1976), 102; Brading, 26, 37 and 90; idem, *Miners and Merchants in Bourbon Mexico, 1763–1810* (Cambridge, 1971), 215–16; and H. W. Konrad, *A Jesuit Hacienda in Colonial Mexico: Santa Lucía, 1576–1767* (Stanford, 1980), 214.

5. Magnus Mörner, "The Spanish American Hacienda: A Survey of Recent Research and Debate," *Hispanic American Historical Review,* LIII, No. 2 (May 1973), 209; and Keith, *"Encomienda, Hacienda* and *Corregimiento* in Spanish America: A Structural Analysis," in *Hispanic American Historical Review,* LI, No. 3 (August 1971), 438.

6. Lockhart, "Capital and Province, Spaniard and Indian: The Example of Late Sixteenth Century Toluca," in Altman and Lockhart, 105.

7. Brading, *Haciendas and Ranchos,* 3 and 8; Manuel Burga, *De la encomienda a la hacienda capitalista* (Lima, 1976), 17; and Keith, *Conquest and Agrarian Change,* 76–79.

8. Brading, *Haciendas and Ranchos,* 118–19, 133, 143, and 203. One example of estate fragmentation is Oyotún, ca. 1613. Heirs' claims increased the debt burden and the frequency of sale of Collús in the 1660s, La Otra Banda in the 1730s, Sipán in 1699, and Cayaltí in the 1750s. See Appendix 3.

9. For examples of one heir buying out the others, see La Punta in 1692 or 1697 and 1764; Santequepe, ca. 1735; and Ucupe, ca. 1649. Appendix 3.

10. Cushner, 56; Harris, "A Mexican Latifundio: The Economic Empire of the Sánchez Navarro Family, 1765–1821" (Ph.D. diss., University of Texas, 1968), 114; Super, 248; Ward Barrett, "Morelos and Its Sugar Industry in the Late Eighteenth Century," in Altman and Lockhart, 158; and Keith, *Conquest and Agrarian Change,* 110.

11. Robert Keith, in *Conquest and Agrarian Change,* 110, rejects the term *entrepreneur* when applied in a strict and unqualified sense.

12. In the long run, this life-style contributed to their disappearance from the elite. Brading, *Miners and Merchants.*

13. François Bourricaud, et al., *La oligarquía en el Perú* (Lima, 1969) and Mörner, 187. On the relatively open elite of Lima, see Fred Bronner, "Peruvian Encomenderos in 1630," *Hispanic American Historical Review,* LVII, No. 4 (November 1977), 633–59; and Taylor, 160.

On the longevity of the "great families" of Mexico City, see John E. Kicza, "The Great Families of Mexico: Elite Maintenance and Business Practices in Late Colonial Mexico City," *Hispanic American Historical Review*, LXII, No. 3 (August 1982), 429–57.

14. David M. Szewczyk, "New Elements in the Society of Tlaxcala, 1519–1618," in Altman and Lockhart, 139. Examples of successful upward mobility of the landowning group by members of other ethnic groups were exceptional in Lambayeque. From the point of view of these individuals, social mobility was limited.

It would be interesting to know how the success that peninsulares had in acquiring land and position in the late eighteenth and early nineteenth centuries affected their sympathies toward the crown during the Independence movements and how their success affected the growth of creole nationalism in this area.

15. Mörner, 203; and Chevalier, 312.

16. For the situation in Mexico, see Chevalier, 56 and 89.

17. Harris, *The Sánchez Navarros*, 97; idem, as cited by Mörner, 193; and Orlando Fals Borda, *El hombre y la tierra en Boyacá* (Bogotá, 1973), 10.

18. Konrad, 164 and 338. This situation contrasts with that in Oaxaca, where Indians were more successful in using the colonial legal and bureaucratic system to defend their lands. Taylor, 67–110, especially 77–78 and 82–89, 195–96, and 201.

19. Keith, *Conquest and Agrarian Change*, 132 and 135. See Favre and Pablo Macera Dall'Orso, "Feudalismo colonial americano: El caso de las haciendas Peruanas," *Acta histórica*, XXXV (Szeged, Hungary, 1971) on the manorial estate.

Glossary

ALCABALA:	sales tax.
ALCAIDE:	manager, administrator.
ALCALDE:	town mayor, municipal magistrate.
ASIENTO (DE PAN LLEVAR):	center of operations of a farm (producing food-stuffs) or ranch.
AUDIENCIA:	advisory and judicial body in the Spanish-American kingdoms under the Council of the Indies and the crown of Spain that served as an appellate and supreme court for the area under its jurisdiction.
BACHILLER:	the honorific title of a secular priest.
BOTIJA:	jug.
CABILDO:	town council.
CACICA:	female Indian chief.
CACIQUE:	Spanish term for an indigenous regional leader, often used as a synonym for curaca, Indian chief.
CAJAS DE COMUNIDAD:	general treasuries of Indian communities.
CAPELLANÍAS:	chantries, ecclesiastical benefice or chaplaincy.
CASA DE PURGA(R):	sugar purification house.
CENSO ENFITEÚTICO::	long-term lease by which the owner of a property transferred the usufruct to another in return for a yearly rent.
COFRADÍA:	sodality or religious brotherhood.
COMPADRAZGO:	ritual or fictive kinship, a relationship between the parents and godparents of a child, establishing quasi-kinship ties between the two couples which implied a recognized, unwritten agreement for mutual aid.
COMPADRE:	godfather, benefactor.

441

COMPOSICIÓN DE TIERRA:	legalization and confirmation of land title; the fee paid to the crown for such a review and regularization of title.
COMPUESTO:	legalized, as for landholding.
CORDOVÁN:	tanned leather or goatskin, hide.
CORREGIDOR:	district governor; ———— de indios: district governor with jurisdiction over Indian communities; ———— municipal: district governor with jurisdiction over Spaniards. By the seventeenth century one person could hold both positions simultaneously.
CRIADO:	servant, retainer.
CURACA:	Indian chieftain or regional ethnic leader.
CHACRA (CHACARA):	field, small farm.
DEFENSOR DE BIENES DE DIFUNTOS:	administrator of decedent estates and the probate of wills.
DIEZMO:	tithe.
DOMINIO DIRECTO:	dominion, ultimate control and disposition, especially of land.
DOMINIO ÚTIL:	usufruct, use, especially of land.
DON:	Spanish term for gentleman, indicating respect.
DOÑA:	Spanish term for lady, indicating respect.
EJIDO:	land reserve for common use of Indian communities.
ENCOMENDERO:	Spaniards granted Indians in trust. They had the right only to levy tribute labor and had no property rights over the land of the Indians under their authority.
ENCOMIENDA:	Grant of Indian labor of specific Indian communities to a Spaniard in return for protection and religious instruction.
ENGANCHE:	System of labor recruitment, whereby landowners, sometimes through a middleman, advanced Indians money and supplies in return for a period of contract labor.
ESTANCIA:	Cattle ranch.
ESTANCIERO:	livestock raiser, rancher, ranch owner.
FACTOR Y VEEDOR:	comptroller.
FAMILIAR:	lay representative of the Inquisition.
FIEL EXECUTOR:	inspector of weights and measures.
FINCA:	small farm.
FLOTA:	escorted fleet of ships, plying the Atlantic between Spain and the Americas.

FOLIO:	page of a colonial manuscript.
FORASTERO:	literally "stranger," Indian who left his community of origin, often severing ties with kin, to escape forced labor and other colonial taxations.
FUERO:	privilege, especially trial by one's peers.
GANADERO:	rancher, cattle raiser.
GARÚA:	heavy mist that falls in winter along the Pacific coast.
HACENDADO:	owner of large estate(s).
HACIENDA:	mixed farm, large estate.
HATO:	fold, place chosen by shepherds to eat and sleep near their flocks or herds; center of operations (usually of a ranch).
HIDALGO:	a member of the lower nobility in Spain; noble.
HUACA:	Indian shrine, temple or place of worship.
HUERTA:	fruit or vegetable garden.
INGENIO:	water-powered mill, usually associated with sugar or rice production.
LABOR (DE PAN SEMBRAR or DE PAN LLEVAR):	small farm producing grains and other foodstuffs.
LABRADOR:	owner of a small farm, farmer.
LEGAJO:	bundle, especially of documents.
LEÓN:	wild species of cat.
MASO:	handful or small bundle, especially of tobacco.
MAYORAZGO:	entailed estate; holder of an entailed estate.
MAYORDOMO DEL CABILDO Y DE CONSEJO:	advisor, trustee (of the council).
MERCED:	grant, especially of land by the Spanish crown.
MITA:	system of rotational, draft Indian labor, levied upon able-bodied males.
MITAYO:	draft Indian laborer.
MITIMAES:	Indian colonists, living apart from their main community of origin.
MORADOR:	town resident without vecino status, sixteenth century.
OBRA PÍA:	act of charity, good work.
OIDOR:	literally "listener," judge of the royal audiencia.
PORTERO:	doorman.
PROTECTOR DE INDIOS:	colonial official whose job was to defend the Indians.
PRIMICIAS:	gift or donation to the church of the first fruits of production.

RANCHO:	small farm.
REALENGA(O):	belonging to the crown, especially in reference to vacant lands.
REDUCCIÓN:	Indian relocation plan and resulting settlements.
REGATÓN:	Regrater or, popularly translated as haggler or huckster, a derogatory word for retailer.
REGIDOR:	town council alderman.
REPARTIMIENTO:	forced sale of goods by the corregidor to the Indians, often at elevated prices.
RESIDENCIA:	judicial review of an official's term of office.
RESIDENTE:	town resident without vecino status, sixteenth century.
SEGUNDA PERSONA:	literally "second person," refers to second in command or lieutenant of an Indian chieftain.
SÍNDICO:	lay representative or trustee of the church.
TASA:	colonial tribute list.
TENEDOR DE BIENES DE DIFUNTOS:	probate judge.
TENERÍA:	tannery. Soap-making and tanning operations were frequently combined and centered in one location. The resulting complex was called a "tina y tenería."
TIERRA BALDÍA OR VACA:	abandoned land.
TIERRA REALENGA:	crown lands.
TINA:	soap-making facility.
TRAPICHE:	mill, especially one run by animal power.
TRIBUTARIO:	tribute payer.
VECINO:	propertied citizen, householder in a city; ———ciudadano: householder who was not an encomendero; ———feudatario: householder who was an encomendero.
VILLA:	Spanish town.
VIÑA:	vineyard.
VISITA:	inspection tour, administrative review.
VISITA DE LA TIERRA:	review of land titles and claims.
VISITADOR:	visitor, inspector.
YANACONA:	Indians serving the Spanish, in return for wages and/or allotments of food, clothing, and so forth.

Bibliography

Acosta Saignes, Miguel. "Los pochteca." *Acta antropológica* 1, no. 1 (1945): 1–62.

Altman, Ida. "A Family and Region in the Northern Fringe Lands: The Marqueses de Aguayo of Nuevo León and Coahuila." In Ida Altman and James M. Lockhart, *Provinces of Early Mexico.* Los Angeles, 1976.

Altman, Ida, and James M. Lockhart. *Provinces of Early Mexico.* Los Angeles, 1976.

Angulo, Domingo. "Cartulario de los conquistadores del Perú: El Capitán Juan de Barbarán." *Revista del Archivo Nacional del Perú* 4, no. 2 (1926): 187–206.

————. "Diario de la segunda visita pastoral que hizo de su arquidiócesis el Ilustrísimo Señor Don Toribio Alfonso de Mogrovejo Arzobispo de Los Reyes." *Revista del Archivo Nacional del Perú* 1–2 (1920–22): 49–81, 227–79, 401–19, and 37–78.

————. "Fundación y población de la Villa de Zaña." *Revista del Archivo Nacional del Perú* 1, no. 2 (1920): 280–99.

Araujo, Alejandro O. "Reseña histórica de Saña" (typescript). Eten, Peru, 29 November 1957.

Arenas Pérez, Victor, and Héctor E. Carmona, eds. *Anuario de Lambayeque.* Chiclayo, 1947.

Arroyo, Luis. *Los Franciscanos y la fundación de Chiclayo.* Lima, 1956.

Bachmann, Carlos. *Monografía de Lambayeque.* Lima, 1921.

Bakewell, Peter J. "Zacatecas: An Economic and Social Outline of a Silver Mining District, 1547–1700." In Ida Altman and James M. Lockhart, *Provinces of Early Mexico.* Los Angeles, 1976.

Balzo, Conde Bertrando del, ed. "Familias nobles y destacadas del Perú en los informes secretos de un virrey napolitano (1715–25)." *Revista del Instituto Peruano de Investigaciones Genealógicas* 14 (1965): 107–33.

Barrett, Ward. "Morelos and Its Sugar Industry in the Late Eighteenth Century." In Ida Altman and James M. Lockhart, *Provinces of Early Mexico*. Los Angeles, 1976.

———. *The Sugar Hacienda of the Marqueses del Valle*. Minneapolis, 1970.

Bauer, Arnold J. *Chilean Rural Society from the Spanish Conquest to 1930*. New York, 1975.

———. "The Church and Spanish American Agrarian Structure: 1765–1865." *The Americas* 28, no. 1 (July 1971): 78–98.

Bazant, Jan. *Cinco haciendas Mexicanas*. México, 1975.

Blaisdell, Darius Othaniel. "Aspects of Life in Lima in the Sixteenth Century, Based on the Libros de Cabildo de Lima." Master's thesis, University of Texas, 1956.

Borah, Woodrow W. *Early Colonial Trade and Navigation Between Mexico and Peru*. Berkeley, 1954.

Borde, Jean, and Mario Góngora. *Evolución de la propiedad rural en el Valle de Puangue*. 2 vols. Santiago, 1956.

Bourricaud, François, et al. *La oligarquía en el Perú*. Lima, 1969.

Bowser, Frederick P. *The African Slave in Colonial Peru, 1524–1650*. Stanford, 1974.

Boyd-Bowman, Peter. "La procedencia de los españoles de América." *Historia Mexicana* 18, no. 1 (México, 1967): 37–71.

———. "A Spanish Soldier's Estate in Northern Mexico (1642)." *Hispanic American Historical Review* 53, no. 1 (February 1973): 95–105.

Brading, David A. *Haciendas and Ranchos in the Mexican Bajío: León 1700–1860*. New York, 1978.

———. *Miners and Merchants in Bourbon Mexico, 1763–1810*. Cambridge, England, 1971.

Bronner, Fred. "Peruvian Encomenderos in 1630." *Hispanic American Historical Review* 57, no. 4 (November 1977): 633–59.

———. "Tramitación legislativa bajo Olivares: La redacción de los arbitrios de 1631." *Revista de Indias* 165–66 (Madrid, 1981): 411–43.

Brüning, Enrique. *Estudios monográficos del Departamento de Lambayeque*. Chiclayo, 1922–23.

Bueno, Cosme. *Geografía del Perú virreinal, Siglo XVIII*. Lima, 1951.

Burga, Manuel. *De la encomienda a la hacienda capitalista*. Lima, 1976.

———. "San Jacinto de Ucupe: Una estancia colonial en el Valle de Zaña." *Análisis* 2–3 (1977): 184–200.

Burkholder, Mark A. "From Creole to *Peninsular*: The Transformation of the Audiencia of Lima." *Hispanic American Historical Review* 52, no. 3 (August 1972): 395–415.

———. *The Politics of a Colonial Career*. Albuquerque, 1980.

Burzio, Humberto F. "La moneda primitiva en el Perú en el siglo XVI." *Boletín de la Academia Nacional de la Historia* (Buenos Aires) 20–21 (1947–48): 404–18.

Cabero, Marco Aurelio. "El Capitán Juan Delgadillo, Encomendero de Saña." *Revista histórica* 2, Trim. 1 (1907): 92–117.

————. "El conquistador Don Juan Roldán de Ávila." *Revista histórica* 3, no. 1 (1908): 94–123.

————. "El Corregimiento de Saña y el problema histórico de la fundación de Trujillo." *Revista histórica* 1, nos. 2–4 (1906): 151–91, 337–73, and 486–514.

————. "En la época de la conquista." *La Industria* (Chiclayo, 31 October 1971): 8.

Capitán A., José Pablo. "421 aniversario de [la] fundación de Ferreñafe." *La Industria* (Chiclayo, 13 December 1971): 2.

Casas, Bartolomé de las. "The Brevíssima Relación." In Francis A. MacNutt, *Bartholomew de las Casas*. New York, 1909.

Centro de Estudios de Historia Eclesiástica del Perú. *Monografía de la diócesis de Trujillo*. 3 vols. Trujillo, 1930–31.

Céspedes del Castillo, Guillermo. "La renta del tabaco en el virreinato del Perú." *Revista histórica* 21 (1954): 138–63.

Chapman, Anne. "Port of Trade Enclaves in Aztec and Maya Civilizations." In Karl Polanyi, ed., *Trade and Market in the Early Empires*. Glencoe, 1957.

Chevalier, François. *Land and Society in Colonial Mexico*. Berkeley, 1963.

————. "The North Mexican Hacienda." In Archibald R. Lewis and Thomas F. McGann, eds., *The New World Looks at Its History*. Austin, 1963.

Cieza de León, Pedro de. *The Incas*. Norman, 1959.

Cobo, Bernabé. *Historia del Nuevo Mundo*. Madrid, 1956.

Coleman, Katherine. "Provincial Urban Problems: Trujillo, Peru, 1600–1784." In David J. Robinson, *Social Fabric and Spatial Structure in Colonial Latin America*. Ann Arbor, 1979.

Comas, Juan. "Historical Reality and the Detractors of Father Las Casas." In Juan Friede and Benjamin Keen, eds., *Bartolomé de las Casas in History*. De Kalb, 1971.

Comisión del Estatuto y Redemarcación Territorial. Ley 10553. *La demarcación territorial y política del Departamento de Lambayeque, Informe de la Asesoría Técnica*. Lima, 1947.

Cook, Noble David. "The Indian Population of Peru, 1570–1620." Ph.D. diss., University of Texas, 1973.

Corbitt, Duvon. "*Mercedes* and *Realengos:* A Survey of the Public Land System in Cuba." *Hispanic American Historical Review* 19, no. 3 (August 1939): 262–85.

Covarrubias, Sebastián de. *Tesoro de la lengua Castellana o Española*. Barcelona, 1943.

Crist, Raymond E. *The Cauca Valley, Colombia: Land Tenure and Land Use*. Gainesville, 1952.

Cushner, Nicholas P. *Lords of the Land*. Albany, 1980.

Dahl, Robert A. *Modern Political Analysis*. Englewood Cliffs, N.J., 1963.

Davies, Keith A. "The Rural Domain of the City of Arequipa, 1540–1665." Ph.D. diss., University of Connecticut, 1974.

Dobyns, Henry F. "An Outline of Andean Epidemic History to 1720." *Bulletin of the History of Medicine* 37, no. 6 (1963): 493–515.

Eisen, Arlene. "The Indians in Colonial Spanish America." In Magali Sarfatti [Larson], *Spanish Bureaucratic-Patrimonialism in America*. Berkeley, 1966.

Escobedo Mansilla, Ronald. *El tributo indígena en el Perú Siglos XVI y XVII*. Pamplona, 1979.

Espejo, Cristóbal. "La carestía de la vida en el siglo XVI y medios de abarataria." *Revista de archivos, bibliotecas y museos* 24–25, nos. 1–14 (1920–21): 36–54, 169–204, 1–18, and 199–225.

Evans, Madelaine Glynne Dervel. "The Landed Aristocracy in Peru: 1600–1680." Ph.D. diss., University College, London, 1972.

Fals-Borda, Orlando. *El hombre y la tierra en Boyacá*. Bogotá, 1973.

Faron, Louis C. "From *Encomienda* to *Hacienda* in Chancay Valley, Peru: 1533–1600." *Ethnohistory* 13, nos. 3–4 (1966): 145–81.

———. "A History of Agricultural Production and Local Organization in the Chancay Valley, Peru." In Julian H. Steward, ed., *Contemporary Change in Traditional Societies*, III. Urbana, Ill., 1967.

Favre, Henry. "Evolución y situación de las haciendas en la región de Huancavelica." In Henry Favre, Claude Collin Delavaud, and José Matos Mar, *La hacienda en el Perú*. Lima, 1967.

Febres Villarroel, Oscar. "La crisis agrícola del Perú en el último tercio del siglo XVIII." *Revista histórica* 27 (1964): 102–99.

Ferry, Robert J. "Cacao and Kindred, Transformations of Economy and Society in Colonial Caracas." Ph.D. diss., University of Minnesota, 1980.

Feyjóo de Sosa, Miguel. *Relación descriptiva de la ciudad y provincia de Trujillo del Perú*. Madrid, 1763.

Fisher, John R. *Government and Society in Colonial Peru: The Intendant System, 1784–1814*. London, 1970.

Florescano, Enrique. "Colonización, ocupación del suelo y 'frontera' en el norte de Nueva España, 1521–1750." In Álvaro Jara, ed., *Tierras nuevas*. México, 1969.

———. *Estructuras y problemas agrarios de México: 1500–1821*. México, 1971.

———. *Origen y desarrollo de los problemas agrarios de México (1500–1820)*. México, 1976.

———. *Precios del maíz y crisis agrícolas en México (1708–1810)*. México, 1969.

Flory, Rae, and David Grant Smith. "Bahian Merchants and Planters in the Seventeenth and Early Eighteenth Centuries." *Hispanic American Historical Review* 58, no. 4 (1978): 57–94.

Ford, Thomas R. *Man and Land in Peru*. Gainesville, 1955.

Foster, George M. *Culture and Conquest: America's Spanish Heritage*. Chicago, 1960.

Frank, André Gunder. *Lumpen-Bourgeoisie, Lumpen Development*. New York, 1972.

Friede, Juan. *El indio en lucha por la tierra, historia de los resguardos del macizo central colombiano*. Bogotá, 1944.

Fuentes, Manuel A., ed. *Memorias de los virreyes que han gobernado el Perú*. 6 vols. Paris, 1859.

Gama, Sebastian de la. "Visita hecha en el valle de Jayanca (Trujillo)." *Historia y cultura* 8 (1974): 215–28.

Ganster, Paul B. "Aspects of Indian-Spanish Relations in the Moche Valley, Peru, During the Colonial Period." Paper presented at the Annual Meeting of the American Society for Ethnohistory, St. Paul, Minn., October 1974.

García Calderón, Francisco. *Diccionario de la legislación Peruana*. 2 vols. Paris, 1879.

Gibson, Charles. *The Aztecs Under Spanish Rule: A History of the Indians of the Valley of Mexico, 1519–1810*. Stanford, 1964.

———. *Spain in America*. New York, 1966.

Glade, William P. *The Latin American Economies*. New York, 1969.

Góngora, Mario. *Encomenderos y estancieros, Estudios acerca de la constitución social aristocrática de Chile después de la conquista, 1580–1660*. Santiago, 1970.

González Sánchez, Isabel, comp. *Haciendas y ranchos de Tlaxcala en 1712*. México, 1969.

———. "La retención por deudas y los traslados de trabajadores tlaquehuales o alquilados en las haciendas, como sustitución de los repartimientos de indios durante el siglo XVIII." *Anales del Instituto Nacional de Antropología e Historia* 19, no. 48 (1966): 241–49.

Greenfield, Sidney M. "An Alternative Sociological Model for the Analysis of Brazilian Agriculture." Latin American Center Discussion Paper No. 14, University of Wisconsin, Milwaukee, 28 September 1968.

Hamilton, Earl J. "American Treasure and Andalusian Prices." *Journal of Economic and Business History* 1, no. 1 (1928): 1–35.

———. *American Treasure and the Price Revolution in Spain, 1501–1650*. New York, 1970.

———. "Wages and Subsistence on Spanish Treasure Ships, 1503–1660." *Journal of Political Economy* 37 (1929): 430–50.

Haring, C. H. *The Spanish Empire in America*. New York, 1963.

Harris, Charles H. *A Mexican Family Empire*. Austin, 1975.

———. "A Mexican Latifundio: The Economic Empire of the Sánchez Navarro Family, 1765–1821." Ph.D. diss., University of Texas, 1968.

———. *The Sánchez Navarros: A Socio-economic Study of a Coahuilan Latifundio, 1846–53*. Chicago, 1964.

Hemming, John. *The Conquest of the Incas*. New York, 1970.

Hoberman, Louisa Schell. "Merchants in Seventeenth-Century Mexico City: A Preliminary Portrait." *Hispanic American Historical Review* 57, no. 3 (August 1977), 479–503.

Hunt, Shane. "The Economics of Haciendas and Plantations in Latin America." Research Program in Economic Development, Discussion Paper No. 29, Princeton University, October 1972.

Ibáñez, J. W. *Informe: Acompaña prueba instrumental y pericial fotográfica. Deduce la falsedad de piezas que indica.* Chiclayo, 1920.

Jara, Álvaro, ed. *Tierras nuevas.* México, 1969.

Jiménez de la Espada, Marcos, ed. *Relaciones geográficas de Indias.* 4 vols. Madrid, 1881–97.

Juan, Jorge, and Antonio de Ulloa. *A Voyage to South America.* 2 vols. London, 1772.

Keith, Robert G. *Conquest and Agrarian Change: The Emergence of the Hacienda System on the Peruvian Coast.* Cambridge, 1976.

————. "*Encomienda, Hacienda* and *Corregimiento* in Spanish America: A Structural Analysis." *Hispanic American Historical Review* 51, no. 3 (August 1971): 431–46.

————. "Origins of the Hacienda System on the Central Peruvian Coast." Ph.D. diss., Harvard University, 1969.

Kicza, John E. "The Great Families of Mexico: Elite Maintenance and Business Practices in Late Colonial Mexico." *Hispanic American Historical Review* 62, no. 3 (August 1982): 429–57.

Konrad, Herman W. *A Jesuit Hacienda in Colonial Mexico: Santa Lucía, 1576–1767.* Stanford, 1980.

Kosok, Paul. *Life, Land and Water in Ancient Peru.* New York, 1965.

Lambert, Jacques. *Latin America: Social Structures and Political Institutions.* Berkeley, 1967.

Larco Herrera, Alberto. *Anales de Cabildo, Extractos tomados de las actas de los años de 1550–1612.* nos. 1–4. Lima, 1917–20.

————. *Anales de cabildo. Ordenanzas de la Ciudad de Trujillo (3 setiembre 1555).* Lima, 1917.

Lecuanda, José Ignacio de. "Descripción del partido de Saña o Lambayeque." In Manuel A. Fuentes, ed., *Biblioteca Peruana de história, ciencias y literatura,* II. Lima, 1861.

León Barandiarán, Augusto D. *Mitos, leyendas y tradiciones Lambayecanas.* N.p. (Lima ?), n.d. (1938 ?).

Levillier, Roberto, ed. *Gobernantes del Perú: Cartas y papeles (Siglo XVI).* Madrid, 1921.

Lewis, Leslie. "In Mexico City's Shadow: Some Aspects of Economic Activity and Social Processes in Texcoco, 1570–1620." In Ida Altman and James M. Lockhart, *Provinces of Early Mexico.* Los Angeles, 1976.

Lima, Municipalidad de. *Libros de Cabildo de Lima.* 19 vols. Lima, 1935–55.

Lissón y Chavez, Emilio. *La iglesia de España en el Perú.* 6 vols. Sevilla, 1943–46.

Liza Q., Jacinto A. "La Ciudad de Ferreñafe." *Firruñap* 3, no. 25 (1966): 64–66.

Lizárraga, Reginaldo de. *Descripción colonial.* Buenos Aires, 1928.

Lockhart, James M. "Capital and Province, Spaniard and Indian: The Example of Late Sixteenth Century Toluca." In Ida Altman and James M. Lockhart, *Provinces of Early Mexico.* Los Angeles, 1976.

———. *"Encomienda* and *Hacienda:* The Evolution of the Great Estate in the Spanish Indies." *Hispanic American Historical Review* 49, no. 3 (August 1969): 411–29.

———. "The Evolution of the Great Estate." In Helen Delpar, ed., *The Borzoi Reader in Latin American History.* New York, 1972.

———. *Men of Cajamarca.* Austin, 1972.

———. *Spanish Peru, 1532–1560.* Madison, 1968.

Lohmann Villena, Guillermo. *Informaciones genealógicas de Peruanos seguidas ante el Santo Oficio.* Madrid, 1957.

———. "Apuntaciones sobre el curso de los precios de los artículos de primera necesidad en Lima durante el siglo XVI." *Revista histórica* 29 (1966): 79–103.

López de Velasco, Juan. *Geografía y descripción universal de las Indias.* Madrid, 1971.

Loredo, Rafael. *Los repartos.* Lima, 1958.

Lynch, John. *Spain under the Hapsburgs.* 2 vols. New York, 1964.

McBride, George M. *The Land Systems of Mexico.* New York, 1923.

MacLeod, Murdo J. *Spanish Central America: A Socio-economic History, 1520–1720.* Berkeley, 1973.

Macera Dall'Orso, Pablo. "Feudalismo colonial americano: El caso de las haciendas Peruanas." *Acta histórica* 35 (Szeged, Hungary, 1971): 3–43.

———. *Instrucciones para el manejo de las haciendas Jesuitas del Perú (siglos XVII–XVIII).* Lima, 1966.

———, and Felipe Márquez Abanto. "Informaciones geográficas del Perú colonial (1803–1805)." *Revista del Archivo Nacional del Perú* XXVIII, nos. 1 and 2 (1964): 133–88.

Malca Olguin, Oscar. "Ordenanzas para corregidores del XIII Virrey . . . 1624." *Revista del Archivo Nacional del Perú* 19, no. 1 (1955): 155–81.

Malpica, Carlos, and Gustavo Espinoza. *El problema de la tierra.* Lima, 1970.

Martínez, Héctor. "Evolución de la propiedad territorial en el Perú." *Revista de economía y agricultura* 1, no. 2 (1963–64): 98–108.

Marzahl, Peter. "The Cabildo of Popayán in the Seventeenth Century: The Emergence of a Creole Elite." Ph.D. diss., University of Wisconsin, Madison, 1970.

Matos Mar, José. "Las haciendas del Valle de Chancay." In Henry Favre, et al., *La hacienda en el Perú.* Lima, 1967.

Meléndez, Carlos. "Los orígenes de la propiedad territorial en el valle central de Costa Rica durante el siglo XVI." *Revista de la Universidad de Costa Rica (San José)* 27, sem. 2 (1969): 53–71.

Mellafe, Rolando. "Frontera agraria: El caso del virreinato peruano en el siglo XVI." In Álvaro Jara, ed., *Tierras nuevas.* México, 1969.

Méndez Rúa, Ángel. *Boceto histórico de la iglesia de Lambayeque.* Lambayeque, 1935.

Mendiburu, Manuel de. *Diccionario histórico-biográfico del Perú.* 8 vols. Lima, 1874–90.

Moreyra y Paz-Soldán, Manuel. *Antecedentes Españoles y el circulante durante la conquista e iniciación del virreinato.* Lima, 1941.

———. *Apuntes sobre la historia de la moneda colonial en el Perú.* Lima, 1938.

Mörner, Magnus. "The Spanish American Hacienda: A Survey of Recent Research and Debate." *Hispanic American Historical Review* 53, no. 2 (May 1973): 183–216.

Navarrete, Martín Fernández de, ed. *La colección de documentos inéditos para la historia de España.* 113 vols. Madrid, 1842–95.

Ots Capdequí, José María. *España en América: Las instituciones coloniales.* Bogotá, 1952.

———. *El régimen de la tierra en la América Española durante el período colonial.* Ciudad Trujillo, Santo Domingo, 1946.

Pardo, Manuel. "El Partido de Saña o Lambayeque en el siglo pasado." In Jacinto López, *Manuel Pardo.* Lima, 1947.

Parsons, Talcott. "On the Concept of Political Power." *Proceedings of the American Philosophical Society* 107, no. 3 (1963): 240–65.

Phelan, John Leddy. "Authority and Flexibility in the Spanish Imperial Bureaucracy." *Administrative Science Quarterly* 5, no. 1 (1960): 47–65.

Phipps, Helen. *Some Aspects of the Agrarian Question in Mexico: A Historical Study.* Austin, 1925.

Poma de Ayala, Felipe Guamán. *Nueva corónica y buen gobierno (1615).* Paris, 1936.

Ramírez-Horton, Susan. "Chérrepe en 1572: Un análisis de la visita general del Virrey Francisco de Toledo." *Historia y cultura* 11 (1978): 79–121.

———. "Land Tenure and the Economics of Power in Colonial Peru." Ph.D. diss., University of Wisconsin-Madison, 1977.

———. "Sources for the Study of Peruvian Hacienda History." In John TePaske, ed., *Research Guide to Andean History.* Durham, 1981.

———. "The Sugar Estates of the Lambayeque Valley, 1670–1800: A Contribution to Peruvian Agrarian History." Master's thesis, University of Wisconsin, Madison, 1973.

[Ramírez], Susan, and Douglas Horton. "Sources for the Investigation of Peruvian Agrarian History." Land Tenure Center Paper No. 84, University of Wisconsin, Madison, February 1973.

Ramos Pérez, Demetrio. *Trigo chileno, navieros del Callao y hacendados limeños entre la crisis agrícola del siglo XVII y la comercial de la primera mitad del XVIII.* Madrid, 1967.

Real Academia Española. *Diccionario de la Lengua Castellana.* Madrid, 1783.

Rivero-Ayllón, Teodoro. *Lambayeque: sol, flores y leyendas.* Chiclayo, 1976.

Roel Pineda, Virgilio. *Historia social y económica de la colonia.* Lima, 1970.

Rostworowski de Diez Canseco, María. *Curacas y sucesiones, Costa norte.* Lima, 1961.

———. "Mercaderes del Valle de Chincha en la época prehispánica: Un documento y unos comentarios." *Revista Española de antropología americana* 5 (1970): 135–77.

Rowe, John H. "The Kingdom of Chimor." *Acta Americana (México)* 6, nos. 1 and 2 (1948): 26–59.

Rubiños y Andrade, Justo Modesto. "Un manuscrito interesante: Sucesión cronológica . . . de los curas de Mórrope y Pacora en la Provincia de Lambayeque . . . (1782)." *Revista histórica* 10, no. 3 (1936): 289–363.

Sáenz, J. Walter. *Racarrumi*. Lima, 1975.

Schwartz, Stuart B. *Sovereignty and Society in Colonial Brazil*. Berkeley, 1973.

Silva Santisteban, Fernando. "Las ruinas de Saña." *La Prensa* (Lima, Perú), 4 October 1971, Magazine section, pp. 20–21.

Simpson, Lesley Byrd. *Exploitation of Land in Central Mexico in the Sixteenth Century*. Berkeley, 1952.

———. *Many Mexicos*. Berkeley, 1941.

Spain, Consejo de las Indias. *Recopilación de las leyes de los Reynos de las Indias*. 4 vols. Madrid, 1681.

Spalding, Karen. "El kuraca y el comercio colonial." In Karen Spalding, *De indio a campesino*. Lima, 1974.

Stein, Stanley J. "Bureaucracy and Business in the Spanish Empire, 1759–1804: Failure of a Bourbon Reform in Mexico and Peru." *Hispanic American Historical Review* 61, no. 1 (1981): 2–28.

Suárez de Castro, Fernando. *Estructuras agrárias en la América Latina*. San José, Costa Rica, 1965.

Super, John C. "The Agricultural Near North: Querétaro in the Seventeenth Century." In Ida Altman and James M. Lockhart, *Provinces of Early Mexico*. Los Angeles, 1976.

Szewczyk, David M. "New Elements in the Society of Tlaxcala, 1519–1618." In Ida Altman and James M. Lockhart, *Provinces of Early Mexico*. Los Angeles, 1976.

Tannenbaum, Frank. *Ten Keys to Latin America*. New York, 1963.

Taylor, William B. "Landed Society in New Spain: A View from the South." *Hispanic American Historical Review* 54, no. 3 (August 1974): 386–413.

———. *Landlord and Peasant in Colonial Oaxaca*. Stanford, 1972.

———. "Town and Country in the Valley of Oaxaca, 1750–1812." In Ida Altman and James M. Lockhart, *Provinces of Early Mexico*. Los Angeles, 1976.

Tibesar, Antonine. *Franciscan Beginnings in Colonial Peru*. Washington, D.C., 1953.

Tord Nicolini, Javier. "El corregidor de indios del Perú: Comercio y tributos." *Historia y cultura* 8 (1974): 173–214.

Tosi, Joseph A., Jr. *Zonas de vida natural en el Perú*. N.p., 1960.

Trujillo, Consejo Provincial. *Actas del Cabildo de Trujillo, 1549–1604*. 3 vols. Lima, 1969–70.

Tutino, John M. "Provincial Spaniards, Indian Towns and Haciendas: Interrelated Agrarian Sectors in the Valleys of Mexico and Toluca, 1750–1810." In Ida Altman and James M. Lockhart, *Provinces of Early Mexico.* Los Angeles, 1976.

Ugarte, César A. "Los antecedentes históricos del régimen agrario Peruano." *Revista universitaria* 1, no. 2 (1923): 318–98.

———. *Bosquejo de la historia económica del Perú.* Lima, 1926.

Valdez de la Torre, Carlos. *Evolución de las comunidades indígenas,* Lima, 1921.

Vargas Ugarte, Rubén. "La fecha de la fundación de Trujillo." *Revista histórica* 10, no. 2 (1936): 229–39.

———. "Fragmento de una historia de Trujillo." *Revista histórica* 8, nos. 1 and 2 (1925): 86–118.

Vassberg, David E. "Concerning Pigs, the Pizarros, and the Agro-Pastoral Background of the Conquerors of Peru." *Latin American Research Review* 13, no. 3 (1978): 47–61.

Vázquez de Espinosa, Antonio. *Compendio y descripción de las Indias Occidentales.* Madrid, 1969.

Vicens Vives, J.*Historia social y económica de España y América.* 4 vols. Barcelona, 1957–59.

Villarán, Manuel Vicente. *Apuntes sobre la realidad social de las indígenas del Perú ante las leyes de Indias.* Lima, 1964.

Viñas y Mey, Carmelo. "La sociedad americana y el acceso a la propiedad rural." *Revista internacional de sociología* 1, no. 1 (1943): 103–47; 2, nos. 2–3 (1943): 247–84; 3, no. 4 (1943): 159–78.

Vollmer, Günter. *Bevölkerungspolitik und Bevölkerungsstruktur im Vizekönigreich Peru zu Ende der Kolonialzeit (1741–1821).* Zurich and Berlin, 1967.

Wachtel, Nathan. *The Vision of the Vanquished.* New York, 1977.

Weeks, David. "The Agrarian System of the Spanish American Colonies." *Journal of Land and Public Utility Economics* 23, no. 2 (1947): 153–68.

Whetten, Nathan L. *Rural Mexico.* Chicago, 1948.

Whyte, William Foote, and Giorgio Alberti. *Power, Politics and Progress: Social Change in Rural Peru.* New York, 1976.

Zavala, Silvio. *La encomienda indiana.* México, 1935.

Zevallos Quiñones, Jorge. "Don Luis de Velasco y los corregidores." *Revista del Archivo Nacional del Perú* 17, no. 2 (1953): 123–43.

———. "Lambayeque en el siglo XVIII." *Revista del Instituto Peruano de Investigaciones Genealógicas* 1–3 (1946–48): 89–152, 53–116, and 83–125.

Index